From the *Kirkus Reviews* response to the first edition of this book: *Happily Hippie: Understanding, Celebrating and Defending a Living Ethnicity*:

> Dougan argues for the continued relevance of hippies in this work of popular social science. The hippies, with their roots in the 1960s American counterculture, have given the world many things, from the popularization of the environmental movement and organic food to the introduction of yoga and meditation in the West and figures such as Jim Henson and Steve Jobs. In this debut book, Dougan argues that the hippies have never gone away, despite attempts by the media to undermine them and by the political right to demonize them. He writes that "we can't understand modern American politics and history" without the hippies; "it's like watching a play, and since one of the most important characters is invisible or can't be acknowledged, we're puzzled." Over the course of the book, he attempts to convince readers that hippies bear all the characteristics of an ethnic group and that they're persecuted by mainstream society, even as they offer it prized cultural contributions. He then goes into hippie-specific issues—yes, including marijuana—and calls for the creation of a "Hippie-American" ethnic organization to promote social equity for its members. Dougan's case for the continued existence of a vibrant counterculture is persuasive. . . . A detailed . . . analysis of 50 years of hippie culture.

HAPPILY HIPPIE

Meet a Modern Ethnicity

On the fiftieth birthday of Hippie culture, I dedicate this book to those who've dared to walk a path less traveled, to dance to the beat of a different drummer. Carry on wayward daughters and sons; let us continue this work so well begun.

I am a burning bush: I am on fire,
and yet, I am not consumed by the flame . . .

PAUL DOUGAN

Rev. date: 08/17/2017

To order additional copies of this book, contact:
Xlibris
1-888-795-4274
www.Xlibris.com
Orders@Xlibris.com
759761

Table of Contents

Chapter One

Rethinking "Hippies": An Introduction

"All truth passes through three stages. First, it is ridiculed.
Second, it is violently opposed. Third, it is accepted as being self-evident."
—Arthur Schopenhauer

I almost called this book *Rethinking Hippies* because it takes a subject people have strong opinions about and rethinks it. This book is about paradigm shift, and if you'll allow me, I'm going to shift several of your paradigms. I'm going to re-explain reality, or a large part of it, to you. I'll do this using something I call *Ethnic-Hippies Theory*, the idea that Hippie culture is a living ethnicity; by "living," I mean that it has survived the 1960s and exists today, that it has a future. By "ethnicity," I mean just that, and we'll discuss the term in depth below.

Americans usually respond negatively to the word "Hippie." Yes, we'd expect that from bigots, but it also true of many who've had or have Hippie identity; they wince at "hippie" because it strikes at their self-esteem: America has turned "hippie" into an epithet and shamed many who were once willing to claim Hippie identity into feeling they have something to feel guilty about and deny. So, for readers who cringe at "hippie," please calm yourself, and read what follows with an open mind. One of this book's purposes is therapeutic; that is, we're going to take the anxiety and fears so often associated with being identified as Hippie and sooth them. After reading this book, you may feel a whole lot better than when you started.

When I began writing *Happily Hippie*, I feared readers would avoid a book with the H-word in the title. I considered the options and decided I liked none: the reason people often feel so badly about the term "hippie" (prejudice) is the very issue this book addresses. However, I found an acceptable and appropriate use of language that arose naturally from an ethnic approach: the terms *Hippie-America* and *Hippie-American*. They communicate ethnic status, including all the rights and respect that should entail.

Another way of thinking about the word *Hippie* is that the word needs re-defining. Readers will find a reference-book-type definition of Hippie on this book's website, HappilyHippie.net; see "Redefining *Hippie*"

*   *   *

Here's a book preview:

First is this introduction—**Chapter One**. This book isn't nostalgia; it's not a personal memoir. Rather, it's a combination of argument and what I call "popular social science"; that is, it's writing that attempts to be scientific in its approach (using objective evidence and sometimes consulting scholarly texts) but that isn't academically stuffy.

After this book-by-chapter preview, in the second part of this first chapter, I'll tell you a bit about myself. The introduction's final section regards writing matters: source citing, who I see as my audiences, even why I'm capitalizing *Hippie* and *Counterculture*.

In Chapter Two, "Ethnocide in the American Mind: Rumors of our Death are Greatly Exaggerated," I'm going to take that demeaning cliché, Hippies Were Just a Thing of the Sixties, and show how it's a socio-political myth constructed by American neoconservatism and the War on Drugs. Hippiedom never died; rather, it became socially invisible, meaning that although almost everyone at some level knows that Hippiedom lives on, publically we deny its existence, see the subject as unpleasant and impolite. Hippies Were Just a Thing of the Sixties is, in fact, the ethnocidal wishful thinking of American bigots, nothing more.

If this book is about paradigm shift, we begin here. I'm taking the decade-specific paradigm of Hippies, wadding it up and tossing it into the recycle bin.

Among other arguments, this chapter undercuts Hippies Were Just a Thing of the Sixties in its assertion of generational transfer; that is, Hippie parents often produce Hippie kids, and sometimes those Hippie kids grow up and produce another generation of Counterculturists. In addition, I'm going to show the reader two demographic maps of Hippie-America.

> **Generally, in its treatment of Hippie-America, socially conservative bigots have been the same old dog doing the same old trick—only with a new toy.**

Chapter Three, "A Most Important Secret: Why the Counterculture Counts," also demonstrates the continuing relevance of Hippie-America by showing how Hippie-hating and Hippie-baiting have for almost five decades been what makes mainstream American politics tick, how in election after election, the Republicans have essentially said, "Hey, the Democrats are just a bunch of hippies!" and by doing so have shoved the nation to the hard right.

We'll examine American political history from the mid-1960s right through the election of Donald Trump.

I believe that without Ethnic-Hippies Theory, EHT, we can't understand modern American politics and history; it's like watching a play, and since one of the most important characters is invisible or can't be acknowledged, we're puzzled. This chapter clarifies that confusion by showing readers how that invisible character is affecting the larger national drama.

The next four chapters, four through seven, are the ethnic proof.

Chapter Four, "The Better Lens: Ethnic-Hippies Theory," begins the ethnic proof by demonstrating how our current definitions and paradigms of Hippiedom don't really make sense. The phrase "the sixties generation," for instance, doesn't explain either those of that generation who didn't go Hippie or the many Hippie-Americans of today who weren't born until after the 1960s ended, sometimes by several decades.

Chapter Five, "Hippie as Ethnic; Counterculture as Ethnicity," is a deductive (general-to-specifics) proof of Hippie ethnicity; that is, it takes a definition of *ethnicity*, and then proceeds to prove that Hippie culture fits it.

We're going to use the definition of *ethnicity/ethnic* from *The Harvard Encyclopedia of American Ethnic Groups*, and then, because that definition neglects certain obvious matters, such as ethnic costume, we're going to amend it. The chapter opens with an essay refuting the sometime misunderstanding that ethnicity requires racial/biological distinctiveness.

Chapter Six, "Waddling Well: What a Relatively Short, In-Many-Ways-Typical Trip It's Been," is an *in*ductive (specifics-to-general) proof of Hippie ethnicity. The "waddling" is as in "If it walks like a duck, if it looks like a duck, if it quacks like a duck—it's probably some kind of duck." The rest of the chapter title is a play on the Grateful Dead lyric "What a long, strange trip it's been." So, I'm going to take things we see as typical of traditionally recognized racial and ethnic groups and show how we can see these same things in regard to Hippiedom and how society treats it; for example, I'm going to take 15 stereotypes applied to various racial and ethnic minorities and show how these same stereotypes are routinely applied to Hippie-Americans.

At this point, then, I'll have double proven the ethnic nature of Hippie-America. One intellectual obstacle remains: "If Hippiedom is an ethnicity, where did it come from? It doesn't have the usual origins of an ethnicity."

Chapter Seven, "The Birth of Hippiedom: Stand and be Delivered!" explains Hippiedom's unusual origins, the *ethnogenesis*, of Hippie culture. It concludes that Hippie culture is a "synthetic ethnic minority": it's synthetic in both how it formed (with the decisive intervention of technology, especially mass media) and in its culturally eclectic content. In the historical background, of course, is widespread social dissatisfaction, a malaise with mainstream Western culture, leading to what social scientists call a *revitalization movement*.

Chapter Eight, "God Bless the Freaks: Hippiedom's Greatest Hits," is a catalogue of the amazing contributions of Hippie culture to this nation and to the world. We're going to look at the creation of the personal computer, at modern mid-wifery, at the recycling industry, at the Muppets, at *Cirque du Soleil*; we're going to explore Countercultural business empires. We'll be taking a Hippie tour of Hollywood—directors, actors and comedians. We're going to look at the world of sports, including some World Series-winning baseball teams and US Olympic medalists, and much more.

Chapter Nine, "'Now, Lay Back on the Couch, Please': Healing Your Inner Hippie," deals with the psychological aspects of Hippie identity. Counterculturists have, of course, been subjected to a regimen of social shaming; this chapter discusses the attitudes that keep some in the "Countercultural closet" and an alternative to them: Hippie pride.

Chapter Ten, "Drug Laws and Hippie-America—We Are Not Criminals: We're a People Criminalized," is EHT applied to the prohibition of marijuana and other drugs. It is history that demonstrates how the true purpose of American drug laws has been to persecute minorities and that today's drug laws persecuting Hippie-America are more of the same. I point out that there is no correlation between drug laws and the extent to which people use or abuse a drug, neutralizing the protecting-the-public-health argument that is the mainstay of the War on Drugs. I prove Gateway is illogical and ridiculous—an argumentative embarrassment. I show how War on Drugs pseudo-science is biased and silly. I cover other health matters and issues and show how Hippie-America is the driving force behind today's legalization movement.

Chapter Eleven, "Once Upon a Soapbox: A Collection of EHT Essays," is a series of shorter pieces on a variety of EHT-related subjects:

Weaknesses of the Counterculture:
    "Take me to Your Guru"
    "Sex, Drugs and Rock 'n' Roll!"
Dumb Demagogues 'R' Us: The Scariest Halloween Ever!
Fun Media Analysis with EHT: Five Examples with Accompanying Ridicule
    Males with long hair, Bad Guys with Black Hats
    Good Will Hunting Fights the Abominable Hippie!
    Farscape: How Bigotry is Born
    Fox's *24*: "Oh, the treasonous Counterculture!"
    Happily Hippie's Hall of Shame Award: "And the loser is . . ."
Hippie-America and Vietnam: If Anything, Heroism and Social Responsibility
"Dirty Hippie Protestors" Spittin' on "Our Brave Boys"!
Slouching Towards the Third Reich
The Infamous Case of Dr. Jeffrey MacDonald: "Helter Skelter" Meets "The Ballad of the Green Berets"
Seeing "Redneck": Country-Western culture as an American ethnicity
A Love-Haight Letter to the Left: The Devil Reads *Pravda*; The Democrats Usually Disappoint; The Center-Left Shines
Paul's Addiction
Mr. Paulie's Psychedelic Experience: Toto, We're not in Kansas Anymore
My Hippie Dream: A Life Where Soul Meets Body

Chapter Twelve, "A Problem's Solution: Building a Hippie-American Ethnic Organization," sketches out what a Hippie-American ethnic organization (HAEO) might look like and a simple plan for starting one. Although the most obvious function of such a group would be the promotion of social equality for its members, there are other things an HAEO could do.

If Hippie-hating and Hippie-baiting have done tremendous harm, imagine how much good might be done by going in the opposite direction, by building an HAEO that works to make Hippie-America respectable.

Chapter Thirteen, "The End of a Book, the Start of an Organization," summarizes this book and ends with a call to organize.

*   *   *

Who am I? In contrast to the stereotype of the spacey hippie (with a small *h*), the reader will find me well-organized and lucid. Indeed, one of my hopes as a writer is that in the course of this book, I will defy almost every negative stereotype readers may have of Hippie-Americans.

I am a *Hippie nationalist*; that is, I'm one who seeks civil rights and social equality for Hippie-Americans and Counterculturists everywhere.[1]

Since much of this book is about ethnicity, I'll tell you what I know about mine. While I see myself as Hippie-American, that doesn't preclude other forms of ethnic identification. Apparently, I'm about three quarters German-American, and the other fourth or so is either Scotch or Scotch-Irish.[2] I don't, however, remember those two ethnic backgrounds being prominent in my house while growing up or later; mostly, I think, I was a middle-class kid raised in white-bread American suburbia where historic ethnic identity had been supplanted by a sort of homogenized corporate allegiance, where instead of Scottish kilts or German food, we identified with John Deere and Company, its logo and its trademark green-and-yellow colors. They were, as my father put it, "the hand that feeds us."

And while my economic background was comfortable, like many of my era, I was dissatisfied with the society around me, starting with my corporate father. In theory, he'd "made it"; yet, he was seldom happy. Tormented by his insecurities and resentments, his life was often about acting out and making others miserable. By my late teens, I knew that I didn't want a lifetime of anger and debilitating insecurity, of always desperately looking for others to be "better than," of unrelenting psychic pain, of being part of the problem and not being part of the solution.

And there was the rest of Establishment society too, with its vicious racism, with its nuclear weapons, with its bullying of Third World Vietnam, with its assassinations, with its disrespect for planet Earth, with its shallow mammon addiction, with its lack of genuine community. So, I "dropped out." I went Hippie because in Hippie culture and identity, I saw the possibility of a better way—a promising path of cultural progress and personal salvation. I have never regretted that choice, and I've always been grateful that I had Hippie culture to be a part of—a beacon of

---

[1]   The term need not mean the intent to create a separate nation state.

[2]   A relative was once told that the family name, Dougan, derives from *Doovan*, which actually means *darkman*, due apparently to some Moorish blood that arrived in the northern British Isles long ago.

light and social revitalization emerging from a misguided mainstream America, a society that's often seemed, in Bob Dylan's words, "not busy being born" but "busy dying." I've sought to be busy being born, and Hippie culture, bless its pointed little head, has helped me do that.

And I believe I'm a lot like Hippie culture in the sense that I'm a good person who, at the end of the day, will likely make the world a better place; yet, I've often been surrounded by people who were eager to deride and undercut me, to always speak disrespectfully and slightingly of me, to—in their deep insecurity and hyper-competitiveness—look for ways to keep me down.

Our racist society has often refused to acknowledge the manhood of African-America males, has refused to let Blacks be adults. So it is with Hippie-Americans: In my mid-twenties, I had gone on an errand to my local True-Value Hardware. A clerk approached me and asked, "May I help you?"—very polite and professional. Then, looking further, he noticed the ponytail on my back and added, ". . . sonny."

And I have been the target of anti-Hippie violence, discrimination, stereotyping, general disdain, condescension and sometimes hatred.

In short, although people have sometimes accused me of making a mountain out of a mole hill when I insisted that there was something to all this stereotyping, discrimination and disrespect, it's always been clear to me that it was American society making a very big deal indeed about the Counterculture and Hippie identity.

> **I whole-heartedly embrace the Countercultural value of Kindness, but enabling bigots, bullies and the abusive isn't helping anyone, and codependence isn't kindness: it's just poor mental health.**

I have a motto: "Treat others respectfully; insist others treat you respectfully." I believe this is true for individuals; I believe this is true for social/cultural groups and for nations.

Let me finish here with a note on attitude: I occasionally meet Counterculturalists for whom the idea of asserting ourselves isn't "nice" or "cool," might hurt someone's feelings, just isn't peace and love. Yes, I whole-heartedly embrace the Countercultural value of Kindness, but enabling bigots, bullies and the abusive isn't helping anyone, and codependence isn't kindness: it's just poor mental health.

*   *   *

8

Here's who I see as my readers: first, those I call *Hippie-American*; second, Counterculturists around the world who I call *Hippie-Irish*, *Hippie-Australian, Hippie-French, Hippie-Japanese* and so forth; third, those of the American liberal/left who call themselves Progressives. I hope this will help them forge a successful politics for a healthy, modern green America; fourth, historians and perhaps political scientists striving to learn how American politics and society work; fifth, the rest of the general public; in other words, non-Hippies interested in the subject or various related topics. You're welcome here, and I hope you'll leave this book feeling you've been treated fairly and respectfully.

When I use the term *Counterculture*, I mean it as a synonym for *Hippiedom*, and I don't include every social movement that originated in the 1960s. As I'll explain later, I have issues with *Counterculture*.

On occasion, I'll occasionally be using *stoner*, or quoting it, as the equivalent of *Hippie*. I don't like this word because it tends to assume all Counterculturalists use marijuana—not so. It also tends to imply that Hippie culture is almost entirely about cannabis—not so.

I am capitalizing *Hippie* and derivations of it as well as *Counterculture* and derivations of it. I do this against the background of a society that often puts the word *hippie/hippy* in quotation marks, treating the word as if it had no legitimacy, like it isn't a real word. These language habits, of course, mirror the condescension and ethnocidal tendencies of the larger society. We usually capi-talize the names of traditionally recognized ethnic groups; since the point of this book, is to assert Hippie ethnicity and, by implication, the Counterculture's right to exist and be treated respectfully; I'm going to capitalize these terms.[3]

> At book's end, don't say, "Gosh, his brain is so-o big!" Say, "I accept EHT because it makes sense to me; going back to old ways of thinking would be like wearing an old pair of glasses."

When I speak of *fascism*, I'm referring to a specific type of totalitarian society and to the political movements and people who seek it; essentially, it's a dictatorship of big business, Wall St. and the wealthiest one-or-so percent with a lot of misguided "little people" tagging along—a kind of capitalist totalitarianism.

---

[3]   Except when I'm quoting others.

The reader will find footnotes; sometimes they'll be traditional informational footnotes that elaborate; often, they're comic-aside footnotes, and I encourage readers not to ignore them—you'll have more fun if you don't.

Also, there are many chapters that might be skimmed should the reader choose: use the bolded headings. I'll often be directing readers to "Book Photos" at *HappilyHippie.net* to view images not available in the text itself, e.g., "See photo #13."

My writing sometimes has a comic edge; the way I see it is, if I'm going to inflict my personality on the reader for almost 400 pages, it better be pleasant and relatively entertaining. Don't assume that because I'm sometimes playful I shouldn't be taken seriously.

Generally, I don't want to "blow the minds" of readers: I want to open and clear your minds. At book's end, don't say, "Gosh, his brain is so-o big!" Say, "I accept EHT because it makes sense to me; going back to old ways of thinking would be like wearing an old pair of glasses."

* * *

Are you ready for some paradigm shifting? Next up is the chapter refuting Hippies Were Just a Thing of the Sixties. Let's get started . . . .

Chapter Two

Ethnocide in the American Mind:
Rumors of our Death are Greatly Exaggerated

"It ain't what you don't know that gets you into trouble.
It's what you know for sure that just ain't so."

—*Mark Twain*

In modern America, that Hippie culture is dead is *de rigueur*. Consider contemporary books about Hippies or the Counterculture: aside from *Happily Hippie*, none I am aware of asserts that Hippiedom hasn't died. Here's a blurb for a 2004 release: *"Hippie*, by Barry Miles, chronicles a period between 1965 and 1971 that has not lost its fascination because we are still living within its legacy" (www.boston.com)—very typical in its relegation of Hippies to the past, in its facile assumption that Hippie culture died young.

This widespread parroting of Hippies Were Just a Thing of the Sixties is largely the result of media coaching, and news reports are larded with examples illustrating this peculiar way of thinking and speaking. Two cases:

New York Times reporter Evelyn Nieves writes in 1999, "In the San Francisco Bay area, Marin County is considered a kind of resting home for old hippies and New Age followers . . . ." Why call these Hippies "old"? Why the "resting home" remark? Are these Hippie-Americans all senior citizens? And why are the younger Hippie types ("New Age followers") considered something other than Hippies? Truth is, just as particular ethnic groups are predominant in other towns or regions, Hippies of a variety of ages are predominant in Marin County; yet, Nieves carefully parses her language in deference to Hippies Were Just a Thing of the Sixties.

In 1991, the *New York Times* ran a story "A Move for Marijuana Where the 60's Survive": in the small town of San Marcos, Texas, a group of Hippie-Americans have been engaging in civil disobedience against marijuana laws. They are described as "refugees from the 1960's," "residents who pride themselves on dwelling largely in the 60's," and the situation is called a "throwback to the 60's" by the reporter. The District Attorney explains, "We have a little time warp here in parts of Hays County." The sheriff comments, "They are just old hippies going through a life change." So, every time Hippies are mentioned in this piece, whether it's by the reporter or those being interviewed, a comment about being "old" or belonging back in the 1960s is very deliberately added.[4]

Bottom line: Virtually all popular discourse and scholarly work assumes, "Hippies were . . ." and never says, "Hippies are . . ." as if doing so were taboo. It's like our society is using a style manual that reads, "Every time you use the word *hippie*, you must add language pointing out that Hippies no longer exist. If you use the word *hippie*, say, eight times, you must add the appropriate deadening language eight times. There are no exceptions to this rule." We've reached an understanding that when we speak of "hippies," we must always remind ourselves and others that Hippie culture is dead.

> **Virtually all popular discourse and scholarly work assumes, "Hippies were . . ." and never says, "Hippies are . . ." as if doing so were taboo.**

In fact, that American society and media feel the need to append every mention of "hippie" with an essentially derisive comment about how Hippies no longer exist is a kind of overcompensation; that is, the way they use language expresses a certain insecurity about something. Why the obsessive need to constantly remind us that Hippies Were Just a Thing of the Sixties? The answer is simple: it's not true, and at some level, we all know it's not true, as I'll explain below. If this ethnocidal way of thinking and speaking were not rigidly reinforced, it would quickly collapse as it has no basis in fact.

* * *

Hippies Are Just a Thing of the Sixties is usually just assumed—a sort of "everyone knows" common knowledge. When we are given evidence, it usually consists of some combination of the following:

1) The "death-of-the-Hippie" parade that some Haight-Ashburyites staged in fall 1967, with great media attention, and the collapse of the late-1960s scene in that neighborhood.

---

[4]   In the same vein, consider the popular phrase "aging Hippies": all people age, so why say "aging" unless you're trying to remind your audience that Hippies are supposed to be a thing of the past?

2) The Manson-family killings in California, beginning in July 1969.

3) The violence at the Countercultural Altamont music festival in Oakland in December 1969, some 14 weeks after Woodstock.

4) The deaths of three major Countercultural artists, first, Jimi Hendrix and Janis Joplin, a mere two weeks apart in late 1970, and then, The Doors singer Jim Morrison in July of 1971.

Let's look at each:

The "death of the Hippie" parade was an event staged in Haight-Ashbury in October of 1967 by the Diggers, a Hippie collective known for its community services such as distributing free food. By the end of that summer, the Summer of Love, Haight-Ashbury had been overrun with new arrivals and infested with predatory dealers hawking bad drugs. So, this event was a protest against the degradation of the Haight-Ashbury neighborhood and media exploitation of that scene. Organizers—and the Summer of Love wasn't spontaneous, it was an event called for by a group called Council for the Summer of Love (*Wikipedia* "Summer of Love")—felt that it was in the community's best interest if no one else was, in singer Scott McKenzie's famous words, "going to San Francisco."

Participant Mary Kasper comments, "We wanted to signal that this was the end of it [the emigration to San Francisco], don't come out. Stay where you are! Bring the revolution [Hippie culture] to where you live . . . (qtd. in *Wikipedia* "Summer of Love"). Thus, this "mock funeral," as it's usually called, was more a plea to stay out of Haight-Ashbury than an admission of Hippiedom's death.

And yes, the "scene" in Haight-Ashbury did seem to collapse. Still, as many as 100,000 may have journeyed to Haight-Ashbury for the 1967 Summer of Love (*Wikipedia*, "Summer of Love"). How big is the Haight? Not counting the parks, roughly 130 to 140 regular-size city blocks, far as I can tell.[5] Do the math, and we're talking over 700 extra people per block in an already crowded urban area. Add to the mix, police hostility, exploitative criminal elements, other issues, and it should be no wonder the early Haight wilted. But today, this neighborhood is still Hippie dominated—the Countercultural Haight-Ashbury Free Clinics,

---

[5]   I looked at some maps of San Francisco to arrive at this rough figure.

for example, are about to celebrate their 48th anniversary—so why should we say that Hippie culture failed or died just because this early scene was overwhelmed? In fact, the early Haight's nadir might be attributed to the vast popularity of emerging Hippie culture.

Well then, what about **the Manson killings**? They've been widely interpreted as revealing a dark side of the Counterculture, a bad streak so virulent it could only signal the end of the entire entity. Well, you'll find no apologist for Manson and his "family" here nor denial of their Hippie identity though a fair look at Charles Manson—who'd been raised in a vicious prison environment and, among other things, repeatedly raped—would show him to be more the product of larger American society than Hippiedom.

But why assume the Manson killings typify Hippie culture or symbolize its death? Considering that the blame for the 1971 Jeffrey MacDonald killings points to MacDonald himself—as correctly judged by the courts—and not to drug-crazed Hippies as MacDonald claims, the Manson killings remain singular and exceptional. While those murders may point to certain weaknesses in early Hippie culture (a tendency of some to blindly follow "gurus" and to abuse amphetamines), they fail as evidence that Hippie culture died. If, by the way, millions of Hippie-Americans had concluded that the Manson murders revealed the true face of their allegedly peace-and-love culture—that they had been betrayed and were now part of an evil and menacing movement—and as a result, they left the Counterculture, this argument might work. Evidence of such a mass reaction to the Manson killings within Hippiedom is non-existent.

So, **how about Altamont?** There was one murder and three accidental deaths at this infamous Rolling Stones concert (there were also four children born there) (*Wikipedia,* "Altamont"). For a largely hostile national media, the success of Woodstock—"three days of peace, love and music"—mere months before had likely been galling; they jumped on Altamont, and as with the above two incidents, it is now regularly seen as emblematic of Hippiedom's demise. While there can be no doubt that organizers of Altamont failed in tragic ways, why should one particularly bad Countercultural concert be seen as evidence of the death of an entire culture? If Altamont had started a pattern of horrific rock festivals, that assumption might make some sense. It didn't. Indeed, Altamont would seem to be one in a thousand. Rock concerts, many overtly Countercultural, have become a staple of modern American and international culture, gatherings where we rarely read of a violent death.[6] Altamont, then, isn't even proof of the death of Countercultural rock concerts, let alone of the death of Hippie culture.

Okay, what about all those dead Hippie rock stars—Jimi, Janis and Jim? In the media's rush to write Hippiedom's obituary, **JimiJanisJim** plays prominent, partly because all three deaths seem to have been drug related. So, we're left with the demise of three Countercultural icons in less than a year. But that's *all* that it is—the separate deaths of three famous Hippies in a relatively short time. Joplin was alone and depressed one night in Los Angeles when her fiancé and a close friend failed to show. She bought and used some street heroin which turned out to be far more powerful than she expected; she died. Jimi Hendrix—by all accounts gentle and kind but a bit troubled, perhaps, by his meteoric stardom—died in his sleep partly due to barbiturate abuse. And anyone who has ever seen Oliver Stone's 1991 film *The Doors* knows that Jim Morrison, while talented, was a lunatic—most people, Hippie or otherwise, have never drunk human blood. Morrison wasn't a "normal" Hippie; he wasn't a normal anything. He was a freak's freak.

To treat these three and their early deaths as representative of the entire Counterculture is unfair. Since then, how many Hippie rock stars have survived and prospered? Mick Jagger still looks pretty lively to me; why doesn't society see him as a symbol of the Counterculture's survival and vitality? In these deaths, we have the exception, not the rule, and only a hostile, prejudiced media and society would see them as proof of complete cultural collapse. A fairer assessment of these tragedies would be as caveats on the perils of drug abuse and the difficulties of stardom, nothing more.

Author LeRoy Ashby's account of the alleged demise of Hippiedom from his *With Amusement for All: A History of American Popular Culture since 1830* is fairly typical:

---

[6]   There have been occasional rock-concert deaths and violence, and the webpage "10 Rock Concerts which Resulted in Bloodshed" (http://www.socialsciencecareers.org) lists some; generally, however, violent rock concerts, especially Countercultural ones, are the exception, and rock concerts remain vulnerable to some of the same violent events (fans stampeding and trampling others, etc.) that plague other mass gatherings.

At the Rolling Stones' free concert outside San Francisco [Altamont], hundreds of fans suffered drug overdoses, and the Hells Angels motorcycle gang stabbed an eighteen-year-old youth to death. "Altamont was the end of the sixties," said Jefferson Airplane's manager, Bill Thompson, referring not to the calendar but to movement sensibilities—"the whole feeling." (410)

Ashby adds other alleged evidence for Hippies Were Just a Thing of the Sixties thrown at us so fast, it's overwhelming: first, President Nixon's invasion of Cambodia; second, the breakup of the Beatles; third, JimiJanisJim; fourth, Don McLean's 1972 song "American Pie" with the chorus lyric "The day the music died"; fifth, "A number of musicians pulled away from politics and moved towards songs that were mellow and introspective—indeed almost 'clinically depressed'" (411)—Countercultural acts mentioned are the band Chicago, James Taylor, Carole King and Joni Mitchell; and finally, "Such turning inward reminded the former student radical Todd Gitlin of the Ghost Dance phenomenon almost a century earlier among the Plains Indians as their culture disintegrated" (411).

What's wrong with this obituary? Almost everything. First, the claim of "hundreds" of Altamont drug overdoses is likely an exaggeration, and more importantly, notice how Altamont is used in a symbolic, impressionistic way. Second, although the manager of Jefferson Airplane would seem an admission-against-interest source, Thompson speaks of the death of a "feeling," not the death of a culture. If he does mean the death of Hippiedom, then his personal experience contradicts that as the best days Jefferson Airplane, in terms of record sales and popularity, lay before them. Third, the invasion of Cambodia invigorated the anti-war movement, and as I'll show below, Hippiedom and the anti-war movement were never one in the same, anyway.

Fourth, okay, so the Beatles broke up, they still had their own musical careers, and Ashby's quoting of a rock critic who says of the breakup that "we can't be Beatles fans anymore" (411), and thus apparently Hippie, sounds silly—as if there aren't both Beatles fans and Hippies today. Fifth, as Ashby admits, "American Pie" is actually about the deaths of non-Hippie, early-1960s rockers Buddy Holly, Richie Havens and the Big Bopper (411). Sixth, "mellow and introspective" songs? There were never such songs *during* the 1960s, is that it? And how did we get from "mellow and introspective" to "clinically depressed"? As for the alleged Countercultural shift to non-political music, with perhaps the exception of Joni Mitchell's "Banquet," I can't think of a single overtly political song any of the mentioned groups or artists ever made to begin with—James Taylor may do liberal fundraisers, but his songs are rarely, if ever, political. Lastly, Todd Gitlin's alleged Ghost Dance/"cultural disintegration" comment—spare me. It's melodrama, faulty analogy and hyperbole without a speck of evidence that Ashby shows us, and when I read Gitlin's *The Sixties: Years of Hope, Days of Rage (1987)*, I found Ashby's paraphrase of Gitlin inaccurate and misleading: Gitlin never says Hippies Were Just a Thing of the Sixties, even contradicts it. What we have here is simply the sloppy yet stylish retelling of a modern American myth.

The various pieces of alleged evidence for Hippiedom's "fade to black,"[7] then, are subjective fluff. The above-mentioned events have been blurred into an emotionally evocative whole, thrown into a coffin and quickly covered with media dirt, lest anyone ask for an autopsy. A fair inquiry, however, fails to find a corpse; the story of the Counterculture's collapse, collapses. There is no convincing evidence that Hippie culture tanked some time near the end of the 1960s however widespread this false belief might be.

If we are going to read this period in early Hippie culture symbolically, then it's better a symbol of a young Counterculture's loss of an adolescent sense of invincibility/immortality than a symbol of its demise. In the lives of individuals, we see such losses as necessary to growing up, as events that mature and prepare us to reach our full potential. They don't spell death: they herald a coming of age.

> **If we are going to read this period in early Hippie culture symbolically, then it's better a symbol of a young Counterculture's loss of an adolescent sense of invincibility/immortality than a symbol of its demise.**

*　　*　　*

---

[7]   This, from a 2001 *New York Times* review of T.C. Boyle's novel *Drop City*.

We're now going to consider several rationales people cling to in their attempts relegate Hippiedom to the 1960s.

Let's begin with the **got-a-haircut-and-a-job-and-therefore-can't-still-be-a-Hippie argument**. It assumes, wrongly, that Hippies and employment are mutually exclusive. While bigots have wallowed in the stereotype of the parasitical and unemployed Hippie, it's difficult for anyone to live for long without work, and the vast majority of Hippie-Americans *do* work, always have. In late 1969, for example, the *New York Times* carried an article entitled, "Hippies Praised for Plant Work," noting the high regard the manager of a light industry had for his largely Hippie workforce (Smith). Also, the Hippie take on work has never been so much that work is bad and being lazy and unproductive is good, but that one should try to find meaningful work, a so-called "right livelihood." As such, that millions of Hippie-Americans are gainfully employed in almost all sectors of the economy doesn't mean they aren't Hippie or that they've ceased to be Hippie.

As for the male haircuts, consider two relevant concepts: *job discrimination* and *forced assimilation*. That is, employers are often reluctant to hire the overtly Hippie, especially men with long hair; help-wanted ads specifying "clean cut" have been commonplace. So, to get a job, Hippie males often conform to employer expectations and get a haircut, shave, etc., something that falls into the category of *forced assimilation* since this process is essentially coercive. Incidentally, although one can find "longhairs" working various jobs today, there remains a dress code in various professions that forbids hirsute males. I remember a Hippie neighbor who in the late 1990s had gotten his locks chopped. When I inquired, this business major told me he had gotten an internship at a local amusement park, and they had told him that his long hair was "unprofessional." Needless to say, after his haircut, he didn't have a new cultural identity (nor was he any more or less professional); he was just a Hippie man with relatively shorter hair for, at least, the semester.

Thus, the perception that there are fewer males with long hair can be explained largely as evidence of discrimination and harassment and attempts by Hippie-Americans to adapt to a hostile society, not the death of Hippie culture.

Also, how are we to explain today's long-haired males? If long hair on men is seen as a sort of litmus test of how alive Hippie-America is,

18

then the many contemporary longhairs would seem to contradict Hippies Were Just a Thing of the Sixties.

*   *   *

Let's now consider some other rationales for maintaining that Hippies no longer exist—the Vietnam War-ended argument, the just-a-phase-of-life-now-past explanation, the "arbitrary-definition argument"—and we'll look at the term *neo-Hippie.*

Yes, **the War in Vietnam did indeed end** in the early 1970s—about the same time as the alleged death of the Counterculture. Problem: This notion blithely assumes that Hippiedom and the anti-War in Vietnam movement were one and the same.[8] Hardly—the equation doesn't work on either end:

There has always been a "spiritual," New Age wing of the Counterculture that isn't necessarily political, and others are just apolitical. Not all Counterculturists, then, are or were "protestors."

Then again, only the simpleminded think the anti-War in Vietnam movement was entirely Hippie. By war's end, polls showed a strong majority against that war; the "anti-war movement" had come to represent all kinds of Americans. Dr. Benjamin Spock, Dr. Martin Luther King, Jr., the Berrigans, Senator Eugene McCarthy— these prominent anti-war leaders were not Hippie-American.

In short, the Counterculture and the anti-War in Vietnam movement grew up in the same neighborhood, the same hothouse of that era, and yes, there was definitely some overlap: there were politicized Counterculturists who were actively opposing that war. All well and good—none of it proves that when the anti-War in Vietnam movement ended, Hippiedom died alongside it.

Next, here's how the 2009 *World Book* encyclopedia explains the alleged end of the Counterculture: "The majority simply left the ***hippie stage of their lives*** behind while trying to hold on to at least a few of the ideals that once inspired them" (emphasis added). Gosh, that was beautiful! As I watch us ride off into the sunset, methinks I shed a tear. Problems: Well, it does sound like a variation of, "Hey, those kids just

---

[8]   For a popular example of this stereotyping, see *Forrest Gump* (1994): in it, anti-war protestors are exclusively Hippie.

grew up and got jobs," but it's also presumptuous in its supposition that being Hippie is merely a life phase, something one "outgrows." If it is, then why do a majority of people never go through it? Also, why do so many never "outgrow" their Hippie identity?

Now, the Hippie haters would respond, "Precisely because they've never grown up; thus, the phrase *overgrown Hippie*." But the Counterculture's accusers have no proof that these "overgrown Hippies" are in fact immature, and in their assumption of childishness, they echo the accusations of traditional racial and ethnic stereotyping. In short, this objection is evidence of bigotry, not of the collapse of the Counterculture.

Next rationale: **the arbitrary 1960s-specific definition of *Hippie*.** In other words, there are those who, for no clear reason, insist on relegating Hippies to the 1960s—just, as I suppose, some might relegate "flappers" to the Roaring Twenties and insist that by definition, the term correlates with that decade and has no meaning beyond it. Logically, this is a tautology, a circular argument that goes nowhere. Because this approach trivializes and de-legitimizes, stiff adherence to it often indicates prejudice, and it tells us nothing that would prove the death of Hippiedom. It's an attitude, not an argument.

Lately, we hear the term **neo-Hippie** *(new-Hippie)*. The idea, apparently, is to confer Hippie identity but to do so in a way that indicates someone isn't a "Sixties hippie." Oftentimes, the person being referred to is, by my count, simply a younger Hippie-American. The strength of the term is that it acknowledges that, yes, there is a contemporary Counterculture. The weakness of the term is, in distinguishing between "new" Hippies and, presumably, "old" Hippies (the reason for the *neo* prefix), it assumes some kind of cultural interruption, most likely, acceptance of the myth that 1960s Hippie culture died.

*   *   *

Now, we'll look at some Countercultural accomplishments and events that are post-1960s; in short, **if Hippies Were Just a Thing of the Sixties, how do we explain these things?**

To begin with, it's common knowledge that urban Haight-Ashburys were followed by a **back-to-the-land movement** and the creation of Hippie communes. People seem to agree that this happened in the early-to-mid 1970s (Tennessee's The Farm was started in 1971, for example). *Wikipedia*:

When the Summer of Love finally ended, thousands of hippies left San Francisco, a large minority of them heading "back to the land." These hippies created the largest number of intentional communities or communes in the history of the United States, forming alternative, egalitarian farms and homesteads in Northern California, Colorado, New Mexico, New York, Tennessee and other states. . . . Judson Jerome, who studied the American commune movement, estimates that by the early 1970s, about 750,000 people lived in more than ten thousand communes across the United States. ("History of the Hippie Movement")

In this same vein, what happened to all those who flocked to Vermont in the late 1960s and early 1970s? Did all those Hippie-Americans move there just to abandon their culture?

Invention of the Personal Computer: As "Hippies," a *History Channel* video, notes, "In April 1977, Steve [Jobs] and his partner, Steve Wozniak, introduced the Apple II, the first commercially viable personal computer." There's ample evidence that the "two Steves" are/ were Hippie-American. Wozniak adds, "We were so influenced by the People's Computer Company in Menlo Park [CA], the same area that the hippie thought had come from. . . ." Nineteen seventy seven—isn't that six-to-seven years after the alleged end of Hippiedom?

Hippie websites: As history majors will recall, the internet didn't really come of age until long after the 1960s. So, being that Hippie culture is molding in the grave, we wouldn't expect to see Hippie websites, would we? How can you tell a website is Hippie? Well, let's consider self-identifying sites, those with *Hippie* in the name. Here are ten from 2008: www.HippiePower.com; www.Hippie Mommy.com; www.UKHippy.com; www.StopHippieProfiling.org; www.Hippy.com (Hippyland); www.HippyGourmet.com; www.Hippieshop.com; www. HippieMuseum.org; www.HippieLawyer.com; www.HippieChristian. org. Not only are there many overtly Hippie websites, notice their variety.

Rolling Stone: I refer to the magazine, about to celebrate its fiftieth anniversary, it's maiden issue (November 9, 1967) bearing a cover photo of Beatle John Lennon in costume for his appearance in the film "How I Won the War." Today, *Rolling Stone* is a pillar of American journalism, an important and influential voice. And it's relatively easy to document its Hippie heritage and continuing Countercultural identity; for example, its headline on a piece on the Countercultural band Phish reads, "Phish Reunite Hippie Nation" (Frick). Yes, and the reason the magazine contains such headlines is because *Rolling Stone* is the most prominent journalistic voice of "Hippie Nation."

The Rolling Stones: I refer to the still-performing rock band. Long seen as Countercultural—remember, among other things, Mick Jagger and Keith Richards' sensational marijuana arrest in London in 1967—the Stones rock on. And it's particularly noteworthy since for a while, people had these preconceptions about Countercultural rock bands: like Hippie culture itself, as they aged, they would dry up and die. In fact, Jagger and many others have redefined not only "rock star" but what it means to age.

The Muppets/Sesame Street: Though their creator, Jim Henson, has left this life, *Sesame Street* and its Muppet characters endure. Yes, Henson's creation is still on the air, still shooting new shows, still as popular as ever. This powerful phenomenon arrived late Sixties (first show November 10, 1969) and continues to be cutting edge and award winning. *Sesame Street* is the longest running children's show in history. I'll document its Hippie heritage and identity in Chapter Eight.

Dr. Andrew Weil: In October 2006, *Time* had Dr. Andrew Weil on its cover, hailing him as America's most-trusted authority on health; his success typifies the success of Hippie-based modes of healing, that holistic, East-meets-West blend properly known as *Integrative medicine*. It and Weil can safely be considered Countercultural; thus, for the healthy changes he's helped wrought, *Psychology Today* refers to Weil as "one of the most subversive hippies of them all" (Ryan).

Natural/organic foods: Pioneered and developed largely by Hippie culture, natural/organic foods may be the last laugh on those who would consign Hippies to the past. The website Food Navigator—USA reports (2015), "US organic goods market to grow 14% [annually] from 2013-2018" (Daniels). Countercultural cuisine, diet and food production, then, have become so successful over the last decades that not only do they demonstrate a thriving Counterculture in the present, they are, I believe, the future of food.

*   *   *

Next, **younger Hippies, especially Hippie kids and grandkids**—how do those convinced Hippies ended with the1960s account for them? They can't. What they've done is to live in a *Family Ties* fantasy world. *Family*

Ties, of course, was the 1980s television show that launched the career of actor Michael J. Fox, who premiered as the very un-Hippie son of Hippie parents (*Wikipedia* obligingly describes them as "former hippie parents"). While such a portrayal was politically welcome in the 1980s world of neoconservative ascendance,[9] it never had much to do with reality. As Chelsea Cain, the author of *Wild Child: Girlhoods in the Counterculture*, puts it, "You can take the girl out of the counterculture, but you can't take the counterculture out of the girl" (qtd. in Powell's Books).

> **Younger Hippies, especially Hippie kids and grandkids— how do those convinced Hippies ended with the1960s explain them? They can't.**

I've documented Hippie children and grandchildren. And I'm referring, of course, not just to biological offspring, but to progeny who demonstrate Hippie identity. So far, I've identified and photographed at least one three-generation family (**see Photo #1**); it stands to reason, there are many more. Soon, there will certainly be fourth-generation Hippie families—if there aren't already. For now, let's quickly look at one celebrity example of generational transfer.

Bill Walton—first, a college basketball star at UCLA, then a famous pro player at Portland and Boston, then a widely watched sportscaster— often doesn't appear overtly Countercultural, yet his Hippie identity is relatively easy to establish, both in the past and in the present. Walton and his wife have a son, Luke, who was a star of the Los Angeles Lakers and later an NBA coach. Luke Walton's Hippie identity is even easier to establish than his father's; just look at him; particularly, at his visible body art as described by *Wikipedia*: "On his right arm, there is a tattoo of four Grateful Dead-type dancing skeletons, each one with a basketball; the skeletons represent Luke and his three brothers" ("Luke Walton"). So, Luke Walton is literally marked with Hippie identity, and the tattoo suggests a larger Hippie family.

Again, I do not believe that *all* Hippie offspring "inherit" their parents' cultural identity. Non-biological, cultural "inheritance" usually

---

[9]   I do not mean to portray *Family Ties* as completely anti-Hippie. In particular, the program depicted the Keaton parents as responsible and loving; this, a welcome contradiction of the Hippie-as-neglectful-parent stereotype.

involves a measure of choice, and some choose other paths. Still, far as I can tell, most Hippie offspring remain Hippie, continue to exhibit aspects of Hippie ethnicity and identity, largely because having grown up in that milieu, it's who they are, and it's what they've chosen to remain even if they don't always call themselves "hippie."

It's June 2009; I'm leafing through the alternative *Boulder Weekly* when what does my eye espy? A picture of a local boy working his way up a climbing wall. Something about his hair catches my attention. Are those dreadlocks? They *are*, and a closer look shows an amulet and perhaps an earring as well. He looks Caucasian, so it's unlikely he's Native American or Rastafarian.[10] Ooh . . . I think I smell patchouli!

"Dreadlocks and limbs flying every which way, Liam Vance slithered from hold to hold with swift, decisive movements," writes Sam McManis (33). Turns out, this 13-year old is a rock-climbing wonder, a future Olympian should rock-climbing ever go Olympic. Hippie-American Liam Vance was born about 1996, long after the alleged end of Hippiedom, and across America, there are likely millions like him. If Hippie culture died decades ago, how can such children be explained?

Hippy.com, a website with over 75,000 registered users, has a special forum for "young hippies." Webmaster Skip Stone comments: "I was very surprised to find when I started Hippyland that I wasn't just attracting old hippies like myself. There seems to be a large contingent of young people who consider themselves hippies. If Hippyland is any indication, they are legion. In fact, 85% of Hippyland's huge audience is under 30." Hippies Were Just a Thing of the Sixties, then, can't explain the youthfulness of contemporary Hippie-America, in general.

*   *   *

Next, we're going to look at **another problem with Hippies Were Just a Thing of the Sixties: on an individual level, it usually makes little sense**. If a person has identifiably Hippie traits, if a person is Hippie before midnight December 31st 1969—or whenever the axe allegedly

---

[10]   And as I'll also demonstrate in Chapter Eight, modern rock climbing is a Hippie-dominated and -developed sport.

fell—does that person wake up the morning after a non-Hippie, an "ex-hippie"?

Consider the renowned computer designer, entrepreneur and all-around genius, the late Steve Jobs whose Countercultural past is common knowledge. Okay, so at what date exactly did Jobs cease to be Hippie? The question, of course, falsely assumes he did. For his 2005 book, *What the Dormouse Said: How the 60s Counterculture Shaped the Personal Computer Industry,* author John Markoff interviewed Jobs:

> iTunes [then newly created by Jobs] . . . included a simple visualization feature that . . . [resembled a psychedelic light show].
>
> . . . Jobs turned to me with a slight smile and said, "It reminds me of my youth . . . Jobs . . . had experimented with drugs and pursued a countercultural lifestyle both before and after helping found the quirky computer maker [Apple]. . . . . Jobs has maintained deep emotional ties to the era in which he grew up.
>
> He . . . still believed that taking LSD was one of the two or three most important things he had done in his life, . . . He also said that his countercultural roots often left him feeling like an outsider in the corporate world of which he is now a leader. (pp. xvii, xix)

Ergo, long past his youth, long past the end of the 1960s, Jobs still had Hippie identity.[11] In fact, he couldn't escape it: it'd been seared into him by his life experiences, and like many Hippie-Americans, he had a certain sense of otherness, of not quite fitting in.

Yes, I do think there are some who have truly abandoned Hippie identity, allowed themselves to be completely assimilated, but they're a minority. For the vast majority of Hippie-Americans, their distinctive cultural identity didn't suddenly die. It lives on albeit sometimes muted. In short, since having Hippie identity almost always means far more than

---

[11] Jobs reportedly refused standard Western medicine when he first learned of his cancer, something he also reportedly regretted (CBS *60 Minutes*); still, it's clearly a Countercultural sort of thing.

having once owned a pair of bell bottoms, at the level of the individual, Hippies Were Just a Thing of the Sixties is unrealistic.

* * *

Next I'll explain my claim that today, using an ethnic definition, **ten-plus percent of America is Countercultural**—that would be over 30 million Hippie-Americans. I'm also going to make a regrettably even-rougher estimate of the Counterculture's international size. The point, of course, is to demonstrate that not only do Hippies still exist but that they and their communities dot the globe and comprise a substantial portion of American and world population. We've been trained to trivialize Hippiedom; when we see it today, in its tens of millions, that acts as an antidote.

Being Hippie isn't the sort of thing one finds listed in demographic data or genealogical charts, so any attempt to quantify Hippie populations must for now remain in the realm of estimation. Still, I believe we can make reasonable and intelligent estimates: using evidence from the media, particularly two demographic maps of Hippie-America and some lists of Hippie cities and colleges, I can show how widespread is the modern Counterculture. I'll then add what I call "the eyeball method" (what we can see and deduce in our daily lives).

From media reports, we can glean that virtually every part of America has Hippie-Americans. North and South, the Midwest, the East Coast and the West Coast, in the cities and in the countryside—Counterculturists are everywhere. A few states have reputations as being Hippie, or more precisely, disproportionately Hippie: California, Oregon, Vermont, Colorado and Washington.

California has so many Hippie communities that I once heard a woman on a talk show disparagingly refer to it as "the flower-child state." It's not just the Haight-Ashbury neighborhood, either, or even Berkeley across the bay. We earlier mentioned Menlo Park in the Bay Area where the PC hailed from. Apparently, Humboldt County is renowned for its marijuana growers, many of whom would be Hippie-American. Laurel Canyon, as in Joni Mitchell's *Ladies of the Canyon*, has a Hippie history, and, as my demographic map (see below) would seem to confirm, there are a large number of Counter culturalists in the larger Los Angeles area, and, of course, San Francisco remains heavily Hippie. Suffice it to say, a sizeable portion of the state's large population is Hippie-American.

Here's a blurb about Oregon from Hippy.com: "Just about any city in Oregon West of the Cascade Mountains is a Hippy Haven. Oregon is the only state where hippies enjoy a majority at the voting booths come election time. There's a saying going around "Hippies don't die. They just move to Oregon. During the past few years hippies have been moving to Oregon in droves . . ." (Hippy Havens 2). And both Oregon and neighboring Washington have been among the first states to legalize marijuana, implying a large Countercultural population.

> If we string these West Coast states together, I think we could see a swath of Counterculturists coming north from southern California, up through San Francisco, Portland and Seattle, across the border into Vancouver and possibly continuing north.

If we string these West Coast states together, I think we could see a swath of Counterculturists coming north from southern California, up through San Francisco, Portland and Seattle, across the border into Vancouver and possibly continuing north.

Vermont is increasingly seen as a Countercultural state by national media. Some speculate that the Hippie migration to Vermont was inspired by a 1972 *Playboy* article praising the state's clean air and often-open countryside laced with mountains: "Get 225,000 counterculturalists to settle in the Green Mountain State and exercise their franchise—and you've begun a unique social experiment" writes journalist Tim Madigan; he quotes a Countercultural Vermonter: "I think we should put a glass dome over the state and preserve it. . . . It's only half a million people, but . . . the food is organically grown. Everybody is still a hippie. The stereotype is absolutely true." And when one researches Hippie culture, as I do, Vermont comes up a lot—Ben & Jerry's ice cream, for instance.

Colorado, where I live, is disproportionately Hippie. The most prominent Hippie-American population is in Boulder, and fall semester 2009, in a Boulder high school, there was a sign hanging over the cafeteria reading, in part, "I come from a hippie town in Colorado." I agree: not everyone in Boulder is Hippie, but the town, in both reputation and fact, is a Countercultural enclave. However, Boulder is not alone, and many mountain and ski towns, in particular, have a distinct Hippie presence. Of course, Countercultural singer John Denver immortalized Colorado with his song "Rocky Mountain High," and the late Countercultural author Hunter S. Thompson was based in Pitkin County (the Aspen area). It's also a state with a very active legalization movement which in 2012 legalized marijuana.

Often Hippie communities spring up around university towns; no matter how conservative the state, it has colleges, and that often means Hippie communities. Someone once told me a story about "all these little hippie houses" near some small town in rural Kansas where she used to live—the town had a college campus. And in many states—Wisconsin, Iowa, Colorado and Texas, for examples—the largest Hippie communities are located in and around important university towns: Madison, Iowa City, Boulder and Austin, respectively. I once heard late-night television host Colin Ferth joke that in Texas when people go into Austin, they "take off their cowboy hats and put on an earring."

Often, I think, a sizeable Hippie community becomes a hub, and after several decades, the towns around it become more and more Countercultural. You can see it in California's Marin County just north of the Bay Area. You can see it around Boulder, Colorado. You can see it in the *New York Times* article we saw earlier from San Marcos, Texas—a suburb of Austin. So, when we identify a town with a noticeable Countercultural community, it often means adjacent areas have also become disproportionately Countercultural.

Another reason I estimate there are tens of millions of contemporary Counterculturists is because there are also individual Hippie-Americans scattered throughout the nation in areas not predominantly Hippie. In the 2006 *Frontline* film "Country Boys," for example, one of the subjects is a twenty-something self-described "hippie" living in rural Appalachia.

Now, "The First Demographic Map of Hippie America," as I call it: Let me explain my methodology, how I created this map: I began with the assumption (partially proven at this point, but I'll supply more evidence in Chapter Seven) that natural/organic food is essentially Hippie-American food. Find the locations of natural/organic groceries, co-ops and farmer's markets, and we can probably assume that these businesses are supported by a local Countercultural community. This isn't to say, by the way, that each and every individual eating natural/organic food is Hippie, just that it's safe to assume a strong correlation between essentially Hippie food, Hippie-food eaters and Hippie-Americans.[12] Yes, the methodology is inexact, but if we can create a map of natural/organic food sellers, we should be able to create a crude demographic map of Hippie-America.

I began by reinforcing the link between various natural/organic food chains and Hippie culture. I researched and found five major chains to be Hippie-American: catering to a Hippie-American clientele and/or seen in the public eye as "hippie": Whole Foods, Sprouts, Natural Foods (Vitamin Cottage), Trader Joe's and Fairway.

Of course, I wanted to look at independent natural/organic grocers (small businesses) and natural/organic coops and farmers' markets, too. I believe it's safe to assume these venues are Hippie-American.

As luck would have it, there's a website, www.Allstays.com, that lists all of the above under the category "All Food Co-ops, Natural Food Stores, Health Food Stores." The site's information is somewhat dated, but it lists the big chains as well as the smaller companies; plus, it's divided up by states and has a map for each—oh, happy day! See below.

Now, it turns out my map may not be the first demographic map of Hippie-America. Thus, in 2015, the *Washington Post* published another such map compiled by the national real-estate firm Estately (Swanson).

The Estately map (see below) uses five criteria:

> The number of communes and intentional communities per capita in each state, the number of food co-opers per capita in each state, the number of local Etsy stores per capita selling hemp, patchouli and tie-dye products; and the percentage of Facebook users who express interest in the Grateful Dead, Phish, cannabis, tie-dye, peace, LSD, Bob Dylan or hippies. (Estately also looked at the cities with the most hippies.) (Swanson)

I find their first four criteria relatively good excepting the "Etsy"[13] one: First, the Etsy website doesn't look particularly Hippie-American

---

12   Also, I think that many non-Hippie Americans still aren't quite comfortable with so-called "health food" for various reasons, that they would think an Amy's frozen dinner, for instance, was "kind of weird."
13   Etsy is a website selling the artistic goods of small artisans, some of whom are likely Hippie.

although if you're looking for a tie-dyed jump rope, you've come to the right place—it does sell some clearly Hippie goods. But the more obvious problem here is that Etsy is, yes, a website. Thus, how can anyone calculate "the number of local Etsy stores per capita" as if they were real, non-cyber stores with people walking in the door?

Despite that apparent problem, below is the Estately map,[14] called"10 Best U.S. States for Hippies" (the #1 state is Vermont, #2 is Maine, #3 is New Hampshire, #4 is Oregon, #5 is Colorado, #6 is Montana, #7 is New Mexico, #8 is Wisconsin, #9 is Washington, and #10 is Idaho). Also, at the website Hippyland (www.hippy.com), the reader will find an excellent list of Hippie communities organized state by state ("Hippy Havens"). An advantage of the Hippyland list, by the way, is that it ventures overseas.

Finally, the *Huffington Post* reported in August 2013, "The *Princeton Review* has assembled a list of the best colleges for the *Birkenstock-wearing, tree-hugging clove-smoking vegetarians*" (emphasis in original). Apparently, the small colleges listed are largely on the East and West Coast, and mid-America has been to some extent neglected (*Huffington Post*). On that webpage, however, the reader will find links to several other Hippie-college lists.

Another way of seeing the national breadth of Hippie-America is to consider where its many famous rock bands hail from. Think about it, and you'll see they are from across the nation, including the South—Tom Petty and the Heartbreakers from Gainesville, FL; R.E.M. from Athens, GA; Lynard Skynard from sweet home Alabama; The Allman Brothers Band from Georgia; the late Stevie Ray Vaughan from Austin, TX; and many more.

*   *   *

(The reader will find easier-to-read, color versions of the following two maps at HappilyHippie.net.)

---

[14]   The Estately map was designed by Estately's Marketing Manager, Ryan Nickum, and we thank him for his generosity in allowing us to use it.

"The First Demographic Map of Hippie-America"

The Estately Map of Hippie-America

10 BEST U.S. STATES FOR HIPPIES

Bunch of Squares

Most Hippies

Estately

As for the "eyeball method," most of us know what items of appearance we associate with Hippie identity, from tie-dyes to long hair and beards on men to a natural look for women, etc. So, look around, and you'll see people with those appearances; I find the percent varies from place to place, but that ten-plus percent seems a good general number. When I go to Denver, for instance, I see about ten percent of the people looking identifiably Hippie.

Now, the eyeball method understates; if we estimate how many Hippie-Americans there are solely by external appearance, we'll miss many. Consider Bill Walton, Steve Jobs and Ben Cohen and Jerry Greenfield of Ben & Jerry's. As mentioned, when we see Walton in the broadcasting booth, his ethnicity isn't evident. Same with Jobs, based on photos I've seen. Likewise, Ben Cohen and Jerry Greenfield self-identify as Hippie-American, yet they don't necessarily appear distinctively Hippie (unless, of course, they're wearing Ben & Jerry's tie-dyes).

Clearly, there are tens of millions of Hippie-Americans, but how many "tens of millions"? Let's try this: I'm estimating there are almost as many Hippie-Americans as blacks, and African-Americans make up 13.2% of the US population (CDC). Let's roughly estimate, then, the Hippie-American portion of the US population at ten-plus percent—over 30 million people.

*   *   *

Now, let's look at **the larger world—how many Counterculturists are in it?** As mentioned, any figure can only be even rougher than the United States estimate.

Today, Hippies are a presence in variety of nations: the United States; Canada; areas of Latin America; all the European nations, including Iceland; Russia; Japan; Australia; New Zealand; South Africa; Israel, and places where we might not expect to find them. In early 2008, for example, the Associated Press carried the following:

> Omar Osama bin Laden bears a striking resemblance to his notorious father—except for the dreadlocks that dangle halfway down his back. Then there's the black leather biker jacket.
> The 26-year-old does not renounce his father, al-Qaida leader Osama bin Laden, but in an interview with The Associated Press, he said there is a better way to defend Islam

than al-Qaida's militancy: Omar wants to be an "ambassador for peace" between Muslims and the West. . . .Of course, many may have a hard time getting their mind around the idea of "bin Laden: peacenik."

Yes, Osama bin Laden's eldest son is Hippie-Arabian. The point: There are Hippie-Arabs too, and somewhere out there where we don't necessarily expect to find Counterculturists, we will.

So, if there are roughly 33 million Hippie-Americans in the United States, then I'm going to estimate that for every one Hippie-American, there are about two Counterculturists living elsewhere. Thus, my necessarily very rough estimate results in a very round international number—100 million.

* * *

"Please, don't call me a hippie!": Coming out of the Countercultural Closet

"A rose by any other name would still be a rose."

—Shakespeare

Perhaps one reason why post-Sixties Hippie-America seems invisible is because many Counterculturalists cringe at the word *Hippie*. In short, while there are tens of millions of Hippie-Americans, not all of them call themselves "Hippie," and some resist the term vehemently.

Why mention it? For starters, it raises a question: "If someone doesn't call herself or himself Hippie, how can you?" One way to think of this question is to phrase it in terms of social science: If a member of a group isn't a *self-identifier, self-describer* or *self-designator*, how can you say he or she is a group member?

First, label-avoidance can be seen in other ethnic groups; for example, according to *Wikipedia* ("Names of the Romani people"), Romani do not like to be called *gypsy;* they self-describe as "Roma." Their reluctance to be labeled with an apparently disrespectful term is understandable; however, it doesn't mean they aren't part of that ethnicity that much of the world knows as *gypsy*; they're simply refusing the name the larger society has given them.

Here's a post-1960s example of Hippie-Americans who won't be called "hippie." In 1999, *New York Times* reporter Ann Powers profiled some young people following the Countercultural band Phish. "With their natural-fiber clothing, vegetarian diets and predilection for trippy music, the members of the jam-bands scene seem to be carrying on the legacy of their hippie forbears"; further, she comments, they "appear to have stepped from photographs of [Woodstock]." But don't call them Hippie. One objects, "I don't know what a hippie was." Another adds, "The term is such a convoluted stereotype. It's an explosive cliché." Powers concludes, ". . . many [such] young people disassociate themselves from the image of the stoned hippie living in a hazy fantasy." Yet, as Powers clearly notes, these people have all the objective qualities of Hippie identity; indeed, her article is titled in part "A New Variety of Flower Child in Full Bloom." So, yes, a dispassionate observer would rightfully conclude that, even though they're reluctant to use the H-word, these post-1960s people are indeed Hippie.

Self-designation (in this case, using *Hippie*) isn't crucial to ethnic identification. In other words, if, like Powers, I can show you, using objective criteria and evidence, that someone has the traits of Hippie identity, then I can classify that person or people as "Hippie"—even if he, she or they dislike the term.

In any case, disagreements over particular names does not make either my US or international estimate of the numbers of Counterculturists in today's world unreasonable.

Lastly, I've spent many pages demonstrating the falsity of Hippies Were Just a Thing of the Sixties to prove to you, the reader, something you already know. As I once heard a disapproving Coloradan say, "The Sixties may be over with, but they sure don't know it up in Boulder." He implicitly admits, then, that Hippiedom lives, that "the Sixties" aren't actually over, and what he really means is, "The Sixties are *supposed* to be over with, and they aren't in Boulder." Saying "Hippies were just a thing of the sixties," then, isn't so much *des*criptive as it is *pro*scriptive. It's a policy statement posing as a description of reality.

> **Hippies Were Just a Thing of the Sixties, by creating/ asserting invisibility, turns Hippie-Americans into second-class citizens. That's why we, as a society, repeat it; that's what it really means.**

In short, Hippies Were Just a Thing of the Sixties is the ugly canard of neoconservatives, their intolerant attempt to have their ethnocidal intentions treated as fact. However, Hippie-America lives. It's massive, and as we'll see in Chapter Eight, it's marvelous.

* * *

Chapter Three

A Most Important Secret:
Why the Counterculture Counts

Reviled and demonized, then trivialized by the official
culture it so exuberantly opposed, the counterculture
of the 1960s nevertheless remains the 2,000-pound
gorilla in the china closet of recent American history.
—Jay Stevens, author

For fifty years, the status of that invisible ethnicity I call Hippie-America has been of singular importance; trivialization of it is foolhardy. Here I'll prove that the Counterculture and America's attitudes towards it have, since the mid-1960s, been a key factor in who goes to Washington; I'll contrast this thesis with that of the renown economist/pundit Paul Krugman, who in his *The Conscience of a Liberal* argues that the primary target of modern rightist demagoguery has been African-Americans.

Krugman correctly notes that the "movement conservatism"/ neoconservatism which has dominated American politics for much of the last forty years seeks primarily to transfer wealth upwards. Of course, getting the poor and middle-classes to vote against their own economic interests requires manipulation and demagoguery, aka *red herrings*: emotionally evocative issues largely irrelevant to the matter at hand. These are the fuel of nascent fascism.

Krugman writes, "The most important, sustained source of this [conservative] electoral strength has been race—the ability to win over a subset of white voters by catering, at least implicitly to their fear of blacks" (206).

Now, I will not engage in a politically sectarian contest about which minority, African-Americans or Hippie-Americans, is more oppressed. Given the ugly history of racism in America, I don't doubt that African-American oppression has been more long-lasting, institutionalized and usually intense than the persecution of the Counterculture. That's not the point. The question

> **The question is, since the mid-1960s which group, African-Americans or Hippie-Americans, has been the primary target *in the arena of American politics*, the demagogic fuel of neo-conservatism?**

is, since the mid-1960s which group has been the primary target *in the arena of American politics*, the demagogic fuel of neo-conservatism?

Krugman quotes President Lyndon Johnson's comment to staffer Bill Moyers after the passage of the 1965 Voting Rights Act—enfranchising blacks, primarily—that he, LBJ, thought the Democrats had just lost the South for the rest of their lifetimes (99). Indeed, the South soon turned Republican and has remained so.

Also around 1965, Hippiedom was born. Like predators smelling the newborn flesh of another species, conservative demagogues began exploiting this sensational new culture. Let's begin here with a late-1960s look at two founding fathers of American "backlash" politics: the neocon icon Ronald Reagan of California and the infamous segregationist George Wallace of Alabama.

Unfolding in California was the early political career of a future President, one **Ronald Reagan**—movie star, former liberal union leader; later, a GE corporate spokesman. Now reborn as a militant conservative, he ran for governor. Krugman:

> In the 1966 elections voters would express their dismay at the polls, giving Republicans major gains in Congress. In California . . . Ronald Reagan became governor by campaigning against welfare cheats, urban rioters, long-haired college students—and the state's fair housing act. (81)

Specifically, Reagan promised "to send the welfare bums back to work" and "to clean up the mess at Berkeley" (*Wikipedia*, "Ronald Reagan"). Translation: Reagan's primary scapegoats were Hippies ("long-haired college students," "the mess at Berkeley") and African-Americans ("welfare bums/cheats") though we should bear in mind, that for many voters, Hippies were "welfare bums" too.

Krugman:

> The youth rebellion infuriated many Americans—Ronald Reagan in particular. During his campaign for governor of California, he promised to "investigate the charges of communism and blatant sexual misbehavior on the Berkeley campus." He spoke of "sexual orgies so vile I cannot describe them to you," and at one point claimed to have proof that the Alameda county district attorney had investigated a student

dance which had turned into "an orgy," where they had displayed on a giant screen "pictures of men and women, nude, in sensuous poses, provocative, fondling." In fact there was no such investigation—like the welfare queen with her Cadillac, the dance-turned-orgy was a figment of Reagan's imagination. (95)

For Reagan and the angry right, what was happening in Haight-Ashbury and across the Bay in radical Berkeley were twin demons: non-conformist, bohemian culture and dissident, largely leftist politics. Conservative, "God-fearing" Californians were indignant, resentful and enraged, presenting a political opportunity for Governor Reagan.

In his speeches, Reagan said things so ugly about Hippies that they probably have no equivalent in modern two-party politics. He joked, "A hippie is someone who looks like Tarzan, walks like Jane and smells like Cheetah" (qtd. in "Making Love, Not War")—overt Social-Darwinism and saying, as governor, that a group of Californians stink. But the Hippie haters couldn't get enough; the *New York Times* reports:

> He [Reagan] won a decisive victory in 1966 by vowing to "clean up the mess in Berkeley," and his popularity soared again this year [1967] when he denounced the new outbreak of student unrest [this *student unrest,* to some extent a euphemism for *the Counterculture*]. (Roberts)

In 1969, what had begun as a tussle with the teacher's union at UC-Berkeley spread and in the context of Vietnam protests had further radicalized and mobilized the local largely Hippie community. A siege ensued at "People's Park," an area of that the school's administration wanted as a gym and that locals wanted turned into a park. Author Ron Jacobs calls it the "Showdown in the Counterculture Corral." The conflict escalated, and Reagan declared in regard to student "troublemakers," "If there has to be a bloodbath, then let's get it over with!" (Reagan Quotes)—and he was prepared to walk his talk. Reagan sent into Berkeley, first, Alameda County Sherriff's deputies and, then, thousands of National Guardsmen. The first Guardsmen, however, were local and tended to fraternize with the Countercultural demonstrators. Then, *Wikipedia* explains:

. . . local National Guardsmen were sent home and replaced with National Guardsmen from the more conservative Orange County south of Los Angeles; this "fixed" this problem in the view of the governor's office. Citizens who dared ask questions of National Guard commanders, or engage them in debate, were threatened with violence. . . . [Also,] Berkeley city police officers were discovered to be parking several blocks away from the Annex park, removing their badges/identification and donning grotesque Halloween-type masks . . . to go inflict violence upon citizens they found in the park annex. ("People's Park")

Eventually, the Orange County National Guardsmen used teargas and buckshot on the mostly Hippie protestors. One was shot dead, one was blinded, and at least 128 were wounded ("People's Park"); Reagan, then, led a public war against this Countercultural community—a sort of organized lynch mob in which conservative Californians were encouraged to hurt Hippies. Apparently, the Governor's fascistic demagoguery and repression were popular enough to help win him re-election in 1970.

So, Ronald Reagan's early successes in California relied heavily on fears and hatred of Hippies.

In 1968, George Wallace, the Alabama governor and infamous white supremacist, threw his hat into the presidential ring. Running as an independent, he hoped to lure a substantial portion of the conservative vote from Republican Richard Nixon and drive the nation towards the right. Early in his career, Wallace had been a liberal

> Wallace taunted Counter-cultural protestors: "Oh, I thought you were a she; you're a he! Oh, my goodness," "Come up here after I've finished my speech, and I'll autograph yuh sandals for ya," "All he needs is a good haircut; if he'll go to the barber shop, I think they'd cure him."

judge who treated African-Americans respectfully; then, he lost a 1958 bid for governor and privately declared, "I was outniggered, and I will never be outniggered again!" (qtd. in "George Wallace"). The key to Wallace's political success in Alabama, according to the Wallace campaign's executive director Tom Turnipseed, had been "Race and being opposed to the civil-rights movement" (qtd. in "George Wallace").

But if race-baiting had worked at home, Wallace apparently felt he needed to modify his message for a broader national audience, and his presidential campaign speeches tended to pander to prejudice against Hippies, not blacks.

On the campaign trail, Wallace taunted Countercultural protestors: "Oh, I thought you were a she; you're a he! Oh, my goodness," "Come up here after I've finished my speech, and I'll autograph yuh sandals for ya," "All he needs is a good haircut; if he'll go to the barber shop, I think they'd cure him" (qtd. in "George Wallace"). Explains Turnipseed: "Governor Wallace used to love to use the long-haired hippie agitators, the folks who were out in the front lines of the civil-rights movement, the anti-war movement. He felt like his constituency just really disliked [them] the most" (qtd. in "George Wallace").

Wallace's Finance Director, Seymour Trammell, adds:

> That would be the kind of pictures [Wallace quarreling with "hippie" protestors] we would want; when that would be on television . . . people would just . . . send whatever dollars they had right into the campaign headquarters, and by doing that, we were able to finance the campaign. (qtd. in "George Wallace")

Hippies, then, became Wallace's new "niggers," anti-Hippie hatred the lifeblood of his campaign. And just as his old appeals to racism long sustained Wallace politically, his new appeals to anti-Hippie prejudice worked political wonders. No, Wallace didn't win, but his campaign mobilized millions of angry Americans, invigorating forces of prejudice and ethnic chauvinism and shoving the nation in a more intolerant, repressive direction.

Let's next consider who in 1968 was elected President: Republican **Richard M. Nixon**. Like many rightist politicians of the time, Nixon was the resurfaced remnant of a tarnished McCarthyism. Screaming, "Communist!" had lost some of its political magic; new targets and scapegoats were needed. Of course, late-1960s riots in the African-American hearts of blighted urban America helped Nixon, giving him a pretext for a fascistic military response that left numerous "Negroes" dead. And when the keystone of Nixon's successful campaign became

Law and Order, voters took this as code for a crackdown against black "rioters."

But, historians concur, it was also code for a crackdown on the Counterculture. Remember, it wasn't just the inner cities that were in turmoil; the heavily Countercultural campuses were revolting: Vietnam was in full swing, escalating daily, and the military draft was on.

So, despite the advice of his own Schafer Commission to legalize marijuana, Nixon chose to crack down on pot and initiated the first "War on Drugs" (Baum 11-12). White House tapes show that Nixon's zealotry for pot prohibition was part and parcel of various prejudices, specifically against "blacks, Jews, and the Counterculture" (Common Sense for Drug Policy).

In addition to targeting inner-city blacks, Nixon's war on "crime" was also a war on the Counterculture and was understood as such by voters. The evidence, then, would seem to show Nixon exploiting Afrophobia and prejudice towards Hippies about equally.

Let's look at the Democrats for a bit: Their 1972 presidential nominee was the anti-war, liberal Democrat from South Dakota, Senator **George McGovern**. That campaign first faltered when a few weeks in McGovern had to change his vice-presidential choice.

> **According to author and researcher Martin Torgoff, in 1972, ". . . the Republican Party accused the Democrats of being the party of 'acid, amnesty, and abortion.'"**

Generally, the McGovern campaign was heavily Hippie-baited, perhaps a historical first. Politicized Hippies were looking for a way to "work within the system," as they'd been told they should. Some began working for McGovern. There was nothing necessarily Hippie about George McGovern; the idea that Hippie-Americans have ever dominated the Democratic Party is fantasy. Nonetheless, the McGovern campaign was and is commonly seen as being Hippie; in fact, this perception was so prevalent 22 years later, when Republican Newt Gingrich began crying "counterculture McGoverniks," that most people took his assumption that the Counterculture and the McGovern campaign were one as an established truth.

A conservative pundit typifies this historical take on the McGovern campaign: ". . . George McGovern, the far-left Democrat Party radical who was the candidate of the 'hippie' 1960s counterculture movement" (Ryan).

And according to author and researcher Martin Torgoff, in 1972, ". . . the Republican Party accused the Democrats of being the party of 'acid, amnesty, and abortion'" (272). The "acid" and, to some extent, the "amnesty"[15] are references to the Counterculture.

Partly because of the McGovern campaign's Countercultural trappings, the conservative head of the AFL-CIO, George Meany, refused to endorse the Democratic nominee and went with the Republicans, something unique in modern American politics (Plumer). Add it all up, and a heavily Hippie-baited McGovern was badly beaten by a Richard Nixon Watergate bound—soon to be the most disgraced president in American history.[16]

Nixon's successor, Republican **Gerald Ford**, wasn't re-elected. One Ford Administration incident, however, is worth recalling: during the 1976 campaign, Ford's Secretary of Agriculture, Earl Butz, was caught making a vulgar racist was then forced to resign. So at that time, overt Afrophobia had begun being punished—make a racist comment, and you could lose your job.

In 1976, Democrat **Jimmy Carter** went to Washington. His connection with the Counterculture was fairly close; in his outlook towards Hippie-America and marijuana issues, Carter was way ahead of his time. For starters, he had Hippie kids; indeed, in a *Rolling Stone*, interview, Carter notes resentfully that his sons were sometimes abused by police for having long hair (Brokaw 58). And Carter has an appreciation for Hippie culture; for example, he can quote Bob Dylan lyrics and played Dylan's music "almost constantly" at his Georgia governor's mansion; he described himself as being "deeply immersed in the culture of the countercultural Allman Brothers [Band]" (Brokaw 58). Here also was a President who said one of the most sensible things ever about the marijuana-and-health argument: "Penalties against possession of a drug should not be more damaging to an individual than the use of the drug itself; and where they are, they should be changed" (qtd. in Torgoff 272).

---

[15] The reference is to amnesty for "draft dodgers" who fled to Canada and elsewhere.

[16] By the way, no one argues that a reason the McGovern-Shriver ticket lost was because that campaign was too close to African-America.

And, like McGovern, Carter's campaign was getting Countercultural support. The Allman Brothers, according to Carter, were his "key fundraisers" (Brokaw 58). Carter's personal Countercultural friends (Willie Nelson, Bob Dylan and Hunter S. Thompson) were also on board —Thompson's endorsement blared on, literally, the cover of the *Rolling Stone* (Brokaw 55). I recall reading of a Carter campaign staffer's response to a complaint that the Counterculture wasn't getting enough back in return from Carter: "What do you want us to do? Make Greg Allman Minister of Drugs?"

Carter's Countercultural connections followed him into the White House although his first crisis had nothing to do with Hippies. In 1977, Carter's Director of the Office of Budget and Finance, Burt Lance, a Carter friend from Georgia, became enmeshed in scandal, and Carter, who had run as a moralist, was accused of hypocrisy. His numbers went down, and an energy crisis, leading to humiliating lines at American gas stations, hurt him more.

Then, public drug use by Carter staff became a thorn in his administration's side. In July 1978, Carter's progressive new drug czar, Peter Bourne, was caught sniffing cocaine at a Washington party hosted by NORML. A second drug-related issue arose; Bourne soon resigned. Critics were turning Carter's connection with the Counterculture into a political liability, and the situation escalated with accusations of pot-smoking and other drug use by Carter aides. Thus, only four days after Bourne's dramatic departure, Carter was forced to publicly warn his staff about "using illegal drugs" (Baum 116). Generally, Carter was seen as being too close to the Counterculture.

Add a recession, and the 1979 Iranian Hostage Crisis was the final blow. So, a number of things made Jimmy Carter a one-term President; prominent among them was Hippie-baiting. In contrast, there is no clear evidence that Carter's undoing had anything to do with Afrophobia.

Then, it was 1980, and Jimmy Carter had to face an angry, self-righteous **Ronald Reagan**. It's a myth, apparently, that Carter lost in a landslide (Brokaw 58); still, neoconservatism won Washington.

Reagan began his campaign with an appearance in Philadelphia, Mississippi, a small town whose only previous national significance was as a place where in 1964 three civil-rights workers were murdered by white supremacists. Clearly, Reagan's visit was an affirmation to the racist right. Still, Reagan's campaign wasn't overtly Afrophobic, and the Philadelphia appearance seems more a disturbing historical footnote than the first act in a race-baiting play.

Of course, Reagan hadn't forgotten how well his appeals to anti-Hippie bigotry worked in California, and Torgoff notes, "Presidential candidate Ronald Reagan would wield one of his most effective political cudgels in the election of 1980 when he charged that not only were Democrats soft on crime and Communism, but they were the party of pot, too" (280).

Torgoff quotes legalization activist Keith Stroup regarding Reagan's demagoguery:

> I think it [Reagan's victory] was . . . a cheap way to get reelected. If you paint your opponent as soft on crime, soft on drugs, you could beat them—it was that simple. It became an easy way to tar people, to destroy their careers and lives . . . . It didn't matter if you were a middle-class person who held a respectable job and went home once a week and smoked a joint or you were a heroin addict on the street corner; we were all lumped together. It was Lester Grinspoon of Harvard who began calling it *psychopharmacological McCarthyism*. (qtd. in 423)

The Reagans soon launched a crusade, one that would save the nation from the menace of "drugs," a term that was understood to mean the substances other cultures were using, not the drugs[17] respectable Mrs. Reagan and her kind were taking. And of course no distinctions between use and abuse—no "excuses," no moral shirking—would be allowed.

In October 1982, President Reagan told the nation: "The mood toward drugs is changing in this country and the momentum is with us. We're making no excuses for drugs—hard, soft, or otherwise. Drugs are bad and we're going after them" (qtd. in Baum 162).

Later, author/researcher Martin Torgoff tells us: ". . . president and First Lady **Nancy Reagan** appeared on television together to make an

---

[17]   Nancy Reagan's daughter, Patti Reagan Davis, has described her mother as "addicted" to prescription diet pills (CNN). And of course, many neocons—Rush Limbaugh, for instance—have documented drug-abuse problems.

45

> Nancy Reagan called the new campaign Just Say No, and one of its key phrases, "zero tolerance," was for Hippie-America *intolerance* in the traditional racial/ ethnic/ religious sense.

appeal for a national crusade against drugs, comparing it with the Second World War, and urging Americans to adopt an attitude of 'outspoken intolerance'" (355).

Nancy Reagan called the new campaign Just Say No, and one of its key phrases, "zero tolerance," was for Hippie-America *intolerance* in the traditional racial/ethnic/ religious sense. Billions of dollars of propaganda and repression would end drug use in America, and by implication, the Counterculture—now often known as simply "the drug culture." Congress couldn't have been more acquiescent. Drug-testing became a national obsession—yes, the wicked marijuana users[18] would be rooted out that America might again be clean, pure and strong.

On the legal front, mandatory minimums became law; we began to see life-without-parole sentences for people whose only "crime" was being involved with marijuana, a drug from which no one has ever directly died.

A country mobilized to attack the enemy within looked like a lynch mob. It was a hard time to be Hippie-American; I felt vaguely like a Jewish-German probably felt upon the election of Adolf Hitler. Neoconservative Reagan appointee Myles Ambrose, director of a federal Office of Drug Abuse Law Enforcement, sounded particularly Nazi-like: "Drug people are the very vermin of humanity" (qtd. in Baum 83). Hippies had become the official national enemy; it was payback time, and the Counterculture was going to get a good dose of what it allegedly deserved. In a short time, what a long and awful way the country had come from sane, humane Jimmy Carter.

In 1988, Reagan's second term ended, and he was succeeded by his Vice-President **George H. W. Bush**. In the campaign, Bush attempted to race-bait the Democrats with the infamous Willie Horton television ad. Horton was a black murderer who had been paroled by the Democratic nominee, Governor Michael Dukakis of Massachusetts. Though criticized for the commercial, Bush triumphed.

---

[18] Drug testing almost exclusively identifies marijuana users.

On taking office, however, his demagoguery and scapegoating seemed directed at the Hippie-America. On September 5, 1989, in his first televised address to the nation from the Oval Office, Bush called the drug crisis the "moral equivalent of war" and the "gravest threat to our national well-being" (qtd. in Torgoff 427). A Hippie-hating zealot, a philosophy professor without a speck of medical background, William Bennett, became the new Drug Czar—head witch-hunter.

Congress was busy as a lynch mob too—you simply couldn't be too hysterical about drugs. Torgoff describes 1989:

> Senator Phil Gramm and Congressman Newt Gingrich wanted to round up masses of drug users, herd them onto military bases that would be converted into prisons [as in concentration camps], and make them pay the court costs. Not to be outdone, Congressman Richard Ray, a Georgia Democrat, proposed the Pacific Islands of Wake and Midway for the same purpose. Police Chief Daryl Gates of Los Angeles declared that casual drug users should be "taken out and shot" because they were guilty of "treason." The Delaware State Legislature debated bringing back the whipping post for drug users, a punishment that may very well have been too mild for William Bennett, who at the time told Larry King that the beheading of drug dealers was "morally plausible." (428)

* * *

Now, let me briefly interrupt our chronology: I need to prove **the link between neoconservatism's War on Drugs and its emphasis on persecution of the Counterculture**. After all, other American minorities have been heavily impacted by the War on Drugs. It's generally accepted, for example, that the double standard in crack/cocaine laws targets blacks. Again, my purpose is not to paper over the horrors of racism or to deny its vicious impact. My purpose is to expose the underlying bigotry that is the fuel of the right's rise—how does neoconservative demagoguery work?

Two things: first, by examining neoconservative philosophy, we can see its overt emphasis on persecution of the Counterculture, not blacks. Second, I'll show how neoconservatism has been engaged in a deliberate attempt to destroy Hippiedom, that in regard to the Counterculture, it has clear ethnocidal intentions whereas its Afrophobia seems more muted, harder to prove.

First, **neocon philosophy**: How to prove it **is inherently anti-Hippie**, that hatred of Hippies is as integral to neoconservatism as anti-Semitism was to Hitler's fascism? Well, aside from the electoral evidence already mentioned, let's go to the ideology's source, the "Godfather of Neoconservatism," Irving Kristol, who died in September 2009. Associated Press notes Kristol's powerful influence and tells us that Kristol's seminal political life was characterized by two principal thrusts: "an emphatic rejection of communism and the Counterculture." Kristol himself is quoted as saying, "If there is any one thing that neo-conservatives are unanimous about, it is their dislike of the Counterculture" (AP, "Godfather").

> **It's clear from its rhetoric and practice, neoconservatism has long wanted Hippiedom dead. There's a term for the attempt to remove an ethnicity from society: *ethnic cleansing*.**

Or consider the beliefs of Kristol's pupil, another influential neocon ideologue, William Bennett: "[The drug problem] comes from this tradition of freedom and liberty, which gets distorted into license and 'do your own thing' and the gospel of the Sixties" (qtd. in Baum 291). "Do your own thing," "Gospel of the Sixties"—can you say *Hippie*?

Okay, so no Secret Decoder Ring needed here: necocons hate the Counterculture; they're overt about it. It's at the very heart of neoconservatism. In contrast, if white supremacism and Afrophobia are at the heart of neoconservatism, shouldn't we see it in Kristol's obituary? Shouldn't we hear Bennett excoriating African-America?

It's clear, then, from its rhetoric and practice, neoconservatism has long wanted Hippiedom dead. There's a term for the attempt to remove an ethnicity from society: *ethnic cleansing*. Two examples:

Consider first the strange case of **James Watt**, Reagan's neoconservative, Christian-right Secretary of the Interior, who in 1983 attempted to ban The Beach Boys from performing at the Fourth of July celebration at the National Mall. Watt, who was fantastically ignorant about popular culture, had never heard the Beach Boys, but he knew their music was rock 'n' roll, and correctly associated it with Hippie culture, with what he called "the wrong element" (UPI). Here policy and principle were one: neo-conservatism would outlaw Hippie-America from national affairs.

Then, consider this from author, researcher and former *Wall St. Journal* reporter Daniel Baum who quotes **an anti-marijuana activist urging** in **1981 the appointment of Carlton Turner** as Reagan's drug czar: "It is hoped by legions of hopefuls [an organized letter-writing campaign was under way] that the government in Washington will come forward with a new approach to the whole drug problem in America, which will mean turning the nation away from the wretched Drug Culture that is rotting it at the core" (qtd. in 146). Turner was soon approved, and he proclaimed, "I was hired by the President of the United States to clean up America" (qtd. in Baum 137). Also, "We have to create a generation of drug-free Americans to *purge* society" (emphasis added) (qtd. in Baum 152).

So, neoconservatives have been speaking the language of ethnocide, practicing ethnocidal policies. And it's clear that the group they've been trying to eliminate is Hippie-America; it stands to reason, then, that Hippie-hating and Hippie-baiting are at the heart of their demagoguery, not Afrophobia.

*   *   *

In 1992, the neoconservatives stumbled at the polls, but not for a lack of anti-Hippie appeals. Columnist David Broder describes **the keynote speech at the 1991 Republican national convention**:

> Through almost gritted teeth, Marilyn Quayle [wife of Republican vice-president Dan Quayle] declared that those people in Madison Square Garden [the Democratic National Convention], who were claiming the mantle of leadership for a new generation, were usurpers. . . . And then she drew the line that has not been erased: "Remember, not everyone joined in the Counterculture. Not everyone demonstrated, dropped out, took drugs, joined in the sexual revolution or dodged the draft. Not everyone concluded that American society was so bad that it had to be radically remade by social revolution. . . . The majority of my generation lived by the credo our parents taught us: We believed in God, in hard work and personal discipline, in our nation's essential goodness, and in the opportunity it promised

those willing to work for it. . . . Though we knew some changes needed to be made, we did not believe in destroying America to save it."

In short, the Republicans ran mostly against the Counterculture, not blacks. Their basic campaign message: We're not Hippies; the Democrats are.

Somehow, it wasn't enough, and the allegedly Countercultural **Clintons, Bill and Hillary**, came to Washington. Maureen Dowd of the *New York Times* explains the Republican response:

> Ever since Bill Clinton was elected, conservatives have been acting as though the Oval Office had been festooned with macramé and bongs, as if there were some crazy free-love, war-protesting, pig-hating, Bobby Seale supporting, Carlos Castaneda-reading, Bob Dylan-grooving hippie running the country. ("G.O.P.'s Rising Star").

"But now Newt Gingrich, echoing other Republican moralists, like William Bennett and Dan Quayle, has brought the counter-culture back—not for a reunion concert, alas, but as a scapegoat with flowers in its hair."—Frank Rich of the *NYT*.

Well, if Hippie-baiting hadn't done the job in 1992, it redeemed itself big time two years later in Bill Clinton's first mid-term election. The Republicans, led by Speaker of the House, **Newt Gingrich** of Georgia, were pushing something called The Contract with America. Vehement, vengeful—Gingrich angrily branded the Clintons, "Counterculture McGoverniks" (Dowd, "G.O.P.'s Rising Star"), this the cutting edge of his campaign. Dowd paraphrased Gingrich: ". . . before America got what conservatives scoffingly call the welfare state and hippies, things were on the right track" ("G.O.P.'s Rising Star"). Columnist Frank Rich of the *New York Times* comments:

> But now Newt Gingrich, echoing other Republican moralists, like William Bennett and Dan Quayle, has brought the counterculture back—not for a reunion concert, alas, but as a scapegoat with flowers in its hair. Not only is the counterculture

being held responsible for the excesses of Bill Clinton—a non-inhaling Fleetwood Mac fan, of all unlikely hippies—but for everything immoral, violent and sexually explicit in American culture today.

The Republican Party won the elections handily, gaining control of both houses of Congress for the first time in decades; Dowd concluded, ". . . the Republican leader [has] dragged his party from a 1992 slough to a nasty and successful attack mode" ("G.O.P.'s Rising Star"). Gingrich, then, had effectively Hippie-baited the Clinton Administration, pushing the nation further to the repressive right.

Those who lived through the Clinton administration will remember the strange state of governmental affairs that eventually led to impeachment: in addition to the three historical branches of government—the legislative, the judicial and the executive—there was the **Special Prosecutor's Office of Ken Starr**, a new *de facto* branch of government seemingly designed to harass the executive. When neoconservative Starr failed to prove much else, he went after Bill Clinton's extra-marital sex life.

Thing is, according to sociologists, bigots often engage in denial and projection, putting unseemly qualities in themselves onto racial and ethnic others (Levin 176).

As noted, neoconservatives tend to see the Clintons as Hippie, as cultural others. Well, if bigots view Hippies much the way they do other ethnic minorities, then they likely have a deep-seated need to see allegedly Hippie Bill Clinton as particularly lustful and lewd— "Yes, it's the hippies who are like that; it's not us decent, God-fearing real Americans." Of course, during the time of this witch hunt, the indiscretions of several prominent conservatives were also discovered: pro-life crusader Indiana senator Birch Bayh, drug warrior and former New York Mayor Rudi Giuliani, and eventually Gingrich himself. The rightist moralizers, it turned out, were "fornicators" too, but their outrage was reserved exclusively for "countercultural" Bill Clinton and his appalling "lack of character." Thus, the Republican fixation with Bill Clinton's sexual behavior that so hurt his Presidency may well have been rooted in anti-Hippie bigotry.

Incidentally, in 1994, **executives at** the oil giant **Texaco were secretly taped making anti-black slurs**, creating a public scandal. Two high-level executives were suspended, and in 1996, partly because of the tape, Texaco lost a 175-million-dollar lawsuit filed by its African-American employees (Grant). This again illustrates how, increasingly, openly Afrophobic speech has been punished.

At this point, let's look briefly at **Pat Buchanan**, the former Nixon speechwriter and Reagan advisor who ran for the Republican Presidential nomination in 1992 and 1996; in 2000, he ran for president as an independent. Today, a widely heard pundit, Buchanan believes the nation is enmeshed in a "culture war," that "the counterculture, the adversary culture, the Woodstock generation has pretty much prevailed and captured the commanding heights of American culture . . ." (qtd. in Caban), and this, in turn, is leading to the demise of not just the nation but of Western Civilization.

When in 1994 *Forrest Gump* premiered, that mainstay of American conservatism *The National Review* hailed it as "Best Picture Indicting the Sixties Counterculture"; in the same vein, Buchanan promptly declared that Forrest Gump, the film character, was his campaign's mascot (Gordinier).

In 1996, he bashed Department of Education "bureaucrats," telling crowds, "The American people do not need some character . . . sitting up there in sandals and beads telling them how to educate their children" (qtd. in Rowland).

Buchanan, then, has not been shy about his Hippie-hating and Hippie-baiting. Although Buchanan is occasionally accused of being anti-black, the evidence tends to be indirect. In contrast, his prejudice towards the Counterculture is overt—a staple of his politics. In fact, before George Wallace died, he hailed Buchanan, claiming him as a political heir for, among other things, his vitriol against the Counterculture (Byrne).

In 2000, the Democrats fielded Al Gore of Tennessee against Republican **George W. Bush** (Bush the junior). Early on, Bush made a campaign visit to white-supremacist Bob Jones University, later claiming he hadn't known of its no-blacks-allowed policy.

He publicly signaled his dislike of the Counterculture, his bigotry, in an interview with *Gentleman's Quarterly* (*GQ*) as reported by Dowd: "[George W. Bush] said that when he was at Yale in the 60's, he did not share the musical tastes of the counterculture. He said he liked the Beatles before their 'weird, psychedelic period' [translation: before they went Hippie]" ("Cultural Drifter").

I don't have solid evidence of Al Gore being Hippie-baited (though it may well have happened); perhaps, tying him to the allegedly

Countercultural Clintons was enough. In an election decided by a neoconservative-dominated Supreme Court and widely perceived as stolen, Bush, of course, prevailed. Not a year afterwards, 9/11 happened, and suddenly these reactionaries had a new pretext for repression: the "War on Terror."

Now, you might think this would mean a neglect of the War on Drugs and persecution of the Counterculture. Instead, neoconservatives sought to elide the two (**the War on Drugs and the War on Terror**); so, instead of fighting a war on two fronts, they could attack on one. Radley Balko, a policy analyst of the libertarian-leaning Cato Institute, reports:

> **"[P]eople who plant and tend the [marijuana] gardens are terrorists who wouldn't hesitate to help other terrorists get into the country with the aim of causing mass casualties."—Bush Drug Czar John Walters**

On the heels of the "I Helped" commercials that began last January [2002], the Drug Enforcement Administration has again engaged in a propaganda campaign aimed at likening drug-using Americans to the most notorious financiers of terrorism.

This time, it's a traveling museum exhibit entitled "Target America: Traffickers, Terrorists and You." The exhibit harmonizes chunks of World Trade Center rubble and pictures of the scarred Pentagon with paraphernalia seized in international drug busts, and offers a "history" of the links between the drug trade and terrorism.

The aim? Stain the hands of the growing decriminalization movement with the blood of Sept. 11 victims. It's shameless, exploitative and not even remotely accurate.

President Bush himself stated, "If you quit drugs, you join the fight against terror in America" (qtd. in Campbell). And here's what his last Drug Czar, a William Bennett acolyte named John Walters, said about pot growers, ". . . people who plant and tend the [marijuana] gardens are terrorists who wouldn't hesitate to help other terrorists get into the country with the aim of causing mass casualties" (qtd. in Mojoey). Walters offered not a shred of evidence.

The first George W. Bush administration, in contrast, had a painstakingly crafted multiracial face. African-American General Colin Powell became Secretary of State; Bush's important National Security Advisor, Condoleezza Rice, was not only African-American but female. If this was an administration trying to send some coded message to the Afrophobic right, they were certainly bungling it.

Of course, before George W. Bush could get to a second term, he and the Republicans had to get past the 2004 **Democratic ticket headed by** Massachusetts senator **John Kerry**. The election was a squeaker, and there is credible evidence that in Ohio and New Mexico, Republicans stole it (Kennedy). Then again, the GOP employed their favorite tactic, and Kerry was heavily Hippie baited.

In particular, an anti-Kerry group called Swiftboat Veterans and POWs for Truth launched an attack on Kerry, spotlighting his leadership role in Vietnam Veterans Against the War (VVAW), a group of anti-war veterans, the great majority of whom were visibly Hippie. In fact, the conservative Sinclair Broadcast Group ordered its 40 television stations to air a scathing "documentary" on Kerry's VVAW work, "Stolen Honor: Wounds That Never Heal," in the weeks before the election. Columnist Michael Graham writes:

> Campaigning on Kerry's military service certainly makes him more relatable to Mr. and Mrs. Typical American. However, it also makes Kerry's record as an anti-war activist relevant, too. This was always the Achilles heel, calf, thigh and lower torso of the Kerry "war hero" strategy. Do you really want Mr. and Mrs. Typical flipping through photo albums of John Kerry hanging out with hippies and throwing away the ribbons from his medals? . . . John Kerry . . . launched his political career as a long-haired, ribbon-throwing, fist-shaking, [Jane] Fonda-friendly peacenik.

Conservative blogger Linda Goodman writes, ". . . after watching the political advertisements crafted by the Swift Boat Veterans for the Truth . . . some, mostly older folks, ask, 'Was he really one of those awful hippies?'" ("Dateline D.C.").

Conservative columnist Beverly Eakman goes farther, calling young Kerry "a scruffy-looking hippy-type." And David Broder adds that the outburst over Kerry's postwar record ". . . is explainable only as the latest outburst of a battle that has been going on now for more than three decades. . . . On both sides, the unending culture war is as searing as it was when it first burst into flames." Yes, and as we saw in Broder's description of the 1991 Marilyn Quayle speech above, that "culture war" is really a war on the Counterculture.

Meanwhile, **back at the Bush Ranch, second term**, the Administration's face looked more multiracial than ever: African-American woman Condoleezza Rice had been promoted to Secretary of State, and Hispanic Alberto Gonzales became Attorney General. Yet, the Bush Administration ramped up marijuana arrests (Common Sense for Drug Policy). An ideology demonizing the "drug culture"— a euphemism for the Counterculture— seems to have been a constant in these two Bush Junior administrations, and in 2007, Dowd would write of Bush and VP Cheney's "scolding social policy designed to expunge the Age of Aquarius" ("Ozone").

But, "Dubya's" late-term approval ratings were the worst in history (CBS News, "Bush's"). The 2006 mid-term elections saw a Democratic landslide, giving that party a majority in both House and Senate, something they hadn't seen in twelve years. The smart pundits said 2008 would certainly produce a Democratic president.

In August 2006, **Virginia Governor George Allen** was a rising Republican star, rising, that is, until a public gaff in the form of a racial epithet brought the Presidential hopeful tumbling down—seems to have destroyed his political career. No, the target of the prejudice wasn't black, but the incident well illustrates how damaging any credible charge of racism had become.

In November 2006, following the new Democratic domination of Congress, Representative **Nancy Pelosi** of San Francisco became the first woman to be elected as Speaker of the House. The neocon response was to set up a national howl about Pelosi's "San Francisco values." Outgoing GOP Speaker Dennis Hastert launched the attack; he was soon joined by other prominent conservatives such as talk-show host and "culture warrior" Bill O'Reilly. As for Hippie-baiting, O'Reilly assailed San Francisco's "setting up city-wide pot shops" (SFist), and of course, for much of the nation, San Francisco remains a symbol of Hippie culture.

Then, in October 2007, in a bit of pre-election positioning, the Republicans found a way to Hippie-bait the Democrats, particularly **future presidential candidate Hillary Clinton**. Turns out that Clinton and fellow New York Democratic Senator Charles Schumer had attempted to fund something called the Bethel Woods Center for the Arts, located in Woodstock, New York. The request mentioned that the museum, among other things, was preserving "the 1960's and its continuing legacy" (Murray). The media then reported Republicans had killed what they had begun calling the **"Woodstock Museum."** As reported by the *NY Daily News*, Senator John McCain, the future Republican nominee, gleefully grasped the opportunity:

> "I heard that Woodstock was quite a cultural event," the former Vietnam prisoner of war deadpanned, referring to the 1969 counterculture music festival in upstate New York. "I happened to be in prison at the time.[19] Though I wasn't able to see it, I understand that it was quite a pharmaceutical marvel. But let me tell you, I don't think we ought to be spending one million of your tax dollars to have a museum there." (qtd. in DeFrank)

Of course, Hillary Clinton didn't win the Democratic nomination. Had she, the Republicans would likely have generated an orgy of Hippie-baiting, sounding something like "Hippie Hillary Countercultural Clinton!" We know this partly because in anticipation of her presidential nomination, numerous hate-Hillary books hit the market, and these "exposés" often stressed the Clintons' alleged Hippie identity; for example, Edward Klein has a lurid-in-tone chapter called "Grooving at Cozy Beach" about the young couple's very own Summer of Love. We are talking allegations of drug use, premarital sex and—gasp!—listening to Jefferson Airplane albums!

In September 2008, relatively late in the primary season, former Tennessee Senator **Fred Thompson** entered the Presidential race, hoping to be a new Ronald Reagan, someone who would galvanize and lead a contentious GOP. Of course, Thompson fizzled and left the race in January 2009 but not before doing something noteworthy: while his official

While Fred Thompson's official platform promised "Security/ Unity/Prosperity," his campaign issued a tee-shirt that seemed to show his real electoral strategy—the demagogic dark side behind the noble façade. It read "Kill the terrorists. Protect the borders. Punch the hippies."

---

[19]   Other accounts have McCain punning, "I was tied up at the time."

platform promised "Security/Unity/Prosperity," his campaign issued a tee-shirt that seemed to show his real electoral strategy—the demagogic dark side behind the noble façade. It read "Kill the terrorists. Protect the borders. Punch the hippies" (Curt). (**See photo #4.**)

"Punch the hippies"?! It's amazing, really; I can't imagine a mainstream political campaign being so overt in its hostility and scapegoating of any other American group. Yet, when Thompson exited the race, the conservative *National Review* headlined its piece, "Maybe He Should Have Punched More Hippies" (Geraghty).

Given, finally, the not particularly Countercultural Democratic nominee, **Barack Obama**, the Republicans just kept on keeping on, and Senator **John McCain**'s first television attack ad was called "Love." "It was a time of uncertainty, hope and change—the Summer of Love," the spot began. The video showed a long-haired male strolling across a campus (Montopoli). Yeah, we get it—the Sixties, Hippies. The ad then extolled McCain's character: a real American war hero. And the Hippies? They're the foil, the epitome of everything McCain and his party are not—they're the Democrats.

McCain soon surprised the nation with his deliberately sexy VP choice, the woman governor with folksy appeal, **Sarah Palin**. *Rolling Stone* illustrator Victor Juhasz portrayed her (correctly, in my opinion) as McCain's attack dog—a reactionary pit bull (Taibbi). And where did the grinning demagogue sink her teeth? That wild-man Sixties "terrorist," William (Bill) Ayers, who in Palin parlance had been "palling around with" Obama in Chicago. Late in the campaign, this seemed the GOP's number-one issue—"Can't have a President who pals around with terrorists!"

A "Sixties radical," Ayers was a member of the Maoist-inspired Weather Underground; he participated in three small bombings, targeting property, not people (*Wikipedia*)—thus the "terrorist" label. Also, judging from his physical appearance both in the late Sixties (long hair and flamboyant glasses) and today (an earring in each earlobe), Ayers is Hippie-American. For neocon demagogues, then, he must have seemed a gift; they'd been trying to lump "terrorism" with the Counterculture; here was an apparent incarnation of both, and ("Oh, it's too good to be true!") an actual associate of Obama's. Well, sort of: apparently Obama's contact with an older, more moderate Ayers probably didn't constitute actual "palling"—most likely, the two were never in the same bowling league. But never mind: the Republican plan was guilt by association, and *any* association, however distant, would do.

Undoubtedly, then, one motive behind the GOP obsession with William Ayers was to play on prejudice towards the Counterculture, to once again Hippie-bait the Democrats. **Please see Photo #5**, the cartoon of Bill Ayers; notice how prominent are Ayers'earrings. He's ridiculed as stupid, scruffy and dirty (there's obvious grime on his jacket). Together, these comprise a standard stereotype of a "Sixties person" and evidence exploitation of anti-Hippie bigotry.

Now, during this same campaign, there were racist attacks on African-American Barack Obama's candidacy, "humor" wallowing in demeaning stereotypes. But these attacks remained on the anti-Obama fringe and never played a prominent role in the official GOP campaign. That's partly because they were usually reported with a sort of indignation, and the McCain campaign well understood that any overt Afrophobia would be disastrous.

Finally, here's an amusing **2010 example of** the **Hippie-baiting of House Speaker Pelosi** by a conservative Congressman from Georgia, Jim Marshall, as described in the *SFWeekly.com* story "Democratic Candidate Portrays San Francisco as Haven of Dirty Hippies." Joe Eskenazi reports that Marshall's campaign produced a video portraying Pelosi's "San Francisco as a den of bizarre, gyrating hippies" and adds:

> "Georgia is a long way from San Francisco," brays an announcer in a syrupy drawl of the sort that makes one anticipate he'll soon remark on life and boxes of chocolate. "And Jim Marshall is a long way from Nancy Pelosi." These pearls of wisdom are accompanied by images of trippy hippies engaging in some manner of zonked-out dance closely approximating The Monkey.

Finally, let's consider the **2016 campaign** culminating in the election of **Donald Trump:**

An insightful column by the widely read Paul Waldman, "Hillary Clinton, Bill Clinton, and the Long But Fading Shadow of the 1960s," suggests that Hippie-hating remains at the heart of modern American politics, something he ascribes to a sort of late-1960s national sibling rivalry: "If you were in that first group [anti-Hippies] back then, you may still be mad, not just for what you missed out on but because so many of the questions people were arguing about back then—civil rights, Vietnam, sexual liberation—have been settled, and your side lost. Many of those people looked at Bill Clinton and saw every hippie they ever wanted to sock in the jaw." And Waldman quotes from a piece by Hanna Rosin in *The Atlantic*, making essentially the same angry, frustrated, late-1960s-rivals case, arguing it's an important aspect of today's anti-Hillary politics.

The conservative website Joe the Plumber, on Oct. 19th, published a piece about, the van Clinton travels in called "WIKILEAKS: Hippie Hillary Clinton's Gas Guzzling Hippie Van Has a Bed; Mood Lighting!" (Osborn). The piece never explains why they call Clinton "hippie," but they do, and the tone here implies that Clinton is a spaced-out and possibly promiscuous person—in keeping with stereotypes of Hippie-Americans.

A prime opportunity for Hippie-baiting occurred when Clinton, asked by a college student about activism, responded, "I come from the '60s . . . ." Rosin reports: "Republican strategists went wild, suggesting that this daffiest of statements was the beginning of the end for Clinton. Some envisioned the clip starring in hard-hitting anti-Hillary general-election propaganda, shown alongside lava lamps or other '60s accouterments."

Thing is, we never saw that commercial; surprisingly Trump didn't bite, reserving his demagoguery, it seems, largely for Mexicans and Muslims.

So, we see some anti-Hippie prejudice on the surface, much underlying the larger anti-Hillary vote. Though the Trump campaign apparently decided to pass on Hippie-baiting Hillary, it also seems clear that the nation wouldn't even be in a position to elect the likes of Mr. Trump without decades of anti-Hippie demagoguery pushing America to the far right.

*   *   *

Let's now take a look at some **extra-political evidence** to illustrate how in American Public-Speak, bigotry towards African-Americans is now seen as unacceptable whereas trashing Hippiedom seems to be rewarded—this showing the larger social context of the demagogic political rhetoric.

We'll begin by examining a **piece by** the pundit/commentator **George F. Will**, one of the most respected voices of American neoconservatism.

In 1995, on the death of Grateful Dead icon Jerry Garcia, Will launched into a demagogic rant in *Newsweek*, scapegoating the Counterculture, branding it "infantile," holding it responsible for everything from inner-city rot to moral decay. The basis for this is stereotyping: a shameless overgeneralization based on the case of a Countercultural couple who allegedly abandoned their baby to run off and follow the Grateful Dead. So here, employing that fallacy known as a *hasty generalization*, Will displays a textbook case of bigotry.

Yet, one might also see Will opining on the evils of racism when, baseball expert and enthusiast he is, he discusses the treatment of Jackie Robinson (*Baseball*, Vol. 6). And he seems to have a genuine understanding of the evils of Afrophobia. Go figure: regarding bigotry towards Hippie-Americans, he's ignorant and deeply complicit; regarding bigotry towards African-Americans, he seems astute and upset.

Or consider **mainstream entertainment, particularly television shows:** images of African-Americans are now mostly respectful, eschewing negative stereotyping. Virtually every Hollywood television script is built around a carefully constructed diversity, featuring women and men, African-Americans, Asian-Americans, Hispanic-Americans, European-Americans and sometimes others. On the outside tend to remain the "bad guys," targets of the War of Drugs and/or the War on Terror: Hippies and Arabs.[20]

Lastly in the social realm, consider the case of **Michael Richards**, comedian and formerly *Seinfeld's* beloved Kramer. In 2006, he exploded onstage in racist rant—screaming "nigger" at African-American comedian Sinbad several times—something he was later unable to take responsibility for or to adequately explain to leading members of the black community. Today, a cloud hangs over Michael Richards—his career hanging by a thread, if not dead. Again, in American PublicSpeak, overt Afrophobia has become taboo.

*   *   *

In **conclusion**, it seems almost a law of political science: rightists rely heavily on demagoguery as a way to manipulate the body politic; bigotry

---

[20]   Please see the 2006 documentary *Reel Bad Arabs: How Hollywood Vilifies a People* (Shaheen and Earp).

Although neoconservatives have clearly been trying to link the Counterculture to international anti-American terrorism, they don't appear to have tried to link African-America to the same—Osama bin Laden, we're supposed to believe, hung out with Hippies, not blacks.

is a tool for the fascistic. "If the Jew did not exist," said John-Paul Sartre, "the anti-Semite would invent him" (qtd. in Levin 39).

At the heart of neoconservatism, that political movement that's driven the nation rightward, is hatred of Hippies, not Afrophobia. Likewise, although neoconservatives have clearly been trying to link the Counterculture to international anti-American terrorism, they don't appear to be trying to link African-America to the same—Osama bin Laden, we're supposed to believe, hung out with Hippies, not blacks.

How to explain the willingness of reactionary demagogues to openly target Hippie-Americans while increasingly avoiding openly attacking blacks? African-America is organized, and people have come to recognize Afrophobia as evil. Those who publicly trash blacks face a powerful opponent in the form of African-American organizations and leadership and in widespread social condemnation. Prejudice against Hippie-Americans, however, seems respectable, even evidence of morality, and it's a political freebie.

Consider: if in virtually every national election since 1968, Hippie-hating and Hippie-baiting have been effective tactics for rightists (and the fact that they have so consistently used them would seem evidence for their effectiveness), then they have what golfers call a *handicap*.

And it's a mistake to assume that anti-Hippie demagoguery is a thing of the past, that the further we get from the 1960s, the less important it will become. Stubbornly mumbling, "The Sixties are over with" has never made it so. If we ever see a Bernie Sanders nomination in the Democratic Party, a surge of support for Jill Stein and the Greens or perhaps an electable Libertarian, Hippie-baiting will likely re-emerge with a vengeance.

Ethnic-Hippies Theory reveals a direct relationship between the ability of neoconservatism to exploit hatred of and prejudice towards Hippie-America and neoconservatism's political power. The relationship is like that of a bow and arrow—the further back the bow is drawn, the farther the arrow flies; without the Counterculture as a foil, neoconservatism couldn't have become the powerful force it has. To a significant extent, then, the world suffers because Americans have been taught to hate Hippie-Americans and because there has been no effective response to that hatred.

Chapter Four

The Better Lens: Ethnic-Hippies Theory

"Usually the first problems you solve with the new paradigm
are the ones that were unsolvable with the old paradigm."
—Joel A. Barker

Here, we're going to look at the many other paradigms people have about Hippie culture—the muddled clichés we routinely recite about Hippiedom, the clumsy language we use when we think and speak of it. As I do this, I'm going to show the reader how Ethnic-Hippies Theory (EHT) works better than those commonly accepted yet flawed concepts. At the end of it all, we should realize that our usual ways of thinking about Hippiedom don't really work, and given that EHT works better, I'm hoping readers will be ready to change their minds, to shift their paradigms.

What are those conventional paradigms? Chapter Two refuted two: "Just a Phase of Life People Usually Outgrow" and, of course, a decade-specific definition. Here, I'll disprove some others: The Sixties Generation/ The Woodstock Generation, "dropouts," ideological definitions, the Mythical definition, "Just a fad or a fashion," a subculture, the Counterculture, and "the drug culture." As I discuss these dysfunctional definitions, I'll explain why an ethnic perspective works better.

* * *

"The Sixties Generation": First, not everyone of that generation went Hippie. Being a Baby Boomer didn't automatically make you Countercultural; indeed, some of the most vociferous Hippie haters— people like Rush Limbaugh or Pat Buchanan—are those of that generation who didn't go Hippie. On the other hand, probably a majority of today's Hippie-Americans had yet to be born when the 1960s ended. In short, a single-generation explanation makes little sense.

"The Woodstock Generation": If "Woodstock" is, at least, more explicitly Countercultural than "Sixties," all the problems of a single-generation explanation just mentioned hold here.

In contrast, EHT handles the multi-generational nature of Hippie-America with ease: Yes, some are inheriting Hippie identity, in much the way that a child/offspring of any parent might inherit their parents' culture; also, some post-1960s people have chosen Hippie identity in just the way that those original 1960s Hippies did. Dysfunctional paradigms either see Hippiedom as something that lasted five years, or they see it as a one-generational blip on the historical timeline. Ethnic-Hippies theory sees an ethnicity that's fifty years old and that now involves people of all ages.

"Dropouts": A few years back, I was reading about hostels in a travel book for Europe; the author mentioned who travelers might find working in these hostels, including the occasional "hippie dropout." It struck me as strange; I mean, if someone has a job somewhere, then how is that person a "dropout"? And why is this tag stuck on the Hippie and no one else who's mentioned as maybe working in a hostel?

As for "dropping out," the term, I believe, derives, from psychedelic pioneer Timothy Leary, who coined the motto "Turn on, tune in, drop out," and "drop out" was usually interpreted as going Hippie. Well, be that as it may, going Hippie isn't really dropping out, at least not out of society, something that, in practice, is almost impossible to do—even the most independent communes remain part of a larger economy and society. As far as "dropping out" of mainstream *culture*, I suppose you could describe going Hippie that way though it strikes me as unnecessarily negative, as if joining an immense revitalization movement of society were an act of despair.

Well, EHT would tell us that we might expect Hippiedom to be subject to hostility and disrespect. Clearly, *dropout* has a negative connotation: an unmotivated, apathetic, life-is-just-too-hard-so-I-decided-to-quit loser. Thus, as this term is usually used, it stereotypes and communicates prejudice.

Ideological definitions of *Hippie*/A "Hippie Philosophy": It's common for people to speak of "the hippie philosophy," as if they knew what it was and were sure there was only one. Sometimes, people like to speculate, asking "deep" questions like, "What do *you* think the Hippie philosophy is?"[21] The question seems to have a Quest-for-the-Grail quality to it—will Galahad be able to grasp the true mystery of Hippiedom? But there is no "Hippie philosophy"; it's a mistake to assume any kind of shared cookie-cutter ideology among the wide diversity of individuals comprising Hippie-America. After all, members of other minority groups don't always agree, do they?

---

[21]   This makes a great party game!

64

The assumption that all Hippie-Americans are straight-up liberals is a political stereotype.[22] Many would call themselves Libertarians, a party and philosophy usually thought of as to the right. Apparently, Mike Love of the Beach Boys, who having gone to India alongside the Beatles, Mia Farrow and others has serious Countercultural pedigree, is a Republican and was a personal friend of the late Nancy Reagan.[23] Or I, for example, am a registered Green; often, I feel uncomfortable being called a liberal since I don't wish to be grouped with the political likes of Hillary Clinton and a center-right Democratic Party.

Consider the matter of religion: the belief systems among Counterculturists run the gamut from atheism to a wide variety of religious beliefs or influences. Although most Counterculturists would probably describe themselves as being on a spiritual path, and many espouse New Age theologies, there is no agreed upon Hippie religion.

If the Counterculture is an ideologically based entity, if underlying it is some common philosophy, why does no one seem entirely sure what that philosophy is? And why do individual Hippies have such a rich variety of beliefs and opinions?

An ethnic approach works much better here. As we'll see, one criterion that the *Harvard Encyclopedia of American Ethnic Groups* includes in its definition of *ethnicity* is "values." EHT, then, says there are certain

> **There is no "Hippie philosophy"; it's a mistake to assume any kind of shared, cookie-cutter ideology among the wide variety of individuals comprising Hippie-America.**

describable values that are imbedded in the Counterculture, and most people would likely agree with that. The thing is, values tend to be more abstract than specific positions on particular issues. To one person, Peace might mean strict pacifism; to another, it might mean proportionate violence in self-defense. Many would likely interpret this value as something spiritual. Also, Freedom means different things to different people. Values can be applied in various ways, and this accounts for the broad ideological diversity within Hippiedom.

---

22   Nor are all liberals Hippie-American.
23   As evidenced, no doubt, by the Beach Boys delivering several live musical tributes to Nancy Reagan upon her death in 2016 (Hawkes).

Then, there's what I call the **Mythic Definition of** *Hippie*; it sounds something like this: "Oh, today's *so-called* hippies are just a bunch of pathetic wanabees. I mean, the *real* hippies back in the 1960s believed in peace and love and were so enlightened! Not like these kids today who just look like hippies but are really so far from the *real* hippies." It's odd that an argument allegedly based on a reverence and respect for Hippies is in practice dismissive and contemptuous of today's youthful Counterculturists, saying, in effect, "They're not *good* enough to be real hippies, the presumptuous phonies!"

The problems of this approach to defining *Hippie* are many. For starters, it turns the Counterculture into a finishing school for gurus and holy people, and it romanticizes the early Counterculture, an essentially mythical approach that turns Haight-Ashbury and other early enclaves into something unreal populated by unreal people. Sure, among those early Haight-Ashburyites were the visionary and far-sighted like the Diggers or the Merry Pranksters. But do, then, only a tiny elite qualify as "true Hippies"?

Most Hippies today have the same basic values of peace and love and kindness as did the "true hippies" of the 1960s, and many would describe life as a spiritual journey of sorts. And in any given population—then or now—some will always be more mature, more enlightened, wiser. Those clinging to the Mythic Definition seem to assume that almost *all* Hippies *then* fit their lofty requirements and that *almost no* Hippies *now* do, especially younger Counterculturists. There is, however, no reason to assume that in terms of enlightenment, Hippiedom has gotten worse; indeed, considering the youthfulness of so many early Hippies, it's a safe bet that the maturity of the average Hippie has increased. In any case, you don't need to be Gandalf the Grey to call yourself Countercultural.

Again, an ethnic approach describes Counterculturalists far better because it's so much more inclusive and forgiving.

One particularly dismissive alternative to EHT is to see Hippie culture as a **mere fad or fashion**—bell bottoms, long hair on men, flowered dresses on women, and not much more; often, this superficial approach is combined with Hippies Were Just a Thing of The Sixties in that the "fashion" they speak of is usually late-1960s. Yes, it's true that Hippiedom has had a marked impact on fashion, but there's always been more to Hippie culture than just a particular look; the Hippies Were a Fashion approach neglects natural/organic foods and a score of other things that exemplify Hippie culture; so, it's one more way of trivializing the Counterculture.

Yes, Hippiedom is a **"subculture"**; then again, the term is so broad it might mean any number of groups. Computer "hackers," for instance, or the Teddy Boys in England. *Ethnicity* is the more precise and accurate term for Hippiedom, so why not use it?

"The Counterculture": I use the term with some reluctance. It derives from Theodore Roszak's *The Making of a Counter Culture: Reflections on the Technocratic Society and its Youthful Opposition* (1969), and you'll notice that Roszak says "*a* Counter Culture," implying there might be many countercultures, and not "the counterculture," as the term has evolved and is now popularly used. But Roszak apparently isn't Hippie, so why is he naming our culture? And in this book, Roszak tries to elucidate a Hippie philosophy that's pretty much what Roszak thinks and not necessarily what Hippiedom thinks, as if to say, "Hello, lowly creatures. I have appointed myself your guru." Particularly ridiculous is Roszak's argument that the Counterculture is or should be virulently anti-technology; yet, as we'll see, Hippie-America invented that technological wonderment, the personal computer—oops!

An ethnic approach, on the other hand, isn't baffled by Hippiedom's technological prowess: ethnic groups invent things all the time; it's one of the ways we recognize them.

Of the many non-ethnic ways of defining Hippie culture, **"The Drug culture"** is the most insidious and evil. The phrase is the invention of neoconservatism's War on Drugs. Thus, even though the users of drugs in America hail from a variety of racial and ethnic groups, "the drug culture," refers exclusively, it seems, to Hippie-America. Since it's assumed that "drugs" are bad and are killing our innocent youth, sticking this label on an entire ethnicity is flagrant vilification, sort of like saying to the American public, "Sic 'em!"

And this propagandistic label lies: it takes a full-fledged ethnicity with numerous facets and simplistically—murderously—reduces it to one allegedly hateful thing: drug use. It attempts to portray an entire culture as a group of people with a drug problem and to portray the nation as having a drug problem because the "drug culture" exists within it. So, whether conservatives want to jail "drug addicts" or liberals want to treat them for their "illness" (Big Brother vs. Big Nurse), for those using the "drug culture" paradigm, that's all Hippie-Americans have ever been: a national drug problem in the course of being solved and eliminated—or so we're supposed to believe.

*   *   *

These non-ethnic paradigms and definitions, then, consistently fall short; in contrast, Ethnic-Hippies Theory explains reality far better and with ease.

Chapter Five

Hippie as Ethnic; Counterculture as Ethnicity

There's lots and lots of us, more than anybody thought before.
We used to think of ourselves as little clumps of weirdoes.
But now we're a whole new minority group.
                              —Janis Joplin at Woodstock[24]

This chapter is a deductive proof of Hippie ethnicity. That is, I'm going to take a definition of *ethnicity* and show how well the Counterculture fits it. However, before we go there, I'm going to raise and respond to a sometime counterargument: "Ethnicity requires racial distinctiveness, doesn't it?"

*   *   *

Ethnicity and Race: Not the Same

Some might prematurely write off "Hippie ethnicity" due to misconceptions about ethnicity and race: ethnicity, they think, always involves race; without racial distinctiveness, there is no such thing as ethnicity. This isn't true, but because some seem confused, let's spend a bit of space clarifying. First, here's what three prominent ethnographers say:

Richard T. Schaefer, author of the text *Racial and Ethnic Groups*, writes, "The designation of a racial group emphasizes physical differences as opposed to cultural distinctions" (8). Also, "Minority groups that are designated by their ethnicity are differentiated from the dominant group on the basis of *cultural* differences . . ." (emphasis added) (8).

". . . ethnicity is not transmitted genetically from generation to generation . . . ."—Rudolph J. Vecoli, editor of the *Gale Encyclopedia of Multicultural America* (xxi).

"In its current usage a biological connotation sometimes adheres still to 'ethnic,' but not necessarily: some groupings are defined by . . . their language or religion or some other criterion," notes ethnographer

---

24   Source: Quoted in *With Amusement for All: A History of American Popular Culture Since 1830* by LeRoy Ashby, 2006, University of Kentucky Press, Lexington, KY, p. 410

William Petersen in "Concepts of Ethnicity" (235). He adds that while *ethnic* derives from an "originally biological context, the meaning . . . has broadened to include cultural characteristics . . . ." (234).

Think of it this way: How we perceive and define race is culturally conditioned—"race is a socially constructed concept" (Schaefer, 12)—and at times in American history, we've had very different racial categories than the "rainbow" we now assume—Irish and Italians, among many others, were seen as separate races. Still, race, however it may be perceived, involves biology and DNA. It begins in the body.

Ethnicity, on the other hand, begins in the brain. Thoughts may have objective manifestations; a German, for instance, may choose to dress in a certain way, to listen to certain music, etc. but her or his distinctive ethnic traits originate in the mind, not in the genes.

Another way of understanding the difference is this: race is dumb in the sense that our body inherits it, and we have no control over it. Ethnicity, on the other hand, is mutable and subject to choice and change (Waters, 69-70). People can make decisions about their ethnicity precisely because it is lodged in the mind. Also, when we speak of ethnicity being "inherited," we shouldn't assume this involves biological inheritance; as Vecoli notes above, culture can be inherited apart from genes.

Well, if confusing race and ethnicity is wrong, why do so many do it?

First, in the USA, we've been trained to blur the two by affirmative-action forms. Often, they've had the same strange section: "Ethnicity: Check one." And then accompanying one of the boxes below has been the word *Caucasian* or *White*. But *Caucasian* and *White* refer to race, not ethnicity.

Second, distinctive races often have distinctive cultures, so race and ethnicity sometime seem to go hand in hand. Thus, sometimes race/biology and ethnicity do overlap and so seem the same; Petersen implies that long ago, this was always the case.

But more often than not today, this perfect correlation isn't so. Consider the Amish. Ethnographers consider them an ethnic group (*Harvard Encyclopedia of American Ethnic Groups*). They are, after all, culturally distinct and possess the traits of an ethnicity. Yet, no one believes the Amish are a distinct race. In other words, a geneticist would be unable to distinguish an Amish person from a non-Amish person of northern-European descent.

Bottom line: although race and ethnicity sometimes overlap, ethnicity does not require racial distinctiveness.

* * *

Hippie Ethnicity: A Deductive Proof

What exactly does *ethnicity* mean? Turns out, there is no single, agreed-upon definition of *ethnicity*; however, the best, most nuanced and developed definition I found is in the introduction to *The Harvard Encyclopedia of American Groups* (*HEAEG*). It doesn't focus on a particular trait; rather, it sees ethnicity as embodied in a nexus of factors.

Before we look at the *HEAEG* definition, however, let's quickly consider two related aspects of ethnicity that might not be apparent from examining a list of ethnic traits, no matter how well constructed. First, as mentioned, ethnicity often involves choice; second, contrary to the popular belief that ethnicity is fixed, static and survives only as a relic of a now-dead past, ethnicity is dynamic. And sometimes ethnicity is dynamic precisely because individuals *are* making choices about it. Sociologist Mary C. Waters explains:

> The common view among Americans is that ethnicity is primordial, a personal, inherited characteristic like hair color. Most people assume that ethnic groups are stable categories and that one is a member of a particular ethnic group because one's ancestors were members of that group. . . . The idea [held by sociologists] that membership in an ethnic group need not be hereditary, or directly related to common lineage, is a direct challenge to this view. . . . This [false] belief that ethnicity is biologically based acts as a constraint on the ethnic choices of some Americans, but there is nonetheless a range of latitude available in deciding how to identify oneself and whether to do so in ethnic terms. Whites enjoy a great deal of freedom in these choices; those defined in "racial" terms as non-whites much less. . . . ethnic identity is a social process that is in flux for some proportion of the population . . . ethnic identification is, in fact, a dynamic . . . social phenomenon. (69-70)

So for some, ethnic identification may change over time as individuals make choices about their ethnicity.

And then, there's another, larger, dynamism at work here: entire ethnicities adapt and evolve. Rap music and hip-hop may be identified as part of African-American culture today, for instance, but fifty years ago, that wasn't the case.

So, bearing in mind that individuals often make choices about their ethnic identities and that those choices may change, that an ethnicity is like a living, growing organism, as much process as product, here's the *HEAEG* definition:

> Ethnicity is an immensely complex phenomenon. All the groups treated here are characterized by some of the following features, although in combinations that vary considerably:
>
> 1) common geographic origin;
> 2) migratory status;
> 3) race;
> 4) language or dialect;
> 5) religious faith or faiths;
> 6) ties that transcend kinship, neighborhood, and community boundaries;
> 7) shared traditions, values, and symbols;
> 8) literature, folklore, and music;
> 9) food preferences;
> 10) settlement and employment patterns;
> 11) special interests in regard to politics in the homeland and in the United States;
> 12) institutions that specifically serve and maintain the group;
> 13) an internal sense of distinctiveness;
> 14) an external perception of distinctiveness.
> ("Introduction," vi)

One of the first things you may notice about this definition is that, scholarly as it is, there are absences even a lay reader should notice. I will, then, supplement this *HEAEG* definition with four categories which I hope the reader will agree are reasonable and necessary.

First, what about "ethnic costume"? Dress/costume is an aspect of ethnicity (Kennett) virtually everyone is aware of; we all seem to know that ethnic groups are partly characterized by their norms of appearance—hairstyles, jewelry, and/or body markings, and the way they dress: think of *lederhosen,* think of Germans; think of kilts, think of Scots; see a certain shirt or type of knitting, think Guatemalan, and so on; thus, it shouldn't seem a stretch to add a category called "**norms of appearance.**"

There's another fairly obvious item missing from the *HEAEG* definition, "**cultural artifacts.**" Ethnic groups produce certain products which then tend to be associated with that group. Those artifacts might be plants or animals they've bred or modified, or they might be man-made items such as musical instruments, pottery, art, furniture, housing, or particular products. Archeologists have, after all, long used cultural artifacts to draw conclusions about which ethnicities or peoples inhabited a certain area during a certain time. So, artifacts are used to identify cultural/ethnic groups; the *HEAEG* definition says nothing clearly about this.

The third category I'll add—the "**distinctive drugs and recreational substances**" a group uses—may be a bit less obvious but is still well within reason. Throughout prehistory and history, different cultural groups have used different substances whether for recreational, religious, aphrodisiacal, performance-enhancing or medicinal purposes, including the reduction of pain and stress—sometimes for all. In the beginning, these substances were derived from the natural environments those groups formed in. Later, such a substance may in some way emigrate or be adopted by and identified with a another culture; thus, the English became renown as drinkers of tea (caffeine) though tea isn't grown in the British Isles; Sir Walter Raleigh brought tobacco (nicotine) to England, but he got it from Native Americans.

These substances, then, become a part of a group's ethnicity; they are interwoven into its culture. Furthermore, outsiders often associate these substances with particular cultures/ethnicities.

People who argue, "But my culture doesn't use drugs" are people in denial: I doubt there's been a society in history, or prehistory, that hasn't been a "drug culture." After all, human beings have created and used drugs as tools: they've usually had some positive purpose. That doesn't mean drugs can't be used negatively, even catastrophically; it doesn't mean there's no such thing as drug abuse, but the notion that it's always someone else, some other group, who's using "drugs" is a self-serving fantasy. Somewhere scattered about the world, there may be "drug-free"

> If a cultural group had all the features of an ethnicity but only lasted one generation, would we consider it an ethnicity? I doubt it. When we think of ethnicity, we think of something passed down to some extent from generation to generation.

individuals, but aside perhaps from Mormons, it's doubtful there has ever been a truly "drug-free" society or culture.[25]

Bottom line: these substances (drugs), the ways they're used, and the identity of the groups that create/cultivate and use them are interwoven.

Lastly, let's add the category of **generational transfer**. Think of it this way: if a cultural group had all the features of an ethnicity but only lasted one generation, would we consider it an ethnicity? I doubt it. When we think of ethnicity, we think of something passed down to some extent from generation to generation. This additional trait, then, should seem a natural.

*   *   *

So, our list of fourteen ethnic traits has grown to eighteen. Let's now apply that expanded definition to the Counterculture. As we work through the ethnic-trait list, I'll be awarding a point for each category that the Counterculture seems to fully qualify in. For categories that have two or three parts, I'll award two or three points, respectively. Where the Counterculture seems to qualify somewhat, I'll award half a point. This point system, incidentally, is *not* the *HEAEG's*: it's mine. It makes it easier to see how well the Counterculture fits this expanded definition.

*   *   *

---

[25] Even America's pioneers were "on drugs." Thus, in *The Botany of Desire*, Michael Pollan discusses Johnny Appleseed: The apples in those orchards Appleseed planted were inedible "spitters" (21-23); instead, the settlers used them to make hard cider. Yes, Sweet Betsy of Pike was a ciderhead; her husband Ike, a tippler.

Applying our definition of *ethnicity* to Hippiedom

Common geographic origin: At first glance, it might appear that this wouldn't apply to Hippies since we aren't a traditional immigrant group. But on closer inspection, we can see that Hippies do have a sort of common geographic origin: the developed nations of the world. Generally, we tend not to find Hippies originating in Third World countries, and they only live there in noteworthy numbers due to emigration from the industrialized Western states, i.e., Hippie colonies in Goa, Katmandu, etc. Let's give the Counterculture a half a point here.

Migratory status: "Migration"—defined as "to move from one country *or region* and settle in another" (emphasis added) ("Migration")—need not mean crossing a national border. And indeed, much of the Hippie story involves migration—"If you're going to San Francisco . . . ." In Colorado, where I live, there are several towns or areas that have large populations of Hippies; most of those Hippie residents came from elsewhere in the United States. The same could be said of the Hippie enclaves in most American states. Regarding Vermont, reporter Tim Madigan explains:

> [I]n the 1960s, Vermont changed, a transformation reportedly triggered by a magazine article that let slip about the cheap living possible in a beautiful, unsullied place. Perfect, in other words, for tens of thousands of hippies . . . The counterculture arrived in Vermont en masse in their VW buses. Communes sprouted in the hills. Thousands of the immigrants . . . persevered, transforming state politics and culture from the dairyman's bedrock conservatism to the transcendentalist ethos of the beat poet and candle maker. . .

In this category, let's give the Counterculture a full point.

Race: No, the Counterculture is not a racial group; indeed, one of the things remarkable about the Counterculture is that while it's predominantly Caucasian, there are members of other racial groups. No credit for this trait.

Language or dialect: Clearly there is no distinct Hippie language. The Counterculture does, however, possess something resembling a dialect; that is, there are a number of particular words associated with Hippiedom. Rex Weiner and Deanne Stillman are researchers who in

1979 published *Woodstock Census,* a study of Hippie-America. They note, "Another feature of the counter-culture is that its members adopted their own vernacular" (42). In *On Writing Well,* writing teacher William Zinsser reminds us of "all the wonderfully short words invented by the Counterculture in the 1960s as a way of lashing back at the bloated verbiage of the Establishment: *bag, scene, trip, rap, crash, trash, fuzz et al"* (45). Give Hippiedom a half point here.

Religious faith or faiths: As mentioned, a look at the religious beliefs of Hippies shows a diversity. On the other hand, there are the so-called "New Agers"; if not a formal religion, this movement is religious in nature and is producing its own distinctive churches and institutions. No, not all Counterculturalists can be considered New Age; still, the great majority of New Agers are, I think, Countercultural; let's award a half point here.

Ties that transcend kinship, neighborhood, and community boundaries: The function of this criterion is no doubt to distinguish the ethnic group from the homogeneous neighborhood, or the small town from the large, closely knit family or clan; it easily applies to the Counterculture.

As already noted, there are Hippie communities or enclaves across the Western world and throughout the United States. The Christiana community in Denmark is but one example of a non-American Hippie enclave. And regarding the United States, Weiner and Stillman write:

> . . . this group [Hippies] seems to have formed its own intercommunal links that . . . transcended the old American boundaries. No matter where you were, Alaska or Mississippi, if you joined Woodstock Nation, you became part of something that was bigger . . . than your own home town. (27)

Since we've already seen the geographic scope of the Counterculture, I'll present no further evidence and give the Counterculture a full point here.

Shared traditions, values, and symbols: That the Counterculture is only fifty limits the amount of Countercultural **traditions**; nevertheless, they do exist. Weiner and Stillman cite rock concerts as "important convocations of the counter-culture" (63). And as we earlier saw in the 1999 *New York Times* story about young Hippie types following Phish (Powers), such Countercultural events are not simply a thing of the past.

Lollapalooza, for instance, is a contemporary Countercultural music-festival venue.

4/20 seems an emerging Hippie holiday, and *tradition* can mean, "The passing down of elements of a culture from generation to generation . . ." and "a time-honored practice or set of practices" ("Tradition"). Weiner and Stillman: "The group experience and the ritual of using drugs," as one respondent notes, were 'more important than getting high. . . .' The counter-culture was passed, hand to hand, like a burning joint" (111). Give the Counterculture a full point here.

Next, let's explore Hippie **values**. Some values seem to permeate the Counterculture: questioning authority and emphasizing the natural, healing, kindness, informality and personal freedom.

Later, we'll look at thirteen Hippie values; for now, let's give the Counterculture a point here

And **symbols**? For starters, the peace sign certainly has a Counter-cultural connotation. Images of the seven-pronged marijuana leaf also serve as a Countercultural symbol; tie-dyes have come to symbolize Hippie culture. In the context of vehicles, there are Grateful Dead symbols/stickers; they clearly symbolize not just the band but Hippie culture in general, and an image search of the internet will reveal several Hippie-American flags. Give the Counterculture another point.

Literature, folklore, and music: As for **literature**, the reader will see ample evidence for this in various parts of Chapter Eight in the Literature, R. Crumb, and, I think, "alternative" newspapers sections. Add another point to the Counterculture's ethnic tally.

Is there Hippie **folklore**? First, what exactly is "folklore"? The *HEAEG's,* Roger D. Abrahams defines the term as a group's "ways of entertaining and instructing each other [including] proverbs, prayers, curses, jokes, riddles, superstitions . . . tales and songs, [also] certain types of story—anecdotes, testimonies, reminiscences—that emerge on both casual and ceremonial occasions" (370-71); in addition, *folklore* often deals with the issues the group has in interacting with nonmembers; thus, it ". . . involves an analysis of traditional means of expression as they [ethnic groups] undergo self-conscious scrutiny both from group members and from outsiders (370).

Of course, at the broadest level, this could mean any Countercultural music since that would involve Hippies "entertaining" one another through "songs." But if we want to get more specific and consider that aspect of dealing with non-members and the larger society, there are a number of Hippie songs that would fit here: Arlo Guthrie's "Alice's Restaurant," (the amusing tale of Hippie Arlo's encounter with the police and then his draft board); Charlie Daniels' "The Ballad of Uneasy Rider" (Daniel's harrowing narrative of his escape from and triumph over a gang of Hippie-hating bullies), and Ed Sanders' "The Iliad" (the darkly comic story of a Hippie type jumped by a bigoted thug). I could heap on more evidence here; for now, let's give Hippiedom another full point.

And then there was **music**. Hippie music. *Lots* of Hippie music. If it's an overstatement to say "Rock music is Hippie music," it would be impossible not to notice the predominance of Hippie-types in the rock world for the last fifty years; the list is so long and probably so obvious it need not be cited. In fact, I recall hearing of some Tennessee Hippies who once filed some kind of anti-discrimination suit arguing that to be successful in their chosen careers as rock musicians, their long hair was necessary. Let's add another point to the tally.

Food preferences: Proving the existence of Hippie cuisine is, pun intended, a piece of cake—a whole-grain cake with natural sweeteners. For starters, in 1989, Warren J. Belasco, professor of American studies at the University of Maryland, Baltimore County, published *Appetite for Change: How the Counterculture Took on the Food Industry, 1966-1988*. The book describes not just Hippie food but the impact it has had on mainstream cuisine. Reviewer Joan Jacobs Brumberg paraphrases:

> These "freaks" (a term Belasco uses fondly) rejected the beef-based, adulterated cuisine of their families and opted instead for foods that were "natural" or lower on the food chain. The call for a decentralized food supply generated a network of rural communes and urban food co-ops, where disaffected youth developed a new way of eating . . . .

And there are several essentially Hippie cookbooks, including *New Farm Vegetarian Cookbook* (Hagle).[26] The Moosewood Restaurant in Ithaca, New York went celebrity with the 1977 release of *The Moosewood Cookbook* (Katzen). The place is clearly Hippie; when I last looked, I counted on the shelves almost 20 cookbooks from Moosewood alone.

---

[26] The Farm is an enduring Hippie commune located in Tennessee.

A close look at the booming natural-foods industry—whether they be coops or privately owned chains like Whole Foods—will show Hippie types founding and/or running these businesses (Adler 57; Taylor). It's easy to prove there's Hippie food. Give it up for the Counterculture—a full point.

Settlement and employment patterns: Settlement patterns are relatively easy to document; like members of other ethnic groups, Hippies tend to cluster.

Of course, we discussed Hippie demography in Chapter Two, and, as mentioned, there are Hippie enclaves across the globe. In 1987, the *New York Times* carried "Off Canada, The Hippies are Evolving," telling of the Queen Charlotte Islands, south of Alaska and west of British Columbia:

> If there are underlying patterns to Hippie settlement, three factors seem to predominate: a relatively tolerant atmosphere (such as in college towns or in traditionally open San Francisco), being with and around other Hippies, and being close to nature; in particular, I think, mountains.

. . . once regarded . . . as a Bolshevik rabble, most of the hippies have become near yuppies. Not all the way to BMW's, to be sure, but far enough to be seen as solid citizens . . . . an area of the village of Queen Charlotte known as Hippie Hill, once a cluster of lean-tos and cabins separated by vegetable plots is a suburban community of $50,000 [then a respectable price] houses. (Burns)

If there are underlying patterns to Hippie settlement, three factors seem to predominate: a relatively tolerant atmosphere (such as in college towns or in traditionally open San Francisco), being with and around other Hippies, and being close to nature; in particular, I think, mountains.

We'll give the Counterculture another full point here.

Employment patterns: Weiner and Stillman summarize some of their survey results as indicating that members of "Woodstock Nation" are employed in two general areas: non-competitive fields and those emphasizing human as opposed to material products (25). Among such careers is certainly teaching, and as a teacher, I've always noticed a strong contingent of Counterculturists among educators.

Another area where Hippies seem to be congregating might be called the healing arts. I notice a lot of Hippie massage therapists, nutritionists, mid-wives, therapists and healers of various sorts, and Hippiedom seems to have pioneered Integrative Medicine.

I also notice that here in Colorado, where marijuana is now legal, a number of those developing and working in the legal marijuana/industrial hemp industries are Countercultural.

In the United States today, I doubt that any ethnicity is strictly limited to a single field of employment, so let's award a full point here.

Special interests in regard to politics in the homeland and in the United States: Though there are Hippies who don't use marijuana, the intertwining of marijuana and the Counterculture is substantial; not only is cannabis widely used within the Counterculture, but the association of Hippies and cannabis in the public mind is widespread, and I believe cannabis remains illegal largely to punish the Counterculture. As such, marijuana-legalization issues are Countercultural "special interest" issues.

Laws punishing use of other Countercultural drugs—LSD, Ecstasy, etc.—also create a special political interest for the American Counterculture.

Around food issues, the Counterculture has special interests in laws pertaining to natural and organic foods and farming, use of hemp in foods or for biodiesel and so forth. Give the Counterculture a full point here.

Institutions that specifically serve and maintain the group: From its earliest days, Hippiedom has had group-serving organizers and organizations.

Wikipedia tells us, "The original Council for the Summer of Love was created in 1967 by The Family Dog, The Straight Theatre, The Diggers, *The San Francisco Oracle* and about twenty-five individuals" ("Summer of Love").

Rolling Stone magazine, nearing fifty, would also qualify as a Countercultural institution; of course, there are other prominent Countercultural periodicals, particularly *High Times*, which, through the efforts of then editor-in-chief Steven Hager, created other Countercultural institutions. The first, known as the Cannabis Cup, is a contest held annually in Amsterdam where cannabis growers and connoisseurs from around the world gather to partake—sort of like a giant, international wine tasting for Counterculturists. Celebrating its 27th birthday in 2014, the Cup has clearly become a tradition. Then there's an institution associated with the Cannabis Cup: The Counterculture Hall of Fame. Younger than the Cup itself, "The Counterculture Hall of Fame," Hager reminisces, "became a major part of the Cup at the 10ᵗʰ Cup [1998], when Bob Marley became the first inductee." The list of other inductees reads like a Countercultural Who's Who.

The Counterculture, then, is generating group-serving institutions in much the way an ethnicity might be expected to. Let's award a full point here.

An internal sense of distinctiveness: As William Hedgepeth, who authored a study of Hippie communes, *The Alternative*, noted, "They're learning now, as have the militant young blacks, to spot their own soul brothers and draw together in common cause—which begins with the molding of an independent cultural identity . . ." (181).

Also, this criterion works in a dynamic interplay with the next: "an external perception of distinctiveness"; that is, as mainstream society tends to set the Counterculture apart in its mind and act on that, so that set-apart, Hippie group feels distinctive and develops a sense of clannishness. As Charles Reich stated in *The Greening of America* (remember, that bestseller was published in 1970 when the first Hippies were generally seen as a "youth culture of dissent"):

> . . . an entire culture including music, clothes, and drugs, began to distinguish youth . . . . And the more the older generation rejected the culture, the more a fraternity of youth grew up, so that they recognized each other as brother and sisters from coast to coast. (241)

Of course, the best proof here is the "freaks" label the Counterculture seems to have largely placed on itself. Definitely a full point here.

An external perception of distinctiveness: I'll start with an anecdote: I visited a medieval Renaissance fair outside Chicago sometime in the 1980s. The fair had many Hippie types, both as staff and visitors. I had a ponytail, a mustache and was pretty overtly Hippie myself. After a few hours there, we visitors began to recognize each other. Several times I had seen a middle-aged woman, husband in tow, who had that coiffed hair dyed to just the "rich," blond that women of "impeccable taste" aspire to. As she passed me, her ladyship was heard to murmur in a voice that by some inexplicable acoustic phenomenon happened to float *my* way, "Well, I see the *drug culture* is here today." Yes, she did perceive me as a member of a distinct group.

> **As she passed me, her ladyship was heard to murmur in a voice that by some inexplicable acoustic phenomenon happened to float *my* way, "Well, I see the *drug culture* is here today." Yes, she did perceive me as a member of a distinct group.**

We'll be examining Hippie stereotypes in the next chapter. In any case, that the larger society tends to stereotype Hippies clearly shows that they see the Counterculture as a distinctive group. Add another point to the Counterculture's ethnic-trait tally.

Norms of appearance: Long hair, especially on men, has, of course, become a recognized Countercultural norm of appearance. Yet, many male Hippies no longer have long hair; some, perhaps, never did. I once met a 25-year old who announced, "Yup, I've always been a hippie." Under his baseball cap, he had prominent earrings and a shaved head. Remember, Mr. Clean, the cleaning-product logo? That's how I think of it: the Mr. Clean look, only with more earrings.[27]

So yes, for males, earrings can connote Countercultural identity; for both sexes, tattoos and things like pierced noses. Sometimes Hippies of both genders wear dreadlocks. Countercultural women are often characterized by a de-emphasis on makeup and long-flowing skirts among many other distinctive and recognizable fashions. A head scarf on a man often indicates Hippie identity, and Weiner and Stillman note that male facial hair often has Hippie overtones (40). Hemp jewelry and tie-dyes also deserve mention.

The various aspects of Hippie appearance are, no doubt, well known to the reader, so let's add one point.

Cultural artifacts: An invention/machine such as the personal computer should qualify as a cultural artifact.[28]

Or for the museum minded, a 1999 *New York Times* article (Brown) tells of a San Francisco Museum of Art show entitled "Far Out: Bay Area Design 1967-73"; the show includes a variety of early Hippie artifacts.

---

[27] Think comedian and game-show host Howie Mandel.
[28] To be documented and discussed in Chapter Eight.

Also, in 2009, the Denver Art Museum hosted an exhibit entitled *The Psychedelic Experience: Rock Posters from the San Francisco Bay Area, 1965-71* (Wilson); sometimes, on PBS's *Antiques Roadshow*, Countercultural artifacts, such as music posters and other items, are appraised.

Traditionally, one important type of cultural artifact has been the plants a people breed and grow—the Aztecs, for instance, are renowned for their maize. Apparently, the Counterculture has generated a range of new crops; researcher Craig Dreman writes in a 1989 article "Hippie Ethnobotony":

> From my perspective as a seed supplier, I've noticed that cultural hippies are still the major introducers of new vegetable varieties in North America. Six or seven seed suppliers (out of an industry total of 250), all of them "alternative," collectively introduced the majority of the 1,271 new varieties of vegetable seeds in the last three years.

We'll give the Counterculture a full point here.

Distinctive drugs and recreational substances: Marijuana use has helped shape and define the Counterculture. Also, LSD and other hallucinogens have been the source of much psychedelic art, including, perhaps, tie-dye; for many Counterculturists, psychedelic experiences are an important aspect of their identity, and in recent years, Ecstasy has become somewhat popular among younger Counterculturists. Add another point.

Generational transfer: The 1994 film *Tie Died: Rock 'n Roll's Most Dedicated Fans* quotes a "Deadhead": "So there really is a whole culture that's grown out of the Grateful Dead phenomenon and continues to thrive, and will continue to thrive because our children are picking up all of the[cultural] stuff from us and hopefully their children will pick it up from them" (qtd. in Behar).

In 1997, *The Seattle Times* carried "'90s Kids Follow the Lead of '60s Parents: 30 Years Later, Counterculture Ideals Hold Appeal." Reporter Nancy Kruh writes:

> That was then [the 1960s] and this is now [1997], . . . Yet the similarities between the children of the '60s and these under-25 "grandchildren" are undeniable.

...They look the same. (Male: long hair and maybe a beard, rock band or tie-dye T-shirts, and jewelry made of silver or macrame. Female: long hair and gauzy, loosely fitting "sack" dresses, silver or macrame jewelry, Birkenstocks or bare feet and a dab or two of patchouli oil.)

They eat the same tofu and trail mix; they burn the same incense. They decorate their walls and skin with . . . peace signs. They read Jack Kerouac, Ken Kesey and Anais Nin. They watch "Easy Rider," "Woodstock" and "The Graduate." They listen to the '60s troika of the tragically dead: Janis Joplin, Jimi Hendrix and Jim Morrison of the Doors.

If they're into an illegal drug, it's usually marijuana. If they're into religion, it's usually of the "great spirit in the sky" variety.

[M]embers of this new generation say they are far more a sequel to the '60s than a remake. As they emulate the styles of a 30-year-old counterculture, they believe they are pursuing their own contemporary identity and individuality.

"I can say, yeah, I'm a hippie," says Todd Campbell, a 25-year-old long-haired musician who works at Whole Foods supermarket in Richardson, Texas . . . .

And consistent with argument I've made—that younger Counterculturists are both choosing and *inheriting* Hippie ethnicity—Kruh adds:

The hippie ways have filtered into the consciousness of this generation . . . . For some, parents . . . participated in some aspect of the '60s counterculture; for others, a chance discovery or a recommendation of a

Thus, out of 23 possible points, the Counterculture scored twenty and a half. Given that many universally recognized ethnicities would certainly score less than a perfect 23, Hippiedom's 20.5 demonstrates well its ethnic nature.

book, movie or musical group has introduced them to the

decade. . . . the neo-hippie culture is far less a movement than a lifestyle.

So, there's evidence of generational transfer here; some young are inheriting Hippie identity. For the Counterculture, add one final point to our ethnic tally.

*   *   *

Thus, out of 23 possible points, the Counterculture scored twenty and a half. Given that many universally recognized ethnicities would certainly score less than a perfect 23, Hippiedom's 20.5 well demonstrates its ethnic nature.

Chapter Six

Waddling Well: What a Relatively Short, In-Many-Ways-Typical Trip It's Been

*"If it walks like a duck, if it looks like a duck, if it quacks like a duck—
it's probably some kind of duck."*

—Proverb

Here, we have an inductive proof of Hippie ethnicity: I'll start with specifics and move towards the generalization of ethnicity. Let's ask, "What specific traits do people correctly associate with ethnicity?" and then look for these same traits in Hippiedom and how society treats it. I found an abundance of such parallels, and what follows is an edited list.

First up: an examination of 15 Hippie stereotypes and how they mimic stereotypes of members of traditionally recognized racial and ethnic groups. Then, we'll segue way into an examination of some of the results and symptoms of prejudice— social invisibility, scapegoating, forced assimilation/ethnocide and a variety of other ugly behaviors. We're also going to examine the sources of prejudice in individuals, and we'll discuss the *authoritarian personality*. The last part of the chapter will focus more positive parallels such as couples and weddings.

* * *

Stereotypes of Hippies: A Foul Potpourri of Traditional Prejudices

We know that traditionally recognized racial and ethnic minorities— in America and elsewhere—have often been stereotyped; certainly, Hippies have been stereotyped. But what exactly is a stereotype? Some sociologists don't think stereotypes are necessarily bad (Baron). Is it a stereotype to say, for instance, that Italian-Americans love Italian food? Yet stereotypes are often employed in an insulting, demeaning manner; they can be used to trivialize, humiliate, intimidate, and de-humanize people. So, where does the legitimate use of criteria to define a group end; where does bigotry begin?

Well, there is often an element of truth to stereotypes;[29] yet, they distort. Imagine all the traits that society admires in people: courage, intelligence, industriousness, a sense of responsibility and so forth. At the opposite end of the spectrum would be qualities universally disrespected: cowardice, foolishness, laziness, irresponsibility and so on. Groups of people, including ethnic groups, are composed of individuals—people who perhaps share cultural qualities that allow them to be grouped but who are individuals nonetheless. Some will be sinners, some will be saints, most will be a mixture of the two—the common stuff of humanity. What stereotyping does is to point to those individuals at the bottom of that judgmental hierarchy and imply or openly argue that these "bad" human beings represent the group. Thus, the degraded—even though exceptional within the group—are seen by bigots as the norm. Usually, stereotypes accentuate the negative, eliminate the positive, and forget Mr. In Between.

Let's begin with that most ugly of stereotypes, the notion that the target group is **subhuman and primitive.** Certainly, Social Darwinist attitudes have long been applied to ethnic and racial minorities in America. White supremacists have for centuries accused non-whites of being biologically inferior to white European-Americans. Blacks, in particular, have been stereotyped as of the jungle, animalistic, barbaric— as a sort of pre-human. Asians, Hispanics and others have been similarly targeted.

In his highly popular and long-running comic strip *L'il Abner*, Al Capp drew derisive images of Hippie types resembling something from the left end of "The Ascent of Man"—apelike. In Capp's world, all "protestors" were Hippies; in his strips—one is entitled "Ignoble Savages"—those "Hippie protestors" belonged to—as in *pig*—SWINE (Students Wildly Indignant About Nearly Everything) (Capp166); his caricatures of Hippie musicians (a band called "The Flipped Dimension," for example) also dehumanized, assigning features Social-Darwinists associate with the primitive and subhuman (188). Tens of millions of Americans regularly read *L'il Abner* and were influenced by these Hippies-are-subhuman images.

---

[29]   Occasionally, I'll use the term *neutral stereotype* for a generalization about a group that isn't necessarily negative and seems generally accurate.

During baseball's 2004 World Series and the preceding season, members of the victorious Boston Red Sox attracted much attention—often condescending criticism—for their unconventional appearance, including beards and hairstyles which smack of Hippiedom. *Time* correspondent Bill Saparito speaks of ". . . Johnny Damon, the lead-off hitter whose long hair and beard evoke the style of 'modern caveman'" (42). Mike Lopresti of *USA Today* says of the Red Sox (who, he describes as of "beards and braids and bohemians"), "Possibly the shaggiest *animals* to walk into Busch Stadium since the last time the Clydesdales marched . . ." (emphasis added).

Photo #6: A "straight" man stands in a natural/-organic foods store, looking at and commenting on a bearded, dreadlocked man who's shopping in the back-ground. He says, "I came here for the same reason people go to the zoo. Shh. Look at that thing. Nature is amazing."

For a vivid image of Hippie-as-subhuman thinking, please go to **Photo #6** where the reader will find a three-part image of a man in a natural/ organic foods store. "Straight," he stands in the foreground, looking at and commenting on a bearded, dread-locked man who's shopping in the background. The picture captions: "I came here for the same reason people go to the zoo. Shh." "Look at that thing." "Nature is amazing."

So, there's ample evidence that Hippies are stereotyped as subhuman and primitive.

Part of being not-quite human is being stereotyped as **stupid and inarticulate**, particularly regarding English. Sociologist Jack Levin writes:

> [B]lacks have traditionally been depicted as indiscriminately substituting the "d" sound for "th." Thus, a black might be viewed as saying "dis" and "dat" as in "lift dat bale" or "dis is de place." In a similar way . . . A Mexican character might typically say "theenk" rather than "think"; "peenk" rather than "pink." By contrast, the American Indian has been depicted as devoid of any English at all; his linguistic ability generally limited to "ugh," "kemo sabe," or some monosyllabic grunt. (57)

Just so, Hippies are often portrayed as having simplistic, limited vocabularies and being perpetually at a loss for words; Hippie characters often sound something like, "Er, ah, like, a, hey, man! Like, you know— oh, what was I going to say . . . oh, I forgot. Oh yeah, I know: real far out!" It's a caricature that shouts, "Spaced out and stupid!" *Time* concludes, "Rational, clearly defined words and logical sequences are tools of what they [Hippies] feel is the Ice Age. Thus they are usually wielded clumsily by the real hippies" (20-21).

Another aspect of being primitive is of course being "**dirty**," and the word has often been appended to epithets directed at traditional ethnic groups: "dirty _____!" Waters quotes a 1914 bigot: "The Slavs," remarks a physician, "are immune to certain kinds of dirt. They can stand what would kill a white man" (qtd. in Waters 2).

Consider, this cartoon from some ill-begotten anti-drug campaign in the United Kingdom **(See Photo #7.)** The character, "Bernie Hayzy," is holding a joint and is described as "the unwashed, scruffy, half-awake, spaced out, cannabis using father of the Hayzy Family (and yes, he wears sandals!) . . . ." Notice, of course, the prominent buzzing fly—"Dirty Hippie!" Notice also the missing tooth, usually used by cartoonists to denote stupidity.

The phrase "dirty hippie" is disturbingly familiar. One day in 2003, I was visiting with two neighbors, one of whom apparently was unaware I was Hippie. She had just returned from a fair where she'd been hawking patriotic doodads and had some friction with the couple in a neighboring booth: "Oh, they were *real* hippies: they were all dirty, and their teeth were sticking out of their mouths." Also, the Ronald Reagan Tarzan "joke" mentioned in Chapter Three stressed stinkiness. Capp's cartoons regularly portrayed Hippies with flies buzzing about them like they were living garbage dumps.

Meanwhile, back in the "real world," Winthrop Griffith of the *New York Times*, reports of demonstrators, mostly Hippie, at the 1969 People's Park confrontation in Berkeley, "Their clothing is often garish and their hair shaggy, but most of them are clean and none of the hundreds I sat with 'smelled.'"

Author Mark Kurlansky notes, "A persistent claim of lack of hygiene was used to dismiss a different way of dressing, whereas neither beatniks nor Hippies were particularly dirty" (184).

Let me add, that in August 2009, while attending a local Countercultural music festival (Nedfest in Nederland, CO), I personally tested the dirty/smelly Hippies accusation. Despite the fact that it had rained earlier and that the concert goers were now dancing in damp dirt, I saw only one couple who were visibly dirty—their feet and the bottoms of their clothing were somewhat muddy—and I detected *no one* who stunk.

Then there's the stereotype of minority member as **protestor**. Journalist Lucy A. Ganje notes the stereotype of "Native Americans as Protesters" (43), and journalism professor and media analyst Carolyn Martindale notes stereotypical "portrayals of African-American leaders conducting protest marches, African American citizens agitating for change . . ." (22).

Now there's nothing necessarily wrong with protesting; some would argue it's a civic duty. The problem is the way the media portrays protestors, taking the protests out of context (Martindale 22). Also, "When people are always seen in conflict," Ganje comments, "they're often viewed as troublemakers and a threat to society" (43).

As mentioned in Chapter Two, it's a mistake to see the Counterculture and the anti-War in Vietnam movements as one and the same. Yet clearly, in the Al Capp mode, many Americans do. Indeed, neoconservatives have often elided the two, referring to the "Vietniks" (as in *Vietnam* and *Beatniks*, I assume), and the phrase "hippie protestor" has become common. In a small-town Iowa restaurant in 1984, hung for public view, I found a cartoon showing a stereotypical Hippie couple (flowered pants, peace signs, etc.); its caption, allegedly describing the couple's plans for the day, reads in part: "Later we'll meet at the Federal Building for the mass protest against the stinking, rotten establishment."

Likewise, just as the protests of other minorities is often taken out of context, many bigots also seem to have forgotten about the War in Vietnam, the draft, environmental degradation and any of the specific sources of Hippie protest; rather, "Hippie protestors" are seen as "just a bunch of spoiled kids" whose protests speak to nothing except their own irresponsibility and lack of character.

The protestor parallel leads us to yet another Hippie stereotype that replicates a traditional American ethnic stereotype: minority member as **"un-American."** "With the possible exception of the British, it is difficult to find an immigrant group that has not been subject to some degree of prejudice and discrimination [in America]," notes ethnologist Rudolph J. Vecoli (xxiii), adding, "Although the targets of nativist attacks have changed over time, a constant theme has been the danger posed by foreigners to American values and institutions" (xxiii).

In the twisted minds of bigots, Hippies are "un-American," even "anti-American," and that view has been foisted upon and is now shared by much of the nation.

Here's right-wing talk-show host Michael Savage from his bestseller, *The Savage Nation*: "So, they [Hippies] hate their country. . . .They hate their fatherland, their motherland, or whatever you wish to call it. They care not for America's great history, her great achievements, or her great freedoms" (94).

The neoconservative *Washington Times* has harped away at this bigoted theme in its coverage: they refer to "the counterculture assault on the U.S. military" (West)[30] and the Counterculture's "assault" on the National Anthem[31] (Gaffney)—Hippie as treasonous America-hating traitor.

In Chapter Two, we saw how neoconservatives have tried to link Hippie-America with international terrorism;

> Hippie as treasonous America-hating traitor—the Counterculture, Americans are supposed to believe, is the enemy within, not just the foremost threat to the nation's moral and physical health but to its national security, as well.

the Counterculture, Americans are supposed to believe, is the enemy within—not just the foremost threat to the nation's moral and physical health but to its national security, as well.

Suffice it to say, this Hippie-as-un-American image is indeed only a stereotype. As *Time* quoted one early Hippie, "Man, I dig those Founding Fathers!" (99). Countercultural writer and musician Ed Sanders explains his attraction to early Hippie culture:

---

[30] President Bill Clinton had appointed an admiral they didn't like.
[31] The reference is to Jimi Hendrix at Woodstock. Incidentally, I think Hendrix's rendition of "The Star Spangled Banner" is an awful piece of music, but I think it's presumptuous to assume it's intended to be unpatriotic; a kinder and probably more accurate interpretation of the Hendrix cover is that it's an experimental piece of music that attempts to meld Hippie and mainstream American culture.

It was artistic, literary, political . . . Lust, wild abandon. Love
of freedom, love of America, veneration for the Constitution.
Affection for Thomas Jefferson and Thomas Paine. Love of
Emma Goldman. Delight in the beatniks and the jazz guys.
Reverence for Native American culture. The new technical
innovations involving light and sound. The rock and roll
heroes. . . . (qtd. in Torgoff 198)

Doesn't sound particularly "anti-American" to me. Likewise, Hippies
emerging out of a larger American culture couldn't be "un-American"
if they wanted. How else does one explain Hippie baseball players, for
instance? Or do an online search for Hippie "peace flags"; you'll find
several, and they're mostly variations on the American flag. Hippie-
Americans aren't un-American; they're a particular type of American.

Dovetailing the stereotype of being un-American is the stereotype
of being **against God**; historically, various American ethnic minorities
have been viewed as in opposition to "God," usually as conservative
Protestants have defined the term. Thus, Chinese "coolies," other Asian-
Americans and Native Americans have been seen as "heathens." Much of
the prejudice against the Irish was justified by their Catholicism. And, of
course, Jewish-Americans have been seen as an enemy of the Christian
God, the killers of Jesus Christ. One way angry Americans have justified
their persecution of particular ethnic minorities has been to say, in effect,
"God's on my group's side; *those people* are against God and deserve
punishment. We who punish them are doing God's work!"

Bigots usually see us the Counterculture as the antithesis of
"godly." An example is *Dust of Death: The Sixties Counterculture and
How It Changed America Forever,* a work foolishly described by the
Presbyterian Journal as "One of the most penetrating and significant
books of the [20th] century" (qtd. in Guinness). The author, Os Guinness,
sees the Counterculture as a "movement" that epitomizes "the lemming
like, suicidal rush from the truth of the historic Christian faith" (228). In
other words, the Counterculture is anti-Christian.

Likewise, many conservative Christians see God as the ultimate
authority figure; thus, to be obedient to God is to be obedient to and
worshipful of all authority, including earthly authority. For them, a culture
for which questioning authority seems a core value, a culture associated in
their minds with protest, a culture that openly values pleasure, including
sexual pleasure, is a culture that spits in God's face. And of course, there's

been no shortage of Christian preachers claiming that rock 'n' roll—often associated with Hippiedom—is essentially devil worship.

In reality, again, one finds no uniform philosophy within the Counterculture, anti-Christian or otherwise. Clearly, though, not all Hippies are atheists: consider some of the didactic lyrics of "Ripple," penned by Robert Hunter for the Grateful Dead:

> Reach out your hand if your cup be empty
> If your cup is full may it be again.
> Let it be known there is a fountain
> That was not made by the hands of man. . . .
> You who choose to lead must follow
> But if you fall, you fall alone.
> If you should stand, then who's to guide you?
> If I knew the way, I would take you home. (qtd. in Dodd)

The song is an obvious argument for the existence of God. Thus, not only are there Hippie "believers" (whether they be Jewish, Buddhist, Muslim or of other lesser-known faiths), there are a large number of Hippie Christians. Can you say "Jesus freak"? You know, as in a Hippie who has placed Jesus and some kind of Christian faith at the center of her or his life?[32]

> **That some alleged Christians in America twist the love-thy-neighbor message of Jesus Christ into a rationale for stereotyping and bigotry has, sadly, a long history—usually one steeped in racism and ethnic chauvinism.**

The notion that Hippies are against God, the Christian God, or even traditional Christian religions is silly; that some alleged Christians in America twist the love-thy-neighbor message of Jesus Christ into a rationale for stereotyping and bigotry has, sadly, a long history—usually one steeped in racism and ethnic chauvinism.

Okay, can you say **"welfare bum"**? It's a stereotype often applied with chilling political consequences to traditionally recognized American minorities. Certainly, African-Americans have been a target; while blacks don't constitute the majority of Americans on "welfare,"

---

[32] Better still: hum a few bars of The Doobie Brothers' "Jesus is just Alright."

the media often makes it seem as if they were (Martindale 21). It's been applied to Mexican-Americans too.

Hippie-as-welfare-bum is a staple of anti-Hippie prejudice. A 1996 news story about problems being caused by a few Deadheads (the Hippie followers of the Grateful Dead) is generally fair, noting that the troublemakers are a "few bad apples" who don't represent the majority of Deadheads; it even quotes Grateful Dead spokesperson Dennis McNally who denounces the misbehavers:

> Acting like a parasite is destructive to the social contract. It was not acceptable on tour, and it's not acceptable now. Jerry Garcia worked his ass off for a living and so did the rest of the band. If they [the misbehavers] think their lives are in some fashion devoted to Jerry Garcia, then they should honor him by being a positive force in the community. (qtd. in Woolfolk)

Now, consider how an editor has headlined this piece: "Drifting Grateful Dead followers bite the handouts that feed them," making it sound as if *all* Deadheads—*all* Hippie-Americans—are ungrateful parasites.

Here's how the Hippie-as-parasite stereotype has played out courtesy of our tax dollars: "Wallet," a government-sponsored freevibe. com television commercial, appeared during 2003 (National Youth). In it, a "straight" boy, about 12, takes out his billfold and heads downstairs, explaining, "My brother, he started smoking pot when he was my age; he didn't drop out of school like some other guys, and he didn't go to jail or get hooked on other drugs. He didn't end up on the street or anything like that." The boy then enters the dimly lit basement where his older brother (longish hair, unshaven, barefoot—a stereotypical lazy Hippie) is apparently living. Slumped on a couch, staring mindlessly at a glaring television, the elder brother asks in a surly tone "What do *you* want?" The boy hands him a few dollars and tells the viewer, "He never really did anything—at all."

Yet, far from being parasites, Hippies regularly give to the larger society—to the planet—in a manner that's exemplary. As the reader will see, the section on Hippie philanthropy in Chapter Eight is hefty.

And it seems Hippies aren't just protesting parasites but **promiscuous** too. That's a stereotype often historically applied by bigots to various ethnic minorities, including Polynesians (Brislin 106), Irish-Americans

(Ross 55, 1996), African-Americans, Mexican-Americans and others, now including Hippie-Americans. [33]

Consider this ugly Hippie-as-whore passage from The *Savage Nation*:

> These [hippie] chicks would go to Kabul, do drugs, sex, rock and roll. . . . If you, as a religious [Afghani] person, saw women running around without underwear or brassieres, if you watched them get loaded in your cafes, and you saw that they were doing drugs, they were doing guys, and they were seducing your sons, what would you think? . . .
>
> You'd say that these were the Jezebels of the West. . . .
>
> As an Afghani, you wouldn't have wanted your son to sleep with one of those girls from Berkeley who came over there. You'd be afraid she'd give him a disease and go home. Worse, the hippies didn't even leave babies behind.
>
> All they left was STDs . . . . (101-02)

And of course, Hippie men are often seen as promiscuous too. Perhaps, there is some truth to this stereotype: many male Hippie rock stars have apparently had groupies ever within grasp. The media, and often the stars themselves, publicize their "conquests," creating a popular, and probably exaggerated, image. And all that talk about "love-ins"—well, heck, let's just leap to the conclusion that the

> **"If you, as a religious [Afghani] person, saw [hippie] women running around without under-wear or brassieres, if you watched them get loaded in your cafes, and you saw that they were doing drugs, they were doing guys, and they were seducing your sons, what would you think? ... You'd say that these were the Jezebels of the West."–talk-show host Michael Savage**

---

[33] There was an interesting display of this stereotype in neoconservative Justice Anton Scalia's dissent to the Supreme Court's legalization of gay marriage in June 2015. Scalia wrote, in regard to "Freedom of Intimacy" (promiscuity), "Ask the nearest hippie" (qtd. in Swanson).

Counterculture is a large mass of writhing, naked bodies—an ongoing orgy. Listen to Savage:

> The potheads on the left [hippies] said, "Whatever you're feeling, you should act out." You know, "If it feels good, do it." If you're feeling sexual, do it in the road.
> If you feel like it, make it with a cow or a dog.
> The pot-induced attitudes dredged up sexual perversion in people. Things that should have been suppressed by the norms of any sane society were drawn out of people . . . . (98)

Can you say *polymorphous perversity*?[34] So, is this popular image of Hippies as wildly licentious and lewd a reality? After all, the slogan "Sex, drugs, and rock 'n' roll!" seems to have been a Countercultural battle cry, right?

First, let's not assume that conventional American sexual mores are the standard Hippie sexuality should be measured against. In America, at least, those mores were, and are, Calvinist and flesh-hating; thus, our "animal" nature has been seen as the opposite of our Godly capacity, and while much of socially conservative America may consider sex acceptable for procreational purposes, it's still seen as inherently dirty.

George F. Will, for instance, criticizes the Counterculture for "recreational use of . . . sex," a stricture that would forbid even long-married couples having relations for any purpose other than procreation. Against this background, any open courting of pleasure, especially of sexual pleasure, smacks of Sodom and Gomorrah, seems "dirty." Yes, the Counterculture's valuing of sexuality is partly why "dirty hippies" are "dirty hippies."

Secondly, the Counterculture's critics tend to romanticize the pre-sixties; yet, "The Good Old Days Weren't," as writer Gary Sloan puts it:

> In "A Social History of the American Family," Arthur Calhoun notes that in several colonies between 1650 and 1657 "the extant record of fornication and adultery is appalling." . . . In Rhode Island in the 1700s, half the newlywed women were pregnant at the time of their marriage. Prostitution in the United States was so pandemic after the Civil War that in several cities officials talked

---

[34] Okay, now say it three times really fast!

seriously of legalizing it. . . . Today [October 2000], proportionately more Americans marry than ever before. In the 1880s, the divorce rate in America exceeded that in all other industrialized countries. In the 1800s, there was one abortion for every six births. In the 1920s, one in four pregnancies ended in abortion.

There have always been divorces; there have always been promiscuous people; there have always been brothels; there have always been abortions; and though Sloan doesn't specifically mention it, there have always been STD's.

Third, Hippie promiscuity has tended to be exaggerated by a prurient media—it claims to be shocked, but somehow, fascinated by its own licentious imagination, it just can't stop speculating. As Countercultural cookbook author Lucy Horton notes, "It's a delightful joke on the press, I think, that most rural 'hippie communes' should prove to be centered not on lurid sex or violent politics, but on food" (qtd. in Belasco 77).

Lastly, while sexual mores have changed somewhat since the sixties— and some of that change *is* probably attributable to the Counterculture— the major change has been an acceptance of premarital sex, premarital cohabitation and an openness to seeing sex as healthy. That does not translate into an ongoing orgy; today, most Hippies are probably no more or less promiscuous than members of other social groups.

Another staple of racial and ethnic stereotypes has been that of group member as **childlike**. For generations, white supremacists in America and elsewhere argued that people of color were overgrown children. Thus, an African-American man was always a "boy." Martindale mentions media stereotypes portraying African-Americans as "feckless, ignorant, child-like beings" (21). And colonialism was often justified with condescending, patriarchal attitudes that convinced colonialists they were behaving in a responsible, benevolent manner—as a kind and wise father would to his children. Like children, the colonized were portrayed as unable to determine what was in their best interests.

Well, I know you can say "flower child," and this notion of Hippie as perpetual pre-adult permeates the media. George F. Will opines:

The spirit of the Sixties was, strictly speaking, infantile. For an infant, any appetite is self-legitimizing. . . . The portion of popular culture that constantly sentimentalizes the Sixties also panders to the arrested development of the Sixties generation . . . .

In his commentary on the 2004 Boston Red Sox—a team renowned for their Hippie-looking players—sportswriter Bill Saparito glibly links their hairstyles to "staggering immaturity" (42). He adds of Countercultural Johnny Damon, "His philosophy could be described as *early developmental*" (emphasis added) (42)—you know, as in infantile.

An example of this type of stereotyping is the common phrase "overgrown hippie," implying, again, some kind of never-ending adolescence.

Another traditional, yet modern, stereotype of American ethnicities as been as a **drug addicts**. The Irish, of course, have been seen as drunks. Martindale speaks of African-Americans being stereotyped as "drug addicted" (21). Yes, there certainly are minority persons who are drug addicts; yet, they are a minority within minorities, and mainstream America surely has its drug addicts too, especially if we include alcoholics. Thus, the charge of ethnic-minority member as "drug addict" is often unfairly applied.

Well, the government, mainstream media and American society as a whole have turned the Counterculture into a poster child for drug abuse. The assumption, of course, is that all drug use is drug abuse and that all Hippie-Americans are "drug addicts." "Being a longhair," one Jimm Davis writes, "I personally understand the social stigma associated with the length of my hair and its connection to my presumed dependency to some narcotic." It's like because of JimiJanisJim, the entire Counterculture has been indicted.

What is neglected are the millions of Hippies who use marijuana (and sometimes other drugs) responsibly, who aren't addicted to anything, who are productive, successful citizens. When a worst-case scenario is seen as the norm, that's stereotyping.

> **The government, mainstream media and American society as a whole have turned the Counterculture into a poster child for drug abuse. The assumption, of course, is that all "drug" use is "drug" abuse and that all Hippie-Americans are "drug addicts."**

Laziness, of course, is a charge that for centuries has dogged a number of American minorities. Sometimes, perhaps, the discrimination and other factors leading to high unemployment among minorities has helped foster

98

this accusation, but the unemployed aren't necessarily lazy, and many American minorities—African-Americans, Jewish-Americans, Chinese-Americans, Irish-Americans and Mexican-Americans come to mind—have at one time or another done much of the nation's hardest, dirtiest work.

Laziness and a lack of productivity is usually part of a "hippie pothead" stereotype; that is, people falsely believe marijuana use will lead to "amotivational syndrome," and like the parasitic older brother in "Wallet," Hippies will never do anything with their lives, never amount to much. As we'll see in Chapter Eight, the accomplishments of Hippiedom and individual Hippies are numerous and significant—the antithesis of "lazy" and "unmotivated."

The stereotype of **neglectful, abusive parent** has sometimes been applied to traditional American racial and ethnic minorities. Martindale, for instance, notes "the image of the neglectful and abusive African American mother" (24).

Well now, as I understand it, Hippies are lazy, self-indulgent, welfare bums addicted to drugs and irresponsibly promiscuous to boot, so they must be having kids,[35] and there's no way people like that can be good parents. Certainly, mainstream media have propagated this stereotype.

An episode of the old TV show *Dragnet* showed a Hippie mother who had let her child drown in the bathtub—she was out back getting high on marijuana and got so stoned she forgot the baby. A similar message was sent by a 2005 government-sponsored freevibe.com commercial which shows a toddler about to fall into a swimming pool as the narrator tells us that the babysitters are too busy smoking pot to notice (National Youth, "Pool").

And as mentioned, George F. Will plays heavily on this prejudice in his column on the death of Jerry Garcia:

> If you're going to San Francisco, said a song of the Sixties, "you're gonna meet some gentle people there." If you had gone this June you might have met Wolfgang and Lisa Von Nester. . . . Wolfgang, 23, and Lisa 24, will be sentenced next week by a California judge . . . . He could sentence the Maryland couple to six years in prison for abandoning their 3-year-old son at a

---

[35]   "Hey, they can't abort them all!"

San Bernardino mall on June 2. "I figured that without food and money and without diapers to put on his butt what else could I do," says Wolfgang, who also says, "I walked away in tears." Then he dried his tears and he and Lisa, who were not really without money, abandoned their car and took a bus north to a Grateful Dead concert in San Francisco. . . . Wolfgang and Lisa really represent that survival [of 1960's idealism, i.e. the Counterculture].

The proof that the abusive and neglectful Hippie parent *is* a stereotype is found in the millions of Counterculturists who excel at parenting. Most are painfully conscientious, devoted, responsible and loving. Of a probable Countercultural parent, *The Wall St. Journal* reports, "Tracey Daugherty grew up on Kraft Macaroni & Cheese, but she won't feed it to her 18-month-old son. . . . These days she opts for fresh produce, chicken, fish and an occasional Amy's Organic frozen dinner when pressed for time" ("Eating Up"). I think Daughtery is typical of Hippie parents: highly conscientious about what she feeds her children and about parenting in general.

Yes, there *are* criminally bad Hippie parents, but sadly, poor parenting, incest and damaged, dysfunctional families are frighteningly common—among *all* sectors of society—and considering how many exemplary Hippie parents there are, it's unfair and prejudicial to assume Hippie parents are abusive parents.

Traditionally formed American ethnic groups often complain about being stereotyped as **criminals**.

Well, Hippie-Americans are also often stereotyped as criminals—as the "bad guys." Consider the nineties television program *Baywatch*—at one time the most syndicated show in the world. In episode after episode, the bad guys appear to be Hippie types. In one program, evil poachers are shooting helpless baby seals. The nastiest of the poachers, the one who laughs sadistically as he shoots the poor creatures, is a scruffy, stocking-capped male with shoulder-length hair. In another particularly preposterous episode, the bad-guy/murderer turns out to be a rogue FBI agent. Of course, male FBI agents seldom have ponytails—it violates military dress code—but this one does. Yes, we know he's a bad FBI agent *because* he has long hair.

Yes, it would be different if the villainous longhairs were balanced by heroic longhairs, but this never seems the case. Small wonder, then,

> **Evidently, Matthews' real intent was to remind viewers that Paul McCartney had a "criminal" past in his Japan-ese marijuana arrest in the 1970s, to say, in effect, "Don't forget, America, this guy is a convict." "Rap sheet"! You would think the Beatles had been bank robbers.**

that a columnist for a mainstream American newspaper cries, "Look at the dirtbags and scumballs of the world, and you'll see long hair and beards" (Healy). Yes, when we look at the media—particularly entertainment media where directors have made conscious decisions about how characters will look—that is *exactly* what we see; I'll demonstrate this early in Chapter Eleven.

One last egregious example of stereotyping Hippies as criminals: After some fumbling by organizers, Paul McCartney became the half-time performer at the 2005 Super Bowl for a performance that was supposed to be "family entertainment" for a nation still shocked by the previous year's Nipplegate scandal. But the selection of the ex-Beatle also raised a question: Just how wholesome is McCartney? After all, the Beatles were/are Hippies—you know, the "drug culture"? As I recall, conservative commentator Chris Matthews' next-day comments on his show seemed a heavy-handed attempt to play the Hippie-as-criminal card: Wasn't it "great" that a guy like Paul McCartney, with the "rap sheet" he had, could "go straight" and turn his life around—be rehabilitated. Evidently, Matthews' real intent was to remind viewers that McCartney had a "criminal" past in his Japanese marijuana arrest in the 1970s, to say, in effect, "Don't forget, America, this guy is a convict." "Rap sheet"! You would think the Beatles had been bank robbers.[36]

But there's a flip side to the stereotype of minority member as criminal and villain: minority member as **victim**. It makes sense if you think about it: For people to respect someone, that someone usually has to have two basic qualities: strength and virtue. If someone is strong but wicked, that person is a villain. But if someone is in some ways virtuous or well-intended but weak or ineffectual, then that person will be a victim. And seldom the twain shall meet because when they do,

---

[36]   I will cite no source for this; it is from notes and memory.

then we have a strong, virtuous character who would command respect.[37] So, when Hippies aren't being viewed a villains, they're often being stereotyped as weaklings and easy victims. Two examples:

A short-lived late-1970s NBC program, *Big Hawaii* was about a plantation run by an aristocratic white patriarch and his son.[38] In one episode, a nearby town has been stricken by an epidemic the townspeople mistakenly blame on a local Hippie commune. The son soon discovers the true source of the disease, and when local "hotheads" head for the commune, the son and his manly pals are to the rescue. Well, as everyone knows, Hippie communes have a guru who the others, childlike, unquestioningly follow. "Moonflower" has a headband, slightly long hair, a two-day beard, and dynamic leader that Moonflower is, he's somehow sensed the danger and fled with his "tribe" into the forest, where presumably they're subsisting on nuts, berries, and tree bark. Cowardly, helpless, and unable to defend themselves, they need others—superiors—to do that for them. After much cajoling, the brave son finally convinces the frightened Hippies to emerge; the communards then file out of the forest, single-file, behind the Wise One. It's like a scene from *Bambi*, and Moonflower is a wide-eyed mix of fear, innocence, and cupidity—"Like w-w-wow, m-man!" Finally, the good guys depart, but not before admonishing the hapless Hippies: "You just take, but you never give back"—the parasite stereotype thrown in for good measure.

Entering the national limelight in the fall of 1969 via NBC's "Tonight Show" hosted by Johnny Carson, ukulele-strumming, falsetto-voiced Tiny Tim was a curiosity. Vegetarian with very long hair and a trademark song, "Tiptoe through the Tulips," Tiny Tim (Herbert Khaury) was seen as the quintessential "flower child." And while audiences howled when "Mr. Carson" interviewed Mr. Tim, they were more laughing at the singer than with him. And Tiny Tim seemed oblivious—fluttering away, blowing kisses feverishly at studio audiences, clucking repeatedly, "Oh, Mr. Carson, Mr. Carson," as America convulsed with laughter. *Tonight Show* ratings rose. What exactly was the national fascination?

---

[37] There are exceptions, and Stephen Segal films, for instance, would be one.

[38] It's probably not coincidental that in its treatment of indigenous Hawaiians, this program seemed overtly colonial. The townspeople, by the way, didn't seem necessarily Hawaiian, either, as I recall. It's like this show existed in a racial/ethnic fantasy world.

Yes, Tiny Tim was entertaining in his eccentricity, but the real secret of his sudden success was probably the role he played in the nation's psyche, particularly among insecure men: Tiny Tim seemed the stereotypical "hippie fag"—a weakling and a victim.

Underlying and running through most of these stereotypes ("the mother of all stereotypes"?) is what might be called the "moral argument" for prejudice: the assumption that members of the group in question are **irresponsible and lack character**; therefore, disapproving of them is the moral thing to do—it *shows* character. Since bigotry is now widely seen as evidence of immorality and lack of character, we tend to forget that campaigns of racial and ethnic persecution have always been portrayed as moral crusades. White-supremacists in the Old South, for instance, argued that Afrophobia was crucial to their society retaining its moral fiber and virtue. The same could be said for Nazi anti-Semites in their campaigns against European Jewry.

Just so, neoconservatives usually define the Counterculture as a movement against virtue and character. For instance, a reviewer paraphrases the views of Gerturde Himmelfarb (wife and collaborator of the "Godfather of Neoconservatism," Irving Kristol); she claims, "[T]he counterculture of the 1960s," characterized by ". . . its unbridled sexuality, its flight from tradition and personal responsibility, its flouting of authority and its cultural relativism" has led to America's "moral decay" (qtd. in Posner). The assumption that the Counterculture eschews personal responsibility, in particular, is a staple of neoconservative propaganda expressed routinely by neocon ideologues like George F. Will, Newt Gingrich and William Bennett.

The equation of culture with lack of character is—plain and simple—bigotry. And the Hippie-haters rarely supply any evidence for their insulting assumptions; where they do, it tends to be crude overgeneralizations or they beg the question by making self-serving assumptions, i.e., "hippie protestors" who opposed the War in Vietnam did so for the most shallow, selfish and irresponsible reasons—because opposing that war or refusing to fight in it was the easy way out.

* * *

As we've now seen, prejudice towards Hippies is a foul potpourri of the stereotypes often applied to other victims of ethnic and racial prejudice. Bigots will resist acknowledging Hippie ethnicity since doing so confers a certain legitimacy, but their own behavior belies them: they've stereotyped the Counterculture almost exactly the way they've stereotyped traditionally recognized racial and ethnic minorities—quack, quack.

*   *   *

> **Hippies are socially invisible—not a topic of polite or comfortable conversation. Consider, for example, this bizarre phenomenon: reference books that inexplicably make no reference to *hippies*.**

Social invisibility: In the relevant social sciences, it's recognized that certain groups considered "undesirable" by "respectable" society attain a peculiar status where everyone knows they exist but pretends they don't. Often these "undesirable" groups are ethnic or racial minorities though they might also be gays and lesbians or others. Hippies are socially invisible—not a topic of polite or comfortable conversation. Consider, for example, this bizarre phenomenon: reference books that inexplicably make no reference to *hippies*.

Enter the 1986 *Webster's Third New International Dictionary* which neglects to even mention either *hippie* or *counterculture*. No, I didn't miss them; I checked different spellings and variations—nothing. Actually, *hippie* and *hippy* do appear; the former is defined as "a small heap," the latter, "having or resembling large hips." Obviously the editors didn't omit these two words, just particular definitions of them.

Yes, these terms might be considered slang, but the 1986 *Webster's Third New International Dictionary* is "unabridged": it should include informal language. *Webster's Dictionary* is a respected institution with many editors and proofreaders; the only rational explanation for these omissions is that they're deliberate—the editors have carefully removed these terms/meanings.

And lest the reader conclude this edition of *Webster's Dictionary* is unique, let me note that in the 2007 *Encyclopedia Britannica:* the term *hip-hop* is listed, but there's nothing for *hippie, hippy* or *counterculture*. In addition to being frighteningly Orwellian ("Big Brother has decided you never existed!"), this evidence illustrates well Hippiedom's social invisibility.

And like many American outgroups, Hippie-Americans have played the role of the **scapegoat**. How often have we heard that America's "decline" began in the Sixties with the Hippies? Savage: "The joy of the fifties was unmatched. . . . Then, all of a sudden, the freaks popped up out of the woodwork and ruined America" (95). To Hippies, Savage then directly attributes four modern woes:

1) Teaching homosexuality in schools.
2) "No-fault" divorce and the fallout on the family
3) STDs and costs to society
4) Abortion (95-96)

The way in which he reaches these conclusions is of course twisted and tortured; nonetheless, the result seems always the same: blame it on the Counterculture.

Well, we expect a cheap demagogue like Savage to exhibit cartoonish thinking, but from the eminent George F. Will, we might expect better; instead, we get Savage in a bow tie:

> . . . the band [the Grateful Dead] has promoted much more than music. Around it has hung an aroma[39] of disdain for inhibitions on recreational uses of drugs and sex. During the band's 30-year life the costs of "liberation" from such inhibitions have been made manifest in millions of shattered lives and miles of devastated cities.

Hippies are responsible for America's "devastated" inner cities? It's a ludicrous argument. First, America's ghettoes long predate the Counterculture. And while some think those inner cities have become more devastated in recent decades, there are numerous causes for that: everything from interstates being forced through those communities to the gutting of the social safety net to a weak economy.

First, Will is engaged in gross oversimplification. And if "millions of shattered lives" is a veiled reference to drug abuse or the AIDS epidemic, how is Hippiedom responsible? If someone living in a largely black inner

---

[39] Interesting how Will works in "aroma." . . . Oh, that's right; I almost forgot! . . . Hippies smell!

city decides to use crack or have unprotected sex, it's not because he or she was listening to or being influenced by Hippie-America; why blame the Counterculture?

Lastly here, an obvious way that many Americans scapegoat Hippies is by blaming them for the loss of the war in Vietnam. Thus the vain follies of trying to wage a neocolonial war in a post-colonial era are blamed on the anti-war movement, who are portrayed as synonymous with Hippie-America.

Scapegoating—the trademark tactic of bigots across the globe and throughout history.

For our next parallel, consider something social scientists refer to as **"forced assimilation," a.k.a. ethnocide.** Ethnologist David H. Levinson: "Assimilation is a complex process and can be voluntary or forced (sometimes called *ethnocide*) . . ." (x). Generally, *forced assimilation/ ethnocide* is pressure by the larger society on the outgroup to conform— "You need to look, think and behave as we do." The cultural differences of such outgroups are seen as threatening, so society attempts to mute or destroy those differences.

Let's look at a very particular type of forced assimilation: "giving" someone a haircut. The parallel to traditional racial and ethnic persecution? Two cases from American history: First, European-

> **Let's look at a very particular type of forced assimilation: "giving" someone a haircut.**

American settlers forcibly assimilating Native American males often cut their hair, especially those enrolled in schools explicitly designed to "take the Indian out of them." And in the American West in the late 1800s and early 1900s, these same European-Americans harassed, persecuted and inflicted violence upon Chinese immigrants and Chinese-Americans. White American lynch mobs often gave haircuts to "coolies," cutting off the long braid (*queue*) many Chinese men wore. The purpose was to humiliate, hurt and intimidate. Forced hair-cutting, then, has a history in America as a kind of ethnic rape.

Now, jump to the late 1960s and the advent of long-haired Hippie men. "Keep America Beautiful, Give a Hippie a Haircut" was at one time a popular bumper sticker in America (Lind). Actual billboards blared a similar message (Kurlansky 184). And notice, it's not "Ask a hippie to get a haircut," it's *"Give* a hippie a haircut." And there's a whole body of Hippie folklore, I think, about "longhairs" being forcibly shorn by

Hippie-haters, sometimes by official institutions like courts or draft boards, sometimes by unofficial gangs in violent assaults.

And of course, American history is littered with what are now known as **"hate groups"** who target various minorities. If the Counterculture is an ethnicity, we'd expect to find hate groups hating it. In Chapter Three, I mentioned a sort of crisis in American fascism: the old scapegoats and victim groups are increasingly out of reach politically—defended. The fascist right is confused about which way to go, and like their respectable Republican cousins, some seem to like the idea of placing Hippie-hating at the head of the class. Let's look at three examples: an American fascist who bills himself as "the world's greatest economist," Lyndon LaRouche; a former Klansman who calls himself "America's Most Outspoken Patriot Preacher," Johnny Lee Clary; and the website of the twisted Anti-Hippie Action League.

Lyndon LaRouche and his organizations are widely considered fascist, partly because of Brown Shirt-type attacks his followers have made on socialist groups. LaRouche seems to have settled on Hippie-America ("the drug culture," he would call it) as his preferred scapegoat/target. One of his organizations is called the "War on Drugs" committee. Countercultural activist and author Jack Herer and five members of the California Marijuana Initiative attended one of the committee's 1981 public events; Herer reports:

> They told us that along with new marijuana laws, they expected to implement their most important goal: anyone in the future playing any disco, rock 'n' roll or jazz on the radio, on television, in schools, or in the concert, or just sold rock 'n' roll records or any other music that wasn't from their approved classical lists, would be jailed, including music teachers, disc jockeys and record company executives. (96-7) (Herer also cites the *LA Times* and KNBC-TV as sources here.)

Why? Because all those non-classical genres have the "evil marijuana beat" (qtd. in 97). As Herer and colleagues entered:

> . . . we were asked to sign a petition endorsing a Detroit reporter who had written an open letter to the new President, Ronald Reagan, asking him to give immediate presidential clemency and make a national hero of Mark Chapman, who had murdered

John Lennon of the Beatles six weeks earlier. The letter stated that John Lennon had been the most evil man on the planet because he almost single-handedly "turned on" the planet to "illicit drugs." (96)

Essentially, LaRouche and his followers would like to "feed" on the Counterculture.

Then, consider a character known as **Johnny Lee Clary**—once a professional wrestler known as Johnny Angel. He describes himself as a former Klansman who was brought to God and repented; now, he loves black people! Or says he does. Turns out, Clary has even appeared on *The Oprah Winfrey Show*.[40] His article, "Hippies: A Spiritual and Moral Crisis," on his website (www.RepublicanRebel.com) is a poorly written rant against the Counterculture containing almost every stereotype mentioned earlier in this chapter. Clary also engages in silly scapegoating and associates Hippie-America with international anti-American terrorism.

And his site is laced with menacing "humor"; thus, Clary writes, "Of course if they [hippies] were on a pair of [water] skies [sic], with a couple of good conservatives driving the boat, being pulled [sic] the swamps with an alligator swimming behind the hippie, I bet they would repent and become a Christian, like immediately! That's one way to get a hippie to change!" Well, say one thing for Reverend Johnny Lee—he's a regular Laff-Riot!

Essentially, what we see in Clary isn't so much a man reborn as a Christian, but of black-hating fascist "reborn" as a Hippie-hating fascist with a pseudo-Christian façade. Like much of rightist America, he's simply changed his victim/scapegoat of choice.

Now meet **The Anti-Hippie Action League** (AHAL). Here's a website that encourages violence—including murder—against Hippies, and they consciously attempt to de-sensitize others to such crimes. They do these things as part of a politicized, ideologically driven group, they claim; if they aren't already engaged in organized terror against Counterculturists, it may only be a matter of time. "Ethnically directed physical attack," says Pettigrew, ". . . generally only flares up after group mobilization has taken place. When churches or synagogues are

---

[40]   Oprah!?

desecrated, or homes of 'invading' outsiders are damaged in an ethnic neighborhood, the attack is almost always the work of organized groups" (827).

Viewing the AHAL website is quite the experience. Looking sort of Goth, actually, the homepage's black background is complemented by a deep crimson: an animated graphic of dripping blood. Yes, it has occurred to me this website might be someone's idea of dark humor—a *Saturday Night Live* skit gone badly awry. Some of the propaganda on the site, in fact, is so absurd it *does* border on the comical: One photo under "Hippie Horrors," for instance, shows some Hippie men admiring a newborn, their faces radiant. The accompanying caption, however, speaks of cannibalism: "A group of hippies, passing around an infant prior to its ritual consumption."

But they appear serious, and the AHAL site also includes handy tips for murdering Hippie-Americans, including ideas for planting bombs in Hippie crowds ("Include nails and metal shreds for the added delight of flayed hippie skins"). Make no mistake about it, this is a *terrorist* site, in the true sense of the word.

As a sophomore in college, I was walking along a street near my campus. Suddenly, my glasses shot off my head, and an object ricocheted off a nearby wall. Speeding by, some thugs had thrown a golf ball at me. Probably, I was a target because I was visibly Hippie.

Next on our tour of Uglyville, **targets of hate crimes**. Of course, America has a "rich" history of crimes against racial and ethnic minorities. The many lynchings of African-Americans are infamous, but Irish-Americans, Chinese-Americans, Jewish-Americans and a wide variety of others have also been targeted.

Take all that we've already seen—demagogic politicians and commentators fueling and feeding off of anti-Hippie prejudice; stereotyping, scapegoating and hatred of Hippie-Americans; obsessive bigots and hate groups attempting to organize and direct the bigotry, to lead the lynch mob—add a general fear, frustration, sense of helplessness and rage in "straight" society, and what do we get? Violence towards Hippies. Using the language of sociology, Michael E. Brown describes the phenomenon:

. . .the they-mentality of the persecutors . . . draws lines around its objects as it fits them conceptually for full-scale social action. The particular uses of the term "hippie" in the mass media—like "Jew," "communist," "Black Muslim" or "Black Panther"—cultivates not only disapproval and rejection but a climate of opinion capable of excluding hippies from the moral order altogether. This is one phase of a subtle process that begins by locating and isolating a group, tying it to the criminal, sinful or obscene, developing and displaying referential symbols at a high level of abstraction which depersonalize and objectify the group, defining the stigmata by which members are to be known and placing the symbols in the context of ideology and readiness for action. (113-114)

That "action" would be violence.

As a sophomore in college, I was walking along a street near my campus. Suddenly, my glasses shot off my head, and an object ricocheted off a nearby wall. Speeding by, some thugs had thrown a golf ball at me. It had hit the bow of my glasses; they flew off my face, and I was unhurt, but if not for those glasses, I could have been blinded in one eye or even killed. Probably, I was a target because I was visibly Hippie.

Researchers Stillman and Wiener note a Hippie woman's "worst experience of the Sixties": "Being witness to a beating, with a club, of two males with long hair whose automobile had run out of gasoline, by the owners of the service station (sign on the service station read 'no service to hippies') on the drag in Austin, Texas" (47); they add that in New York City, ". . . gangs of them [hardhats] went on a rampage in 1970, beating up anyone on the street who had long hair" (47).

Not surprisingly, there have been murders. In October of 1983, a 21-year old American, Michael David Kline was pulled off a bus in El Salvador and later found dead, victim of the US-armed and -supported Salvadoran National Guard. Joanne Omang the *Washington Post* reports:

The soldiers . . . said Kline tried to escape, ignored warnings and was shot from about 30 feet away as he ran down the road. . . . The story fell apart quickly. There were powder burns on [Kline], indicating close-range shots, and multiple bruises and burns, suggesting torture, according to photographs. Two shots were fired from the front.

Why was Kline detained to begin with? His mother said he was not a political activist, but simply a tourist (Omang). Salvadoran Guardsmen, however, reported that "he looked 'suspicious' with his long hair, knapsack and rubber sandals" (Omang). This young man, then, was murdered for being identifiably Hippie.

". . . as Hilberg suggests in his *The Destruction of the European Jews*," Brown warns, "the extermination of the forms of lives [culture or ethnicity] leads easily to the extermination of the lives themselves. The line between persecution and terror is thin" (99). Official and media reports seldom say a murder victim was "Hippie," the way they might note the race or ethnicity of another, so we must wonder: how many Hippies have been murdered just for being Hippie?

One form that ethnocidal violence takes is **rape**. We've seen it used as a means of persecution and punishment in various parts of the world experiencing "ethnic strife"; it happened in Bosnia-Herzegovina; more recently, it's happened in Darfur in the Sudan. It's happened throughout history.

> **But why was "Anna" assaulted to begin with? Partly because she was vulnerable, and her assailants were depraved. But also, I suspect, because she was Hippie and because for some, prejudice has made Hippie-American women acceptable targets.**

I've found anecdotal evidence of Hippie rape, and here's a likely example from 1998. In Boulder, CO, a man was on trial, the last of four accused (the first three were convicted) in the east-of-town gang rape of a hitchhiker ("Anna") headed towards the Countercultural Boulder-Nederland area. Boulder *Daily Camera* editor Clint Talbott described a bizarre courtroom scene: "At least two police officers—trained to identify drunks and drug users—testified that Anna did not appear intoxicated. No one testified to the contrary." Yet, despite that there was ". . . no evidence—not one shred, iota or scintilla of evidence, admissible or otherwise—that 'Anna,' the rape victim, had been using illegal drugs," the public defender continued to raise the issue, so much so that the judge repeatedly warned him.

At first puzzled, I realized that the rape victim must be Hippie. By email, Talbott apparently confirmed my suspicion, noting the woman was wearing a tie-dyed tee-shirt in court and seemed one of the "footloose and fancy free." The defense attorney, then, had appealed to prejudices about Hippies: they're all on "drugs," out of touch with the real world, in a psychotic state and therefore untrustworthy. The jury, fortunately, was no more impressed with this Hippie-baiting approach than the judge and convicted the rapist.

But why was "Anna" assaulted to begin with? Partly because she was vulnerable, and her assailants were depraved. But also, I suspect, because she was Hippie and because for some, prejudice has made Hippie-American women acceptable targets.

Often traditionally recognized minorities have been persecuted by government and law. Here now is a section on **official violence** against the Counterculture, and I'll begin by merely mentioning **drug laws directed at the group**, but I'll not discuss this aspect of ethnicity here; I'll cover it in depth early in Chapter Ten.

And given all the laws designed to persecute the Counterculture, it should come as no small surprise to find that many Hippie-Americans are **workin' on a chain gang**. That is, just as a repressive and bigoted society has connived ways to put people of color, in particular, in jail, so, through the War on Drugs, it is doing to Hippie-America. As such, I believe that there are a disproportionate number of Hippie-Americans in our prisons. Indeed, in 2015, one in eight US federal prisoners was in for cannabis-related crimes (NORML), and probably a large number of these people are Hippie-American. *Relix* magazine headlined its February, 1994 issue "Drug Wars: Heads Behind Bars." In it, publisher Toni A. Brown writes of "dozens of . . . incarcerated Deadheads" and says, "Musical preferences and lifestyles are being used as evidence against drug offenders. . . ." Inside, under the title "Heads in Prison," is a photo of seven Hippie-Americans standing in front of a prison building in Florence, Colorado.

In the news of late has been **police profiling,** the practice by police departments of assuming someone is a suspect based on little more than race or ethnicity. HR 95 founders Chris Conrad, Milli Norris, and Virginia Ressner report,

Apparently, in many jurisdictions, courts have ruled that things such a Grateful Dead stickers are due cause for traffic stops—driving while Hippie.

"People who match a 'profile' (a racial or culturally-based stereotype appearance, such as ethnicity, long hair, political or music bumper stickers, etc.) are targeted for harassment in traffic stops and on the streets" (32). Apparently, in many jurisdictions, courts have ruled that things such a Grateful Dead stickers are due cause for traffic stops—driving while Hippie (Miller; Baum 333-34). Here, we can see how on the basis of drug laws, any artifact of Hippie culture can be evidence of a crime, that Hippie ethnicity itself has effectively been criminalized.

One issue ethnic minorities have historically had is **police harassment and brutality.** Many Hippie-Americans have stories of police harassment, intimidation and even violence to tell; consider this appalling example: In September of 1997, the former marshal of Nederland, CO, a small mountain community 15 miles west of Boulder, confessed to and was arrested for the 1971 murder of local Hippie Guy Goughnor. The Boulder *Daily Camera* reported:

> . . . it was well known that [Renner] Forbes . . . had a distaste for 'hippies.' Weeks after Goughnor's death, Forbes told an officer of the Boulder Sheriff's Department that, 'You ought to shoot these bastards [Hippies]. There are plenty of places around these mountains. You could dump the bodies and no one would be the wiser,' according to the arrest affidavit. (Anderson)

The pressures on racial and ethnic outgroups seems to produce a range of **organizational paths**, ideas about how the group should proceed, everything from bowing to assimilationist pressure to working within a political party to forming an ethnic organization to even forming a homeland or nation somewhere. We can see all these various paths being pursued as Hippie-America tries to deal with its oppression.

Some Hippies are actually arguing that last option: armed resistance and creation of an independent nation state. They're called the Green Panthers. Journalist Cletus Nelson reports on this "secessionist" group: "Head quartered in Cincinnati, Ohio, the hard-liners are mainly recognized by drug policy activists for their incendiary publication *Revolutionary Times* [formerly the *Revolutionary Toker*]." Spokesperson Terry Mitchell, who has experience in both NORML and the Libertarian Party:

> . . . envisions a day when a repressive federal government will declare martial law, and the nation will be plunged into civil war—not unlike the post-Cold War conflicts that arose in many

nations, such as the former Yugoslavia. When this time comes, the Panthers plan to be prepared. The armed pot smokers and their supporters hope to stake out a coastal strip of land 20 miles from the Pacific Ocean beginning due north of San Francisco and extending ten miles south of Portland. If they succeed, they will create what they call the first "Stoner Homeland." (13)

And just as Jewish Zionists often argue that Israel is the only alternative to a second Holocaust, "Mitchell is a fatalist who is convinced this is the only choice left for the pot community. 'If we don't win, nothing is lost. We were marked for extermination anyway. . . . It's either gonna be a stoner homeland or a stoner last stand'" (13).

Another ethnic parallel: Although there have always been inter-racial and inter-ethnic **couples,** generally, people pair within their own group—we expect blacks to marry blacks, Hispanics to marry Hispanics, Jews to marry Jews, and so forth, and they usually do. We can find the same pattern in the Counterculture, so much so that someone pairing with another who has Hippie identity is often a strong sign that both are Countercultural—**endogamy**.

Finally, let's look at **ethnic weddings**. *My Big Fat Greek Wedding* is the name of the 2002 film directed by Joel Zwick. We see an Italian-American wedding in the opening scenes of Francis Ford Copolla's *The Godfather*. And we know of Jewish weddings. Native American tribes also have their own wedding ceremonies; weddings seem an integral and distinctive part of any ethnicity.

Hippie weddings aren't hard to document, and they aren't just a thing of the 1960s. A reporter for the *Cleveland Plain Dealer* comments in 2003:

> Mention organic weddings, and the image is of a barefoot couple saying their vows in an open field, the bride with a flower in her hair, the groom dressed in anything but a tuxedo and a guitar in the background playing a wistful song with the lyrics "There is love." In other words, a simple hippie wedding. Today, however, call it organic, and it's anything but simple. (Washington)

Or consider this from South Carolina wedding columnist Lillia Callum-Penso in a 2004 piece called "A Hippie Wedding?":

When I read the wedding invitation, I could tell it was going to be different sort of wedding. As if the stargazing, group hiking and waltz lessons weren't enough to tip me off, a co-worker's response when I told him where it was to be held solidified the feeling.

"Warren Wilson (College)? It is a hippie wedding," he said.

An insert is entitled, "You might be at a hippie wedding if . . . ."[41]
As we saw at length in Chapter Three, Hippie-Americans have often played the **same role in demagogic political appeals** that traditionally recognized racial and ethnic groups so often have, particularly as scapegoats.

Hippiedom also resembles other ethnic or racial minorities in that it has its own **cuisine, distinctive artists, successful entrepreneurs/ businesses** and **famous athletes**; we'll cover those areas in some depth when we look at the Counterculture's accomplishments in Chapter Eight.

* * *

Lastly, let's now look beneath the surface symptoms of bigotry, asking why racism and ethnic chauvinism exist to begin with? Do these causes apply to anti-Hippie bigotry as well? I'll examine the **sources of prejudice in individuals** and show how they apply to Hippie-hating.

So, why are people prejudiced? Well, such questions are not as abstract or unanswerable as they might first seem. Social scientists have been investigating these matters for decades, long before Hippies existed. In particular, many have been both appalled and intrigued by the Holocaust—what causes a society to implode and feed upon itself? They have produced theories—supported by research—about why individuals

---

[41] I found a memoir of a woman who sneaked into a 1999 Hippie wedding in Oklahoma. Apparently, she sent a copy to the groom who then posted it on the wedding's website "unedited." Called "Some kinda heathen wedding . . .," it's a Tom Sawyerish tale, written in vernacular, and the woman—not Hippie and previously quite ignorant about Counterculturalists—learns a wonderful lesson, concluding afterwards, "And they weren't no devil worshipers either, just kind of different" (Oakdancer). I'm pretty sure this delightful piece is for real, and as of December 2014, the webpage was still up. Go to http://oakdancer.com/hfast/HeathenWedding.htm

cling to prejudice, why societies foster bigotry, and how an ethnic slur morphs into a gas oven.

Sociologist Jack Levin speaks of "the gains that accrue to the personality of a majority-group member" (39) who is prejudiced towards minorities, and he lists three basic psychological "benefits" to the bigot: "to displace aggression, protect self-esteem, and reduce uncertainties" (61).

The first, **"to displace aggression,"** is the result of a sense of impotence; thus:

> . . . hostility or aggression cannot always be directed against the true source of a frustration, . . . In order to blow off steam, then, an individual who has experienced frustration may attempt to locate a more vulnerable and visible enemy against whom his hostility can be directed with relative impunity. (41)

Essentially this is scapegoating, and as demonstrated, Hippies are one of America's favorite scapegoats.

For the second, to **"protect self-esteem,"** Levin writes, "It [prejudice] is a method of defending self-image, whereby, for the majority member, a minority group becomes a negative reference group, or a point of comparison against which the values, abilities, or performances of the majority member can be regarded as superior" (46). So here, the deeply insecure find their solace; self-esteem becomes relative to the status of others. And this self-enhancing, "ego-defensive" (47) mechanism often involves psychological projection.

Likewise, today's America is eager to see Hippies as losers and the Counterculture in general as a failure—a self-serving illusion, sucker bait for the insecure.

Regarding the **reduction of uncertainties**, Levin tells us, "Culturally supported prejudices provide ready-made expectations in terms of which individuals can be categorized. What people often do is to fill the gap in the knowledge of others with oversimplified and distorted preconceptions, many of which are based on group membership" (53). Prejudice, then, enables a kind of judgmental shorthand: one needn't get to know individuals in all their diversity and complexity; instead, identifying a person as a member of an outgroup, such as a man having long hair, enables the bigot to make a quick, clear, negative judgment.

116

Levin adds, "Prejudiced persons desire absolute and unequivocal feelings about themselves and others; . . . Members of the majority group are glorified and idealized, whereas culturally designated outgroups become targets for displaced hostility" (59). As conservative icon John Wayne put it: "If everything isn't black and white, I say, "Why the hell not?"'

> Certainly, the War on Drugs has encouraged this kind of self-righteous, simpleminded thinking: "drug" users, including recreational marijuana users, are characterized as immoral menaces to society, whereas those prosecuting that war are seen as public servants and paragons of virtue.

(Brainyquote). By creating a simplistic, good-or-bad image of people, where everyone is a kind of flat character, prejudice makes the bigot's world easier to understand, however incorrectly.

And generally, conservative America has come to see Hippie-America has a kind of moral and social contagion, the antithesis of an idealized "good and decent" America they live in. In particular, I have heard employers make the argument that a drug test, i.e., a marijuana test, will tell them everything they need to know about a prospective employee—a simple litmus test for character.

Before moving on, let's briefly consider how bigots may come to have something called an *authoritarian personality*: specific value and personality traits—particularly an obsession with hierarchy and one's place in it—that many social scientists believe predict prejudice. Pettigrew:

> Central to the syndrome [authoritarian personality] is . . . the refusal to look inside oneself and the lack of insight into one's own behavior and feelings. Authoritarians refuse to accept their emotions and try to deny them. As children, authoritarians may have been punished frequently by stern parents, and in turn felt intense hatred for them. Unable to express these aggressive feelings for fear of further punishment, authoritarians find them threatening and unacceptable, deny them, and begin to project them onto others. If they feel hatred for their parents, they see hatred not in themselves but in the dangerous outside world.

Consequently, authoritarians typically convey an idealized picture of their parents as near-perfect. Generalizing this unrealistic view to include other authorities, they come to view the world in good-bad, up-and-down power terms. They are outwardly submissive to those they see as authorities with power over them, and aggressive toward those they see as beneath them in status. This hierarchical view of authority links directly with ethnic attitudes. High-status ethnic groups are respected, and authoritarians treat them with deference. But low-status groups are disparaged. Prejudice becomes for many authoritarians 'a crutch upon which to limp through life.' Lacking insight into their own inner feelings, they project their own unacceptable impulses onto outgroups whom they regard as beneath them." (825)

Imagine how an authoritarian personality would respond, for instance, to that Countercultural bumper sticker "Question Authority."

Thus, the personality traits producing bigotry towards traditionally recognized outgroups are the same personality traits fueling anti-Hippie bigotry.

*   *   *

Hippie-America, then, isn't just *like* an ethnic group: it *is* an ethnic group. We know that not just because Hippie-America fits a definition of *ethnicity* but because in so many ways, Hippie-America behaves exactly like and is treated exactly like an ethnicity. It waddles like a duck; it looks like a duck; it quacks like a duck. It *is* a duck; it *is* an ethnicity.

Chapter Seven

The Birth of Hippiedom:
Stand and be Delivered!

"God danced on the day you were born."

—Anonymous

Having proven that Hippie culture is an ethnicity using deductive and inductive proofs, the question should now be "How did this new ethnicity get here?" Ethnic-Hippies Theory would make more sense if we could explain Hippiedom's origins.

Let's begin by answering a related question, "If Hippiedom is so clearly an ethnicity, why are we just now figuring this out?" And then we'll have a bit of a Birthday Party as I steer us into a discussion on the origins of Hippiedom and what I call *synthetic ethnogenesis*—the creation of new ethnicity through technological or man-made means. Sound scary? Oh, it is. (A rumble of thunder in the background, a voice shrieking, "Oh, my God! It's *alive*!!!").

* * *

If it's clear that Hippies are an ethnicity, why don't we already know this? Why, five decades after Hippiedom's birth, are we just figuring this out?"

First, let's briefly discuss some related terms: *tribe*, *ethnicity* and *nationality*. As I understand it, a tribe has cultural consistency, but its members are also biologically related—a sort of huge extended family. Ethnicity also involves a cultural consistency, but it transcends biological ties. A nationality is an ethnicity with a country. Italians living in Italy are a nationality; Italians who move to the USA become Italian-Americans, an ethnicity.

There's no reason why anyone should've immediately recognized Hippie culture as ethnic. People have presumed—often wished— Hippie culture would be short lived, a fad. Why would one look at Haight-Ashbury in 1967 and say, "Oh, this is clearly an ethnicity" when important traits such as generational span weren't yet evident, when Hippie cuisine was hardly known?

In addition, the dominant approach to trying to understand Hippie culture has been to look for an underlying philosophy, to try to see the Counterculture as an ideological movement; as mentioned, this simply doesn't work. Further, it tends to lead us astray: we're so busy looking for that "hippie philosophy" that we can't see the ethnicity in front of our faces.

Still, I believe there has often been a sort of intuitive understanding on the part of Hippies that they are an ethnicity, a nationality or something similar. There are those who sense what we really are, that we are predominant in certain geographic areas, that these areas are distinctively Hippie-American. You can also see this attitude in the creation of Hippie-American "peace flags." It's normal for nationalities to create flags; implicit in the creation of these Hippie-American flags seems the understanding that the Counterculture is a sort of nationality without a nation state—an ethnicity.

> **It's normal for nationalities to create flags; so, implicit in the creation of these Hippie-American flags seems the understanding that the Counterculture is a sort of nationality without a nation state—an ethnicity.**

You can also see this intuitive understanding in the Counterculture's self-describing language. While the term *ethnic* is not commonly used, related terms are. For instance, it's common for Hippies to see themselves as "gypsies." Well, of course, very few Counterculturists are actually Gypsy, but what is a Gypsy (a Romani)? She or he is a member of an ethnic group.

Also, you'll notice widespread use of the term "tribe" or a variation. We see it, for example, in the title, *Hair: The American Tribal Love-Rock Musical*. Or consider that Countercultural genre Tribal-Fusion Belly Dance.[42] Again, a *tribe* usually involves biological relationships and is just one step away from an *ethnicity*. Sometimes an ethnicity (say, Native Americans) is an amalgamation of tribes. So it appears that Hippiedom has been tiptoeing around "ethnicity," has stood on the cusp of saying it for decades.

And then again, sometimes people have almost said it; Steven Hager, for instance, calls the Counterculture "a legitimate minority group whose basic rights have been denied" (qtd. in Krassner, "Why?"). And as mentioned in an earlier epigraph, at Woodstock, Janis Joplin said, "We

---

[42]   We'll discuss this in Chapter Eight.

used to think of ourselves as little clumps of weirdoes. But now we're a whole new minority group" (qtd. in Ashby, 410).

Then there's Countercultural icon Stephen Gaskin of the Grateful Dead's "St. Stephen" fame and a founder of that enduring Hippie commune The Farm. Quoted by Paul Krassner, Gaskin says:

> I consider myself to be an ethnic hippie. By that I mean that the ethnicity I grew up with was such a white bread, skim milk, gringo experience that it wasn't satisfying for me. It had no moxie. Now, being a hippie, that's another thing. I feel like the Sioux feel about being from the Lakota Nation. I feel like Mario Cuomo feels about being Italian. It makes me feel close with Jews and Rastafarians. I have a tribe, too. ("The Communal")

Yes, though he also uses "tribe" to describe Hippiedom, Gaskin does, correctly, call it an ethnicity.

On inspection, then, we see that this widespread absence of an ethnic perspective isn't so strange: it wasn't obvious at first; we've always been on the edge of understanding this, but there remains a nagging question—"If we're an ethnicity, where did we come from? what is our ethnogenesis?"

* * *

Synthetic Ethnogenesis

Today, we tend to think of ethnicity as deriving from immigration and nationality, how did Hippie ethnicity originate,

Before we can discuss *synthetic ethnogenesis*, however, we need to discuss more traditional forms of ethnogenesis. In other words, if we're going to call Hippie ethnogenesis "synthetic," then what does "natural" ethnogenesis look like?

Let's start with Jared Diamond's *Guns, Germs and Steel: The Fate of Human Societies*. In this impressive work, Diamond explains prehistory and traces the origins of culture and society, using the latest scientific evidence from a variety of fields. Diamond says it all starts with geography, citing various features of the natural environment, what he calls *ultimate causes*; these would include the availability of domesticable plants and animals and an "east-west axis" (86-7) (domesticated crops, for example, spread faster east-west than they do north-south). Regarding the creation, development and expansion of Polynesian culture, for instance, Diamond lists "at least six sets of environmental variables: . . . island climate, geological type, marine resources, area, terrain fragmentation, and isolation" (58).

So, cultures are originally reflections of their natural environments. In most Native American tribes, for instance, local fauna were a primary source of food and clothing; much of their religion, then, has focused on the spirits of the animals they've encountered in their environment. Or the Inuit reportedly have twenty-some different words for various types of snow. Culture, then, first derived from geography.

Later, these "original" cultures interacted with other cultures and at some point no longer became "pure" reflections of their immediate environments. What Diamond calls *proximate causes* intervened. For example, Egyptian culture might have been originally based on the natural environment around the northern Nile, but what happens when Marc Antony falls in love with Cleopatra and Rome conquers Egypt? Things get more complicated; more than the local geography comes into play. Eventually, there arise other forms of ethnogenesis.

Nowadays, especially in the US, we tend to think of ethnicity being the result of immigration, but there's more: The *Harvard Encyclopedia of American Ethnic Groups* lists five types of ethnogenesis: *migration, consolidation, promotion, schism,* and *race crossing* ("Concepts of Ethnicity"). The meaning of *migration* doubtless includes immigration; *consolidation* refers to diverse tribes merging into one recognized ethnicity such as Sioux, Apache, Nez Perce and such becoming Native Americans. I could attempt to define the other esoteric terms; suffice it to say, none of these five types of ethnogenesis can explain the birth of Hippiedom.

I propose something called "synthetic ethnogenesis."

First, that there should be a new way that an ethnicity arrives shouldn't be so surprising. After all, if culture is derivative of our environment, and if that environment is ever changing as inventions and modern technology take our daily lives further and further from nature, then shouldn't the sources of culture become less and less dependent on nature? Just because culture, ethnicity or nationality emerged a certain way in the past doesn't allow us to assume it will always emerge that way.

If we think of previous forms of ethnogenesis as being ultimately "natural," derived largely from natural environment, then what would "synthetic ethnogenesis" look like? It would be a form of ethnogenesis in which non-natural, man-made things—types of technology—were so decisive that the culture could originate independent of a particular geography, independent of "nature."

Now, we know that ethnicity often involves a degree of volition. To some extent, people choose how much they identify with a particular ethnicity or ethnicities they've inherited or come into contact with.

Here, though, we're talking about a different type of ethnic choice: we're talking about people choosing, *en masse*, a particular ethnic identity that they haven't inherited; we're considering tens of millions of individuals across much of the globe who went Hippie, who chose Hippie identity, all at pretty much the same time, in the mid-to-late 1960s.

But how did that identity they chose come to be? Technology, particularly the mass media, allowed it to happen. So whether you lived in Eastern Europe, Australia, the United Kingdom or Kentucky, you were exposed, through the media, to Hippie culture. Yes, the mass media may have been hostile, exploitative and sensationalistic in its coverage of the Counterculture; nonetheless, the seed of Hippiedom was borne on the breeze of mass media. Stillman and Weiner write: "The press helped spread the message, and the Sixties [read "Woodstock Nation"] reached many people through the pages of 'establishment' newspapers and magazines" (33-34).

In his *1968*, Mark Kurlansky notes that in June 1967, the Beatles performed the first live international concert broadcast by satellite (182). He adds that "In 1968, *Life* called the new rock music 'the first music born in the age of instant communication'" (182).

Of course, it wasn't just mass media. As Bill Moyers commented, "When half a million of the young flocked to Woodstock to celebrate their disenchantment with materialism, they came in cars." Would an influential recording like *Sgt. Pepper's Lonely Hearts Club Band* or participation in the Woodstock Music Festival, both in person and vicariously (though recording and film) have been possible without modern technology? No, without those modern, man-made means, international Hippie culture could never have come into being; instead, we would've remained isolated and eccentric pockets of cultural pioneers unable to effectively interact or coordinate with each other.

Now, it can't be that simple. After all, we've had various forms of modern technology for some time. The invention of the radio or television, for instance, didn't automatically create a new, distinctive ethnicity. Why should a new ethnicity emerge to begin with? What would be the motivation?

First, there had to be widespread cultural discontent—the feeling that mainstream cultures were disappointing, that they were broken and unable to provide people with satisfying lives, that they were dooming humanity. This discontent was a prerequisite for people to strike out and develop a cultural alternative, for people to join that emerging culture. These prerequisites were abundant in the Sixties. We tend to forget that it wasn't just the USA that was in turmoil at the time: it was a good part of the world. As Kurlansky shows in his *1968*, from Mexico to France to Czechoslovakia to the United States, the world was in rebellion, this the product of a widespread belief that society and culture as constituted simply weren't working.

This social/cultural discontent was exacerbated by a sense (in America, at least) that we had a "loss of community"; this was facilitated, to some extent, by corporations that deliberately made an employee's "community" the corporation itself; this, done by moving families to a degree unprecedented.

In this milieu of discontent and social breakdown, people began looking for alternatives, for real, immediate change, for new and authentic community. And there in front of them, courtesy of the mass media and other modern technology, was Hippiedom. No matter where you were, no matter who you were, if you were in touch with that mass media, you could decide to go Hippie.

Going Hippie, making that ethnic choice, meant you didn't have to wait for a political revolution to start changing your world; you could begin right here, right now with the food you grew and ate, with how you thought about life, with how you dressed, with how you related to the planet—with just about everything. It wasn't just theory; it was practice. And across the globe, tens of millions choose that Hippie identity.

Second, society would reinforce that choice by stigmatizing and suppressing the Counterculture. I remember about 1970 going into a Burger King with some Hippie friends, two of whom were wearing leather "floppy hats"; soon, we "got hassled." The decision to wear a type of hat may seem superficial, but if you and your peers get persecuted for

124

> Viola! We have a distinctive cultural formation that is soon distinguishing itself across an array of areas from food to folklore to clothing to values— it's more than music. That culture keeps growing and developing; further, it starts transmitting generationally.

such, you start to see yourselves as distinctive, as set apart from a hostile larger society. External pressure, then, helps solidify a culture.

Viola! We have a distinctive cultural formation that is soon distinguishing itself across an array of cultural areas from food to folklore to clothing to values—it's more than music. That culture keeps growing and developing; further, it starts transmitting generationally. Add the solidifying aspect of external hostility. Thus, in spite of a world that wants to discourage it, to relegate it to the 1960s, the mere "subculture" becomes an ethnic group—one that is now turning fifty.

Is there any scientific basis for this new conception of ethnogenesis? Social scientists speak of "revitalization movements," defined as "a deliberate, conscious, organized effort by members of a society to construct a more satisfying culture" (Partridge 76, Westhues 22). Sociologist William L. Partridge adds that "periods of [social] conflict act as a prism" to create revitalization movements and that the Counterculture was born into the polarizations created by the Civil Rights Movement and anti-Vietnam War movements (76). The Counterculture, then, is the largest revitalization movement ever seen, so successful that it's grown into a full-fledged ethnicity with an enduring presence.

* * *

Now, if Hippie culture is synthetic in how it was formed, it's also synthetic in its content—a fusion of various cultural threads. Specifically, we can see Eastern influences, Native American influences, African-American influences, Beat/bohemian influences, influences from various Third World cultures and from American and world history, and probably a few other things, say, marijuana use, hallucinogenic drugs and Rastafarianism. In both form and content, then, Hippiedom is a synthetic ethnicity.

When we speak of evolution, of how life was first formed on earth, we think of disparate strands of RNA floating around in an ocean, pre-life; these were then presumably struck by lightning, fusing them into a simple life form. Think of those RNA strands as the various elements of Hippie culture; think of the turmoil and discontent of the late Sixties as the lightening.

* * *

That completes my proof of Hippie ethnicity: First, I deconstructed those flawed paradigms we've used to explain Hippiedom. Next, we saw how the Counterculture fits an amended academic definition of *ethnicity*. Then, we saw how the nature and situation of Hippie-America closely parallels that of traditionally recognized minorities. Here, we've seen an explanation of Hippiedom's unusual beginnings, of its ethnogenesis.

Time to shift paradigms: when you hear "Hippie," think "ethnic" and all that implies.

Chapter Eight

God Bless the Freaks:
"Hippiedom's Greatest Hits"

"Let me take you there and show you living story . . . ."
> —Genesis (the rock band)

"Good morning, starshine; the earth says hello; you twinkle above us; we twinkle below."
> —Hair

Here, I'll mention the many accomplishments of Hippie-America and the international Counterculture. The point is to show how great a success Hippiedom has been, build cultural pride, and to once again show readers a thriving post-1960s Hippiedom. If you've ever been ashamed of being Hippie, if you've ever condescended to the Counterculture, this chapter should cure what ails you.

Our ground rules: First, an ethnicity should get credit for things the culture as a whole has produced: full credit for things they invented, partial credit for things others have invented but that the ethnicity has developed and made available to society. Second, an ethnicity should get credit for things that individual group members have produced or invented, and closely related to this would be the success stories of individual members.

* * *

How I Identify Someone or Something as Hippie

I've mentioned the phenomenon of the Countercultural person who's uncomfortable being called Hippie; this, the product of a national campaign to stereotype and vilify Hippiedom. To be classified as Hippie, then, often seems like being identified as a drug user or drug abuser—the War on Drugs makes no distinction—and as a criminal and menace to innocent youth, not to mention being a traitor to the nation and a host of other odious things.

My response to those who might feel defamed by being classified *Hippie* is this: First, my intent is not to belittle or embarrass; on the contrary, people should be proud to be associated with the Counterculture; they should be happily Hippie. Second, I'm only going to use publicly available sources, and I'm going to show readers my evidence and sources—there's nothing up my sleeve. Now, if a reader wants to interpret my evidence differently, wants to disagree with the conclusion I've drawn from that evidence, that's her or his right. Third, I'm going to be careful; I will not intentionally pound a square peg into a round hole.

Another issue is whether someone who was once clearly Countercultural remains Countercultural today. As mentioned, I do think there are genuine ex-Hippies, those who seem to have left a Hippie past behind, who have assimilated; yet, many more "ex-Hippies" remain Countercultural, only they're discouraged from saying so in a society intent on seeing Hippie culture and individuals as 1960s specific. So, bearing in mind that both types of "ex-Hippies" exist, wherever I can, I will prove contemporary Counterculturality.

I'm about to list and to some extent weight specific criteria, but let me note that the *best identifications are made by a series of overlapping criteria*. With two early exceptions, the criteria listed here are merely predictors; some predictors are better than others. The more predictors, the stronger the predictors—the more likely Hippie identity is.

In addition, I'll usually be rating the strength of my Hippie identification using what I'll call an **HICR, a Hippie-Identity-Confidence Rating**. Why? I believe it gives this book more social-scientific validity, more intellectual integrity; that is, I am attempting to apply objective criteria to people and institutions, and I'm trying to be consistent and transparent as I do that. If I don't use HICRs, particularly with individuals, I worry I'll look like a tabloid journalist, more gossiping than proving.

On the other hand, I sometimes won't use an HICR, especially early on here, believing that the evidence I've provided for Hippie identity is in itself adequate and nothing more needs saying.

The HICR scale is ten point. Think of five as the midpoint where someone is as likely Hippie as not; think of 7.5 as where I actually start calling someone Hippie/Countercultural. One way, to think about an 8.5, for example, is that I'm saying there's an 85% chance this person is Hippie/Countercultural, a 15% chance that she or he isn't.

Incidentally, an important factor in these scores is simply how much information I was able, with a reasonable amount of work, to find on these people or institutions, not necessarily how Hippie they are or might be.

* * *

Hippie-Identification Criteria List

Self-identification: If a person or institution calls itself Hippie or Countercultural, that in itself is cause to classify him, her or it as such because in a hostile environment to claim Hippie identity is an admission against interest. On the other hand, denial of Hippie or Countercultural identity should be taken with a grain of salt; it may merely mean a discomfort with the term.

Public identification as Hippie/Countercultural: If the media consistently say that someone or something is Hippie/Countercultural, who am I to disagree? For example, the media consistently describe UK entrepreneur Richard Branson as "countercultural," and I see neither Branson nor anyone else disagreeing, that's good enough for me, and it should be good enough for you. Think of this as a *common-knowledge identification.*

Incidentally, this media identification of someone as Countercultural/Hippie may take the form of euphemism: *Earth Mother, stoner, Aquarian, Sixties person* and so forth.

Identification in either of these first two criteria means an HICR of 10.

Strong interest in Hippie culture: I find writers, for instance, who are obsessed with what they call "the Sixties counterculture." They've devoted hundreds, probably thousands, of hours to the subject. It's their passion. People so dedicated to the analysis of Hippiedom, so fascinated by it, are far more likely than not Hippie themselves. Call this a very strong indicator.

Also, I think actors and actresses who choose to play Hippie parts or who play roles where they get to look Hippie are likely to be Countercultural, and this is especially true when we see a pattern of such parts. Call this a good indicator.

Member of a rock band or practitioner of some art form or practice that tends to be Hippie: Counterculturists often form rock bands. Again, no, not every rock band is or has been Hippie; still,

Hippiedom and playing rock music have often intertwined, so much so that the guitar-playing Hippie has become a neutral stereotype. This is a good indicator.

As for other art forms, some are of Hippie origin and so Hippie dominated that their performers scream Counterculturality; a good example is a tribal-fusion belly dancing: if a woman is involved in that scene, the likelihood of her being Hippie skyrockets.

Much the same could be said of boarding sports: surfing, skateboarding and snowboarding. Add what's called *hacky-sacking* among youth. Add certain "rad" nature-centered sports like rock climbing as well. Call these good indicators.

Display of Hippie/Countercultural symbols: Look for peace signs, tee-shirts that are tie dyed or display the name of a Countercultural rock band/concert or celebrities (Jimi Hendrix, for instance), references to Woodstock, Grateful Dead memorabilia, and/or Countercultural bumper stickers. Call this a very good predictor.

Jobs: Not everyone who works in the natural/organic foods industry, for example, is Hippie. Yet, since the workers in that industry are disproportionately Countercultural, being one increases the chance that someone is Hippie. I think this holds true for certain other professions such as natural healers, including massage therapists and such. Call this a moderate/helpful indicator.

Appearance: That someone looks Countercultural is strong evidence that they are. If a man has a ponytail, and he isn't of some other ethnicity where males might have long hair, that's a strong Countercultural predictor—guys who aren't Hippie almost never wear their hair in ponytails. Let's add here newer ways of men wearing long hair, the *mun* (male bun), for instance. Call such hair styles strong Countercultural identifiers.[43]

Let me note, by the way, that while long hair on a male often signifies Hippie identity, it is not crucial.[44] Given the intense pressure society has

---

[43] About the only exceptions to this might be certain types of "bikers" or professional wrestlers, I think.

[44] I should probably tell you that while in the past I often had very long hair, for many years now, I've had relatively shorter hair myself, and I think that a man having long hair even some of the time, past or present, is still a strong indicator.

placed on long hairs to "Get a haircut!" many Hippie males no longer have long hair; a few never did. Yet, because they display Hippie traits in other areas, they might still be classified as Hippie. Sometimes, I'll show the reader a picture of a male when he had long hair—strong predictor.

I'm also going to include here tattoos and nose and other piercings though I think they're only a moderate predictor since many Counterculturists don't have tattoos or piercings, and some non-Hippie groups have both.

Values: If someone prominently displays such values as, say, a devotion to and belief in nature and the natural, that can be evidence of Counterculturality. One way that values can reveal themselves, by the way, is in one's heroes; if someone lists several Counterculturalists high on their personal-heroes list, it tends to indicate Counterculturality. Strong indicator here.

Valuing the natural often means **environmentalism**, being green. No, not every environmentalist is Hippie; however, a strong environmental interest makes Hippie identity more likely; this is a moderately good predictor.

Reside in disproportionately Countercultural areas: No, not everyone who lives in San Francisco or Vermont is Countercultural. Still, is it a complete coincidence that Tribal Fusion Bellydancing comes from San Francisco? That Ben & Jerry's ice cream comes from Vermont? Generally, call this a weak-to-moderate indicator; on the other hand, I will occasionally present evidence showing that someone has a home in a neighborhood or community considered a Countercultural enclave. Call that a good indicator.

Food: If someone demonstrates a strong interest in natural/organic foods, that can be evidence for Hippie identity—if I can prove, for example, that the muffins someone regularly eats for breakfast are whole-grain, sweetened naturally and organic, that suggests Counterculturality. A preference for natural/organic foods is, I think, a relatively strong predictor. Being vegan is a strong predictor; being vegetarian, a moderately good predictor.

On the cover of the *Rolling Stone* (or the subject of the *RS* interview): Yes, the old Dr. Hook and the Medicine Show lyric says it all: after years of researching and reading *Rolling Stone* (*RS*), I'm convinced that it mirrors Hippie identity well. Thus, if someone is on the *RS* cover or is the subject of the *RS* interview, that can be evidence of Counterculturality. If someone repeatedly makes the *RS* cover, that makes Countercultural identity even more likely. Yes, many non-Hippies have been on the *RS* cover or covered prominently within (Barack Obama, African-American rappers, celebrity pundits, punk rockers, Taylor Swift, and increasingly Country-music talents); still, attention from *RS* can be a strong clue to Hippie identity.

And what holds true for *RS* generally holds true for the rest of the Countercultural press: *High Times, Relix, Mother Earth News*, certain New Age journals and several others I won't list here —who are these journals interviewing, who are they writing about, and who is writing for them?

Documented use of or familiarity with particular drugs: Obviously, not everyone who uses "drugs" is Countercultural, and some Hippies eschew drugs entirely. Still, as we've seen, particular drugs often have racial/ethnic identity, and there remains a strong connection between Hippie identity and particular substances—generally, marijuana, LSD or other hallucinogens and Ecstasy—which can be strong evidence of Hippie identity.

A couple of sub points here: First, we're going to run into situations where someone is accused of marijuana use, and he or she vehemently denies it. Ultimately, the reader can decide for him or herself, but I tend to see allegations of pot use, when they seem substantiated by context and evidence, as more likely true than not.

In particular, let me emphasize that *my identifying someone or something as Countercultural does not assume that the person uses drugs or that the institution supports drug use; especially, it does not assume drug abuse or support thereof on the part of the individual or institution.* Director Stephen Spielberg, for example, talks of his many friends who used LSD and appears to be Hippie-American, yet he claims to be drug free, and I have no reason to doubt it. While something like Steve Jobs' LSD use is a very strong indicator of Hippie identity, I can argue someone or something has Hippie identity while making no mention of Countercultural drug use or abuse.

Interest in the East or Native American culture: Most of the West's recent opening to the East has come through the conduit of the Counter culture. Some clear Eastern association in a person not of Asian descent, then, increases the likelihood of Counterculturality; this may include practitioners of so-called "New Age" spirituality, which has Eastern roots. In a similar vein, a strong interest in Native-American culture evidenced in a non-Native American can also be a Countercultural indicator. I see these as strong predictors.

Practitioner of meditation and/or yoga: As we'll see, both of these arrived in the modern Western world courtesy of the Counterculture. I see either of these as a good indicator of Hippie identity; together, as a very good indicator.

Parentage/Personal history: Again, Hippie parents tend to have Hippie kids. If I can prove to you that someone's parents are Hippie, it makes it more likely that he or she is Countercultural. Then again, not all Hippie offspring turn out Hippie, so call this only a moderately good predictor.

When I began writing this chapter, it never occurred to me to consider the cultural phenomenon of the godfather/godmother. Yet, it came up several times, and I now regard a clearly Countercultural godfather/godmother as an excellent identifier.

A Countercultural history is a strong predictor: that is, someone once did LSD, lived in a Hippie commune, etc.

Countercultural names: Is there any chance that someone with a name like Wavy Gravy isn't Hippie? Yes, certain names are distinctively Hippie; often, they've been adopted. In show biz, they can be single names like Bono and The Edge from the Hippie-Irish rock band U2. Strong predictor.

Countercultural networking: Pay attention to this one. Hippie types tend to socialize, work with and often mate with other Hippie types. When, for example, we look at the arts, we find Hippie rock bands working with early Monty Python; we see the "American Python," Terry Gilliam, working with Tom Stoppard; we see Stoppard working with Andrew Lloyd Webber; we see Lloyd Webber working with Terry Gilliam and

> **Generally, that people keep Countercultural company in their professional lives, and particularly in their personal lives, is a strong clue that they're Hippie; endogamy is a very strong indicator, particularly in longer-term relationships.**

so forth. So, if a particular person keeps popping up in the histories of documented Counterculturalists, that is a strong clue to Hippie identity.

Now, **the mating thing:** Hippie types tend to pair off with other Hippie types, a phenomenon known as *endogamy*.[45] This isn't an iron-clad rule: Frank Sinatra, for example, was briefly married to a young and demonstrably Hippie Mia Farrow, I won't call him Hippie. What's interesting about this aspect of Countercultural networking, however, is how well it usually works, and in a world where people "change partners," it can be an excellent way to track Hippie identity, particularly of celebrities.

Generally, that people keep Countercultural company in their professional lives, and particularly in their personal lives, is a strong clue that they're Hippie.

One last criterion: someone **appearing barefoot at work or in public** seems Countercultural—pretty good indicator.

*   *   *

Now, on to our list of Countercultural achievements. I'll begin with what I've come to call *The Big Four*: 1) The personal computer (PC) and related inventions 2) Natural/organic foods 3) Integrative medicine and related health practices 4) the Counterculture's impact on environmental awareness and the environment itself—the greening of America and the world.

*   *   *

The Personal Computer:
Brought to you by Hippie-America

Probably the most significant invention of recent history has been the personal computer; what other creation has transformed modern life as has the PC? Hippie-Americans have played such a dominant role in the development and dispersal of this technological wonderment that in

---

[45]   Technically, of course, *endogamy* means marriage, but I'll use it here in a slightly broader sense—for romantic pairings.

fairness, we can say the PC is a Hippie invention.[46] And, no, we needn't measure the length of Bill Gates' hair in the early 1970s to prove this.

There were, of course, computers prior to the personal-computer revolution. They tended to be large mainframe machines controlled by East Coast corporations; the public had no access to them (Markoff). The contribution I'll document here is the creation of that machine made for multi-purpose, individual use, the *personal* computer, the PC. In *What the Dormouse Said: How the 60s Counterculture Shaped the Personal Computer Industry* (2005), author and *New York Times* senior writer John Markoff explains this East Coast-West Coast dichotomy:

> . . . there was no discrete technological straight line to the personal computer on the East Coast. What separated the isolated experiments with small computers from the full-blown birth of personal computing was the West Coast realization that computing was a new medium, like books, records, movies, radios, and television. . . . Personal computers that were designed for and belonged to single individuals would emerge initially [on the West Coast] in concert with a Counterculture that rejected authority and believed the human spirit would triumph over corporate technology, not be subject to it." (xv)

Markoff adds:

> Beginning in the Sixties . . .the Midpeninsula, a relatively compact region between San Jose and San Francisco [twenty-or-so miles south of Haight-Ashbury], became a crucible not only for political protest and a thriving counterculture but also a new set of computing paradigms. (xiv) . . . during the mid-Sixties the [Grateful] Dead literally became the house band for the Midpeninsula, their concerts offering a ready-made identity for members of all of the area's unruly threads of political and cultural unrest. The group had emerged directly from a set of wrenching, mind-expanding LSD parties orchestrated by Ken

---

[46] Nowadays, we think of personal computers in two basic categories: PCs and Macs. Here, I use the term *personal computer* as I believe author John Markoff does: to refer to both types before these categories existed.

Kesey and his Merry Pranksters called Acid Tests, which would transform the culture of the Midpeninsula and ultimately the rest of the country. (xvi, xvii)

In terms of individuals involved in the PC's creation and early evolution, there are more characters than in a Russian novel. Most, however, are Countercultural—perhaps because of the anti-Establishment nature of the project or its promise of mind expansion and personal freedom. A great many of the founders had transformative experiences with LSD. Some were affiliated with the anti-Vietnam War movement and early environmentalism. Two important cyber pioneers and Counterculturists already mentioned, of course, are Steve Jobs and Steve Wozniak, the founders of Apple. The late LSD advocate and Counterculturist Dr. Timothy Leary described them as "barefoot, longhaired acid-freaks" (qtd. in Fahey).

Among the key institutional players in this hothouse of cyber creativity, Markoff tells us, was "the Homebrew Computer Club, a ragtag [read *Countercultural*] group that began meeting in the San Francisco Midpeninsula in the spring of 1975" (xx). Another was a Countercultural entity called The People's Computer Company housed in nearby Menlo Park whose first newsletter proclaimed, "Computers are mostly used against people instead of for people; used to control people instead of to free them. Time to change all that—we need a . . . Peoples Computer Company" (qtd. in *Wikipedia*, "People's Computer Company").

And Markoff describes a particular faction of the nearby Stanford Research Institute (SRI):

In the midst of this engineers' world of crewcuts and white shirts and ties arrived a tiny band distinguished by their long hair and beards, rooms carpeted with oriental rugs, women without bras, jugs of wine, and on occasion the wafting of marijuana smoke. Just walking through the halls of the SRI laboratory gave a visitor a visceral sense of the cultural gulf that existed between the prevailing model of mainframe computing and the gestating vision of personal computing. (xxi, xxii)

Also, *Time* reviewer Michael Krantz says of the 1999 TNT film "Pirates of Silicon Valley," "Apple, for [Steve] Jobs, was a messianic imperative: give the world a Mac [MacIntosh computer], and the rest of the Flower Power agenda would follow."

The 1996 PBS series *Triumph of the Nerds: The Rise of Accidental Empires* notes, "The California counter culture was crucial to the PC's development" (Part I), adding, "The Windows software system that ended the alliance between Microsoft and IBM pushed [Bill] Gates past all his rivals. . . . where did the idea for this software come from? Well not from Microsoft . . . . It came from the hippies at Apple" (Part II).[47]

"Hippies," a *History Channel* video, notes:

> But ironically the arena in which the hippies would have the greatest impact on the future of the planet wasn't cultural. It was technological: In April 1977, Steve [Jobs] and his partner, Steve Wozniak, introduced the Apple II, the first commercially viable personal computer. "We were so influenced by the People's Computer Company in Menlo Park, the same area that the hippie thought had come from. The whole hippie thinking was that, basically, the big, wealthy power structure should be undone, and we want to turn the balance over and make the small individuals more important. It was basically bringing this power, this mastery of their [individuals'] own universe, away from the powers that be, the huge, big, rich corporations. . .," says Wozniak. (Kleinman)

Then, in a 1995 *Time* article, "We owe it all to the hippies . . . The real legacy of the Sixties generation is the computer revolution,"[48] Counterculturalist Stewart Brand, founder of the *Whole Earth Catalogue,* notes that not only was the early PC of Countercultural heritage, but in wave after wave of innovation, Hippies have been pioneering cyber technology ever since. This includes having a profound impact on the Internet. Here is a paraphrase of Brand's piece:

---

[47] If the reader wonders why Bill Gates doesn't figure more prominently in this history, I suspect the reason is right here: Gates apparently got his "Windows software system" from Apple, making the original PC, then, pre-Microsoft.

[48] Readers may find a copy at http://members.aye.net/~hippie/hippie/special_.htm

Those new to the Internet are surprised to find themselves in a "kind of cultural Brigadoon—a flowering remnant of the '60s, when hippie communalism and libertarian politics . . . , provided the philosophical foundations of not only the leaderless Internet but also the entire personal-computer revolution."

There are at least four generations of cyber pioneers, Brand believes, and he cites Steven Levy's *Hackers: Heroes of the Computer Revolution* (1984) in regard to the first three. Brand quotes Levy regarding Countercultural values as applied to computers and cyberspace: 1) Computers should be easily accessed, and that access should be complete, 2) Information must be free, 3) Decentralization is good, and don't trust authority 4) That computers can be used to make art and create beauty, 5) Computers can change life and this world for the better.

The first generation are those just mentioned, mostly "geeks" and computer-science academics, who culled the PC from the mainframe computer and invented things like *time sharing*; the second generation are those who created the first PC. Brand mentions Steve Wozniak and Steve Jobs and establishes their Hippie identities. He also mentions one Lee Felsenstein, an early collaborator of the "two Steves," as they became known, who created the Osborn 1, the first moveable computer, and Brand establishes Felsenstein's Countercultural credentials—a member of the New Left and a journalist for the Countercultural *Berkeley Barb*. The success of this second generation—many became very wealthy at a young age— encouraged them to retain their Hippie identities, Brand says.

Then, in the early 1980s, the third generation created the first "apps," games and educational software. Brand says that Mitch Kapor invented Lotus 1-2-3, a seminal spreadsheet program that allowed IBM to work like an Apple PC. Brand establishes Kapor's Countercultural credentials (he taught transcendental meditation) along with those of John Perry Barlow, who with Kapor co-founded the Electronic Frontier Foundation (a Washington lobby group seeking civil liberties in the cyberworld) and who has penned Grateful Dead lyrics.

Next, apparently part of this third generation, Brand mentions Jarod Lanier, and then establishes his Hippie identity, telling us Lanier was raised in a dome (on a Hippie commune in New Mexico, I'm guessing), has busked in the subways of NYC and wears long dreadlocks. Brand says Lanier largely created the concept of virtual reality and developed some of the early technology for it.

Enter one Danny Hillis, who is quoted as seeking to create "a machine that could be proud of us"; to him Brand accredits the creation, development and building of huge parallel-processing supercomputers. Brand tells us Hillis is a longhair.

And Brand credits Whitfield Diffie with a seminal encryption system—one the bases, I assume, for internet commerce, which requires financial privacy. Diffie's Counterculturality is quickly noted; then, Brand quotes Diffie who sounds relatively New Age as he speaks of how in cyberspace generosity will lead to prosperity.

Brand adds a fourth generation to Levy's three and says that using the Countercultural/hacker values Levy mentions, they have essentially created the Internet from its Department of Defense precursor, ARPAnet, and made available various types of freeware and data-sharing technologies. Brand cautions us that not everyone involved in the PC's creation and development is Countercultural; specifically, he mentions Nicholas Negroponte of MIT and Bill Gates of Microsoft. Still, Brand maintains that the Counterculture is largely responsible for invention of the PC and closes by predicting that these Countercultural cyber-influences will continue to reveal themselves in the coming centuries.

If you find the Counter-cultural provenance of the personal computer doubtful, consider the Hippie birthmark on your own machine. In the music program, you will find an application that lets you watch a psychedelic lightshow that visualizes music.

Indeed, *History Channel's* "Hippies" notes of Brand himself, "the Internet [was] brought to you in part by another high-tech hippie, Stewart Brand . . . in the 1980s and 1990s, he was instrumental in forming the paradigm that led to the world wide web."

And here's the frosting on the argumentative cake: far as I can tell, there's not a single book or researched article seriously disputing that the PC came largely from the Counterculture. I did find a 2005 internet column called, "Do we owe it all to the hippies?" Author Charles Cooper of CNET News writes, "You could just as easily argue that heavy investment in military research was the moving force [behind the creation of the PC]." Although military research was apparently a factor in the creation of the internet, no one, far as I can tell, seems to consider the military a major player in creation of the PC, and if some expert or historian does, Cooper needs to quote her or him. Cooper adds that attributing the PC to Hippies "remains an unconventional reading of contemporary history," but he gives no examples of a "conventional" reading. More to the point, perhaps, and explaining his feeble attempts to demonstrate a true controversy, Cooper correctly notes that the attribution of the PC's creation to Hippiedom "has the makings of a feisty barroom debate." In short, he has no real evidence to the contrary; rather, he's worried about how his prejudiced-against-Hippies readers will take this. He spends the rest of his piece summarizing Brand and Markoff.

For there to be a real controversy, there has to be a real opposition—some at least semi-scholarly book or article arguing that the PC doesn't have predominately Hippie roots. Apparently, there isn't. As such, the claim that Hippies invented[49] the PC is fast passing from the realm of opinion into the realm of fact—even if that fact isn't yet widely known or accepted.

As for **the internet**, first, if it weren't for the PC, how important and useful would the internet be? Second, as we've just seen, Hippiedom played a prominent role in the creation of the internet and of the software and programming underlying it and the PC.

For these impressive and astonishing cyber contributions, America and the world owe Hippiedom a great debt. And note that in terms of inventions attributable to an ethnicity, one couldn't do any better than this. Beatnik that.

*　　*　　*

---

[49] By "invented," I do not mean the commercialization of the PC and development of the PC industry, rather the creation of the machine itself.

Natural\Organic Food, Hippie Food, Healthy Food

Let me begin by showing that the Natural/Organic food industry is indeed of Hippie origin. A 1987 *Newsweek* piece mentions the grocer Whole Foods Market, then in Austin, TX as having Hippie origins (Adler 57); today, of course, that chain is prominent throughout much of the nation having swallowed the nation's second-largest natural foods chain Wild Oats, which also had Hippie roots (Taylor) and, in turn, Countercultural Alfalfa's (Taylor) was acquired by Wild Oats in 1996. The apparently Countercultural Bread and Circus—once "the largest natural food retailer in the Northeast" which originally sold "natural foods and wooden toys, hence the unusual name"—became a part of Whole Foods in 1992 (Whole Foods Market). Of course, this is a growing industry, and new chains are always jumping in. As I mentioned in my first demographic map in Chapter Two, all these natural/organic chains test out essentially Hippie.

I also consider these groceries Countercultural because of what I see when I walk into them: In the advertising and in-store PR, you see certain Hippie values, particularly what's Natural, what's Healthy, what's Green and what's Kind, e.g., philanthropic or about social-justice issues. Second, you see the Countercultural dietary emphases mentioned below. Third, the workforce in these stores and the people shopping there look disproportionately Hippie.

White Wave, producer of Silk soy milk, has Hippie roots as described by *The Wall St. Journal*:

> Steve Demos started making tofu in a bathtub in the late 1970s. An earring-adorned Buddhist who once lived in a cave in India, he sold the tofu at a tai chi class he was taking in Boulder, Colo. As his venture grew into an organic-food company called White Wave Inc., he sought to "prove that there is greater profitability in the green approach." He spent thousands of dollars in 2001 to relocate prairie dogs White Wave displaced when it built a soy-processing plant in Utah. (Adamy)

Other Counterculturists, *Colorado Biz* reports, launched "Horizon Organic Dairy—initially known as Horizon Organic Yogurt," becoming another of "Boulder's natural-foods pioneers — known humorously by some as the 'Boulder Natural-Foods Mafia' . . ." (Taylor). And there are

numerous other Countercultural food and health-product companies—
Burt's, Annie's, Amy's, and, of course, the legendary Ben & Jerry's Ice
Cream. Incidentally, Natural/Organic foods are the rising stars of the
grocery marketplace (Daniels; Organic Trade Association).

*   *   *

If the ubiquity and commercial success of Countercultural food is
undeniable, where has all this Hippie food gotten us? I'll now prove that
what I'll call the "Hippie diet" is healthier than mainstream American
cuisine. Also, since people are fixated with body fat, I'll show how
Hippie cuisine is likely far less fattening.

Here are what I consider **the essentials of Hippie diet**: an emphasis
on plant foods, a de-emphasis on meat, a preference for whole grains
and natural sweeteners, and an eschewing of additives combined with
minimal processing.

Let's begin with the **emphasis on plant foods**.[50] No, not all
Counterculturists are vegetarians, but many are, and generally Hippiedom
has welcomed vegetarian dishes into its menus and has created a cuisine
that's less meat centered. What's good about this trend?

First, all modern nutritionists and dietary theorists, from the
mainstream AMA to "alternative" practitioners, seem to agree that we
need to eat lots of anti-oxidants which, by neutralizing damaging "free
radicals," fight cancer, aging and other deleterious effects. Although
vitamins and supplements may help, the best source for anti-oxidants
remain fresh fruits and vegetables.

Also, all seem to agree we need fiber. For years, the AMA, for
instance, has advocated a "high-fiber" diet as a way to fight cancer,
among other ailments. Fresh fruits and vegetables are a major source of
fiber in the human diet.

Next: **a de-emphasis on meat** and, of course, when meat is eaten,
an emphasis on natural/organic meats raised in environments better
than that of commercial feedlots. While animal-rights activists and
vegetarians often dispute the claim that such "natural" environments

---

[50]   By "emphasis" here and "de-emphasis" below, I mean relative to mainstream
American culture.

are indeed more humane, nobody seems to doubt that keeping hormones and antibiotics out of meat makes it safer, healthier.

Yes, meat is a major source of protein. But it turns out that most Americans eat an excess of protein[51] anyway; secondly, most modern nutritionists and health experts seem to agree that plant proteins tend to be healthier; generally, everything meat can do nutritionally, plant products can do better. Among other things, we tend to digest vegetable proteins more easily, and then there's the issue of "bad fat," the kind alleged to cause heart disease and a variety of other ailments. While dietary writer Gary Taubes argues that "bad fats" do not lead to heart disease (454), the AMA and many others still believe they do and would like to see us eat less "bad fat," red meat, in particular.

Another issue with meat is that it's at the top of the food chain; as such, if it's commercially raised, it tends to be loaded with toxins—all the poisons from below tend to accumulate in the animal's flesh. In food writer Michael Pollan's words, "You are what you eat eats" (Goodreads). Of course, when an animal is raised naturally—hormone and antibiotic free, among other things—such problems are greatly diminished.

Let's not neglect the important environmental argument for eating less meat. In 2009, Paul McCartney began spearheading a campaign called Meat Free Mondays. His convincing argument: meat production is one of the largest contributors to global warming, responsible, according to a 2006 UN study, for "a staggering 18% of man's global greenhouse gas emissions" (Vaugn). In addition, meat production consumes far more water than vegetarian products per pound of food, and commercial feedlots are a major contributor to water pollution. Also, acres upon acres of rain forest in Brazil and elsewhere are being decimated to create short-term grazing land for cattle destined for burgerhood; as such, eating less meat is a boon for the environment.

Next, let's look at that Hippie **preference for whole grains.** Hey, who took my Wonder Bread? Well, it's not like all Countercultural bread is 100% whole grain; still, it tends to be noticeably more so than its mainstream counterparts. And we see this embedded in that Countercultural notion of "whole foods"—*whole foods* tend to mean whole grains.

---

[51] The website Mercola.com tells us, "Most Americans consume three to five times more protein than they need."

Let's talk about wheat: a grain of wheat, de-hulled, has three parts: the bran, the germ and the endosperm. White flour" is the starchy endosperm (with some vitamins added). There are four basic nutritional advantages whole-wheat flour has over white-wheat flour: 1) it has more protein; 2) it has more vitamins and minerals than "enriched" white flour;[52] 3) it has more fiber (remove the bran and germ, and you remove all the fiber); 4) it's lower glycemic (of which, more in a moment).

Much the same is true of other grains; whole-grain brown rice, for example, is superior to white rice: it has more vitamins; it has more fiber; it has more protein; it's lower glycemic.

Sugar, sugar, honey, honey—you are my candy girl, and though it embarrasses and chagrins me to admit it, you have got me wanting you. Let me explain the value of **natural sweeteners**. America has an epidemic of type-2 (acquired) diabetes; it's a major health problem, affecting tens of millions, adding tens of billions to our annual health-care costs. There seems to be a consensus that the primary environmental cause of type-2 diabetes is high-glycemic food—chemically simple carbohydrates that enter the blood stream too quickly, are too quickly digested, causing blood-sugar (glucose) levels to spike. The body responds with an insulin surge, and those eating large quantities of high-glycemic foods regularly, then, are on a glucose-insulin roller coaster. (Actually, a better analogy is probably the clutch in your car: suppose you used that clutch many more times than it was designed for and were doing strenuous things with it like shifting from first to fourth. Well, you're going to destroy your clutch—you have diabetes!)

Natural foods tend to be lower glycemic; this is particularly true in the world of modern sweeteners—what a nutritional *Twilight Zone* Big Food has created. One glycemic index (which sets glucose at 100) rates the synthetic sweetener maltodextrin at a shocking 150 and high-fructose corn syrup at a worrisome 87. Refined table sugar (sucrose) clocks in at a hefty 80. In contrast, here's how the same glycemic index rates some natural sweeteners: evaporated cane juice, 55; organic sugar, 47; barley malt syrup, 42; raw honey, 30; brown-rice syrup, 25; and fructose, 17 (Organic Lifestyle Magazine). Natural sweeteners, then, are always lower glycemic.

---

[52]   *Vegetarian Times* reports, "[A]bout 30 nutrients are removed, but by law only five must be added back [to "enriched" white flour]" (Barley).

Eschewing of additives combined with minimal processing:
Remember, at one time, "respectable" America led by Big Food and
their nutritionists resisted natural/organic foods vehemently: according
to Joan Jacobs Brumberg's review of Warren Belasco's *Appetite for
Change: How the Counterculture Took on the Food Industry, 1966-1988:*

> . . . the food giants (and their handmaidens in government and
> academe) began to argue that "life before processing was barely
> worth living." Removal of additives meant the return of rickets,
> pellagra and scurvy; the elimination of preservatives implied
> botulism, salmonella and dysentery. By eating organically, the
> United States would become just like Bangladesh.

In a similar vein, let me quote Belasco:

> In *Nutrition, Behavior, and Change* (1972), Helen H. Gifft and
> Marjorie B. Washbon pronounced that "food faddism stems
> from acute or chronic psychological aberrations, including
> psychosis." Special claims for honey, molasses, wheat germ, and
> whole grains had little scientific veracity and had "overtones
> of magic." The compulsion of some people to embrace such
> delusions probably indicated "their need for emotional support
> when coping with worries about food." (163)

Crazy Hippies! Well, here's a battle the Establishment has lost rather
badly. A rule of modern nutrition has become, in Pollan's pithy phrasing,
"If it came from a plant, eat it; if it was made in a plant, don't" (qtd. in
Wiltwinny). Its corollary is that the more processed food is, the less
nutritious. Generally, consumers are now urged to avoid products with
added ingredients they don't recognize.

And of course, the environmental benefits of organic farming and
"natural" food creation are immense. For starters, pesticides, antibiotics,
growth hormones and the variety of chemicals used to stimulate mono-
crop production end up in our water. Indeed, commercial feedlots are
infamous as water polluters. About a third of Chesapeake Bay, for instance,
is considered a "dead zone," this largely the result of agricultural-chemical
runoff, "nutrient pollution" (Fears)—and it's not just a problem on the US
East Coast. Basically, we're killing our planet, and organic farming and
natural-food raising are crucial to the survival of our traditional ecosystem.

Let me now explain my claim that what I call the "Hippie diet" is inherently **less fattening**. First, America, in particular, has an epidemic of obesity; history has seen nothing like it. Second, there are several causes for obesity; some are not necessarily nutritional; yet, most would agree that we are largely what we eat and that the nutritional factor predominates. Third, as it turns out, fat doesn't necessarily make you fat. It seems like common sense that it would, but it doesn't. Bad fats *may* clog up your arteries and give you heart disease, but during the last decades, Americans have been eating more and more low-fat or no-fat foods; during that same period, obesity in America has grown steadily. As Pollan quips, "Oddly, America got really fat on its new low-fat diet . . ." (43).

Fourth, if dietary fat isn't making America obese, what is? Well, obesity and diabetes have a high correlation, suggesting a mutual underlying cause: refined high-glycemic carbohydrates, aka, "bad carbohydrates." It's not natural for a population to be obese; evolution would never construct such creatures. The primary nutritional cause of obesity, then, must be that we're eating something unnatural, something that our previous evolution hasn't vetted us for. Well, there've always been "bad fats" in our diet to some extent—presumably man was eating some red meat from early on. And if we extend our admittedly simplistic good-bad analysis to protein, we would certainly see the evolutionary eating of both "good proteins" and "bad proteins."

What we wouldn't find would be synthetic, refined "bad carbs," the ubiquity of which is a modern phenomenon. The kind of food/candy many eat out of vending machines, the refined sugary, white-flour breakfast cereal and artificially sweetened soft drinks they buy at the supermarket, the glazed donuts they eat for morning "coffee break"— they're all unnaturally high glycemic. Pollan adds, "[M]any date the current obesity and diabetes epidemic to the late 1970s, when Americans began binging on carbohydrates, ostensibly as a way to avoid the evils of fat" (43). Yes, and those "carbohydrates" would've been largely *refined* carbohydrates, things like white flour, white rice, and synthetic sweeteners. On a

> So, when the Counterculture brought its value of "natural" to cuisine, the result was genius. As it turns out, what's good for our bodies and the land actually has more to do with Mother Nature than the interests of Big Food/Big Agriculture.

glycemic index, then, the score of much modern American "food" must be historically and evolutionarily unprecedented.[53] Bottom line: fat isn't making America fat; refined carbohydrates most likely are.

Suffice it to say, Hippiedom's emphasis on the natural has saved the day: whole grains and natural sweeteners are significantly lower glycemic than their mainstream counterparts. Imagine for a moment that all Americans began eating a Hippie diet, replacing white flour, white rice and synthetic sweeteners with whole grains and natural sweeteners. Most likely, our epidemic of obesity/type-2 diabetes would wane. Modern mainstream fare is too often high glycemic and thus fattening; generally, Hippie cuisine tends to be low glycemic and likely non-fattening.[54]

Generally, Hippie food is healthy food, and the Counterculture's dietary influences have helped America and the world. Blumberg notes:

> . . . whole grain loaves replaced Wonder Bread; red meat gave way to combinations of beans, nuts and cheese; granola bars and yogurt became staples of even the kindergarten diet; and consumption of fresh produce skyrocketed. Between 1973 and 1983, our national consumption of broccoli per capita grew by 214 percent.

Also, in terms of the grocery shelf, a major culinary contribution of the Counterculture has been a variety of new products, including vegetarian burgers, new kinds of milks (soy, almond, coconut and cashew), new grain products (quinoa, chia, granola and many others),

---

[53] And I suspect this is truer the lower one goes on the socio-economic scale with poorer people more likely to be doing the binging and to be eating cheap, relatively high-glycemic meals. As Pollan notes, "the cheapest calories in the supermarket will continue to be the unhealthiest" (Goodreads).

[54] In fairness, there are other plausible theories about excessive body fat; one is that the foods we eat are too acidic, and that to protect ourselves, our bodies create fat cells deal with this acid, according to a study by Dr. Lynn Frasetto at the University of California (All Day Energy Greens). Thing is, one of the most acidic foods mentioned is "sugar," which most likely means, high-glycemic, non-natural sweeteners; generally, I'm betting that the Hippie diet I've described would be less acidic and thus probably still non fattening.

whole-grain pasta, natural/organic-type meats, some new vegetables, organic fruits and vegetables, smoothies (Naked and Odwalla are commercial brands) and a variety of healthy prepared dinners—these to name but a few. Courtesy the Counterculture, the grocery store has been reinvented; shoppers smile, pleased with their new, interesting and healthy choices.

When the Counterculture brought its value of "natural" to cuisine, the result was genius. As it turns out, what's good for our bodies and the land actually has more to do with Mother Nature than the interests of Big Food/Big Agriculture.[55]

*   *   *

Integrative Medicine and Healing Practices

Most of these healing practices were borrowed by the Counterculture from the past, the Third World or the East. So, the Counterculture gets partial credit for the social benefits of these things. We'll look at five areas here: meditation, yoga, acupuncture/herbal medicine, modern midwifery and the revival of breastfeeding.

Courtesy the Counterculture, **meditation** has become widespread in the Western world. As *Time* notes in an August 2003 cover story, "The Science of Meditation," in 1967, "Promoting his own brand of meditation, this guru [Maharishi Mahesh Yogi] won the Beatles as converts and began a resurgence of meditation in the Western world that still flourishes today" (Stein, Joel).

So Hippies—especially the Beatles, but also Mike Love, Donovan Leitch, Mia Farrow and others—brought meditation to the West; now this once seeming exotic practice has become common. Sharon Begley of *Newsweek* notes "meditation has become as mainstream as aerobics," and Time's Joel Stein offers:

---

[55] Let me add here that Hippie culture has such a huge impact on diet, nutrition, cuisine and agriculture that to fully understand modern American food history, we need EHT. What many miss regarding this progress towards national food health is the cultural connection, the underlying impetus of the Counterculture.

... it's becoming increasingly hard to avoid meditation. It's offered in schools, hospitals, law firms, government buildings, corporate offices and prisons. There are specially marked meditation rooms in airports alongside the prayer chapels and Internet kiosks. Meditation was the subject of a course at West Point, the spring 2002 issue of the *Harvard Law Review* and a few too many locker-room speeches by Lakers coach Phil Jackson. . . . Ten million American adults now say they practice some form of meditation regularly, twice as many as a decade ago.

Okay, is meditation beneficial to society? Stein continues:

... the current interest is as much medical as it is cultural. Meditation is being recommended by more and more physicians as a way to prevent, slow or at least control the pain of chronic diseases like heart conditions, AIDS, cancer and infertility. It is also being used to restore balance in the face of such psychiatric disturbances as depression, hyperactivity and attention-deficit disorder (ADD). In a confluence of Eastern mysticism and Western science, doctors are embracing meditation not because they think it's hip or cool but because scientific studies are beginning to show that it works, particularly for stress-related conditions.

Begley notes, ". . . research on it [meditation] has achieved a respectability that astonishes those who remember the early floundering."

Of late, I think meditation has combined with other Countercultural influences to form the *mindfulness movement*. In fact, some school districts are now using mindfulness training to help problem students, and mindfulness promises to have a powerful social impact—all for the better and largely, like Western meditation, of Hippie impetus.

The contemporary wave of interest in **yoga** stems from the Counterculture and is unprecedented in scope. *Time* tells us: "Yoga was little known in the U.S.—perhaps only as an enthusiasm of Allen Ginsberg, Jack Kerouac and other icons of the Beat Generation—when the Beatles and Mia Farrow journeyed to India to sit at the feet of the Maharishi Mahesh Yogi in 1968" (Corliss). Yes, the Counterculture brought yoga to the West, and with an impact far greater than that of the Beats or any others.

Time reported in 2001, "Fifteen million Americans include some form of yoga in their fitness regimen—twice as many as did five years ago; 75% of all U.S. health clubs offer yoga classes" (Corliss). Yoga seems to be everywhere; in much of the USA, yoga studios and businesses are now common.

Is yoga beneficial? The large number of practitioners just mentioned would suggest that a great many feel it is. Not that there aren't doubters; *Time* mentions the "western medical establishment's skepticism of yoga" (Corliss). Still, yoga is a form of exercise, most exercise is good, and there are some studies supporting yoga's virtues; thus, *Time* concludes, "Breathing exercises have been shown to decrease blood pressure and lower levels of stress hormones. Stretching the body through various poses promotes better drainage of the lymphatic vessels, the body's waste-removal system. Holding postures may build muscle tone, which enhances physical well-being and protects delicate joints against injury" (Corliss). Personally, I find that yoga relieves chronic muscle pain and acts as effective preventative medicine. Yes, yoga is good for society.

Another of the Eastern influences[56] brought West by Hippiedom would include **acupuncture and herbal medicines**. Hippiedom obviously didn't invent acupuncture or herbal medicine; yet, Hippiedom has of late introduced them to the Western world and been the means of their increasing popularity (Tierra).

Today, contemporary Hippies are often the practitioners of these healing techniques. Yes, mainstream medicine often remains in opposition. Yet, many patients have had positive experiences with these therapies. I, for instance, have heard that the scientific data on the use of Echinacea is unimpressive, yet I know for a fact that at times in my life, large doses of that herb have given me dramatically successful results where other therapies had failed.[57]

And in practice, many integrative practitioners have found an effective symbiosis of the mainstream and the "alternative." Countercultural Dr. Andrew Weil is an example; his practice employs elements of both traditional Western medicine and Eastern influences (Marshall). He

---

[56] Some of this herbal medicine also has its roots in Native American and other "folk" cultures.

[57] In fairness, I've have less success with homeopathic medicine. So, if a particular alternative approach doesn't work, don't use it; if it does, do. It's good that we have a choice.

has, of course, become one of the most trusted and respected names in modern American health and healing.

Thus, even if every "alternative" therapy isn't effective for everyone, having the option of acupuncture, herbal remedies and other "alternative" therapies makes the world a better place; much of the credit here goes to the Counterculture.

Midwifery has ancient roots; yet in mid-20th century America, this was a tradition lost—until the Counterculture rediscovered it. Ina Mae Gaskin is a founder of the enduring Hippie commune, The Farm; in an article called "The Midwife of Modern Midwifery," Salon.com says, "From her Tennessee commune, Ina May Gaskin almost single-handedly inspired the rebirth of midwifery in this country" (Granju).[58]

Gaskin explains how it all started:

> Before we ended up at the Farm and were traveling around the country, one of the women in our group went into labor. Rather than go to the hospital or accept welfare, the woman had the child with her husband in attendance, with no complications. This was the first of almost a dozen babies born in the caravan and hundreds more in and around the Farm without the use of a physician. I'd decided that midwifery was my calling . . . . (qtd. in Gurvis 126)

The benefits of midwifery? Well, it saves health-care costs and gives people a safe alternative to hospital care, creating a birthing situation many prefer. Having midwifery as a viable birthing option isn't just about the natural: it's about personal freedom in one of the most memorably human experiences a family will ever have.

Breastfeeding is as old as humanity itself. Yet, in postwar America, the practice was fading, partly due to widespread, often doctor-recommended use of manufactured baby formulas. Hippie culture was

---

[58] Michael Tierra notes of the Countercultural Black Bear Ranch commune, "Other members such as Yeshi and Geba were and continue to be in the forefront of the homebirth, midwife movement."

151

> **Hippie culture was one of the main influences that brought breastfeeding back and made it a new "normal."**

one of the main influences that brought breastfeeding back and made it a new "normal."[59]

The Le Leche League International, which advocates breastfeeding, predates Hippiedom. And that group, founded in 1956 by seven Catholic women, tended to be socially conservative (Amazon. com). But Hippie types, particularly "earth mothers" became a force in that organization; journalist Margaret Talbot mentions "Hippie parents . . . who met one another at the food co-op or at La Leche League meetings or at folk-dance fundraisers for Guatemalan refugees." And generally, the Counterculture picked up the ball and ran with it. A 1970 *Newsweek* article noted, ". . . the hippies seem to be in the forefront of a back-to-the-breast movement" (qtd. in Blum 44).

And in her *At the Breast: Ideologies of Breastfeeding and Motherhood in the Contemporary United States*, Linda M. Blum notes that in the early 1970s, the AMA tended to "belittle" breastfeeding advocates. She adds, "The feminist health movement, the 'hippies,' and the Nestle boycott together added a subversive, anti-capitalist interpretation to 'natural' mothering" (44). Yet, within a few years, the MDs came around decisively. Blum: "Finally, in late 1978 the American Academy of Pediatrics (AAP) changed its official position to state that 'human milk is superior to infant formulas . . . [I]deally, breast milk should be the only source of nutrients for the first four to six months' (Clark 1978)" (44).

Sociologist Julie E. Artis of DePaul University speaks of "the culmination of three decades of increasing consensus among medical and public health professionals that, as the saying goes, 'breast is best' that there is no better nutrition for the first year of an infant's life than breast milk." So, that which was first a consensus within Hippie culture and American feminism is now a strong consensus within American medicine and society: mom's milk is the way to go.

* * *

---

[59]   In 1971, only 24% of American new mothers breastfed; in 2009, that percentage had risen to 75 (Artis).

Hippies and the Environment: Have a Green Day!

"Hey farmer, farmer, put away the DDT now, give me spots on my apples
but leave me the birds and the bees . . ."

—Joni Mitchell

In high school, Hippie me had some friction with my parents: my mother
was annoyed by my reluctance to spray the backyard apple tree with
pesticides. My father was put off by my "rebelliousness" when I resisted his
order to pour several gallons of motor oil down a storm sewer. Nowadays, of
course, that's illegal. Yes, times and our attitudes towards the environment
have changed dramatically. Again, Hippie culture has led the way.

"The environmental movement, and especially the notion of
sustainability, was fueled by the hippie movement," says Beverly
Seckinger, interim director of the University of Arizona School of Media
Arts (Everett-Haynes). An obvious example is **recycling**, now a mainstay
of American life. What we tend to forget as we pull that recycling bin out
to the curb is that, yes, it all started with Hippies.[60] In *Waste and Want:
A Social History of Trash,* Susan Strasser writes:

> Like the origins of garage sales, those of contemporary recycling
> lie partly in the counterculture of the late 1960s and early 1970s.
> In its earliest manifestations, recycling was not the province
> of municipalities and big waste companies but an activity of
> counterculture environmentalists. Hippie activists organized
> voluntary recycling centers to which individuals brought their
> glass and paper. These centers were not small businesses so
> much as offshoots of social and cultural movements. Recycling
> was linked to a counterculture ethos . . . . (283)

An example of a still-vital Hippie recycling business is Boulder,
Colorado's Eco-cycle. Its founders were identified as Countercultural in
1983 by *Newsweek* (Adler), and today Eco-cyle thrives.

In communities across the nation, local governments have created
waste-disposal programs that include not just recycling but increasingly,

---

[60]   In modern America, at least: we did, after all, have recycling in WW II, for
instance.

composting. It's a huge national movement, and almost certainly, it too has its roots in Hippie culture.

Organic farming: Of course, as we discussed earlier, natural/ organic foods are essentially Hippie cuisine. And organic farming has been good for the planet. Whereas much of our top soil has been abused and depleted of its nutrients, organic farming is healing the earth; by looking to the past, it lights a path towards a sustainable future. Where mainstream society has seen the land as a mere commodity, the Counterculture has reinvigorated an ethos of respect for the land and soil, for rivers, lakes and oceans.

Many regard the now-institutionalized **Earth Day,** started in 1971, as having Hippie origins. The general consensus seems that the Counterculture was a leading player in the willingness of the general public, and thus some politicians, to accept a national (now international) day devoted to environmental awareness. Even the US Department of State acknowledges this in a document entitled "The Counter-Culture and Environmentalism."

Generally, Hippiedom has been on the leading edge of emerging environmental awareness and interest.

Worthwhile though that is, there's so much more; Hippiedom has again translated idealistic theory into hard-headed practice. In his *Counterculture Green: The Whole Earth Catalog and American Environmentalism*, Andrew G. Kirk explains how and why, noting especially the seminal role of Stewart Brand's Countercultural *Whole Earth Catalog* which debuted in 1968.

Reviewers Jane and Michael Kirk say of *Counterculture Green*:

> The *Whole Earth Catalog* itself became the voice of a new kind of environmental advocacy that, rather than shunning science as nature's enemy, embraced it as the key that could unlock the door to personal freedom and create a post-scarcity social utopia. Advances like pictures from space, personal computers, geodesic domes and even nuclear power[61] were all part of what

---

[61] Perhaps this seemed true at the time, but I think it's clear that for many years now, there's been a preponderance of opposition to nuclear power within the Counterculture, that this was one corporate-sponsored technology that Hippiedom has chosen not to embrace.

became known as the "appropriate technology movement," for which the *Whole Earth Catalog* was both a resource and a summary. No tree-hugging Luddite or apocalyptic doomsayer, Brand, Kirk writes, had an optimistic outlook shaped by "a love of good tools, thoughtful technology, scientific inquiry and a Western libertarian skepticism of the government's ability to take the lead in these areas." Brand wrote of his own publication, "This is a book of tools for saving the world at the only scale it can be done, one hand at a time."

That impetus has, over the decades, led to the development of today's Countercultural **green practitioners and pioneers**. For examples, in 2006, PBS's *The News Hour with Jim McNeil* interviewed a **biodiesel** pioneer Brent Baker who, wearing an earring and a "soulpatch," looks Hippie. Also, in 2008, *Hudson Valley Magazine* ran the article "These Fuelish Things: Jerry Robock's long, strange trip has taken him from the '60s Counterculture to the forefront of the biofuel revolution" (Levine).

In addition, Hippie culture has spawned thousands of **green businesses**. From house cleaning to home building, Hippies figure out a greener way of doing it. Hippie-Americans have developed innovative, environmentally friendly building techniques, and Counterculturists have been leaders in developing and promulgating various sustainable forms of alternative energy from solar to wind power.

Annual **green conferences** like Bioneers (derived from *biological pioneer*) have their roots in the Counterculture; here's a self-description from Utah Bioneers:

> Bioneers draw from four billion years of evolutionary intelligence and apply the knowledge in practical ways to serve human ends harmlessly. We herald a dawning age of interdependence founded in natural principles of diversity, kinship, community, cooperation and reciprocity. By wedding human ingenuity with the wisdom of the wild, Bioneers are creating a future environment of hope that is within our grasp today. (7th Annual)

Their values sound Hippie to me, and notice how the last sentence ("human ingenuity") seems to echo Brand's outlook towards "appropriate technology."

On the Bioneers website, I found an interview with Gary Hirshberg, "founder and CEO of Stonyfield Farm, the world's largest organic yogurt company," called "The Organic Revolution: From Hippie to Hip to Scale," and yes, I think Bioneers itself is "from Hippie."

Consider also Countercultural periodicals, descendents of *Whole Earth Catalog*: *Co-Evolution Quarterly* and *Mother Earth News*. They and their readers have developed practical, earth-friendly technologies and products.

Generally, as humanity faces an unprecedented environmental crisis—with the North Pole steadily melting, with an accelerating number of global weather catastrophes scientists link to rapid climate change and global warming—thank heaven that five decades ago, Hippies started raising awareness about environmental degradation, started creating practical modes for living greener. It's common to deride Hippies as being "a bunch of dreamers unable to live in the real world." But we've been *successful* dreamers—visionaries; time and again, we've turned theory into effective practice.

> **Thank heaven that five decades ago, Hippies started raising awareness about environmental degradation, started creating practical modes for living greener**

* * *

These first four achievements—the invention of the personal computer, the creation of a thriving natural/organic food industry, the development of "alternative"/integrative medicine and healing, and the creation of green attitudes, practices and technology—should be enough to sell any fair-minded observer on the value of the Counterculture to society. But these are only an impressive beginning; next, we'll consider something more general: **the Counterculture's underlying values and how they've benefited society as a whole.** We'll look at eleven.

The Natural: Modern mainstream American society has often seemed to forget where it came from, in its arrogance saying, "Hey, we don't need nature anymore; we're so much better than it." The old Calvinist order, which pitted God against Nature and saw wilderness as the Devil's playground, would have us believe that humankind's glory lay in its destruction and domination of Nature, not in working in harmony with it. Hippiedom's emphasis on the natural, then, has been a much-needed influence. Above, we saw many of the positive results in natural-organic foods, in the renewal of breastfeeding, and perhaps most importantly, in an emphasis on and consideration for the environment; those are but a few.

Healthy sexuality/physical pleasure: Calvinism and mainstream American culture have often embraced a flesh-hating moralism— "Suffering is good for you." The Counterculture has posed a healthy response, valuing pleasure, valuing the flesh. Yes, for some individuals, this has led to destructive hedonism, but for many more, it has lead to healthier, happier lives. Don't tell your parents I told you this, but there's much emerging evidence showing that a certain amount of sex is good for our health, both mental and physical. Draconian sexual repression and shaming is unhealthy; again, that pre-Sixties society the Counterculture rebelled against was sexually sick.

Informality: One way I can spot Countercultural products in the grocery store is that the business names are so often first names: Burt's, Annie's, Tom's, Ben and Jerry's, etc. Likewise, the Counterculture has been a force for changes as simple as being able to wear jeans—comfortable, informal clothing should not a crime. With its egalitarian impulses and its emphasis on the authentic, Hippie culture has been challenging excessive formality and snootiness for decades. Perhaps no other social group has been responsible for so many tea cups crashing onto the patio. Hippiedom hasn't been about rank; it's been about being real. And in that realness, there's been the prospect of healthy human relations; people can't bond, can't join in that larger divine thing when they're so separated by rank that they can't see one another's humanity. Excessive formality makes the world a worse place; it makes us worse people.

> With its egalitarian impulses and its emphasis on the authentic, Hippie culture has been challenging excessive formality and snootiness for decades. Perhaps no other social group has been responsible for so many tea cups crashing onto the patio.

Fun: Of Countercultural entrepreneur Richard Branson, reporter Alan Deutschman notes, "He's an outspoken advocate for fun in the workplace, not fear and intimidation" (92); in his regard for fun, Branson seems typically Countercultural. Hippies tend to see fun as a human right, but as *The New York Times* once opined regarding the impact of the

157

Counterculture's values on society: "America is still close enough to the frontier experience of relentless work and danger to view any kind of fun with suspicion" ("In Praise of"). Of course, anti-Hippie bigots have often portrayed the Counterculture's valuing of fun as evidence of postponed adolescence, immaturity and social irresponsibility, but any psychologist will affirm that the most productive people use fun as a reward, that fun can contribute to productivity. If some insist on seeing fun as immature, perhaps it's because their own adult lives are so dour and discouraging, and fun is healthy—laughter *is* one of the best medicines. Yes, Hippie culture does value fun, and it should be praised for that, not condemned.

Anti-authoritarianism: That bumper sticker "Question Authority" seems quintessentially Hippie, and we're sometimes hated for this. For the far-right, especially those confused about the real nature of Christianity, God is the ultimate authority figure, a very angry white male sitting on a throne somewhere up in the sky with a gigantic gun rack on the wall behind Him and above that, an American flag the size of Nebraska; by questioning authority, they believe, Hippies are spiting God and richly deserve to be punished.

A calmer, more reasonable approach would note that, no, not all Hippies "hate God," and that questioning authority is a basic premise of democracy. A citizenry that doesn't question authority isn't doing its job. Likewise, the value of rational, critical thinking—which is by nature skeptical—cannot be underestimated. Democracy needs a functioning free market-places of ideas, a citizenry capable of questioning and thinking critically.

And, oh by the way, isn't there something fundamentally American about anti-authoritarianism? If we looked at many of those who rebelled against the British monarchy, fought the American revolution and founded this nation, that might seem their most salient feature.

Personal freedom/individual rights: *The New York Times* says of the 60s: "Only a few periods in American history have seen such a rich fulfillment of the informing ideals of personal freedom and creativity that lie at the heart of the American intellectual tradition" ("In Praise of"). In even the simple acts of men wearing long hair, of people dressing as they choose, of parents deciding how they raise and feed their children, etc., Hippie-America has fought for personal freedom and individual rights—the

> Yes, responsible personal freedom is what America is supposed to be about, what life everywhere should be about.

right to make free choices so long as they don't hurt others, to live and let live. Yes, responsible personal freedom is what America is supposed to be about, what life everywhere should be about.

Creativity/Vision: In recent years, the phrase "thinking outside of the box" has become a cliché for ideas and products we now find admirable. Since its inception, Hippie culture has been thinking outside of the box and doing so both with the forest (humanity, society and the planet) and with the trees (specific technologies, problem-solving strategies, artistic approaches and inventions). We can see this mix in, for example, the influential *Whole Earth Catalog*. And obviously, the Counterculture's creation of the PC involved a striking capacity for creativity and vision.

De-emphasis on materialism/consumerism: No, a vow of poverty isn't required to be Hippie, and there are vastly wealthy Counterculturists. Still, from its inception, Hippiedom has emphasized that just maybe there's more to life than "He who dies with the most toys wins."

In a mainstream society obsessed with material success, that seems to place more value on possessions than people, this is a badly needed influence. Prisoners of their own property and insatiable acquisitiveness, those who gain the world often do lose their souls. Recall young Benjamin Braddock (Dustin Hoffman) of the famous 1967 film *The Graduate*: Braddock is pondering his future, and he's given some advice by Mr. Robinson, who represents mainstream America: "I just want to say one word to you—just one word—*plastics*"—this, a metaphor for a materially comfortable but ultimately unsatisfying life. Braddock winces as if he glimpsed his own death. Hippie culture, then, has wisely defined success in life as something beyond personal wealth.

Tolerance/Respect for other cultures: There's a story that African-American blues guitarist B. B. King told: in 1967, long before the success of black "crossover" artists like Michael Jackson, he'd been booked at the Fillmore West in San Francisco. When he and his band arrived, they thought they were in the wrong place since the line outside was largely "white kids with long hair." Legendary Countercultural promoter Bill Graham finally coaxed the band off the bus and later introduced King as the "chairman of the board," King fondly recollected. As he came onstage, the audience rose to its feet; a deeply moved King recalled that during the course of the show, that audience gave him "three or four" standing ovations (Brown).

And here's an historical moment I'm particularly proud of: at the famous 1963 March on Washington where Martin Luther King gave his "I Have a Dream" speech, the Countercultural folk-singing group Peter, Paul and Mary sang Countercultural Bob Dylan's "Blown in the Wind." Yes, at a time when most of America was still uncomfortable with African-America culture, the Counterculture was treating it with respect, often actively supporting the Civil Rights Movement.

Other examples would be how Hippiedom has cultivated Bluegrass music or the many times I've seen on a Hippie vehicle a bumper-sticker quoting Chief Joseph of the Nez Perce: "The earth does not belong to us; we belong to the Earth"; generally, the Counterculture has been respectful towards Native-American cultures. Of course, we've seen the results of Hippiedom's interest in the Eastern world, and add to this, the interest in the Third World and indigenous cultures shown by much of Hippiedom. While much of America has pursued the reactionary and spiritually dead path of being "better than others," Hippiedom has sought to learn from others.

Now, I'm not saying there's no racism or prejudice in Hippie-America, that it's entirely free of such ugly attitudes. Still, Hippie culture is in many ways a synthesis of various cultural influences; as such, by its nature, the Counterculture has generally respected cultural diversity, has helped break down various forms of ethnic chauvinism and racism. We've been ahead of our time. To a nation and a world tormented by a prejudiced past and present, seriously seeking a multicultural future with liberty and justice for all, this Hippie value is invaluable.

Kindness: "Oh, oh, what I want to know-oh is are you kind?" Jerry Garcia sings in "Uncle John's Band." The value of kindness permeates Hippie culture. You can hear it in its language: There's a type of marijuana commonly known as "Kind Bud." A local (Boulder) Hippie restaurant/brewpub has a beer called "Colorado Kind." There's a recognizably Hippie bumpersticker reading "Have a Kind Day." It's like *kind* has become code for *Countercultural.*

Of course, translating theory into practice is another thing. Personally, I think Hippiedom's done pretty well. And if some individuals fall short, I think many outsiders would be surprised to find how polite, considerate and kind most Counterculturists actually are. In a cynical, often nasty world, Hippiedom has at least valued the right thing. Compare the Counterculture, for instance, to angry neoconservatives carping about

160

"bleeding-hearts" as if compassion and kindness were signs of weakness and an inability to deal with reality.

Our last Countercultural value here will certainly shock the bigots: **Social responsibility**. After all, neoconservative ideologues see irresponsibility as a core Hippie value, and closely following are accusations of selfishness, being childlike, cowardly, etc.—the whole litany of Hippie-hating and Hippie stereotyping—this, in turn, rushing us to the ugly conclusion that the Counterculture is all things evil.

First, neocons assume the War in Vietnam was the most noble of causes, and because the Counterculture was often involved in the anti-war movement, they conclude that Hippies are indeed selfish and irresponsible. If, however, one sees the War in Vietnam as an ill-fated attempt at neocolonialism, that would make protesting that war the socially responsible thing to do.

Also, there are Hippies who've abused drugs, who've behaved irresponsibly in that regard; on the other hand, it's War on Drugs propaganda to assume that all marijuana use is drug abuse and unhealthy, and you can find abusers of drugs in any population. Although neoconservatism and the War on Drugs routinely assume that *any* use of "drugs" is the ultimate irresponsibility, it's a weak, histrionic and hypocritical argument.

That said, look at much of the rest of Hippie culture: the environmentalism, the social activism, the emphasis on "right livelihood," the interest in healing individuals and society, the Hippie parents deeply concerned about how to best feed and rear their children, the recycling of waste, the attempt to save our land through organic farming, the philanthropy, the creation of free software and websites—where does it stop? I see social responsibility as a key Countercultural value.

Hey, what's so funny about peace, love and understanding? Hippie values are humane, progressive and life-affirming; it would be difficult to overstate how badly they're needed in America and the world, what a good influence we've been.

*   *   *

Let's next examine a contribution to world history that will no doubt surprise many: **the Counterculture's role in helping bring down the Iron Curtain**.

First, let's remember that Hippies are hardly exclusive to the USA. As noted, there are and have been Hippies across much of the globe, including behind the Iron Curtain. In particular, consider the former Czechoslovakia. In the early 1960s, there was in this repressive nation, "the temporary lifting of several bans" (Prague-Life.com); this, in turn, allowed the creation of a Czech Counterculture with its own rock music. As author Mark Kurlansky writes:

> With the West no longer completely cut off, Czech youth immediately tapped into the vibrant Western youth culture wearing *Texasskis*—blue jeans—and going to clubs to hear the big beat, as rock and roll was called. Prague had more young people with long hair, beards, and sandals than anywhere else in central Europe. Yes, in the heart of [dictator] Novotny's Czechoslovakia, there were the unshorn rebel youth of the Sixties—hippies . . . . On May 1, 1965, May Day, when the rest of the communist world was celebrating the revolution, the youth of Prague had crowned the longhaired, bearded beatnik, visiting poet Allen Ginsberg, *Kraj Majales*, King of May. (31-32)

Ginsberg was soon deported, but then in January 1968, a new period of openness unfurled in what is now known as the Prague Spring, an attempt at democratic communism/socialism. In August, the Soviets invaded; repression returned. A month later, a Hippie-Czech rock band, The Plastic People of the Universe, was formed; they called Hippie culture "The Second Culture" (Prague-Life.com). In 1974, they organized a Czechoslovakian Woodstock; in 1976, they tried to organize a second, were jailed and "rock and roll was taken to court" (Prague-Life.com). *Newsweek* notes:

> When the long-haired, politically apathetic[62] Czech rock group the Plastic People of the Universe were arrested in 1977 by the country's hard-line communist government . . . the arrest of these gangly youths triggered the drafting of Charter 77,

---

[62] I find *Newsweek's* "politically apathetic" label highly questionable; I think these people were indirectly political as opposed to being part of some official party.

the manifesto criticizing Czechoslovakia's hard-line leaders, whose signatories guided the country's first post-communist government. ("Stop-Rocks")

The English-language Prague-Life.com adds:

If it would be an overstatement to attribute the fall of the Iron Curtain entirely to Hippies, what can be safely said is that the Counterculture played a crucial role in the democratization and opening of those societies. Why, it's enough to make a neocon cry.

The counterculture movement in Czechoslovakia in the 1960s had significant political consequences, setting events in motion that would eventually lead to a revolution [the Velvet Revolution] named after a rock band [The Velvet Underground], and an ideological leader [Vaclav Havel] to be elected the first president of a democratic Czechoslovakia. . . .When Velvet Underground founder Lou Reed met Havel in Prague in 1990, Havel revealed what an inspiration the band had been to the hippie movement of Czechoslovakia, telling him, "Did you know that I am president because of you?"

The Counterculture, then, played a major role in the democratization of Czechoslovakia; yet, they were not entirely responsible, and Czechoslovakia was only one nation under the Soviet thumb. Still, in contrast to the neoconservative notion that credit for the demise of neo-Stalinist dictatorships goes to their idol, Ronald Reagan, James Hershberg, a Russia expert at George Washington University, says:

> . . . It's a lot more complicated than that. If you were to pick one person who ended Soviet communism, it would be Mikhail Gorbachev. If you were to pick a few more, you'd add the Beatles and the counter-culture they represented to a generation of Russians. And then you'd have to mix in all the other factors that led to the stagnation, and ultimately to the unraveling, of the Soviet empire from within. ("Outlook")

Hershberg adds:

> An irony worth noting is that much credit for winning the Cold
> War should go to the people Reagan so disliked as governor of
> California—the hippies, the anti-Vietnam War protesters and
> counter-culture figures who in the 1960s produced the music,
> ideas and ethos of non-conformism that appealed to the educated
> youth suffocating in the communist world. ("Just Who")

If it would be an overstatement to attribute the fall of the Iron Curtain
entirely to Hippies, what can be safely said is that the Counterculture
played a crucial role in the democratization and opening of those
societies. Why, it's enough to make a neocon cry.

*   *   *

Next up, **Hippies and charity**: Despite the widespread belief that Hippies
are selfish parasites, the truth is closer to the opposite: Hippies give vast
amounts to charity, and as the "do gooders" we are sometimes accused
of being, we have done great good.

Countercultural musicians have often been in the forefront of charity,
raising funds by making music; probably, the first was ex-Beatle George
Harrison who along with renowned Indian musician Ravi Shankar
arranged the 1971 **Concert for Bangladesh** in New York City. It featured
a range of largely Countercultural acts, garnered an immediate 243,000
dollars and was followed by a concert film and concert DVDs (*Wikipedia,*
"The Concert for Bangladesh"). Overall, some 12 million dollars was
eventually raised though due to tax problems (the organizers forgot to
apply for tax-exempt status), it took until 1985 for much of the aid to arrive;
current proceeds go to the George Harrison Fund for UNICEF (*Wikipedia,*
"The Concert for Bangladesh"). Thus, even if belatedly, Harrison and
friends helped a great many Third World poor; more importantly, they
probably served as the inspiration for generations of Countercultural
charity-concert projects and in so doing, pioneered what seems a new
genre in the world of philanthropy: the charity mega-concert.[63]

---

[63]   Though these charity mega-concerts are clearly Countercultural in origin, I
do not mean to imply that every participant or performer in them is Hippie.

The series of benefit concerts now known as **"The Secret Policeman's Balls"** appears to be a Countercultural institution. The first (not actually called by that name at the time) was in 1976; these balls have continued and are apparently still being held (*Wikipedia* lists the most recent as having been in 2012). The early shows were organized by those in and around the Countercultural Monty Python comedy troupe, aka, "the Beatles of comedy," particularly John Cleese.[64] Eventually the venue included Countercultural musicians such as Sting, Eric Clapton, Bob Geldof, Pete Townshend, Bruce Springsteen and many others. *Wikipedia* reports, "Media reviews at the time described the 1976 show as a gathering of the tribes"; as we've seen, *tribes* is often a euphemism for *Hippiedom*.

These UK-based shows eventually inspired some American spinoffs: Conspiracy of Hope (1986) and Human Rights Now! (1988). Both shows were heavily Countercultural; indeed, Countercultural impresario Bill Graham was one of the promoters.

Band Aid was a musical group founded in 1984 by Countercultural musicians Bob Geldof and Midge Ure to raise money for famine relief in Ethiopia by releasing the record "Do They Know It's Christmas?" It went on to become the number one Christmas single that season. Soon came **Live Aid**, a massive 1985 international charity concert which was, contrary to original plans, recorded.

Again, a broad array of artists contributed to these events, yet the organizational thrust came from the Counterculture (Bono, among many others, was heavily involved), and a great many Countercultural acts performed. If not all the credit here goes to Hippiedom, most of it does.

Can you sing "I Ain't Gonna Work on Maggie's Farm No More"? When we think of America's small farmers, especially the non-organic ones, we don't usually think Countercultural; yet, Hippie culture has been their staunch ally. At the 1985 Live Aid concert, Bob Dylan commented regarding proceeds, "I hope that some of the money . . . maybe they can just take a little bit of it, maybe . . . one or two million, maybe . . . and use it, say, to pay the mortgages on some of the farms and, the farmers here [the USA] owe to the banks . . . ." (*Wikipedia,* "Farm Aid"). Willie

---

[64]   We'll discuss the Monty Python troupe below; I'll document their Countercultural identity there.

Nelson, John Mellencamp and Neil Young soon developed Dylan's idea into a series of annual concerts known as **Farm Aid**; the first was in 1985; they continue to this day. Dave Matthews has since joined the board of directors, and an annual speech by Young on the environment is now a Farm Aid highlight (*Wikipedia,* "Farm Aid").[65]

As of 2008, interviewer Carol Ekarius tells us, "Farm Aid has granted over $17 million to more than 100 farm organizations, churches and service agencies in 44 states . . . In recent years, some of this support has gone to local efforts that confront the threat of increasing corporate control of agriculture."

When I looked at individual Counterculturists, I found a tremendous amount of philanthropy. **Bruce Springsteen** contributes to a great many charities and progressive causes. **Bono** functions on the international level like some kind of Hippie Pope, redefining what a rock star can be. His ability, often working in conjunction with other celebrities such as Oprah Winfrey, to focus public attention on issues, to raise funds for those causes and to affect international public policy seems unprecedented.

Counterculturalist is actress/activist **Mia Farrow**, a UNICIEF Goodwill Ambassador, has relentlessly and courageously fought for the embattled people of Darfur. Unflinching, she has spoken truth to power, urging a boycott of the 2008 Olympic Games in Beijing (the Chinese have been major supporters of the Sudanese regime persecuting those in Darfur) and even convincing director Stephen Spielberg to withdraw as the Beijing Olympics artistic director—ouch! (Keilberger).

And so many **other major Countercultural celebrities and bands** have been powerhouses for charity. Sting and Paul McCartney have been wonderful; Ringo Starr, David Bowie, Jackson Brown, Bonnie Raitt, Aerosmith, and Mick Jagger of the Rolling Stones are socially active and charitable. Many, including the great Hippie singer Robert Plant, help The Robin Hood Foundation which fights poverty in New York City (*Wikipedia,* "Robin Hood Foundation").

---

[65] Although Farm Aid seems to be of Countercultural origins and governance, not every band that plays Farm Aid is Countercultural; Country-Western musicians and others also contribute. Indeed, one of the program's great assets has been its ability to attract a wide range of top-notch acts from across the cultural spectrum.

Woodstock announcer and Hippie icon Wavy Gravy celebrated his 71st birthday at a benefit for the Berkeley-based **Seva Foundation** of which he is a co-founder. *Seva* (the Sanskrit word for service) was formed in 1978, aiming to "alleviate suffering caused by disease and poverty." They are known in particular for their work in preventing blindness and restoring sight to individuals in India, Nepal, Tibet, Cambodia, Bangladesh, Egypt, Tanzania and Guatemala (Seva Foundation).

> **The degree to which Counterculturists promote charity and progressive social activity—and the consistency and effectiveness with which they do so—seem exceptional. If an underlying Hippie value is *Change the world for the better*, here we see numerous examples of theory turned into practice.**

Also consider **Counter-cultural businesses**: walk down the natural-foods aisle of any commercial grocery store, or go into a natural-foods market and look at the boxes of the natural-foods products. What you'll see is that almost without exception, these companies contribute to good causes.

My apologies for not specifically mentioning the charity of many other Counterculturists—some famous, some not, some rich, some not—but you get the point: Hippies give, and. the consistency and effectiveness with which they do so seem exceptional. If an underlying Hippie value is *Change the world for the better*, here we see numerous examples of theory turned into practice.

* * *

Hippie Contributions to the Arts

Let's begin our trek through Countercultural contributions to the arts with puppets, or in this case, **Muppets**, as in Jim Henson. Of course, Henson always looked Hippie with his longish hair and beard. And many acknowledge that his work was derivative of Hippiedom. Reporter Amy Aldrich comments regarding Disney's acquisition of the satirical and sometimes subversive Muppets:

Henson's humor is less mainstream and more irreverent than the Disney variety [which] dispenses a heavy dose of superficial cheer . . . Henson's Muppets, on the other hand, notice what really goes on in mainstream America and poke fun at it; at overgrown egos, out-of-hand anxieties, the foibles of human beings struggling to make it in an accomplished world. . . . Henson's counter-cultural humor will not be swallowed up by Disney.

Yes, Henson and his work are Countercultural. His wildly successful PBS children's program *Sesame Street* began in 1968 and continues to this day, long after Henson's death. A few of the show's impressive achievements: As of 2006, *Sesame Street* had earned 109 Emmys, the most of any television program. And for decades, it's been seen by children in over 120 nations, including some 77 million Americans who grew up on Fozzie

> **If the two great purposes of art are to instruct and to entertain, it's hard to do much better than this. So, here is no small achievement, no small life; Jim Henson and his work span the globe and belong to the ages.**

Bear (*Wikipedia,* "Sesame Street"). Many are now parents themselves and like their parents before them, they approve highly of a show which teaches racial/ethnic tolerance as well as arithmetic and the alphabet. *Sesame Street* is beloved!

Henson himself is described by the The Mississippi Writers Page as "without a doubt the most famous puppeteer in history" (Padgett). If the two great purposes of art are to instruct and to entertain, it's hard to do much better than this. Here, then, is no small achievement, no small life; Henson and his work span the globe and belong to the ages. **HICR: 10.**

Next, we'll be going to **the theatre**. Let's begin with a man considered "among the greatest living playwrights," **Tom Stoppard.** There's even a scholarly tome entitled *The Cambridge Companion to Tom Stoppard* (Kelly, Katherine). Suffice it to say, when such a prestigious institution takes a playwright that seriously, he's important and successful. His many works include "Rosencrantz and Guilderstein are Dead" (1967), "The Real Thing" (1982—a Tony winner), "Arcadia" (1993), "The Importance of Love" (1997), "The Coast of Utopia" (2004), and "Rock 'n' Roll" (2006). Stoppard's works have been produced on both the London and New York stages. He also co-wrote with Marc Norman the popular 1998 film *Shakespeare in Love*. Okay, I can see you're impressed; why call him Hippie?

First, pictures of Stoppard show a man with longish hair—possibly Hippie, definitely "rumpled." Also, he sometimes uses Hippie language; for example, reviewer Elsye Sommer quotes him: "I really dig words more than I can speak them." He "digs" words.

Our best evidence, however, hails from Stoppard's 2006 play "Rock 'n' Roll." *Newsweek* says its protagonist, Jan, is Stoppard's "fictional alter ego" ("Stop-Rocks"). If in this transparently autobiographical play Jan is Stoppard, who is Jan? Like Stoppard, he's a Czech émigré living in England who's returned to his now-democratized homeland along with his lover, Esme, who is consistently described by reviewers as "hippie" or a "flower child." The play also traces some of Jan's and the Czechs' history. Turns out, Jan himself is very Countercultural, a lover of rock music and, in particular, the aforementioned Plastic People of the Universe who "represented Sixties culture in Czechoslovakia" (Burnett). He's contrasted with his professor at Cambridge, the Marxist reformer, Max; Jan, on the other hand, seems more interested in cultural revolution, in rock 'n' roll. In the conclusion, Jan and Esme attend a 1990 Rolling Stones concert in post-Communist Prague; the implication is that rock and roll and the freedom it suggests has triumphed. Essentially, "Rock 'n' Roll" is a paean to the transformative power of Hippie culture.

In addition, as we might guess from its title, "Rock 'n' Roll" is filled with Countercultural music, including songs from The Grateful Dead, The Beach Boys, Jimi Hendrix, Bob Dylan, Pink Floyd, The Rolling Stones, and The Velvet Underground. Clearly, this is the music Stoppard loves, the music he identifies with. So, we're going claim Tom Stoppard as a great Hippie dramatist. **HICR: 10.**

What about **Countercultural contributions to *musical* theater**? As you might imagine, we'll begin with *Hair: The American Tribal Love-Rock Musical* by James Rado and Gerome Ragni (book and lyrics) and Galt MacDermot (music). Opening on Broadway in 1968, like so many other events of the late Sixties, *Hair* told the world Hippie culture had arrived.

What's so special about **Hair**? "Fourteen national companies ran concurrently with *Hair's* Broadway run, as did a score of international companies" (xiv), author Barbara Lee Horn figures, adding, "literally dozens of *Hair* revival productions have been mounted throughout the United States" (xv); *Wikipedia* notes that Hair productions continue today. Apparently *Hair* was a new subgenre, "the first fully realized concept musical[66] on Broadway" (Horn 129). *Hair* also rejuvenated Broadway audiences, bringing in a younger audience (Horn 133) and it was a boon to African-American actors (Horn 134). *Hair* was important in breaking down the "fourth wall" (Horn 136), that invisible barrier between actors and audience resulting from the ways drama has traditionally been staged. Also, *Hair* has allowed people to participate, becoming a sort of people's play, a dramatic exercise in inclusion.

Generally, *Hair* made the American stage freer. Horn notes, "*Hair's* nudity helped to define permissible limits of free expression within the American theater when the United States Supreme Court twice issued major decisions concerning First Amendment rights based on the show . . ." (134).

There once was a place called . . . **"Spamalot."** And it was on the Great White Way. In 2005, Eric Idle's stage send up of the 1975 film "Monty Python and the Holy Grail" won the Tony Award for Best Musical.

Can we call The Pythons Countercultural or Hippie? Yes, though it may not be as straight a shot as we'd like. There were, after all, six of them: five Englishmen (Michael Palin, Terry Jones, Eric Idle, John Cleese, and the late Graham Chapman) and one American, Terry Gilliam—brought aboard as an animator.[67] Individually, some may be more culturally Hippie than others; photos, for example, show Gilliam and sometimes Idle, Jones or Palin looking particularly Hippie; Cleese, on the other hand, not so much.

---

[66] Apparently, a "concept musical" is one developed during rehearsal (Horn 82), similar, I suppose, to what improvisational jazz or jam-band rock are to music. Thus, *Wikipedia* notes, "The show was under almost perpetual re-write."

[67] English comedian Carol Cleveland is often seen as a kind of seventh Python (*Wikipedia*).

Looking at the bigger Python picture, however, makes our chore easier. For starters, Monty Python's success is due in large to its appreciative fans. The comedy troupers were often called "the Beatles of comedy" ("*Wikipedia,* "Monty Python") because they had much the same audience. We can also see ethnic identity in their professional associations: the Python films were financed by Countercultural musicians and bands, including Pink Floyd, Led Zeppelin, Jethro Tull and George Harrison of the Beatles (*Wikipedia,* "Monty Python"). In addition, Gilliam co-wrote the 1985 film "Brazil" with Tom Stoppard. So we see much Python Countercultural networking.

And Python productions suggest Counterculture. As for their form, Python scholar David Morgan notes:

> This revolution was televised. . . . [The Pythons] were reacting against what they saw as the staid, predictable formats of other comedy programs. . . . what made Monty Python extraordinary from the very beginning was their total lack of predictability, reveling in a stream-of-consciousness display of nonsense, satire, sex, and violence.

And in content, their "humour . . . was considered incomprehensible, subversive, even dangerous, when it was first unleashed on the world," reports the website *Icons: A Portrait of England.* Anyone who has seen two skits in the 1983 film *Monty Python's The Meaning of Life*—the first skewing Catholicism regarding birth control;[68] this, followed by a hilarious parody of Protestantism for its sexual dysfunctionality—knows how biting Python satire can be. Thus, like Hippie culture itself, they have a reputation as anti-Establishment. And as a reviewer notes, "Like most counter-culture,[69] the team eventually defined culture" (Gadsby).

So yes, call Monty Python Countercultural (I'd assign a **HICR of close to 10** here since the group's widely seen as Countercultural, almost common knowledge); chalk up another Tony for Hippiedom.

---

[68] Sample lyric: "Every sperm is sacred, every sperm is great; when the heathens kill them, God gets quite irate."

[69] To be fair, I'm not certain this reviewer is using "counter-culture" as a synonym of *Hippie.*

171

Let's next consider the many accomplishments of the remarkable pair, lyricist **Tim Rice** and, especially, musical composer **Andrew Lloyd Webber**. Together, the two created *Joseph and the Amazing Technicolor Dreamcoat (1968)*, *Jesus Christ Superstar (1970)* and *Evita* (the musical—1976); Lloyd Webber's later stage successes include *Cats* (1983), *Phantom of the Opera* (1986), *Starlight Express* (1984), *Aspects of Love* (1989), *Sunset Blvd.* (1995), *Whistle Down the Wind* (1996) and others. On both Broadway and London's West End, Lloyd Webber rules. He's won so many awards, it's embarrassing.

And it's clear that Rice and Lloyd Weber are products of Hippiedom. Michael Walsh of Smithsonian.com writes of, "Lloyd Webber's transmogrification from skinny, long-haired Counterculture icon to well-fed and tonsured Tory peer," and apparently much the same could be said of Rice. When you look at pictures of the two when younger **(see Photo #8),** they look like a pair of rock stars. As for Webber's canon, critic John Snelson comments that "this negotiation of boundaries between conformity and innovation, culture and counterculture, runs through the heart of his work . . ." (56).

Musical historian James E. Perone supplies examples of Countercultural themes and identity: "The counterculture significance of *Jesus Christ Superstar* lies in the way in which Jesus is portrayed as an almost hippie-like, communal holy man at odds with the 'straight' society of his day and in the rock music of the score" (153); onstage, Jesus

> "The counterculture significance of *Jesus Christ Superstar* lies in the way in which Jesus is portrayed as an almost hippie-like, communal holy man at odds with the 'straight' society of his day and in the rock music of the score."—music historian James E. Perone

and his disciples look like a "tribe" of Hippies. Apparently, *JCS* is a paean to Hippie rights; that is, just as the play seems to scream, "Do not crucify this man: it's wrong!" so the play seems to say, "Stop persecuting Hippies," and it implies that the Counterculture is likely far closer to true Christianity than that "straight" society bent on Hippiedom's destruction.

So whether today Lloyd Webber and/or Rice would self-describe as Hippie today isn't crucial: they hail from Hippie culture, and their work reflects Countercultural elements and themes. As such, in the world of musical theater, the Counterculture may reasonably lay some claim to

172

their accomplishments, which are immense. **HICR: 8.0** (minus points for lack of later-life evidence).

I'll end our trip to the Countercultural theatre with **Trevor Nunn**, one of the most respected directors in the UK, a man with a theatrical résumé so impressive it's intimidating. He has of 2010, for instance, directed on Broadway 32 times, on London's West End, 21 times and on television, 9 times (mostly literary films, one literary mini-series); Nunn has won 26 major drama wards, including a slew of Tonys and Laurence Oliver Best Director Awards; for 18 months he was the director of the prestigious Royal Shakespeare Company, and to top it all off, he's been tapped on the shoulders and head with a big sword by the Queen, something the English call being "knighted."

Why do I think Nunn is Countercultural? First, cultural networking: as mentioned, I began to suspect Nunn is Countercultural because as I researched other Countercultural artists, from Monty Python to Tom Stoppard to Andrew Lloyd Webber, the name Trevor Nunn constantly came up. Second, a Google image search shows me a man who I think looks Hippie, and apparently others feel the same way: I found two internet sources who spoke of Nunn's "hippie hair" (Appleyard, "Interview") or of him wearing his hair "in the carefully barbered Restoration/hippie manner he has always favoured" (Appleyard, "Trevor"). And while facial hair is only a low-to-moderate indicator, Nunn usually wears a mustache and goatee. Generally, Trevor Nunn looks Hippie. Also, that others speak so casually of his distinctively "hippie" hair tells me that others likely consider Nunn Hippie. Plus, in *Shakespeare and the Japanese Stage*, Akihiko Senda speaks of "Trevor Nunn, in his *The Winter's Tale*, . . . represent[ed] the shepards' festival as a wild, hippies' party" (Senda), a directorial decision that implies Hippie identity. **HICR: 9.5.**

Generally, Countercultural contributions to the theatre are substantial.

* * *

Shall we **dance**? I'm thinking of a brand new kind of dance, an emerging genre all its Hippie own: tribal-fusion belly dancing, a subgenre of American Tribal Style (ATS) (*Wikipedia,* "American Tribal Style Belly Dance").

There are several touring tribal-fusion troupes, many California and Bay Area based, almost all female. Sometimes, even their names smack of Hippiedom: Jill Parker and Ultra Gypsy,[70] for example. (For some images of Tribal-Fusion Bellydancers, please Google search *Rachael Brice, Bellydance Superstars* or **see Photo #9**.)

Tribal-fusion bellydance is a synthesis of a broad variety of elements—the reason *fusion* is sometimes in their name. *Wikipedia* tells us:

> The style is an extension of American Tribal Style Belly Dance [also, apparently, Countercultural], incorporating popping (the rapid contraction and release of muscles), hip hop, break-dance, Egyptian or Cabaret belly dance, modern and traditional folk forms, including Gypsy, Flamenco, Balinese and others ("Rachel Brice").

And when you see them, you know this isn't exactly your mother's[71] belly dancing—don't look for high heels: many here dance barefoot. Tribal-fusion dancers look very Hippie in their synthesis of decorative elements: lots of tattoos, facial piercings, occasional dreadlocks, and inclusion of Third World, Native American and other "ethnic" items—where exactly do large hoop earrings come from, anyway? They are moving works of art; in costume, tribal-fusion bellydancer Rachel Brice looks like a Hindu goddess.

The contribution to society? Well, does good art need to justify itself? These innovators have created an authentic, vibrant and thriving dance community with artistic value to both audience and performers, and it's living art with a future—a genre and community that's growing and evolving. In the world of dance, here is a shooting star.

Before leaving *dance*, let me note that the Countercultural musicals noted above also have dance; shows like Andrew Lloyd Webber's "Cats" don't win all those Tony Awards without great dance, and in 2009, "Hair" was nominated for a Tony Award in best choreography (*Wikipedia, "Hair"*).

* * *

---

[70] Again, *gypsy* is often a euphemism for *Hippie/Countercultural*, especially when there is no apparent gypsy blood involved.

[71] Unless, of course, your mother happens to be a tribal-fusion belly dancer.

Please, do **not** try this next artistic genre at home unless you're a highly trained professional. Do we call it *dancing*? *gymnastics*? *theater*? Let's call it what they call it: **Cirque du Soleil**, the circus of the sun.

Kiss the whip-cracking lion tamers goodbye. But the daring young man on the flying trapeze? He's back— only he may be a she, and they're multiplying! What a spectacle are the productions of Cirque du Soleil! Combining striking visual imagery in both costume and stage design, world-class performers who are as athletic as they are artistic, innovative ways of allowing those performers to move through space, interesting subject matter (often narrative), and state-of-the-art technology (the seven parts of the Las Vegas stage of *Kà* all move, its 50-ton center stage actually going vertical) *(Wikipedia, "Kà")*, Cirque du Soleil is an international phenomenon. The world has seen nothing quite like it.

Kiss the whip-cracking lion tamers goodbye. But the daring young man on the flying trapeze? He's back— only he may be a she, and they're multiplying! What a spectacle are the productions of Cirque du Soleil!

> "Cirque Du Soleil has now [2007] been seen by 50 million people in 90 countries worldwide since its founding and is currently performing 15 shows simultaneously, reaching an audiences [sic] of 120,000 people on any given weekend," says the China Europe International Business School (paraphrasing Cirque du Soleil's Asia Pacific Marketing Director, Milan Rokic).

So is this international dance phenomenon Countercultural? First, Cirque du Soleil is going to more or less self-identify for us: Rokic explains that Cirque du Soleil was founded by a "raggedy bunch of counterculture hippies" (qtd. in CEIBA).

If that's where they came from, who they are today? Well, as it turns out, we can see clear Countercultural influences in their ongoing work, particularly their recent success "Love," based on an impressive reworking by the "fifth Beatle" (former manager George Martin) and his son, Giles Martin, of original Beatle tracks. Actually, the "Love" numbers were also based on the input of Cirque's appointed director Dominic Champagne, who would "describe an idea he had and ask us [the Martins] for a particular realization of a song." (George Martin, Liner notes). So this entire show is the joint work of those quintessential Hippies, the Beatles, and Cirque du Soleil.

And it turns out, the genesis of "Love" grew out of a personal friendship between Cirque du Soleil's co-founder Guy Laliberte and Beatle George Harrison (George Martin, Liner notes)—networking.

Cirque du Soleil's shows, in addition, are described by George Martin as a "fantastic world," a description immediately comprehensible to anyone who's witnessed the wondrous, sometime surreal, effect they create—visually stunning, often breathtaking. If these shows are not psychedelic, they're at least surreal: audiences see images vivid, dreamlike and hallucinatory.

So given its Hippie roots and the Countercultural elements it still embodies, let's call Cirque du Soleil another astounding contribution of Hippiedom to the arts.

* * *

Great cultures produce great **literature**, and the Counterculture has produced an array of excellent literature and literati.[72]

Allen Ginsberg: Ginsberg is as known for his life as for his literature; both were influential, and in *Return to Aquarius: Seven Who Created the Sixties Counterculture that Changed America*, authors Peter O. Whitmer and Bruce VanWyngarden include Ginsberg as one of their influential seven.[73] As for his literary accomplishments, in particular,

---

[72] We are not interested here in literature which is seen as influencing the Counterculture but that isn't Hippie in origin—things like the *I Ching*, for example.

[73] The seven are William S. Burroughs, Allen Ginsberg, Ken Kesey, Timothy Leary, Norman Mailer, Tom Robbins and Hunter S. Thompson. I won't discuss all here because I don't see Burroughs or Mailer as Hippie; also, Leary is not so much famous for his literature as for his life. In the same vein, the reader might wonder, "Where's Tom Wolfe, author of, among other things, that famous 1968 New Journalism account of Ken Kesey and the Merry Pranksters, *The Electric Kool-Aid Acid Test*?" Well, I don't think Wolfe is Hippie; he wrote his book as an outsider. *Wikipedia* says of him, "Although a conservative in many ways and certainly not a hippie (in 2008, he claimed to have never used LSD and had only tried marijuana once) . . . ."

Ginsberg won a Pulitzer Prize for poetry in 1995 for his *Cosmopolitan Greetings: Poems 1986–1992*. Here, then, is a poet of accord.

Is Ginsberg Hippie/Countercultural? After all, he was actually a Beat, wasn't he? True enough. Still, as mentioned, Beat culture was one of the many streams that eventually formed the river of Counterculture, and it's possible to be both. Cut to the chase: Ginsberg was widely known as "The Hippie Poet." **HICR: 10**

Ken Kesey was the founder of the legendary acid-use-espousing Merry Pranksters, so I'll have no trouble establishing his Hippie pedigree. And his work is of substance; consider, in particular, his bestseller *One Flew Over the Cuckoo's Nest*, made in 1975 by director Milos Forman into a film which won five Academy Awards, including Best Picture. Clearly, *Cuckoo's Nest* critiques mainstream American society as an asylum run by repressives; Big Nurse (Louise Fletcher) seems an obvious play on George Orwell's Big Brother. Kesey's novel *Sometimes a Great Notion* (starring Paul Newman) also found its way into a 1971 Academy Award-nominated film. Entertaining as well as heavy, his is highly successful work. Whitmer and VanWyngarden include Kesey as one of their influential seven literati. **HICR: 10**

Patti Smith: Well known as a poet/singer/songwriter and kick-ass rocker, Patti Smith is also an author. In 2010, *Just Kids*, her autobiographical account of her long-time relationship with photographer Robert Mapplethorpe, won the prestigious National Book Award for Nonfiction, which merits her mention here. As for Hippie identity, let's call this one common knowledge. **HICR: 10**

Tom Robbins: *Wikipedia* summarizes: "His novels are abstract, often wild stories with strong social undercurrents, a satirical bent, and obscure details. He is probably best known for his novel *Even Cowgirls Get the Blues* (1976), which was made into a movie in 1993 directed by Gus Van Sant and starring Uma Thurman and Keanu Reeves." How good is he? Well, Whitmer and VanWyngarden also count Robbins as one of their seven Countercultural "creators." Thus, Robbins' work is both highly popular and very influential.

Is Robbins Countercultural? *Wikipedia* says that a prominent influence on Robbins was his friend, American writer Terence McKenna, an early proponent of psychedelic usage; indeed, Robbins penned an essay called "The Toadstool That Conquered the Universe" about the psychedelic fungi, *amanita muscaria*; it was published in

High Times in 1976 (Daurer). Robbins also tends to look Hippie **(see Photo #10)**, and his Hippie identity is probably common knowledge.

HICR: 10

Richard Brautigan: He was a poet and novelist who died in 1984; *Wikipedia* says it best: "His work often employs black comedy, parody, and satire. . . . when his novel *Trout Fishing in America* was published in 1967, Brautigan was catapulted to international fame and labeled by literary critics as the writer most representative of the emerging countercultural youth movement of the late 1960s, ... *Trout Fishing in America* has so far sold over 4 million copies worldwide." Apparently, he also collaborated with the Beatles, producing a spoken-word recording for their short-lived label, Zapple (*Wikipedia*, "Richard Brautigan").

His work is also seen as having a Zen Buddist influence, among others (*Wikipedia*, "Richard Brautigan"), so again we see Hippiedom's opening to the East. In photographs, Brautigan looks very Countercultural **(see Photo #11),** and he passes an ethnic-definition test pretty easily; in fact, since everyone seems to agree Brautigan is Hippie-American, we can consider this a common-knowledge proof. **HICR: 10**

T.C. Boyle: Since 1982, Thomas Coraghesson Boyle has published at least 12 novels, including *World's End* (1987), a recipient of the Pen/ Faulkner Award for Fiction; *East is East* (1990); *The Road to Wellville* (1993), made into a 1994 film directed by Alan Parker; *The Tortilla Curtain* (1995); and *The Women* (2009). He's also produced several short-story collections and is regarded as one of America's best contemporary writers.

The Dictionary of Literary Biography says that much of Boyle's appeal lies "in his creation of outrageous characters, bizarre situations, and deliberately inflated comparisons. Hip, erudite, and audacious, his fiction is widely praised for its black comedy, incongruous mixture of the mundane and the surreal, wildly inventive and intricate plots, manic energy, and dazzling wordplay."

Is Boyle Countercultural? Photos on his website show a younger self sporting a huge head of frizzy hair and hanging out with other longhairs; currently, he wears a trademark earcuff; his face is goateed, and notice the amulet **(see Photo #12)**. In the 1980's, he had a rock band called The Ventilators, and National Public Radio notes:

178

... his literary reputation owes much to rock 'n' roll ... The characters and settings in one of Boyle's best-known stories, "Greasy Lake," were directly inspired by Bruce Springsteen's "Spirit in the Night," a song about an all-night party with bikers and rockers at a local hang-out. And in *Drop City*, the Van Morrison song "Mystic Eyes" is used to underscore the novel's central conflict between a hippie commune in Alaska and the locals they incense. (NPR)

Yes, his 2003 novel *Drop City*—originally the name of a Hippie commune in Colorado famous for its geodesic "zomes"—tells the tale of a California Hippie commune forced to relocate to Alaska. *The Kansas City Star* says *Drop City* was written by "an unapologetic child of the psychedelic revolution"[74] (qtd. in *Drop City* jacket notes). In short, yes, Boyle appears Hippie-American. **HICR: 10.**

Hunter S. Thompson: *Gonzo journalism* is when reporters "involve themselves in the action to such a degree that they become central figures of their stories" (*Wikipedia*, "Hunter S. Thompson"), "[it] blurs the distinctions between writer and subject, fiction and non-fiction" (Snelgar), and "was based on the idea that fidelity to fact did not always blaze the way to truth. . . . that a deeper truth could be found in the ambiguous zones between fact and fiction" (Lengel and Weil). It's a subjective, interactive journalism characterized by outrage, profanity and in-your-face analogies and images. It's not polite; it's supposed to grab you by the lapels and slap your face. Gonzo journalism is now a recognized style of writing, and Hunter S. Thompson is its original.

Thompson's most famous work *Fear and Loathing in Las Vegas* was made into a 1998 film directed by Monty Python's Terry Gilliam and starring Johnny Depp, and the *Washington Post* tell us, "His books on politics and society were regarded as groundbreaking among journalists and other students of current affairs in their irreverence and often angry insights" (Lengel and Weil). Narrated by Johnny Depp, the documentary *Gonzo: The Life and Work of Dr. Hunter S. Thompson* was released in 2008.

---

[74] And thank you, T.C. Boyle, for being "unapologetic."

Countercultural credentials? Oh, yeah. A number of Countercultural luminaries attended his funeral—comedian/actor Bill Murray, *Rolling Stone* publisher Jann Wenner, and actors Johnny Depp, Jack Nicholson and Sean Penn and the now-late CBS correspondent Ed (with the earring) Bradley (*Wikipedia*, "Hunter S. Thompson"). So Thompson definitely hung in Hippie circles. Thompson rose to national prominence through *Rolling Stone,* which first featured his writing; also, Thompson once said, "I have always loved marijuana. It has been a source of joy and comfort to me for many years. And I still think of it as a basic staple of life, along with beer and ice and grapefruits—and millions of Americans agree with me" (qtd. in UBR, Inc.).

In fact, Thompson was a Hippie nationalist, this documented in a 1970 *Rolling Stone* piece "Freak Power in the Rockies" (or "The Battle of Aspen") (*Wikipedia*, "Hunter S. Thompson"). Thompson was an activist/organizer, focusing on Hippies and their place in society, the essence of a 1969 mayoral campaign he supported in Pitkin County, Colorado (the Aspen area); at one point, Thompson even armed himself in perceived defense of what he saw as Countercultural rights (*Wikipedia*, "The Battle of Aspen")—not your stereotypical Hippie pacifist. (**See photo #13.**)

The following year, he ran a near-successful campaign for sheriff on what was known as "The Freak Platform." *Wikipedia* notes:

> The platform included promoting the decriminalization of drugs (for personal use only, not trafficking, as he disapproved of profiteering), tearing up the streets and turning them into grassy pedestrian malls, banning any building so tall as to obscure the view of the mountains, and renaming Aspen "Fat City" to deter investors. Thompson, having shaved his head, referred to his opponent as "my long-haired opponent," as the Republican candidate had a crew cut. ("The Battle of Aspen")

And in his campaign for sheriff, Thompson promised that if he was elected, he would never to come to work under the influence of mescaline[75] (*Wikipedia*, "The Battle of Aspen"). So yes, Hunter S. Thompson was definitely Countercultural. **HICR: 10.**

---

[75] Typical politician!

Terry Southern: *Wikipedia* says of him:

> Southern's dark and often absurdist style of broad yet biting satire helped to define the sensibilities of several generations of writers, readers, directors and film goers. He is credited by journalist Tom Wolfe as having invented New Journalism with the publication of "Twirling at Ole Miss" in *Esquire* in 1962, and his gift for writing memorable film dialogue was evident in *Dr. Strangelove, The Loved One, The Cincinnati Kid, Easy Rider* and *The Magic Christian*. His work on *Easy Rider* helped create the independent film movement of the 1970s.

He also wrote several novels, including the best-selling 1963 work, later a motion picture, *Candy*. Terry Southern, who died in 1995, was—is—important.

And the case for Southern being Countercultural/Hippie? First, there's his Countercultural subject matter as in *Easy Rider*; also, one of his best known short stories is "Red-Dirt Marijuana." A memoir of Southern by Gail Gerber (with Tom LaSanti) is called *Trippin' with Terry Southern: What I Think I Remember* and has a psychedelic background on the cover. Southern's picture is actually on the iconic cover of *Sgt. Pepper's Lonely Hearts Club Band* (he's the one wearing sunglasses) (*Wikipedia*, "Terry Southern"); in terms of Countercultural networking, he seems well connected. Photos of Southern show someone who looks relatively Hippie (shoulder-length hair and a beard). The inventor of New Journalism, a skilled satirist, a screenwriting pioneer, a legend—let's call Terry Southern Hippie. **HICR: 10**

Gregory David Roberts is an Australian famous for his epic, largely autobiographical novel *Shantaram,* set mostly in India, particularly Mumbai. And I say "epic" because the protagonist, Lin, starts out as a convict in Australia; he escapes and lands in Mumbai. While some dispute Roberts' claims, he says he set up a small medical dispensary in a shantytown there. He soon begins working for an Indian mafia, whose leader becomes Lin's guru/master. In a rural Indian village, he gets his Indian name, Shantaram, which means *peace*. He's jailed in an appalling Indian prison and later wreaks crazed vengeance on the freakish madam who put him there. He follows his mentor to Afghanistan to fight with the *mujahedeen* against the Soviets and barely survives. He kills someone in a raid on a rival mob. He's disappointed in love. He checks himself into an opium den and has to be rescued from it by old friends. Well, it's a wild ride in a "rad" life.

Influential Oprah Winfrey has Tweeted that she considers *Shantaram* one of her favorite novels (AFP), and for almost a decade, Johnny Depp has been struggling to turn *Shantaram* into a film (*Wikipedia*, "Shantaram")—it may soon actually happen. Also, in October of 2015, a sequel to *Shantaram*, *The Mountain Shadow*, was published.

I think Roberts is Hippie for three reasons: first, his book's film's association with Johnny Depp, two, Roberts' connection with the East, and three, Roberts' appearance: beyond-shoulder-length hair, a large mustache and sometimes wire-rim glasses. **HICR: 9.75**

David Foster Wallace: Wallace died in 2008 at the age of 46; his fame continues to grow. *Time* called his most famous work, the 1996 novel *Infinite Jest*, one of the 100 best English-language novels from 1923 to 2005. His last and unfinished novel, *The Pale King (2011)* was a finalist for the 2012 Pulitzer Prize for Fiction. *Wikipedia* adds, "*Los Angeles Times* book editor David Ulin called Wallace 'one of the most influential and innovative writers of the last 20 years' . . . A biography of Wallace was published in September 2012, and critical literature on his work has developed in the past decade." And in 2015, a biopic of Wallace's life was released, *The End of the Tour*, directed by James Ponsoldt.

As for Hippie identity, Wallace is often seen as Hippie; thus, Ben Liebing reports, "David Foster Wallace was one of those writers definitive of a generation of neo-hippies and hard thinkers" (Liebing). Foster was a marijuana user (*Rolling Stone*, "Six Things"); particularly, Wallace always looked Hippie with shoulder-length hair, a beard, roundish rimless glasses and trademark headscarf.**(See Photo #15.) HICR: 9.75 to 10**[76]

Countercultural Rock, Folk-Rock Lyrics: Many Countercultural lyrics rise to the level of literature. Rock and folk-rock—their often-literary lyrics are a major reason for their success. It's no accident that if we'd never heard the song, that if we'd just read the words, we'd recognize it as poetry, and often very good poetry. Further, musical

---

[76] Try this on: The infamous neoconservative Supreme Court Justice Anton Scalia, (you know, the guy who in his angry dissent to legalization of gay marriage, said of promiscuity, "Ask the nearest hippie") was a huge DFW fan, so much so that in 2007, he arranged a lunch with Wallace.

lyrics have far more social impact than other poetry—compare the sales of poetry books to those of lyrical rock albums. Not close, is it? Good lyrics are the poetry of people's lives. Let me mention here Bob Dylan, Joni Mitchell, Jerry Garcia and add to them literally dozens of unamed others.

Now there's an entire category of literature here that I don't want to neglect: Counterculturists writing **non-fiction**. We might call these writers those of the "popular press"; I suppose I should include myself among them. Again, there are dozens, many highly successful and prestigious writers. As for names, consider, for starters, the many authors I cite in this book as evidence. Would Barbara Lee Horn, for instance, write what appears to be a doctoral dissertation on

> **Many Countercultural lyrics rise to the level of literature. Rock and folk-rock—their often-literary lyrics are a major reason for their success. It's no accident that if we'd never heard the song, that if we'd just read the words, we'd recognize it as poetry, and often very good poetry.**

Hair if she weren't Countercultural? I doubt it.

Generally, in terms of producing noteworthy literature, Hippie culture makes a strong showing.

* * *

Consider now our contributions to the once lowly world of **cartoons and comics**. They've come a long ways, and much of the credit goes to the Counterculture.

Let's begin with that genre of comics associated with Hippie culture: **"underground comix."** *Wikipedia* explains: "Underground comix reflect the concerns of the 1960s counterculture: experimentation in all things, drug-altered states of mind, rejection of sexual taboos, and ridicule of the establishment. The spelling 'comix' was established to differentiate these publications from mainstream 'comics.'" Then noted are several underground cartoonists: Vaughn Bode, Kim Deitch, Justin Green, Rick Griffin, Jay Lynch, Dan O'Neill, Trina Roberts, Gilbert Shelton, Art Spiegelman (covered below), R. Crumb and his apparent mentor S. Clay

Wilson. We won't discuss them all, considering, for brevity's sake, just the best known: R. Crumb.

R. Crumb is a seminal cartoonist. As much as anyone, he stretched the cartoon genre, moving beyond the flat characters of so many *Superman*-type strips. Late 1960s, standing on a street corner in Haight-Ashbury, selling his *Zap Comix* out of a baby carriage (Crumb 84), here was this eccentric genius using cartoons to document Hippie culture, to parody it and mainstream society, and to discuss his every insecurity and sexual yearning. He's been phenomenally successful and influential. As Crumb describes his rise: "From shack to chateau" (Crumb, title). In 2008, the Philadelphia Institute of Contemporary Art opened a show called "R. Crumb's Underground." *New York Times* reviewer Ken Johnson sings praise: "Mr. Crumb—a draftsman of transcendent skill, inventiveness and versatility, a fearlessly irreverent, excruciatingly funny satirist of all things modern and progressively high-minded, and an intrepid explorer of his own twisted psyche—remains the genre's [cartooning's] gold standard."

He's also drawn *New Yorker* covers and is increasingly at home in the world of "fine arts" (Kitchen). Evidence of Crumb's notoriety is the well-received 1994 film biography *Crumb,* directed by Terry Zwigoff.

Is Crumb Countercultural? Although Crumb has experience with LSD and has obviously spent time within Hippie culture, he seems alienated from it (Crumb 95). Still, whatever discomfort Crumb might feel at being classified Hippie, how could we not call him, or at least his work, Countercultural? Consider, for example, his famous album cover for Big Brother and the Holding Company's *Cheap Thrills* or the widely printed "Stoned Agin!" poster that once graced thousands of Hippie walls. The Grateful Dead lyric "keep on truckin" and the related graphic seem to be of Crumb origin. His work is so interwoven with the Counterculture, it would seem absurd to say Crumb's work isn't Countercultural. Also, without that Hippie audience to popularize Crumb, his career may never have flowered.

So personal identity issues aside, let's call this founder of modern comics, or at least his work, Countercultural.[77] **HICR: 9.5**

---

[77]   Ummm . . . it just makes me want to bite into a Devil Girl Choco-Bar and think lascivious thoughts as I eat it!

Garry Trudeau: The comic strip *Doonesbury* was created by Garry Trudeau in 1968[78] for the *Yale Daily News*. In 1975, Trudeau became the first to win a Pulitzer Prize for editorial cartooning, and he was a finalist in 1989. In 1983, Trudeau (collaborating with Elizabeth Swados) turned his popular strip into a Broadway musical. "Out of about 250 comic strips circulated in English-language newspapers throughout the world, *Doonesbury* is in the top 10, carried in 1,400 papers," says Salon Brilliant Careers, adding, "Wiley Miller, who draws a semi-political comic strip called *Non Sequitur*, calls Trudeau 'far and away the most influential editorial cartoonist in the last 25 years'" (Rubien). Like so many Countercultural ventures, *Doonesbury's* success is stunning.

Can we claim Trudeau and his creations as Countercultural? Actually, Trudeau more or less self-identifies: *The Yale Daily News* reports, "Trudeau confronted war in his early *Doonesbury* comics from what *he* calls a 'countercultural perspective'" (emphasis added) (Carlson).

And his work often smacks of Counterculturality: Two of *Doonesbury's* most enduring and popular characters are California Hippie Zonker Harris and his "Uncle Duke," a send up of Hunter S. Thompson. Throughout much of the seventies, several *Doonesbury* characters lived at the fictional Walden Commune. Not only does *Doonesbury* feature prominent Hippie characters, but (applause here), Trudeau has kept them identifiably Hippie through the decades—no mindless parroting of Hippies Were Just a Thing of the Sixties.

In Trudeau's *Doonesbury*, we have a great American institution, courtesy the Counterculture. **HICR: 10**

Tom Toles: Hailing from Buffalo, NY, Tom Toles was first a political cartoonist at the University of Buffalo's student newspaper, *The Spectrum*, during the stormy late Sixties (the staff was so used to having tear gas seep into their office, they purchased gas masks) (Liquori). Toles then became the cartoonist for two local papers, the *Buffalo Courier-Express* (1973-82) and the *Buffalo News* (1982-2002) where in 1990, he won a Pulitzer Prize for editorial cartooning. In 2002, in return for three investigative reporters, two syndicated columnists and a want-ad editor to be later named, he was traded[79] to that pillar of

---

[78] Actually, *Doonesbury's* comic predecessor, *Bull Tales*, began in 1968, and *Doonesbury,* in 1970.

[79] This is, of course, a bit of silliness on my part. Shame on me!

185

American journalism *The Washington Post*. Being "inside the beltway" has made this already important pundit even more influential. In the world of editorial cartooning, Tom Toles is a star; in the world of national politics, Tom Toles is powerful.

First, Toles looks the way Hippie males often look (**see Photo #16**)—a prominent beard, a mustache and longish hair—apparent to readers in Toles' trademark asides where he comments on his cartoon beside a drawing of himself at his drawing table. In 2008 in the D.C. area, Toles began playing drums in the rock band Suspicious Package (*Wikipedia*, "Tom Toles"). Interviewer Irene J. Liguori of *Buffalo Spree* says of Toles, who didn't expect to cartoon after college, "He [Toles] was, *he says*, ready to settle into the Age of Aquarius . . . ." (emphasis added). Lastly, Toles speaks truth to power in a way few others do. A 2006 cartoon, in particular, showing then Defense Secretary Donald Rumsfeld in a doctor's coat, examining a quadruple amputee whose chart reads "US Army" and pronouncing, "I'm listing your condition as 'battle hardened'" elicited an angry protest from the Pentagon (*Wikipedia*, "Tom Toles"). So like the Counterculture itself, Toles is a rebel with a cause. Chalk up a second Pulitzer for Hippiedom. **HICR: 10**

Art Spiegelman: Here's another cartooning genius and rising star, largely because he's one of the most successful practitioners of that emerging genre, the graphic novel. It's serious cartooning combining painting-quality visuals with literary-quality narrative. Spiegelman's *Maus*—there are two volumes: "My Father Bleeds History" (1986) and "And Here My Troubles Began" (1991)—is the story of his father, a Jew who endured Auschwitz. Pulitzer Prize administrators at Columbia University were unable to locate this genre in existing categories and in 1992 awarded Spiegelman a Special Award. Comics critic Alan Moore is "convinced that Art Spiegelman is perhaps the single most important comic creator working within the field" (qtd. in Gravette). For ten years, Spiegelman drew the beloved covers of *The New Yorker*, including the magazine's famous 9/11 cover. In 2005, Spiegelman was named by *Time* as one of their "Top 100 Most Influential People" (*Wikipedia*, "Art Spiegelman").

Impressed? Okay, how's he Hippie? As noted above, he was a pioneering "underground comix" artist, but here's what I think clinches it: *Wikipedia* notes, "In 1973 he co-edited with Bob Schneider *Whole Grains: A Collection of Quotations*, featuring the notable words of Countercultural icons like Timothy Leary, Allen Ginsberg and Bob

Dylan before they got much play in such mainstream reference works as *Bartlett's Familiar Quotations*" ("Art Spiegelman"). Spiegelman and Schneider's book is apparently often mis-shelved as a cookbook, but "whole grains" and everything about this book screams Hippie. Thus, I'm going to call Art Spiegelman Countercultural; I'll place his Pulitzer alongside the others. **HICR: 9.5**

Matt Groening: Can you shout, "D'oh!" *Wikipedia* tells us that Matt Groening is the creator of *The Simpsons*, which began as part of the *Tracy Ullman Show* in 1987 and was then picked up by Fox in 1989 as a stand-alone half-hour show. Now America's longest-running sitcom and its longest-running television series, *The Simpsons* has won 24 Emmys (television's equivalent of the Academy Awards), 26 Annies (the Award of the International Animated Film Association) and a Peabody (an international award for television and radio excellence). The show was also named by *Time* as the 20th century's best television series ("The Simpsons"). *The Simpsons* seems to have originated the rising genre of the animated television sitcom, and not only is the show highly popular in the United States, it has broad international appeal, airing in over 200 countries (Muñoz). Way impressive.

Can we call Groening and his show Countercultural? Easily. First, Groening is a self-identifier: in an interview with *Wired*, he comments, "Yeah, I am a hippie, I admit it," and it turns out some of his artistic inspirations are "underground psychedelic comics and R. Crumb" (Kelly, Kevin). Also, the show itself exhibits Countercultural aspects: first, it has Hippie characters, such as Leo the heavy-metalhead school-bus driver, and frequently features, in animated form, Countercultural bands such as Aerosmith, The Rolling Stones, The Red Hot Chili Peppers, The Who, U2, REM, The Smashing Pumpkins and others (Grierson).

> **Let's summarize the Counterculture's contributions to modern comics and cartoons: first, the highly successful new genre of underground comix— you might even say that the Counterculture re-invented the comic book; second, three Countercultural Pulitzer Prize winners—Garry Trudeau, Tom Toles and Art Spiegelman—and topping it all off, the stupendous success of Matt Groening and *The Simpsons*.**

Second, the show clearly lampoons mainstream America and questions authority; Groening notes, "It annoys the hell out of some critics because we're saying the authorities don't have your best interests at heart" (qtd. in Kelly, Kevin) **HICR: 10**

* * *

Let's ramble on, considering Countercultural contributions to **graphic arts and photography**. We'll look at Countercultural posters, Countercultural record-album covers, Peter Max and photographer Annie Leibovitz.

Countercultural poster art: Here again, Hippiedom seems responsible for the development of a new genre. With the birth of the Counterculture, psychedelic rock posters became popular. Many of these came directly out of Haight-Ashbury where early Counterculturists created concert posters for psychedelic rock bands including the Grateful Dead, Quicksilver Messenger Service and Jefferson Airplane.

Today, you can see rock-poster art sold on PBS's *Antiques Roadshow*—a valued commodity. And increasingly, we see art museums giving this work the respect it deserves. In the spring of 2009, for instance, The Denver Art Museum opened a show entitled "The Psychedelic Experience: Rock Posters from the San Francisco Bay Area, 1965-71." Featured artists were Wes Wilson, Bonnie MacLean, Victor Moscoso, Rick Griffin, Lee Conklin and David Singer and the team of Alton Kelly and Stanley Mouse. Of the exhibit, University of Denver art professor Scott Montgomery comments, "Not every museum would have done this. . . . Graphic design has been relegated a second-class citizen. Rock 'n' roll art has not even been given citizenship" (qtd. in Darcangelo).

Related to Hippie poster art are **Hippie album covers.** Although there were record albums long before the late Sixties, record sales began to grow dramatically at that time, so when Hippie culture revolutionized the album cover, it had an impact—just as lyrics became popular poetry, album covers became popular art. Consider the evolution of Beatle album covers: before the four went Hippie, their album covers were routine; then, the cover of the 1965 album *Rubber Soul* featured a slightly distorted photo of the band taken at a peculiar, upward angle, accompanied by the title in a sort of psychedelic font—interesting and distinctive. Next, the cover of the 1966 album *Revolver* was an integration of ink drawing and photographs; it was artistically sophisticated in a way album covers just hadn't been.

Before Hippie culture, album covers were usually perfunctory and predictable; in the hands of Hippie culture, album covers came into their own as an art form. Suddenly, it wasn't enough to cut a great album: that great album needed an equally great cover. On the website, the reader can see illustrations of several covers:

First, the striking cover of the 1968 album *Crown of Creation* by Jefferson Airplane (**see Photo#17**). Second, in 1971, Airplane alumni Paul Kantner and Grace Slick produced *Sunfighter*. Its cover (**see Photo #18**) is, in my opinion, stunning—a cross between the Lady of the Lake and the most striking baby picture one is likely to see.

Like much successful art, the cover of the Beatles 1968 album *Sgt. Pepper's Lonely Hearts Club Band* is so famous, so recognizable, that it's been widely imitated and parodied. In 1967, the Rolling Stones released *Their Satanic Majesty's Request*, the cover of which displayed the heavily costumed band members "inside" a holographic photo—interesting and original.

Another way the Counterculture pushed the envelope of cover art was by having a musician's own graphic art on the cover. Good examples would be the stylish drawing/painting on the cover of Joni Mitchell's 1970 *Ladies of the* (**See photo #19**), her oil paintings for her 1979 album *Mingus* (if jazz were a painting, here's how it would look) and the cover of Cat Stevens' 1970 *Tea for the Tillerman (see Photo #20)*. There are, of course, many more album covers that the reader will recall.

Sadly, most of these illustrators aren't receiving the accolades they deserve. Neon Park, creator of Little Feat covers, is a name many know; of course, R. Crumb did the *Cheap Thrills* cover mentioned above. Otherwise, these often superb artists seem anonymous, their credit subsumed in the name of a band or artist. That injustice aside, Hippiedom deserves credit for creating this beloved form of popular art.

As Hippie culture was coming into its own in the late Sixties, **Peter Max** became its first recognized graphic artist; in particular, he was on the cover of *Life*; inside was an eight-page profile. Max then signed marketing deals; next thing you know, on your bed, you had Peter Max sheets, and on the bedside table was a Peter Max clock. Max began as a psychedelic poster artist; now there's even a Continental Airlines Boeing 777 called "Peter Max" that he's painted—stunning. He was commissioned by the US Postal Service to create two stamps. He worked

189

with Lee Iacocca, former head of Chrysler, to raise funds for the bicentennial Statue of Liberty restoration. In 2007, the de Young Museum in San Francisco saluted the fortieth anniversary of the Summer of Love with a Max exhibition, and Max issued of new version of his classic "Love" poster for the occasion (*Wikipedia*, "Peter Max"). (**See Photo #21.**) Suffice it to say, the

Is Peter Max Counter-cultural? Well, is the Pope Catholic? Is Ted Nugent a self-hating Hippie? Of course he is!

man's work is as popular as it is gorgeous; we'd be hard pressed to find another contemporary graphic artist so well-known, so successful.

Is Peter Max Countercultural? Well, is the Pope Catholic? Is Ted Nugent a self-hating Hippie? Of course he is! I saw Max a few years back, making an appearance in a local PBS studio. The host asked Max, "So, were you a hippie?" and Max immediately responded: "I *am* a Hippie: I'm *still* a Hippie." Yes, exactly. And just as Hippie culture is a vibrant, living thing, so is the art of Peter Max. He continues to do Hippiedom proud. **HICR: 10**

Annie Leibovitz: The *NY Times* calls her "one of the world's most successful photographers . . ." (qtd. in *Wikipedia*, "Annie Leibovitz"). In 1973, *Rolling Stone* publisher Jan Wenner appointed Annie Leibovitz chief photographer, and before she left the magazine in 1983, she created some of the most talked-about images in journalism. Consider, for example, her amazing 1980 photograph of John Lennon and Yoko Ono taken only hours before Lennon's death—from a side view, a naked Lennon curls in fetal position around a clothed Ono. In 1991, she created a series of controversial nude photos of actress Demi Moore, then pregnant, which appeared on the cover and in *Vanity Fair*. In 2007, the Queen of England commissioned Leibovitz to do official photos for a BBC documentary; when Liebovitz suggested Her Majesty remove her tiara, a scene ensued, and BBC mishandling of it resulted in a scandal (*Wikipedia*, "Annie Leibovitz"). Within the world of photographic portraiture, Leibovitz is an original, a genius.

As her *Rolling Stone* ties might suggest, Leibovitz is Countercultural. Here is her sister Barbara Leibovitz, director of the 2007 documentary *Annie Leibovitz: Life Through a Lens,* describing herself: ". . . I'm the youngest of six in a very hippie family. They were all artists" (qtd. in Johnson, Neala). Include Annie Leibovitz in the "all artists," as clearly

---

190

seems intended, and we have convincing identification of Hippie identity. **HICR: 10**

* * *

Hippies in Hollywood

Next stop in the arts: Countercultural contributions to **cinema**. Let's begin with the Counterculture's early-1970s rescue of Hollywood, something film historians now call *New Hollywood*. Here's how American Cinematique.com describes it: "The New Hollywood filmmakers embraced the counter-culture spirit of the late 60's with a vengeance . . . ."

From the introduction of his 1998 book *Easy Riders, Raging Bulls: How the Sex-Drugs-and-Rock 'n' Roll Generation Saved Hollywood* is the take of film writer Peter Biskind:

> Hollywood . . . was at least half a decade behind the other popular arts. So it was some time before the acrid odor of cannabis and tear gas wafted over the pools of Beverly Hills and the sounds of the shouting reached the studio gates. But when flower power finally hit in the late '60s, it hit hard. . . . "It was like the ground was in flames and there were tulips coming up at the same time," recalls Peter Gruber . . . later head of Sony Pictures. (14)

And Biskind later describes the New Hollywood as "when the Hippies finally did come knocking . . ." (*Easy*, 22)

The wilting of the Old Hollywood, according to Biskind, was due to the widespread adoption of television, a fair-trade decision called the Paramount Case, and what appears to be a withering in the popularity of what were then mainstream American tastes—as if they had run their course.

"But," Biskind writes, "when flower power finally hit in the late '60s, it hit hard. . . . 'It was like the ground was in flames and there were tulips coming up at the same time,' recalls Peter Gruber . . . later head of Sony Pictures."

Bewildered Hollywood moguls were desperate; losing money and market share, they looked to new, creative, "artsy" directors and began again emphasizing the director's role, something known as *auter theory*[80] and promoted in particular by, Biskind adds, Andrew Sarris of the Countercultural *Village Voice* (*Easy*, 16). Goaded by European art films and Japanese cinema, as well, you might say Hollywood went bohemian; American film became, once again, intelligent and important.

Thus, the New Hollywood saved Hollywood and opened a period now widely hailed as a golden age of American film (*Easy*, 16). New Hollywood films began as early as 1967 with Warren Beatty's *Bonnie and Clyde* and ended around 1982 with Ridley Scott's *Blade Runner* (*Wikipedia*).

Claiming New Hollywood was completely Countercultural would be casting our net too broadly—for example, I wouldn't call Woody Allen Hippie. Still, it's clear that the New Hollywood was heavily Countercultural and was an integral part of a larger, emerging Counterculture. Biskind:

> . . . the dream of the New Hollywood transcended individual movies. At its most ambitious, the New Hollywood was a movement to cut film free of its evil twin, commerce, enabling it to fly high through the thin air of art. The filmmakers of the '70s hoped to overthrow the studio system, or at least render it irrelevant, by democratizing filmmaking, putting it into the hands of anyone with talent and determination. (*Easy*,17)

Biskind's description of New Hollywood sounds strikingly similar to Countercultural reasons for inventing the Personal Computer; we hear or infer the same themes: democratization; individual empowerment and personal freedom, particularly of expression; rebellion against the tyranny of moneyed interests, and the deep desire to create art. The invention of the PC and New Hollywood—same content, different forms and arenas.

As it turns out, much of New Hollywood was at Warner Brothers. Biskind:

---

[80] That is, the film is largely the product of the director; he or she is the primary artist who's responsible for it, the "author" of the cinematic book.

"You went to Universal and they all looked like cutouts," recalls Nessa Hyams. Once you got to Warners, you were in the middle of Woodstock. Five o'clock in the afternoon, instead of the clinking of ice in a glass would be the aroma of marijuana wafting down the first floor. Adds Sanford, "It was sort of an asset to be into pot and acid. We were all hippies." (*Easy*, 84)[81]

Biskind believes New Hollywood's actual demise began mid-seventies with the advent of the "block-buster mentality" (*Easy*, jacket) exemplified by the vast commercial successes of Stephen Spielberg's *Jaws (1975)* and George Lucas' first *Star Wars (1977)*. If for Biskind, New Hollywood was the revolution, Spielberg's *Jaws*[82] and Lucas' *Star Wars* hailed the counterrevolution—a renewed dominance of art-and-soul-crushing avarice; in turn, according to Biskind, the responses to the rise of shallow commercialism are the growth of independent film, Mirimax and the Sundance Film Festival.

* * *

At this point, instead of following particular Hollywood movements, we'll look at the careers of Countercultural directors, two Countercultural films of note and an emerging genre, thus stepping from the 1970s into the present.

Steven Spielberg has become one of the most successful, powerful and wealthiest directors in Hollywood. His career began in 1968 with the small film *Amblin'*. What followed were famous films: *E.T.* (1982), *Schindler's List* (1993), *Saving Private Ryan* (1998) and many others. Time and again, Spielberg has made film history, and the Academy Awards shout it. The world is wowed, and Spielberg's stature is such that he was chosen as Artistic Director for the 2008 Beijing Olympics. So, you don't get any bigger than this.

We find the most compelling evidence of Spielberg's Hippie identity in his cultural networking; thus, Spielberg tells interviewer Stephen J. Dubner that in his college days he cared for his roommates' cat,

---

[81] This passage seems to echo John Markoff's description of that PC birthplace, the Stanford Research Institute.

[82] Yes, Biskin believes this is true, apparently, even though early Spielberg work is usually considered a part of New Hollywood.

193

Daytripper, who they had dosed with LSD,[83] and occasionally the tripping roomies themselves. Spielberg apparently eschews all drugs, including caffeine (Dubner), yet it's clear he ran in Hippie circles.[84] His first wife, actress Amy Irving, self-identifies: "I'm an old hippie from San Francisco" (qtd. in Californality.com). His second wife, Kate Capshaw? Maybe: she plays a Hippie character in Spielberg's 1995 *How to Make an American Quilt.*

As for who Spielberg associates with, as Dubner interviews him, Countercultural dramatist Tom Stoppard, who has a long working relationship with Spielberg, stops by; then, "After Stoppard comes lunch, delivered from the Amblin kitchen. Spielberg is having broccoli, endame, a tall glass of carrot-spinach juice and some vitamin E. He is on an anti-cancer, weight-losing kick, prescribed by [Countercultural actress] Goldie Hawn"—apparently, a personal friend. And it was widely reported that another close friend, Countercultural actress/activist Mia Farrow, convinced Spielberg to resign as Artistic Director for the 2008 Beijing Olympics.

Sometimes, Spielberg's Counterculturality shows up in his work: His first film (*Amblin'*) was set in Hippie culture and had Hippie characters (*Wikipedia*, "Stephen Spielberg"). And lastly, Spielberg made the *RS* cover in October 1985.

Yes, Spielberg can reasonably be claimed as Hippie-American, especially bearing in mind that such a classification needn't interfere with other ethnic identifications, such as being Jewish-American. Let's assign a **HICR score of 9.0** here; that is, we'll leave a ten-percent chance that he isn't.

Oliver Stone: Stone's work has been as controversial as it's been popular. He's won three Academy Awards: as screen writer for *Midnight Express* (1978) and as best director for *Platoon* (1986) and *Born on the Fourth of July* (1989); other films include *JFK* (1991) and *Natural Born Killers* (1994).

Is Stone Countercultural? His photos don't necessarily show it, but, yes, he is. First, *Platoon* is semi-autobiographical, and Stone's character (Charlie Sheen) is a stoner/Hippie. In addition, his work sometimes deals

---

[83]   I cannot cite this evidence without saying how much I object to "dosing" an animal—or a human.

[84]   This can make you really dizzy.

with Countercultural subjects such as his 1991 film *The Doors*. And Stone is regularly called Countercultural in the media. For example, one reviewer calls *Platoon*, "Oliver Stone's counterculture view of what went on during the Vietnam War" (Smith, Jada); in reference to Stone's two *Wall St.* films starring Countercultural actor Michael Douglas as Gordon "Greed is Good" Gekko, another reviewer refers to Stone as "Gekko's Counterculture creator" (Thompson). I think we're close to a common-knowledge proof here, so let's assign an **HICR of 9.75.**

Peter Jackson: Given the affinity for the works of J.R.R. Tolkien for which the Counterculture is fabled, we might expect the director of the *Lord of the Rings* trilogy and *The Hobbit* to be Hippie. And New Zealander Peter Jackson appears to be so. First, Jackson looks Hippie with his longish hair, a beard and round wire-rimmed glasses **(see photo #25)**. And it's no accident that many of the actors in that trilogy are Countercultural, that the standards of beauty exhibited by those films appear hippie—lots of men with long hair, etc. Many recognize Jackson as Hippie; for example, reporter Felicia Feaster of the *Charleston City Paper* describes Jackson's 2010 film *The Lovely Bones* as a "trippy adaption" (the reference is apparently to hallucinogens) and describes Jackson himself as "an interesting talent, steeped in the counterculture . . . ." Cinema blogger David Clayton comments on Jackson's "counter-cultural productions": "*Fellowship of the Rings* is more of a 1960s motion picture than anything actually produced at that time. Jackson has made exactly the kind of movie an ambitious director might have made back then had all the high tech resources of film making in the year 2001 been available . . ." **HICR: 9.75**

Quentin Tarantino: Currently, one of the most important directors in Hollywood, Tarantino has been a household name since the stunning success of his satiric 1994 crime film *Pulp Fiction*. Is he Hippie? Well, some photos show Tarantino with longish hair; more importantly, a number of photos show him flashing the peace sign **(see Photo #26.).** As for Countercultural networking, he's often casted and directed Countercultural actors, such as David Carradine and Uma Thurman in *Kill Bill* (2004). He's also a marijuana user: he compared Biskind's 2004 book, *Down and Dirty Pictures: Miramax, Sundown, and The Rise of Independent Film*, to "a bag of pot" he couldn't leave alone (jacket), and he's talked about smoking marijuana with actor Brad Pitt (420 Magazine). Apparently, in a marijuana reference, all the clocks in *Pulp Fiction* are set at 4:20 (Jewster). Also, a reviewer speaks of Tarantino's

Inglorious Basterds (2009) as a "'counter-culture' World War II movie" (Azula). And posing with Thurman, Tarantino has appeared on the cover of the *Rolling Stone.*

Let's call Tarantino Hippie-American and call his work a major Countercultural contribution to modern film. **HICR: 9.75.**

Francis Ford Coppola: Francis Ford Coppola became famous after the first *The Godfather* was released in 1972. He's been voted one of the best directors of all time by various film organizations, ranking from 4th to 21st (*Wikipedia*). He's also an accomplished screenwriter.

> **We sometimes find Francis Ford Coppola writing pieces set in Hippie culture; thus, Coppola says of *The Godfather*, "The original script was set all in contemporary time. It had hippies in it."**

Coppola is Hippie-American. First, he's often seen as Countercultural in the media; thus, a film journalist writes of "a burst of creativity in Hollywood, where figures who spent the '60s soaking up the counterculture and making low-budget exploitation features—Francis Ford Coppola, Martin Scorsese, Jack Nicholson—used their new freedoms and their unorthodox training to transform the face of American film" (Walker).

Second, he looks Hippie. Thus, accounts refer to "Coppola's shaggy haired, bearded, 'hippie' appearance" at the time of *The Godfather* (*Wikipedia*). Today, Coppola's hair is shorter, yet he still looks Hippie, more or less **(see photo #27).**

He has experience with marijuana; for instance, "Francis Ford Coppola admits that he ate one of Bill Graham's pot cookies before delivering a particularly inspired address at the 1979 Academy Awards" (NYMag.com). Plus, Coppola has a winery with an "organic herb and produce garden," and he's created a company, Mammarella, that produces "premium organic pasta and sauces" (Francis Coppola Winery). Coppola and his wife, Eleanor, are apparently green—they run of string of "eco-friendly" resorts (Gosselin). Also, we sometimes find Coppola writing pieces set in Hippie culture; thus, Coppola says of *The Godfather*, "The original script was set all in contemporary time. It had hippies in it" (qtd. in Hogg).[85] In terms of Countercultural networking, notice that Coppola got his pot brownie from the legendary Countercultural music promoter Bill Graham. Also, Coppola's films are often filled with Countercultural actors—as we'll see. He directed Johnny Depp in *Don Juan DiMarco* (1995) and apparently has tried to cast Depp several more times (NotStarring.com). Lastly, Coppola was the subject of the November 1, 1979 *Rolling Stone* interview. The evidence here, then, consistently points towards Hippie identity. **HICR: 9.75**

The Coen Brothers: Joel and Ethan Coen are an astonishingly successful Hollywood team with a reputation for quirky humor. According to *Wikipedia*, between them, they do it all—screenwriting, producing, directing, editing, even cinematography. They've made 15 films (Joel directed ten; Joel and Ethan directed five), including a remake of *True Grit* (2010). Their work has been nominated for 23 Academy Awards, has won six; has been nominated for 17 Golden Globes, has won three—impressive stats.

Countercultural identity? Among their most celebrated films is, of course, the Counterculture classic *The Big Leibowski* (1998). Biskind, however, is going to make this easy for us:

> Like the 1970s, the 1990s was pregnant with change. "I remember the New York Film Festival where *Blood Simple* and *Stranger Than Paradise* premiered," said producer Ted Hope. "All of a sudden the Coen brothers get upon stage, and I recognized them from my local supermarket. . . . I was like, 'Oh, my God, it's those stoners from the neighborhood!" (*Down*, 22)

HICR: 9.75

Tim Burton: Burton's impressive body of work is certainly "freaky," (*Wikipedia* calls Burton films "dark, quirky-themed movies"). From the strange urban folktale of *Edward Scissorhands* (1990) to his

---

[85] Since the *Godfather* films have their provenance in the Mario Puzo novel set in Italian-America, this quotation is confusing. As I understand it, to save costs, the studio, Paramount, originally wanted the story set in contemporary time—then, the early 1970s. Coppola resisted this measure, but apparently before he got his way, he penned a 1970s script, and that is what he's referring to here.

reworking of the seemingly hallucinogenic classic that has inspired so much Countercultural art, *Alice in Wonderland* (2010), Burton seems consistently popular at the box office, and he tends to be respected by critics.

Film writers often recognize Burton as Countercultural—reviewer Todd Gilchrist describes part of *Alice in Wonderland* as being Burton "at his most automatically, reliably counterculture"—and Burton is well integrated into the Countercultural network, counting among friends and colleagues Countercultural Winona Ryder and Johnny Depp among many others; also, Depp is the godfather of his children (*Wikipedia*, "Tim Burton"). He apparently hasn't been on the *Rolling Stone* cover, but he was the subject of the *Rolling Stone* interview in July of 1992. Until recently, Burton was also the endogamic non-husband of Helena Bonham Carter, who I'm going to call Countercultural below, and the guy looks Hippie to boot (**see Photo #28**). Okay, what's to argue? Call this cinematic visionary Countercultural. **HICR: 9.75.**

Here are the names and HICRs of three **directors I pulled** from this section:

Arthur Penn, 8.5   Amy Heckerling, 8.5   Jon Landis, 9.0

Next, consider that new cinematic genre, the "**stoner film**." These movies often revolve around marijuana usage, are set in Hippie culture, are made from an insider's perspective and are usually comedies. The genre's archetype appears to be the Cheech and Chong films. Subsequent examples would be Richard Linlater's *Dazed and Confused* (1993), Kevin Smith's *Clerks* (1994), Tamra Davis' *Half Baked* (1998), *The Big Leibowski* (1998)and David Gordon Green's *Pineapple Express* (2008), among many others.

How valuable is this new genre? Well, as with any genre, some examples are better than others. Still, it's clear there's a strong market for such movies and most do at least succeed as humor.[86] Also, the genre is fairly new; it's developing; let's give it some time to hopefully develop more depth. As genre actor/screenwriter/director Seth Rogen asks, "Are we gonna just make movies about trying to get laid over and over again? Or focus on something that's more relevant—while still being funny" (qtd. in Eells).

---

[86]   On the downside, stoner films often stereotype marijuana users as, well, dazed and confused.

Two important Countercultural films: The first is Sam Mendes' *American Beauty* which won Best Picture in 1999. As for its Counterculturality, its title probably hails from the Grateful Dead album of the same name. And the film clearly champions Countercultural values and themes; as *Wikipedia* puts it, regarding protagonist Lester Burnham (Kevin Spacey), "Lester's attempts to recapture his youth [are] reminiscent of how the counterculture of the 1960s combated American repression through music and drugs; Lester begins to smoke cannabis and listen to rock music."

Next, consider the amazing success of James Cameron's 2010 *Avatar*. There are many reasons Avatar set box-office records; among them are its state-of-the-art special effects, including 3-D and IMAX formats. Still, *Avatar's* content screams Hippie. Social conservatives seem outraged by its environmental themes and vilification of imperialist militaries bent on conquest for wealthy corporations; for example, Mary Papenfuss of *Newser* calls her piece "Right-Wingers Go Ballistic Over *Avatar:* Anti-military Sci-Fi 'Hippies' Giving Conservatives Fits."

* * *

Next, we'll foray into the world of **Countercultural actors**: Hollywood, it seems, is disproportionately Hippie. I've trimmed this list to 20 and then supplemented that with a list of several more actors and their HICRs that the reader can read on the supplementary website, HappilyHippie.net.

Johnny Depp: Depp has, of course, become one of the most popular actors in the world; his work in the *Pirates of the Caribbean* series has been a box-office smash. He's a hard working, extremely accomplished actor who's made many intelligent films. And Depp is about as Hippie as you can get—so much so that he's perfect for our Countercultural networking criteria. Find out who Johnny Depp is working with, and you'll likely find out who is Hippie in Hollywood. I consider him a sort of gold standard in Countercultural identification by networking. As brief documentation for Depp's Counterculturality, let me note that he's been on the cover of *RS* five times; he was in attendance at the funeral of Hunter S. Thompson and narrated Thompson's film autobiography—these among many, many other indicators. Essentially, I think we have a common-knowledge proof here, and as the reader will see as I associate Depp with other Counterculturists, his networking score would be astronomical. **HICR: 10**

Gwyneth Paltrow: The highlight of Paltrow's career would seem winning an Oscar for Best Actress for her role in John Madden's *Shakespeare in Love* which, in turn, won the 1998 Oscar for Best Picture. She's also become important and prominent for her work outside of film, including as a natural-foods chef and a parent.

Countercultural identity? Well, in terms of Countercultural networking, she was once engaged to Countercultural actor Brad Pitt; she's concluded a marriage to the lead singer of the Countercultural band Coldplay, Chris Martin. I also found evidence that many of her women friends are Countercultural, including Jennifer Aniston (US Magazine), Winona Ryder and Madonna (see below and website on all three). Paltrow is often described as a "foodie"; she's published two cookbooks, and she eats what might be called a Hippie diet, one that eschews refined carbohydrates and is very natural/organic, and she practices yoga daily (MacLeod). Her first child has a Hippie-ish name, Apple, and she's become a practitioner of what might be called Hippie parenting (929 Radio). Two websites that list Hippie celebrities, Atomica. com and Crushable.com (O'Rourke), list Paltrow; another website has a piece called "The New Hippie Hollywood: From Gwyneth Paltrow to Shailene Woodley" (Roberts). I think we have a common-knowledge proof here. **HICR: 10**

Barbara Hershey: In a career starting in 1968, as of 2016, Barbara Hershey had made a stunning 51 movies (*Wikipedia*). In 1996, she was nominated for the Academy Award as Best Supporting Actress for her role in *Portrait of a Lady*, and although lacking an Oscar, she's won several important acting awards. And as anyone who's seen Hershey knows, she can act—from her role as the spooky Harriet Bird in *The Natural* (1984) to her role as Lee in Woody Allen's *Hannah and Her Sisters* (1986) to her role as Hillary Whitney Essex in *Beaches (1988)*; she was small-town Indiana school teacher Myra Fleener in the now-classic *Hoosiers* (1986). Here is one hard-working, accomplished professional; *Wikipedia* tells us, "the *Chicago Tribune* referred to her as 'one of America's finest actresses.'"

But why no Academy Award?—one nomination for Best Supporting Actress; that's it. Well, to read about Barbara Hershey is to read about discrimination against Hippie-America. Like millions, in the late Sixties, Hershey went Hippie. Attractive, interesting—she got a lot of attention, appearing regularly on talk shows. And in the Countercultural closet, Barbara Hershey wasn't. She famously breastfed her new-born on *The*

Dick Cavett Show. She changed her name to Barbara Seagull, named her son Free and was parenting with Countercultural actor David Carradine. Much of America saw Hershey as the quintissential Hippie/ Flower Child/Earth Mother, and apparently

> **She was persecuted, stereotyped and discriminated against because she's Hippie-American. Hollywood and America owe Barbara Hershey better; their bigoted mistreatment and disrespect of her says far more about them than it does about this stellar actress.**

much of America, including parts of Hollywood, hated her for it. ". . . the hippie label soon became a career impediment and by the late 1970s she was reduced to appearing in made-for-TV embarrassments like *Flood!* and *Sunshine Christmas*," reports WordIQ.com.

Wikipedia notes that in 1979, Knight News Service published a nasty piece which "referred to Hershey as a 'kook' and stated that she was frequently 'high on something' . . . [Hershey] said that this period of her life hurt her career; 'Producers wouldn't see me because I had a reputation for using drugs and being undependable. I never used drugs at all and I have always been serious about my acting career.'"

You know, being married to an alcoholic doesn't necessarily mean you're an alcoholic; that her ex-partner, David Carradine, was a drug abuser doesn't mean Barbara Hershey was a drug abuser. Hershey, then, was persecuted, stereotyped and discriminated against because she's Hippie-American. It's disgraceful; it's unAmerican. Hollywood and America owe Barbara Hershey better. **HICR: 10**

Sean Penn: Here's a Hollywood heavyweight. Not only has Penn made many important movies as an actor—he's won the Oscar for best actor twice, once for *Mystic River* (2003), once for *Milk* (2008)—but he's become an important director and more recently a kind of citizen journalist.

Penn is, of course, widely seen as Countercultural; when, for example, *NY Times* reporter Evelyn Neives reports on how Hippie the Bay Area's Marin County is, one of her reasons is that Sean Penn can be seen there. His first major role was as a stoner in *Fast Times at Ridgemont High*; he plays a gay Hippie in *Milk*. Penn has been on the *Rolling Stone* cover three times; been the subject of the *RS* interview once. He often looks Countercultural, and his private and personal life both exhibit high degrees of Countercultural networking. Let's call Penn Hippie-American. **HICR: 10**

Julia Roberts: Winner of the Academy Award for Best Actress for title role in *Erin Brockovich* (2000), Julia Roberts is a Hollywood legend; her casting in a film, a guarantee of box-office success. She's started her own production company, and a few years ago was rated the eleventh most powerful woman in America (*Wikipedia*).

Okay, is she Hippie? Well, we have an interesting source claiming she is—her ex-bodyguard says, "Julia is a total hippie . . . she's really green" (qtd. in Polilla). And the ex-bodyguard says of Roberts' then husband, Danny Moder: "he's just as much of a hippie" (qtd. in Polilla)—endogamy. Also, Roberts reportedly eats organic food and practices yoga (WorkOutInfoGuru.com). One blogger writes, "[W]hen beautiful Julia Roberts appeared at the 1999 Oscars ceremony with hairy armpits, the world screamed 'hippy' at the TV" (Kelleher), so we have some public perception of Roberts as Countercultural.[87]

Then, there's the 2004 report of Roberts and then-husband Danny Moder passing a joint in Amsterdam during the filming of *Ocean's Eleven*. An onlooker reported, "From the way she [Roberts] put that cigarette together, and judging by the size of it, it was not an ordinary tobacco roll-up as they would probably not have been sharing it if it was" (qtd. in Larsen, "Oceans"). (Sorry, but I find Roberts' subsequent denial of marijuana use unconvincing, something public figures have felt obliged to do because of War on Drugs hysteria.) Further evidence of Roberts' Counterculturality is in her role as Elizabeth Gilbert in *Eat Pray Love (2010)*. Reviewers uniformly describe Gilbert as a "hippie" following an Eastern religious path. Well, not only are Hippie characters more often than not played by Hippies, but as it turns out, Roberts is now a practicing Hindu (*Wikipedia*, "List of converts to Hinduism"), suggesting that Countercultural Elizabeth Gilbert represents Roberts. Generally, I think there's enough here to comfortably call Julia Roberts Hippie-American. **HICR: 9.75**

Jack Nicholson: Here's one of the best actors in Hollywood—in the world. He won the Academy Award for Best Actor for *One Flew Over the Cuckoo's Nest* (1975), for Best Supporting Actor for *Terms of*

---

[87]   Not to mention the evidence of the unshaven "dirty Hippie" armpits themselves!

Endearment (1983), and Best Actor for *As Good as It Gets* (1997) among many, many other awards.

Is he Countercultural? Again, like his colleagues Dennis Hopper and Peter Fonda, it seems common knowledge that when he was younger, he was, but post-Sixties? In 2011, Nicholson went public with the UK's *Daily Mail* about his continuing use of and fondness for marijuana (Celeb Stoner). There's some Countercultural networking in his professional life, teaming with Peter Fonda and Dennis Hopper in *Easy Rider* and working with director Tim Burton twice—*Batman* (1989) and *Mars Attacks!* (1996). In his personal life, he had a long-term relationship with **Anjelica Huston**; my research shows Huston—who, playing across from Nicholson, won the Academy Award for Best Actress for *Prizzi's Honor* (1985)—was and likely is Countercultural. Apparently Nicholson's relationship with Dennis Hopper was lifelong, and a 1981 *Rolling Stone* interview shows him hanging out in the Colorado ski town of Aspen with Huston, Countercultural music producer Lou Adler, Countercultural musician Jimmy Buffett and his wife, Jane, and *60 Minutes* correspondent Ed Bradley (Cahill), who also was apparently Countercultural. And Nicholson was also acquainted with Aspen-based Hunter S. Thompson. Further, Nicholson has been on the cover of *Rolling Stone* five times.

Well, what's missing here is, I suppose, is evidence of a diet of natural/organic foods, an image of Jack Nicholson with a ponytail (in some of his screen roles, he does have longish hair and occasionally a beard) and an affinity for Hippie roles (I don't think I see anything beyond *Psych-Out* (1968) and *Easy Rider (1970)*). I feel comfortable calling Jack Nicholson Countercultural, but let's keep the **HICR at 9.5**—five-percent room for error.

Michael Douglas: Son of the great actor Kirk Douglas, Michael Douglas came into his own, becoming one of the most important actors in America as well as a noteworthy producer. He's won two Academy Awards—the first for producing *One Flew Over the Cuckoo's Nest*, the second for Best Actor as the infamous Gordon Gecko in *Wall Street* (1987)—and his roles have been highly popular—Jack Colton in *Romancing the Stone* (1984) and *Jewel of the Nile* (1985)—and often important, i.e., as the straying husband in 1987's *Fatal Attraction*, a film that riveted the nation. Not surprisingly, in 2009, Douglas received the American Film Institute's Life Achievement Award.

How Hippie is Michael Douglas? He says of the time before he was "discovered" for the television series *The Streets of San Francisco*, "I just spent time being a hippy," (qtd. in Lipworth), and reportedly, he lived in a commune of sorts. Eventful.com reports:

> When he started his career in the mid 1960s people were all too ready to tag him as "the next Kirk Douglas." He defied all those critics by accepting sensitive, quiet, hippie-type roles, a far cry from the macho, leading-man, all-American hero parts that his father was most famous for. It didn't earn Michael much credibility, but it earned him his own identity.

Douglas has played a number of Hippie parts. Also, there's some Countercultural networking in his life; he is, reportedly, a friend as well as a colleague of Oliver Stone. And while I was unable to discover whether or not Douglas uses or has used pot or hallucinogens (it's probably safe to assume he did when younger), he has been an outspoken advocate for legalization of marijuana and a critic of the War on Drugs (ANI). And he's been on the *Rolling Stone* cover four times (once sharing it with actress Jill Claybaugh). All enough, I think, to call Michael Douglas Hippie-American. **HICR: 9.5**

Brad Pitt: Pitt is now one of Hollywood's favorite leading men, but he's also a serious actor who's earned America's respect; he's twice been nominated for an Academy Award—Best Supporting Actor for his work in *12 Monkeys* (1995) and Best Actor for his work in *Benjamin Button* (2008). Pitt also won the Golden Globe for Best Supporting Actor in *12 Monkeys*. A producer, as well, he's considered one of America's most powerful celebrities by *Forbes*, and in 2007, *Time* called him one of the 100 most influential people in the world (*Wikipedia*).

Hippie identity? First, in his private life and sometimes in his screen life, he often looks very Hippie. He's Counterculturally networked: in 2005, he produced *Charlie and the Chocolate Factory*, starring Johnny Depp; in 2010, he made *Inglorious Basterds* for Quentin Tarantino, and news reports had Pitt and Tarantino smoking pot together while in France for the film (*High Times*, "Brad Pitt"). He also used to be involved with Countercultural actress Gwyneth Paltrow; had a long-term relationship with Countercultural Jennifer Aniston; and now, of course, is ending a long-term relationship and marriage to likely Countercultural Angelina Jolie (*Wikipedia*).

And *Cannabis Culture Magazine* comments: "Pitt, who earned fame with tokers everywhere with his role as a honeybear bong-sucking slacker in 1993's *True Romance,* has appeared in public wearing a T-shirt that reads 'I live for hemp,' and also in a sweater with a large pot leaf emblazoned on it" (Larsen, "Celebrity"). Also, Pitt's been of the cover of *Rolling Stone* five times.

It would be nice to know what Pitt eats and a few other things; still, I think we have enough evidence to call Brad Pitt Hippie-American with an **HICR of 9.5**

Susan Sarandon: She's been nominated for Best Actress a mere five times; she won that Academy Award in 1998 for her role in *Dead Man Walking.* She's also, bless her heart, an activist. Hippie? Oh, yeah: she's a self-identifier, telling *The Telegraph* (UK) in 2010, "I'm still a hippie chick" (Bertodano). **HICR: 10**

Jennifer Aniston: Jennifer Aniston has more than arrived in Hollywood. She first succeeded playing Rachael Green in NBC's highly popular and long-running sitcom *Friends*—a role for which she won a Golden Globe, an Emmy and a Screen Actors Guild Award—and she hasn't looked back. Her films have been successful at the box-office, and some of her roles have won critical acclaim. She's now fabulously wealthy and powerful; of course, tabloid obsession with her personal life is a minor Hollywood industry.[88]

Hippie identity? Anistons's diet is described as "good nutrition made up of whole natural foods" (MovieStarBody.com). She also uses and promotes natural/organic cosmetics. She's a marijuana user; CannabisCulture.com calls her a "celebrity stoner": "As for Aniston, she isn't ashamed to be a toker, telling the media 'I enjoy it once in a while. There is nothing wrong with that . . .'" (Larsen, "Celebrity"). Aniston has been on the cover of *Rolling Stone* twice; her role in *Wanderlust* (2011) was playing a disenchanted "straight" woman who, with her husband, joins a Hippie commune. Included is sex, nudity and a pot-smoking scene.

She has some Countercultural connections in her personal life, reportedly spending Thanksgiving 2009 with Gwyneth Paltrow (US Magazine); add a five-year marriage to Brad Pitt. In addition, I think

---

[88] One of my favorite *The Onion* headlines: "Area Woman Emotionally Invested In Jennifer Aniston's Well-Being."

Aniston, even while being "glamorous," often looks Countercultural—
minimal makeup, simple-looking hair style, etc. Our best evidence here,
however, comes from *Friends* co-star Lisa Kudrow, who says that she
was at first clueless as to how to play Hippie Phoebe Buffay; as such, she
said she'd looked to the real-life Jennifer Aniston for inspiration (Female
First). That a close friend and colleague says she sees Aniston as Hippie
gives us strong evidence she is. **HICR: 9.75**

Madonna: Madonna, of course, defines *superstar*. She began
as a dancer and became a famous singer, but among her many
talents is acting. In 1997, she won the Golden Globe for Best Actress
in a Musical for her role in *Evita*. My favorite Madonna role: as
promiscuous center fielder "All the Way" Mae Mordabito in Penny
Marshall's *A League of Their Own* (1992). Madonna has made some
enemies on the way up, yet as reporter Michael McWilliams notes:
"The gripes about Madonna—she's cold, greedy, talentless—conceal
both bigotry and the essence of her art, which is among the warmest,
the most humane, the most profoundly satisfying in all pop culture"
(qtd. in *Wikipedia*).

Hippie? Well, as a teenager, apparently not: she told an interviewer
her high school was divided into "jocks" and "hippies," and she felt she
was neither (Gross). And early in her career, especially, Madonna didn't
seem all that Countercultural. Still, over the years, she's apparently
become Hippie. Debbi Voller, author of *Madonna: The Style Book,* tells
us: "Madonna's *Ray of Light* album [1998] saw the former Material Girl
look to the East and develop an interest in all things spiritual. The world's
most famous Catholic pop star has now also embraced Buddhism"
(119),[89] so we have an Eastern connection. Also, in a profile called "Earth
Mother," a euphemism for a Hippie woman, Voller describes Madonna
as now "New Age" (121).

In addition, Madonna has experience with Countercultural drugs:
she's reportedly used Ectasy (Friends of Cannabis) and marijuana, telling
David Letterman, for instance, she'd smoked a joint before appearing

---

[89]   Strictly speaking, Madonna currently (2011) practices a mystical form of
Rabbinic Judaism known as *Kabala*. It's still sort of Eastern in its tendency
towards mysticism and—according to *Wikipedia*, as Madonna conceives
it—*Kabala* sees a congruence between "spiritual illumination" and "carnal
ecstasy."

on a previous *Late Show* (CBS). Plus, a 2008 headline speaks of a "hippie-dressing Madonna"—this, in her personal life (Hepp). Further, Madonna eats a "macrobiotic, organic, vegetarian diet"[90] (DuDell) that's in the Hippie neighborhood. She's counterculturally networked in her personal life—a Paltrow pal and former wife of Sean Penn, among other things. And the frosting on the cake: Madonna has been on the *Rolling Stone* cover an astonishing 16 times. Since at least the late 1990s, then, Madonna has displayed Hippie identity. **HICR: 9.0**

Jeff Bridges: Hey, the Dude abides. Bridges received cult status playing "Mr. Leibowski" in the Coen Brothers stoner classic *The Big Leibowski (1998)*, a role AMC's Matthew Klein considers one of his "Classic Ten Iconic Hollywood Hippies." The son of actor Lloyd Bridges, Jeff Bridges has become one of the most accomplished actors in Hollywood. For playing Rooster Cogburn in the Coen Brothers' remake of *True Grit (2010)*, he was for the fifth time nominated for an Academy Award; in 2009, Bridges won the Adacemy Award for Best Actor for his portrayal of Bad Blake in *Crazy Heart*. Generally, Bridges is in the midst of a staggeringly successful career.

Is he Hippie? In his professional life, we see a lot of Countercultural networking—the above mentioned work with the Coens, for instance. He also plays Hippies a lot; his character Bill Django in the 2009 *The Men Who Stare at Goats* is Hippie and of course, so is Jeffrey Lebowski, among others. Not only does he frequently look Hippie on screen, but a Google image search shows, he looks Hippie in his private life—usually sporting a goatee and wearing his hair long, often in a ponytail. Bridges has acknowledged being a

> **Hey, The Dude abides. Jeff Bridge received cult status playing "Mr. Leibowski" in the Coen Brothers now classic *The Big Leibowski (1998)*, a role AMC's Matthew Klein considers one of his "Classic Ten Iconic Hollywood Hippies." The son of actor Lloyd Bridges, Jeff Bridges has become one of the most accomplished actors in Hollywood.**

---

[90] She also insists her children eat that diet (DuDell)—another conscientious Countercultural mother.

marijuana user (Answers. com), and he's twice been on the cover of the *Rolling Stone. Wikipedia* reports that Bridges has studied Buddhism and meditates. In November of 2014, I saw Bridges on the cover of a New Age magazine. **HICR: 9.75**

Woody Harrelson: Most of us first saw Harrelson as loveable, dumb-like-a-fox junior bartender Woody in NBC's long-running and beloved sitcom *Cheers.* He's since moved into film, and if an Oscar eludes him, he's become a highly respected actor in Hollywood—one who directors, critics and the public take seriously.

Hippie? Nearly everything about Woody Harrelson screams Hippie. He's perceived by much of the public as Hippie; a webpage called "Woody Harrelson is a Hippie . . . ." (Hot Momma) is an example. *Wikipedia* tells us that he's a legalization advocate—he sits on the NORML board of directors—who's done civil-disobedience work for that cause. He's a staunch environmentalist who's done protests and bio-diesel promotion (*Wikipedia*). His diet is vegan and raw foodist (*Wikipedia*). His wife is described as "a co-founder of Yoganics, an organic food delivery service" (*Wikipedia*)—sounds Hippie to me—and their three daughters have Hippie-sounding names (*Wikipedia*). He also sometimes plays Hippies in film such as his role as the crazed conspiracy theorist in the apocalyptic 2009 film *2012,* as a stoner surfer in the 1993 stoner-comedy *Surfer, Dude,* and there's plenty of Countercultural networking in his professional life.

Harrelson says, "I do smoke [marijuana]" (FrankDiscussion.net). In his private life, he often looks Hippie—he often has longish hair, and I found several photos of Harrelson wearing a Hippie-style stocking cap and a week-old beard—and we sometimes see a visibly Hippie Harrelson on screen. So, call Woody Harrelson Hippie, and do it with gusto! **HICR: 9.75 to 10**

Helen Mirren: This English actress is important: first, she has an impressive background in theatre, including, beginning in 1965, starring in numerous productions of the prestigious Royal Shakespeare Company; second, she's proven herself in film, winning important acting honors, including the Academy Award for Best Actress for her portrayal of Her Majesty in *The Queen* (2006); third, Mirren's has somewhat reluctantly accepted the Order of the British Empire: she's addressed as "Dame Helen Mirren," and you should bow or curtsey slightly as you say this. And, oh, the ultimate indicator of worldly success— *Wikipedia* says there's a wax statue of Mirren at Madame Tussauds London!

Countercultural? The best evidence that Mirren's is Hippie is that she's widely seen as so by the media—common knowledge. The media seem to agree Mirren is Hippie because she was so publicly Hippie during her younger years. She lived in a Hippie commune that apparently included lots of nudity (Moore); she's had lots of drug experiences, including use of LSD (CelebStoner.com). She's tattooed too (People Magazine).

Has Mirren's Hippie flower faded since the Sixties? Well, the media apparently doesn't see it that way; thus, a 2007 profile of Mirren in *Mail Online* (UK) is headlined "Queen of the Hippies" (Moore). And Mirren's fashion choices are described by a fashion blogger in 2011 as "Hippie Chic" (Reynolds). In short, there's no reason to assume Mirren is no longer Hippie, and there's some evidence she still is. Let's call her Hippie-English. **HICR: 10**

Alicia Silverstone: Her most famous role was as Cher, the Beverly Hills in-crowder speaking a distinctive Valley Girl-type dialect in Amy Heckerling's 1995 adaption of Jane Austen's *Emma, Clueless*. She's succeeded on television and stage as well. Silverstone has won some lesser acting awards and generally established herself in Hollywood.

When we apply the usual tests for Hippie identity, she lights it up. First, Silverstone has authored a book *The Kind Diet*; it's a vegan diet; she's followed this with a 2014 book *The Kind Mama*—advice on pregnancy and birthing. Her website is called *The Kind Life* (*Wikipedia*); earlier, I mentioned how "kind" is often a euphemism for *Countercultural*. She's designed a line of cosmetic brushes and bags for a company called EcoTools; included are hemp materials (ChronicCandy.com), and she's into organic gardening and has solar panels on her house (*Wikipedia*); so, very green. Also, Silverstone is apparently a medical-marijuana advocate (Wenn.com) and has been seen smoking marijuana in public—Hillary Duff was "fuming"! (PopDirt.com). She's a practitioner and advocate of meditation (Silverstone). As for Countercultural networking, she began her career by making music videos for Aerosmith (*Wikipedia*), she speaks of a friendship with Woody Harrelson (Celebslam.com), and she's a personal friend of Hippie rocker Alanis Morrisette (Wenn.com).

Her husband, Christopher Jarecki, is a rock musician who a Google image search shows often looks Hippie. Paul McCartney wrote the forward for her book. She, of course, made *Clueless* with likely Countercultural director Amy Heckerling, and in 2010, she made another film with Heckerling, *Vamps*. Plus, Silverstone has graced the *Rolling Stone* cover. Finally, a Google search shows she's widely viewed as Hippie. Here we have a broad-based, consistent and very clear identification—call Ms. Silverstone Countercultural. **HICR: 10**

Al Pacino: Another Hollywood legend, Al Pacino won the Academy Award for Best Actor for his role in *Scent of a Woman* (1992); he was previously nominated no less than seven times. If nothing else, moviegoers know him as Michael Corleone in two of *The Godfather* films. Pacino has done much Shakespearean work, including teaching appreciation of it. Generally, he's an accomplished and highly respected actor.

Hippie? On screen, Pacino played Serpico a NYC cop who is commonly seen as Hippie/Countercultural. He would seem Counterculturally networked: note his work for Francis Ford Coppola in *The Godfather* films (1972, 1990); he also says Johnny Depp is one of his favorite actors (Daily Mail Showbiz Reporter) and has worked with Depp in *Donnie Brasco* (1997). Also, though Pacino says he's now drug free, he does have experience with marijuana (Answers.com). Al Pacino has been the subject of the *Rolling Stone* interview. He says, "I have been doing yoga and meditating since I was 17 years old" (Pacino).

Most importantly, consider Pacino's appearance: off screen, he usually has longish hair and a goatee. And in 2008, a paparazzi website wrote, "We spotted Al Pacino running errands with his kids in Beverly Hills yesterday, and the actor sported his trademark ponytail and leather jacket" (X17 Online).[91] "Trademark ponytail"? As mentioned, lacking some other long-haired ethnic identity, a ponytail on a male is a strong Countercultural indicator. Yes, let's call this distinguished actor Hippie-American. **HICR: 9.5**

Marlon Brando (last half of his life): Named by the American Film Institute as the Greatest Male Star of All Time, Marlon Brando is a Hollywood legend; many of his roles, as he played them, became iconic: failed prizefighter Terry Malloy in *On the Waterfront* (1951), Stanley Kowalski in *A Streetcar Named Desire* (1954), Fletcher Christian in *Mutiny on the Bounty* (1962), Vito Corleone in *The Godfather* (1976), Kurtz in *Apocalypse Now* (1979), or the otherworldly father Jor-El in *Superman* (1978). Brando, ironically, thought his profession was

---

[91]   I apologize for using paparazzi as a source.

overrated, that there were more important things in life than acting.[92] Still, it would be hard to find an actor more accomplished or esteemed— possibly only Sir Laurence Olivier would trump him—and many who worked with Brando considered him a genius. His contributions to cinema are staggering.

Hippie? For the last half of Brando's life, mid-1960s on, yes. Here's the case: His autobiography, *Songs My Mother Taught Me*, reveals a number of Countercultural values: he prized nature and the environment; he had an openness to sexuality; he respected and valued other cultures (Brando involved himself in the

> **Biographer Patricia Bosworth: "Brando seemed quite enthusiastic about it [*The Godfather*], saying that the movie reflected something metaphorical about corporate mentality. To him, the gangsters parodied establishment values"** (168) So, Brando saw himself as the antithesis of the Establishment— close to self-identification, I think.

struggles of African-Americans and Native-Americans, and he loved and respected Tahitian culture); he valued informality; he felt life was about making the world better, not accumulating material wealth (though Brando did eventually become rich); and he definitely questioned authority. In short, by the mid-1960s, Brando was a Hippie waiting to happen.

Brando also mentions being a marijuana smoker. In addition, he sometimes looked Hippie. Thus, director Francis Ford Coppola describes a 1970 scene he videotaped at Brando's home where the actor was starting to improvise the character Don Vito Corleone: "In my video, you see Brando coming out of his bedroom with his long blond hair in a pony-tail. . . . You see him roll his hair into a bun and then darken it with shoe polish . . ." (qtd. in Bosworth 171). Plus, we sometimes saw a Hippie-looking Brando on screen—in *Missouri Breaks,* he had shoulder-length hair and sometimes a headband, and his Fletcher Christian *ala* ponytail also looks Hippie-ish (indeed, one interpretation of *Bounty* is that of "natural" man rebelling against repressive "civilized" man, a theme with clear Countercultural echoes). In 1976, Brando was interviewed by *Rolling Stone* and appeared on the cover.

---

[92]   I've lost my source for this, but it's Bosworth or the autobiography.

Also, this from biographer Patricia Bosworth: "Brando seemed quite enthusiastic about it [*The Godfather*], saying that the movie reflected something metaphorical about corporate mentality. To him, the gangsters parodied establishment values" (168) Brando, then, saw himself as the antithesis of the Establishment—close to self-identification, I think.

Countercultural networking? He appeared in Terry Southern's *Candy* (1968), playing a lecherous Eastern swami across from Ringo Starr, among others; *Missouri Breaks* looks largely Countercultural; it was directed by Arthur Penn, and Brando writes of it: "There was a lot of pot smoking and partying, my friend and neighbor Jack Nicholson was in it . . ." (433). Bosworth tells us, "Sean Penn has been meeting with him on and off for two years about directing him in *Autumn of the Patriarch*. Johnny Depp directed him in a movie called *The Brave* . . ." (218). In *Don Juan DiMarco* (1995), Brando also acted with Depp, who, like Jack Nicholson, was a personal friend (Bosworth 216). Lastly, for an Eastern influence, Brando was a devoted practitioner of meditation (Brando 443). I doubt he ate a Hippie diet (he often binged on high-glycemic foods and had weight problems);[93] still, there's enough here to say that in the last half of his life, Marlon Brando was Hippie. **HICR of 9.75 for post-1965 life.**

Richard Harris: Born in Limerick, Ireland in 1930, Harris left this world in 2002. I place him after Marlon Brando because he was another of the greatest actors of that generation; his life, private and professional, is legend. Turns out that the young Harris was a champion athlete, a squash player who won "the Tivoli Cup in Kilkee four years in a row from 1948 to 1951, a record surpassed by nobody to this day," *Wikipedia* tells us. In fact, there's a bronze, life-size statue of Harris the squash player in Kilkee, Ireland which was unveiled by—can you say *Countercultural networking?*—Russell Crowe. There are three Harris biographies, *Behaving Badly: The Life of Richard Harris* (2003) by Cliff Goodwin, *Richard Harris: Sex, Death & the Movies* (2004) by Michael Callahan and *A Man Called Harris* (2014) by Michael Sheridan and Anthony Galvin; also, Harris is one of the subjects of *Hellraisers: The Inebriated Times of Richard Burton, Richard Harris, Peter O'Toole, and Oliver Ree*d (2009) by Robert Sellers. (As the reader

---

[93]   I can't remember my source for this. It's probably Bosworth.

may glean from these titles, Harris may have been a world-famous actor, but he was hardly a role model; among other things, he was a serious alcoholic.)

Harris never won an Academy Award though he was twice nominated for Best Actor: for Frank Manchin in *The Sporting Life* (1963) and for Bull McCade in *The Field* (1990) (Ireland has a postage stamp with Harris/ McCade's image—*Wikipedia*). Yet, Harris is so renowned largely because he's played important roles in so many important films. In *Wikipedia's* filmography, I count 74 films, everything from *The Guns of Navarone* (1960) to *Mutiny on the Bounty* (1962) to *The Bible* (1966) to *Camelot* (1967) to *A Man Called Horse* (1970) to Dumbledore in the first two *Harry Potter* films, *the Philosopher's Stone* (2001) and *the Chamber of Secrets* (2002).

Let's talk Hippie identity, how we can claim some of Harris's cinematic accomplishments as Countercultural. First, Harris' Hippie identity in the late Sixties is pretty much common knowledge; thus, Sellers writes of Harris in 1967, "He embraced the party scene in LA, dancing and singing most of his nights away, the oldest hippie in town" (132). And of course, in 1968 Harris sang/narrated that quintessential Countercultural song "MacArthur's Park." On eBay, I found photos described as "Richard Harris in his hippie phase." Of course, such language is open to interpretation: was being Hippie simply a "phase" Harris went through, or is this description the stilted language of dysfunctional, Thing-of-the-Sixties-type paradigms?

Was Harris Hippie post-Sixties? Well, let's Google Image search some post-Sixties photos of Harris and see what the chap looked like. **See, please, Photo #31.** Everything in this late-life, off-stage photo of Harris looks Hippie: his hair, his beard, his glasses, the natural-fiber clothing he appears to be wearing, the informal collarless shirt—and several later-in-life photos of Harris suggest the same. As with Marlon Brando, then, let's call Harris Hippie after 1965 with an **HICR** of **9.75**.

Leonardo DiCaprio: Years ago, I first saw DiCaprio in *What's Eating Gilbert Grape* (1993), starring Johnny Depp. It's the story of a poor Iowa family with an obese, single, stay-at-home mom. Depp's character, Gilbert Grape, is the elder son, playing surrogate father; the younger son, Arnie (DiCaprio), is severely handicapped—Arnie makes Forrest Gump look like a high-performing honor student. I was stunned: how, I wondered, did they ever get such a handicapped child to learn his lines? I mean, I'm pretty sure I'm not stupid, but DiCaprio was so convincing, the role so challenging, that at first it didn't occur to me that Arnie could be the creation of a non-handicapped actor. Not surprisingly, then, DiCaprio won the Academy Award for Best Supporting Actor for that role and has turned out to be one of Hollywood's great successes; indeed, it's safe to say (and I think it's partly because DiCaprio seems to have good taste in the films he chooses to make), he will go down as a Hollywood institution, one of the greatest actors of his time.

Hippie? His parents are Hippie—DiCaprio has said so in interviews (Bloom), and the media also describes them as such (Rader); again, Hippie parents tend to have Hippie kids. Of course, sometimes they don't, but DiCaprio *seems* to self-identify as he describes his family of origin: "We're not the hippie family who only eats organic and the children meditate and go to school of the arts. But we're not apple-pie and republican either" (ThinkExist.com). I think the quote is close to self-identification.

Okay, he was Hippie then, is he Hippie-American now? Well, DiCaprio has thrice been on the *Rolling Stone* cover and once been interviewed by *RS*. He's also a staunch environmentalist; thus, a January 2016 *Rolling Stone* cover story is called "Leo's Crusade: His Toughest Role and a Mission to Save the Planet" (*Rolling Stone*, "Leo"). Finally, when I Google Image searched "Leonardo DiCaprio ponytail," sure enough, **Photo #32** shows a bearded DiCaprio with a "samurai ponytail"—it looks real Hippie when you see it (Brigette). **HICR: 9.75**

Helena Bonham Carter: Bonham Carter became a star playing Lucy Honeychurch in the well-received Somerset Maugham adaption *Room with a View (1985)*. She followed with other literary films, playing Ophelia to Mel Gibson's *Hamlet* (1990) and other serious work, sometimes working with then-partner Kenneth Branaugh as in *Mary Shelley's Frankenstein* (1994). In 1997, she was nominated for Best Actress for her role as the corrupted Kate Croy in the Henry James adaption *Wings of the* Dove (1995). Since then, she's done a series of highly successful films working opposite Johnny Depp and directed by Tim Burton—*Charlie and the Chocolate Factory* (2005), *Sweeny Todd* (2007*), Alice in Wonderland (2010)*. And she recently received another nomination for the Academy Award for Best Supporting Actress for playing Her Majesty in *The King's Speech* (2010). Here's a highly accomplished actress who, I'm guessing, is bound for Best Actress and a Lifetime Achievement Award.

Can we call her Countercultural? In recent street photos, she appears be wearing, I'm guessing, what is called "ashcan," "bohemian-bourgeois" or "boho-chic style," which, as we'll see when we discuss the Olsen Twins below, is considered Countercultural. She's informal and values sexuality, the latter apparent in films she's made such as television's *The Good Sex Guide* (1994), where she plays herself; so, she seems to have some values that can be considered Countercultural. In terms of endogamy, she was in a non-married marriage with Tim Burton, who she's raising children with, and I've called Burton Countercultural. She had a relationship with Steve Martin, who we're soon going to call Hippie-American—all good evidence for a strong indicator.

Here's the thing that made me finally decide to mention Bonham Carter: the godfather to her two children by Burton is Johnny Depp (*Wikipedia*, "Tim Burton"). That's a heavyweight criterion bound up as it is with serious life/identity issues, and it involves Mr. Gold Standard for Hippie-Identification Networking himself, J-o-o-o-hnny Depp, ladies and gentleman! Given some weaknesses in my case here, let's keep the **HICR** at **8.75**.

* * *

There, then, are 20 Hollywood actors and actresses of note who can be called Hippie/ Countercultural. Here's **a list of 25 more** (and their HICRs) that the reader can read about on the website:

Orlando Bloom, 9.5	Viggo Mortensen, 9.75	Winona Ryder, 9.5
Uma Thurman, 9.75	David Carradine, 9.75	Dennis Hopper, 10
Goldie Hawn, 9.5	Kurt Russell, 8.75	Kate Hudson, 10
Ed Begley, Jr. 9.75	Daryl Hannah, 10	Russell Crowe, 9.5
Angelia Jolie, 9.0	Tim Robbins, 10	Meg Ryan, 9.5
Keanu Reeves, 10	Drew Barrymore, 10	Stephen Seagal, 9.75
Ashton Kutcher, 9.75	Shailene Woodley, 10	Jared Leto, 10
Peter Coyote, 10	Donald Sutherland, 9.75	Kiefer Sutherland, 8.5
Matthew McConaughey, 9.75		

Hollywood, then, seems disproportionately Hippie, and Hippiedom's acting successes there are legion—yet another area where we shine brightly.

* * *

215

Hippies and Comedy

Perhaps it's those underlying values of fun and a willingness to question authority (with its subsequent tendency towards satire), but Hippies are some funny folks.

Let's begin with three Countercultural comic institutions: *Monty Python's Flying Circus*, the American humor magazine *National Lampoon*, and the spectacularly successful *Saturday Night Live*.

Let's begin with three Counter-cultural comic institutions. I've already demonstrated how Monty Python is Countercultural; to this, let's add *National Lampoon*, an American humor magazine (1970 to 1998). Journalist Paula Duffy tells us, "[T]he magazine came to define outrageous and cutting edge humor." It was also important because "It all bled into comedy that left the printed page and migrated to radio, live stage shows, television and films, with a host of names that came out of *The Lampoon*" (Duffy); indeed, so many of the early stars of *Saturday Night Live* emerged from *National Lampoon* that it might be thought of as a sort of pre-*SNL*. *Wikipedia* adds that "the magazine and its empire of spin-offs changed the course of comedy and humor."

The magazine's Countercultural identity is pretty well established by the 2016 television film *Drunk, Stoned, Brilliant, Dead: The Story of the National Lampoon*. Not only do we see references to marijuana use, but the staff appears very Hippie with many long-haired males; in addition, as we'll see below, many of these staffers (John Belushi, for instance) have documentable Hippie identity. **HICR: 10**

Last here is the spectacularly successful *Saturday Night Live (SNL)*. That doesn't mean each and every comedian who's ever worked on *SNL* is automatically Hippie; rather, the show has Countercultural roots, many of the program's players have had Hippie identity, and the show as a whole has exhibited Countercultural themes and values. Here are two excerpts from Doug Hill and Jeff Weingrad's 1986 *Saturday Night: A Backstage History of Saturday Night Live*:

The [NBC] crew [during the fourth season] was characterized by one of *Saturday Night's* writers as "a bunch of Archie Bunkers" who on the political spectrum fit "somewhere between the Klan and the Mafia." For their part, the crew members spent much of their time snickering at the *Saturday Night* people in disbelief and disgust, muttering, as they watched the rehearsals, such comments as "This gang just came from Woodstock!" Every day the snack table outside 8G declared the differences between them: The crew had the usual doughnuts and coffee; *Saturday Night* had fresh fruit, vegetables, and nuts. (81)

The image of a bunch of heads [a term for *Hippies*] on *Saturday Night* putting together a show for the heads out there in TV land was definitely a large part of the show's appeal. *Saturday Night* became, in many respects, a passing of the communal joint around a circle that spanned, through television, the entire country. (175)

So, let's call *SNL* Hippie/Countercultural; in regard to individual comedians, think of an *SNL* (or *National Lampoon)* background as a strong Countercultural predictor, but since it's not entirely clear that the show remains Countercultural, let's take off some points here. **HICR: 8.5**

Let's next consider *SNL* star **Tom Davis**, the long-time partner of Al Franken, an act known as Franken & Davis. He's an *SNL* veteran, having worked on the show from its 1975 inception through 1980 and then reappearing with Franken during the 1980s. And his work as an SNL writer helped him win four Emmys. Why start with Davis? He's written a book, *Thirty-Nine Years of Short-Term Memory Loss: The Early Days of SNL From Someone Who Was There.* And in estabishing his own Hippie identity, Davis underscores the Countercultural identity of *SNL*, which he calls "my family"; Associated Press ("New") reports:

Davis, 56, also details his friendship with counterculture legends Timothy Leary and Jerry Garcia (the two tried unsuccessfully to write a screenplay of a Kurt Vonnegut Jr. novel); his own drug use (he first took LSD watching *2001: A Space Odyssey* with friends at a Twin Cities drive-in); and his travel as a young hippie to India in the 1970s. Davis, whose hair and beard now are now gray and stylishly trimmed, says his stories are those of his generation. "We all went to India, we all took the acid, we liked the Rolling Stones and the Grateful Dead, we marched against an unpopular war . . .," Davis says.

And, Davis self-identifies, calling himself and Franken "two young hippie freaks" at one point (6). And I see no reason to assume Davis doesn't remain Countercultural today—he doesn't disown or regret his Hippie past; rather, he celebrates it. **HICR: 10**

Al Franken: Franken was an *SNL*er for seventeen years; he was nominated for an Emmy seven times; he won an Emmy three times. He's also reknown for his radio-host/therapist parody, Stuart Smally. Nowadays, of course, call him the Honorable Alan S. Franken, Junior Senator from Minnesota.

Reading Davis' book there's no doubt that the younger Franken was Hippie—a ten on a ten-point scale. So, the only real question is, has he retained his Hippie identity? And again, there's no reason to assume he's disowned his Hippie past, that he's ashamed of it or necessarily "outgrown" it.[94] And there's clear evidence of Counterculturality in his current life. For starters, Senator Franken's website says, "Minnesota has a vibrant and growing number of small and organic farmers. I support policies that bolster the viability and enhance access to markets for these farmers." He's also green: "Al is staunch advocate of generating jobs in renewable energy in Minnesota and realizes the multi-faceted approach that's needed to become more energy efficient and energy independent," writes Minnesota blogger Aaron Landry, paraphrasing a campaigning Franken. And regarding an Eastern connection, Franken is considered a "Jew-Bu"—someone who is ethnically Jewish but religiously Buddhist (DeMontigny). And yes, Franken is shorter-haired than he used to be, but as we've seen, that isn't a deal breaker, nor necessarily is now avoiding marijuana. Yes, call the senator Hippie-Jewish-American or something with *Hippie* in it. **HICR: 9.0**

Bill Murray: Another pillar of the early *SNL,*[95] Bill Murray is a comic legend—and more. He's had great success as an actor, starring in *Caddyshack* (1980), *Tootsie* (1982), *Ghostbusters* (1984), *What About Bob?* (1991) and *Groundhog Day* (1992)—all smart, successful comedies. And Murray's made serious films too, beginning with an adaption of W. Somerset Maugham's *The Razor's Edge* (1984) and *Lost in Translation* (2003) where Murray's acting earned him an Academy

---

94   For the record, Davis says of Franken in 1980, "Al no longer got high."
95   My favorite Murray *SNL* role: Nick, the airport lounge singer who covers *Also Sprach Zarthustra.*

218

Award nomination for Best Actor and a Golden Globe. In 2012, he played President Franklin D. Roosevelt in *Hyde Park on Hudson*.

It's relatively easy to establish his Hippie identity, past and present. Early on, Davis has Murray involved in the larger Countercultural scene, telling us, for instance, that in November 1978 Murray hitchhiked to the closing of Winterland, the Countercultural music venue in San Francisco, and was "immediately adopted by the Grateful Dead family" (239).

He has a history with marijuana; indeed, in 1970, he was busted (Behr). The website CelebStoner.com claims Murray as a Celebrity Stoner, partly. because of the many stoner roles he's played—the crazed groundskeeper in *Caddyshack* (you'll recall a long, surreal pot-smoking scene tucked into the film); in particular, Murray played Countercultural Hunter S. Thompson in the biofilm *Where the Buffalo Roam* (1980). He's very well Counterculturally networked; not only is there his early *SNL* work and association with the San Francisco Hippie scene already mentioned, but he was a personal friend of Thompson's and an attendee at his 2005 funeral (*Wikipedia*, "Hunter S. Thompson"). Murray has been on the *Rolling Stone* cover three times, once with *Ghostbusters* colleagues; he did the *Rolling Stone* interview once. And to this day, Bill Murray can be found emceeing Countercultural music festivals such as Eric Clapton's Crossroads Guitar Festival in Chicago in both 2007 and 2010—Murray is known for his comic impersonation of a late-Sixties, very visibly Hippie Eric Clapton, *ala* Cream (Chicago Blues Guide). So with Bill Murray, we seem to see ongoing—living—Hippie identity. **HICR: 9.75**

Mike Myers: From Canada way, Myers has made it big. Not only has he been an important television comedian, but he has of course morphed into Austin Powers in three highly successful James Bond parodies (a fourth is on the way). Not to know who Austin Powers is, is not to be culturally literate. More recently, Myers has been the voice of Shrek, in the highly popular series of Pixar-type films of the same name.

Here is the case for Myers as Hippie. He has an *SNL* background, and he worked with Quentin Tarantino in *Inglorious Basterds*—both good in terms of Countercultural networking. His roles are often Countercultural; Wayne of the famous *SNL*-generated Wayne-and-Garth skits and later films is a type of Hippie. And lest the truly dull viewer fails to grasp that Austin Powers is Hippie, the International Man of Mystery loves to exclaim how the Sixties were "groovy, Baby!" Powers 2008 comedy, *The Love Guru,* again focuses on early Hippie culture, parodying Hippie "gurus." Myers has been on the *Rolling Stone* cover[96] and been the subject of the *RS* interview. Also, if the Austin Powers films have any messages, it's probably these: it's good to have fun and laugh at ourselves, and the Sixties (read Hippies) were/are great. For that latter message, I see Myers as a comic Hippie nationalist. **HICR: 9.75 to 10.**

Robin Williams: Much on the minds of many since his tragic and unexpected death in 2014, Robin Williams became a household name for his role as the alien Mork in the late-seventies sitcom *Mork and Mindy.* It seems so long ago, and Williams came *so* far. He quickly moved to the big screen, and by 1987, he had arrived in Hollywood, winning The Golden Globe for Best Actor for playing dissident US Army disc jockey Adrian Conrauer in *Good Morning, Vietnam*; in 1997, Williams won the Academy Award for Best Supporting Actor for his work in *Good Will Hunting*, and he has, of course, made a slew of other films, many excellent; most, successful. As

> Robin Williams was often seen as Hippie; thus interviewer Alison Jones calls her 2006 piece "Robin Williams, the happy hippie."

of 2011, he had won four Golden Globes, two Screen Actors Guild Awards, two Emmys and five Grammys (for comedy albums), and an American Comedy Award. Williams' film résumé is spectacular; yet, he'll likely be most remembered as a stand-up comic of rapid-fire wit, incredible energy and peerless improvisational ability.

And, yes, he too was Hippie. A blogger writes about the legendary Countercultural music promoter Bill Graham:

> On November 3, 1991, a free concert called "Laughter, Love and Music" was held at Golden Gate Park to honor Graham, Gold and Kahn. An estimated 300,000 people attended to view many of the entertainment acts Graham had supported including Santana, Grateful Dead, John Fogerty, Robin Williams, Journey (reunited), and Crosby, Stills, Nash & Young (reunited). (Learyfan)

---

[96] He's also been on the *RS* cover alongside his Wayne's World partner, Garth (Dana Carvey).

Wikipedia notes, "Williams was a close friend of and frequent partier alongside John Belushi." He acted opposite of Steve Martin in a stage production of *Waiting for Godot*. And in 2008, Williams was said to have a home in Canada's "Saltspring Island, a haven of alternative living that has remained virtually unchanged since it welcomed hippies to its shores back in the 60s"; one neighbor was Susan Sarandon (Caton). So, plenty of Countercultural networking. He had experience with marijuana—he joked about it in various stand-up routines. He was somewhat green, favoring eco-friendly vehicles (*Wikipedia*), and he was six times on the *Rolling Stone* cover. Plus, he's often seen as Hippie; thus interviewer Alison Jones calls her 2006 piece "Robin Williams, the happy hippie" (Jones). **HICR: 9.5**

Steve Martin: In 1969, Steve Martin won an Emmy writing for *The Smothers Brothers Comedy Hour*. He later became a household name as a popular *SNL* comedian—think King Tut and one of those "wild and crazy guys!" with Dan Akroyd; this in turn led to film acting. Of late, he plays banjo in a bluegrass band known as Steve Martin and the Steep Canyon Rangers. He's won Grammys for both comedy and bluegrass albums, and he's twice won the American Comedy Award. He's published two books, *Steve Martin: Born Standing Up* (2007) and a novel, *An Object of Beauty* (2010). Altogether, he's accomplished and impressive.

Hippie? A profile of Martin tells us that in the late 60s, early 70s, "Martin graduated to opening for rock performers, where his long hair, scraggly beard, and hippie wardrobe aligned him firmly with the counterculture movement of the era" (AMG). Most of us have never seen Martin looking particularly Countercultural; it will be easier to imagine if we look at the Hippie character Martin played in the 2008 film *Baby Mama* where he has long hair tied in a ponytail **(see Photo #33)**.

As for Countercultural networking, Martin won his Emmy on the Countercultural *Smothers Brothers Comedy Hour*, and he has a strong *SNL* background. He's been thrice on the *Rolling Stone* cover and has once been the subject of the *RS* interview. As for marijuana use, Martin quips, "I used to smoke marijuana. But I'll tell you something: I would only smoke it in the late evening. Oh, occasionally the early evening, but usually the late evening—or the mid-evening. Just the early evening, midevening and late evening. Occasionally, early afternoon, early midafternoon, or perhaps the late-midafternoon. Oh, sometimes the early-mid-late-early morning. . . . But never at dusk"

(420 Magazine). And Martin is a spiritualist of sorts (Martin)—not a clear Eastern connection, but in the New Age neighborhood, perhaps; likewise, he says organized religion isn't for him (Martin), and in that sense, he seems to question authority—a prominent Hippie value. And given the Counterculture's strong presence in contemporary bluegrass (and given that Martin has no apparent Appalachian or Country-Western background), his bluegrass work can be seen as another Countercultural predictor. Let's call Steve Martin Hippie-American. **HICR: 9.25**

> The website Freaking News.com treats Whoopi Goldberg like one of the Hippie family and says in a biography of her, "In the late 1960s, Caryn [Goldberg's real first name] connected to the hippie movement and left home to live in a commune, where she developed a liking to marihuana . . . ."

Whoopi Goldberg: Only four actresses have won the quadruple crown of acting: An Oscar, Tony, Emmy and Grammy. "Da Whoop" is one. And as one of the most successful women in Hollywood, she's also reportedly one of the wealthiest. Far as I can tell, most of America loves Whoopi Goldberg.

Hippie identity: The website FreakingNews.com treats Goldberg like one of the Hippie family and says in a biography of her, "In the late 1960s, Caryn [Goldberg's real first name] connected to the hippie movement and left home to live in a commune, where she developed a liking to marihuana . . . ."

Please **see Photo #34** of Goldberg; here we see her trademark dreadlocks; given no evidence that she's Rastafarian, those dreads suggest Counterculturality. Add to this her roundish wire-rimmed glasses,—think "granny glasses." Even the shirt she's wearing here looks Hippieish with its natural colors and informality. I know the first time I ever saw Goldberg, I thought "black Hippie." There's also evidence of Countercultural networking here: A large part of her early work was with the Countercultural charity Comic Relief. She's once been on the *Rolling Stone* cover. So, it's clear Goldberg was Hippie, and the evidence would seem to indicate that she probably still is. **HICR: 9.75**

George Carlin—the late and the great. He won five Grammys for comedy albums; he was awarded the Mark Twain Comedy Award (given by the John F. Kennedy Center for Performing Arts and described as "America's foremost award for humor") (*Wikipedia*). "In 2004, Carlin placed second on the Comedy Central list of the 100 greatest stand-up comedians of all time," *Wikipedia* notes. He's historically important because a 1978 freedom-of-speech lawsuit based on his "Seven Dirty Words" routine went to the US Supreme Court. His social commentary was lacerating and hilarious; today, George Carlin is legend.

It is likely common knowledge that George Carlin was Hippie, but let me document just a bit. One of his earliest routines was "The Hippy-Dippy Weatherman." *Wikipedia* says of Carlin in the early 1970s, "He lost some TV bookings by dressing strangely for a comedian of the time, wearing faded jeans and sporting long hair, a beard, and earrings at a time when clean-cut, well-dressed comedians were the norm." His was the first host of *Saturday Night Live*. Some of his comedy was about marijuana. **HICR: 10**

Julia Louis-Dreyfus is best known for playing Elaine Benes in *Seinfeld*. Since then, she's had a five-year television run as the star of *The New Adventures of Old Christine*, and since 2012, she's been the lead actor in television's *Veep*. One of the most celebrated female comics in America, as of late 2014, credit her with one Golden Globe, five Emmy Awards (she's been nominated for 18), six Screen Actors Guild Awards, five American Comedy Awards and two Critic's Choice Television Awards. She now has a star on Hollywood's Walk of Fame, and in 2014 was inducted into the Television Academy Hall of Fame (*Wikipedia*).

Regarding Hippie identity, Louis-Dreyfus has high Countercultural-networking scores: she has a *Saturday Night Live* background (1982-85); even better is her endogamy: her husband, Brad Hall, also an *SNL* alum, is a self-identifier; thus, he "speaks proudly of his 'deep hippie roots'" (Seal). They married in 1987; they remain together today and have two children. She and Hall are both committed environmentalists—politically active in that cause—and try to practice what they preach by having an environmentally friendly house and running a green household (*Wikipedia*). Louis-Dreyfus says, "Ever since having kids . . ., I have felt a calling to work to defend the environment . . ." (qtd. in Seal).

Also, Louis-Dreyfus describes her beauty as "natural," and *Shape* comments that she "credits her eco-lifestyle as her anti-aging weapon. 'I buy organic foods whenever they're available and shop at my local farmers' market whenever I can . . .,' reveals Julia" (qtd. in MacLeod). She practices yoga (Shea); in one episode of *The New Adventures of Old Christine*, her character uses marijuana (YouTube, "Smoking")— not as good as information on Louis-Dreyfus herself, but supportive. She's twice shared the *Rolling Stone* cover with her *Seinfeld* co-stars. And lastly, in an interview (5min.com), she comments at one point, "I dig it!"—Hippieish language. All enough, I think, to call Julia Louis-Dreyfus Countercultural. **HICR: 9.5**

Jim Carrey is of course a renown star of film comedy. Famed for his rubber face and extraordinary impersonations, Carrey's films, usually comedies, have been highly successful—he's won two Golden Globes, been nominated four other times.

As for Hippie identity, let's begin with looks. Carrey often appears Hippie in both private life and in film as in his role in *Burt Wonderstone* (2013). People often see Carrey as Hippie; thus, among other examples, a website identifies Carrey in "Hollywood Celebrities Who Embody the Hippie Lifestyle" (Bryan). A 2004 article has Carrey saying he's quit smoking pot (ContactMusic.com), so we at least know he has been a regular marijuana user.

Carrey is widely considered to be very green, and he's seriously New Age: he's a friend and colleague of sorts of the popular metaphysicist Eckhart Tolle (*Wikipedia*); I once heard Carrey on a talk show say that he has a special meditation space in his back yard. Also, Carrey has been on the *Rolling Stone* cover once, has been the subject of the *RS* interview once. As for diet, Carrey "has been a vegetarian for most of his life," (Go n Try) and favors a "vegetable and protein diet" (Pop Blend)—in the Countercultural neighborhood. Let's call Mr. Carrey Hippie-Canadian-American. **HICR: 9.5**

Jon Stewart was the host of Comedy Central's *The Daily Show*, a singular phenomena in that the program parodied the "serious" news channels, particularly the mouthpieces of the far right; yet, it became a popular news show itself, one often taken more seriously than Fox and company. The program's motto is "Where more Americans get their news than probably should" (DVD Talk). Stewart has won no less than 16 Emmys (the Oscars of television) and two Grammys. He and his show were a sensation.

As for Hippie identity, Stewart is a self-identifier: In 2004, former Secretary of State Madeline Albright appeared on *The Daily Show*. Reportedly, she told Stewart, "I want to be in your universe!" to which Stewart quickly replied, "You can . . . all you need is a bong and a Grateful Dead album" (nonprophet81). **HICR: 10**

Finally, here are several **more Countercultural comedians** (and their HICRs) the reader will find on the website:

John Belushi, 10	Dan Akroyd, 9.5	Dana Carvey, 10
Sam Kinison, 10	Russell Brand, 10	Mitch Hedburg, 10
Bill Bailey, 10	Larry David, 9.5	Stephen Wright, 8.25
Gallagher, 10	Cheech & Chong, 10	

In the realm of comedy, then, begin with three important comic institutions *National Lampoon, Monty Python's Flying Circus* and *Saturday Night Live*, add a bunch of world-class Hippie jesters (many of whom are accomplished actors), and again we have an impressive record of achievement—as good, I'd say, as any out there.

* * *

The Hippie contribution to **television** has been less overwhelming than its contributions to film and comedy; still, remember that both *Saturday Night Live* and *Monty Python's Flying Circus* began, at least, on television. We'll call *The Monkees* Hippie—not only because the group members would likely test out Countercultural, but also because of the show's style which seems derivative of the Beatles *Hard Day's Night*. We'll call *That 70s Show* Hippie-American and likely *Dharma and Greg*—their audiences were Counter cultural (a Denver station used to do an hour rerun block pairing the two). There's probably more, but for now, we'll look only at two historically important Hippie-American television programs.

The Smothers Brothers Comedy Hour (*SBCH*): *Wikipedia:* "The show started out as only a slightly 'hip' version of the typical comedy-variety show of its era, but rapidly evolved into a show that extended the boundaries of what was considered permissible in television satire." Indeed, despite *SBCH's* popularity—for the first time in nine years, it knocked NBC's *Bonanza* out of first place in a highly competitive

Sunday-evening slot—*SBCH* only lasted three seasons: 1967 through 1969. The show was cancelled by network censors.[97]

As for Hippie identity, Scott Harris writes for IMDb: "*The Smothers Brothers* quickly tapped into the hippie counter-culture and anti-Vietnam sentiment, eventually causing the network's conservative executives to abruptly cancel the show despite strong ratings and critical acclaim (Harris).

According to Anita Bodroghkozy, writing for the Museum of Broadcast Communications:

> The show's content featured irreverent digs at many dominant institutions such as organized religion and the presidency. It also included sketches celebrating the hippie drug culture and material opposing the war in Vietnam. These elements made *The Smothers Brothers Comedy Hour* one of the most controversial television shows in the medium's history.

In *With Amusement for All*, LeRoy Ashby writes, "Events had radicalized the [Smothers] brothers, turning them into what the press described as 'hippies with haircuts'" (363).

Bodroghkozy adds:

> Another *Comedy Hour* regular engaged in a different kind of subversive humor. Comedienne Leigh French created the recurring hippie character, Goldie O'Keefe, whose parody of afternoon advice shows for housewives, "Share a Little Tea with Goldie," was actually one long celebration of mind-altering drugs. "Tea" was a countercultural code word for marijuana, but the CBS censors seemed to be unaware of the connection. Goldie would open her sketches with salutations such as "Hi(gh)—and glad of it!"

---

[97] Underscoring the importance of this show, there's now a book partly about it, Anita Bodroghkozy's *Groove Tube: Sixties Television and the Youth Rebellion (Console-ing Passions)*, and as of 2011, George Clooney was planning on making a movie about the show and its demise (Harris).

226

Also, the musical acts *SBCH* hosted were recognizably Countercultural, including The Who; George Harrison; Joan Baez; Cream; Buffalo Springfield; Cass Elliot; The Doors; Donovan; Janis Ian; Jefferson Airplane; Peter, Paul and Mary; Spanky and Our Gang; Steppenwolf; and Simon and Garfunkel. In fact, *SBCH* pioneered the first music videos (*Wikipedia* et al).

Generally, when viewers tuned in, they felt they were seeing Hippie culture televised, and *SBCH's* Countercultural nature is widely known—probably common knowledge here. **HICR: 10**

(The reader might ask, "Where's that late-1960s, early-1970s, show *Rowan & Martin's Laugh-In*? Wasn't it a lot like *The Smothers Brothers Comedy Hour*?" Well, when I researched the show, I found its Hippie identity doubtful. Thus, blogger Kliph Nesteroff writes:

> *Laugh-In* was old in style, but draped in the popular fashion of the day. It effectively garnered a genuine hippie aesthetic, but any actual connection to the counterculture was mostly smoke and mirrors. The bulk of *Laugh-In* consisted of eye-catching vaudeville bits that mostly ignored the war, the riots and the protest. It embraced the look and sound of the hippies and had no problem making references to getting high, but generally glossed over political issues. Whereas Tom Smothers found himself on Nixon's enemies list, Rowan and Martin found themselves on Nixon's guest list.

In fact, Nesteroff notes that one of the show's writers was also President Nixon's joke writer, and of course, Nixon himself once appeared on the program, saying, in a lame attempt to soften his image, "Sock it to me.")

Gene Roddenberry and Star Trek: *Star Trek* has become more than a single television show (the original program lasted only three seasons); it's become an institution: numerous television series, a spate of films, "Trekkie" conventions—you name it.

Star Trek, then, is a great Counter- cultural contribution to humanity. To succeed at something, we need a vision to guide us, and *Star Trek* visualizes a sane, humane future, shows us what humanity matured might look like.

Again, we're talking stupendous success, and *Star Trek* is also important (and likely popular) for the values it communicates; that is, millions have been inspired by the *Star Trek* ethos; that ethos, as we're about to see, is a Hippie ethos.

Let's begin our proof of Hippie identity by first looking at Gene Roddenberry who created *Star Trek* and who was involved in the second television series, *Star Trek: The Next Generation* and in many of the *Star Trek* films. In "Star Trek's Gene Roddenberry was a Big Hippie (And Star Trek is All the Better for It)," Eric Stape comments:

> Star Trek's core values remain firmly rooted in that turbulent age of peace, love and hippie sensibilities. Captain Kirk may have commanded the Enterprise, but Gene Roddenberry was head hippy in charge of everything else.

And while Stape doesn't provide a lot of evidence, I found in internet searches that there was a general perception that Roddenberry was Hippie, almost common knowledge.

I also found interesting examples of Countercultural networking. Thus, there was a Roddenberry-Beatles connection. One blogger who's researched this, Reed, writes:

> Supposedly, they [Roddenberry and Paul McCartney] did get together in November of 1976 to work out the story about an invasion from space that would involve Paul's group, Wings, and Paul as an outer space rock singer. However, when Paramount decided to go ahead with reviving *Star Trek*, Roddenberry abandoned his plans with McCartney.

There's even a particular episode of the original *Star Trek* series, "This Way to Eden," where the Enterprise encounters the Catuallans, who enthusiasts describe as "space hippies" (*Wikipedia*, "This Way to Eden").

And some see Hippie influences in the many subsequent films; thus, reviewer Stephen Holden of the *New York Times* writes of *Insurrection* (1998):

228

With its vision of a peaceable kingdom of eternal youth in an agrarian arts-and-crafts paradise in a California environment, "Insurrection'" is an appealing millennial throwback to the hippie dream that is part and parcel of "Star Trek's" utopian ethos.

Stape elaborates on that ethos, on those Hippie values:

Perhaps more than any sci-fi entity it [*Star Trek*] compels audiences to think higher thoughts, to expect more from sci-fi than simple lightsaber fights or flashy starships. It's graphically illustrated the horrors of war time and again. It's shown us the waste and illogic of hatred because of skin color or preferences in mating or religion.

Star Trek, then, isn't just a fabulous commercial success: it's a great Countercultural contribution to humanity. To succeed at something, we need a vision to guide us, and *Star Trek* visualizes a sane, humane future, shows us what humanity matured might look like. [98]

* * *

We'll finish our survey of Hippie contributions to the arts with **music**. Countercultural contributions here are so extensive and important, I could spend many pages documenting them; instead, I'm going to briefly gloss over those contributions. Why? Primarily because they're already so well known it seems unnecessary to cover them in depth here; it's common knowledge that much of the greatest and most popular music of the last fifty years hails from Hippiedom; so, I won't bother telling my readers what they already know. Let's move on.

* * *

---

[98] I'm sorry to qualify this, but I recently saw *Star Trek* (2009). It was terrible—a dumb action film imbued with macho "real-man" values and insecurities. There's nothing in this film that suggests Countercultural values—*Star Trek* gone astray.

Sports and athletes: Well (sing along, please), it's a long road from Haight-Ashbury . . .[99] I mean, early Hippie culture wasn't exactly renowned for its athletes, was it? I find this area interesting because it so well challenges our stereotypes of Hippies; it also shows how Hippie culture has grown and become more clearly ethnic.

Well, there's a lot of ground to cover here, so we'll be skimming the surface; many sports we'll skip entirely. What I'm going to demonstrate is that Hippie-Americans have "arrived" in the world of sports and that the Counterculture has in fact invented or reinvented several sports—rock-climbing and mountain biking, for instance—and often these new, Hippiegenerated sports are Hippie dominated.

> **Well (sing along, please), it's a long road from Haight-Ashbury . . . I mean, early Hippie culture wasn't exactly renowned for its athletes, was it?**

Some background: Counterculturists have often been banned from sports teams, or at least long hair on males was banned, so if a long-haired Hippie male athlete wanted to play, he had to, on the outside, at least, deHippify. When I was growing up in the late Sixties and early seventies, coaches banned long-haired males from teams. An example of this was when legendary UCLA basketball coach John Wooden ordered Bill Walton to get a haircut. It happened sometimes in pro baseball too. When exactly this changed would be nice to know, but when it did come, it was long past the end of the 1960s.

Add to this the whole issue of drug testing, which often penalizes marijuana smokers. An example would be Ricky Williams, long considered one of the best running backs in the NFL, a legend who has at times been banned from the sport because he uses marijuana, because Ricky Williams is Countercultural.

It's against that background that I now paint a picture of Hippie athletic achievement.

Professional Baseball: Well, best to start with America's national sport, right? And what's wonderful about baseball is its rich history. Much of that history, in turn, is racial and ethnic history. Each American minority seems to have its own stars, including discriminatory-barrier

---

[99] As in "It's a Long Road to Tipperary" from *The Bridge over the River Kwai*.

breakers, to have its historical moments of connection to the game. So it is with Hippie-America. Here, instead of focusing on individual players, let's look at two World Series winners.

The first would be the **2004 Boston Red Sox**, a team that will live in baseball annals as the lifter of The Curse, the myth/legend saying that the Red Sox would never again win the World Series because they had long ago traded Babe Ruth. I've mentioned the "subhuman" comments made about Red Sox players based on their sometimes long hair, I showed the reader evidence of the perpetual-child stereotype directed at this team, based on the same, and I've demonstrated a clear association with Hippiedom in the public mind. This doesn't mean, by the way, that every Red Sox player was Hippie, that no other American racial/ethnic groups had any claim to that glory. Bottom line: Hippie-America can take some credit for this historically important baseball team.

Or, consider the **2010 San Francisco Giants**[100] Again, as with the 2004 Red Sox, I will not argue that each and every player on this team was Countercultural; rather, the team and its fans had a strong Countercultural presence, and that there was a clear connection in the public mind between the 2010 Giants and Hippiedom.

The Giants' star pitcher Tim Lincecum (since traded) became emblematic of the team. With his shoulder-length hair and open affinity for marijuana (apparently, when Giant fans cheer, "Let Timmy smoke," they refer to more than the speed of his fastball), Lincecum is seen as a modern Hippie. Indeed, in one of the 2010 NLCS games against Philadelphia, some Philly fans were seen waving placards at Lincecum saying, "Hippy Trash," "Wanna Smoke?" and "The Guy Stinks" (Sullivan). Bigoted Philly fans also waved placards at outfielder Pat Burrell, saying, among other insults, "We're sorry . . . hippie" (Sullivan) though why they would say this about Burrell beats me: he doesn't look Countercultural.

---

[100] Of course, a lot has happened since I first wrote this section; particularly, the Giants have won two more World Series, in 2012 and in 2014. The team seems to have retained its Hippie associations and, to some extent, Hippie identity. Thus, though Lincecum has been traded, long-haired, bearded, Hippie-looking Jason Baumgartner is now also a star of their pitching staff.

When I ran a search using *San Francisco Giants Hippie*, I came across a blog on the official San Francisco Giants website. One comment: "Dirty radical loving hippies always fold under pressure!" A response to it: "They never regained their mojo after Governor Reagan sent in the troops." Bigoted taunting? I suppose, but it's safe to say that some blog contributors here make a Hippie-Giants connection

In August of 2010, Giant management held a Jerry Garcia Night to mark the 15th anniversary of Garcia's death; CNBC reports:

> All living members of the Grateful Dead will be involved in the day. The National Anthem will be sung by Bob Weir, Phil Lesh and Jeff Pehrson, while the seventh inning stretch will be played by Mickey Hart and Bill Kreutzmann. As an added bonus, NBA Hall of Famer and notorious "Deadhead" Bill Walton will be in attendance. Grateful Dead fans paid in between $20 and $50 to sit in a special section of the ballpark. The first 9,000 who bought tickets to the promotion got a Garcia bobblehead, sponsored by Ben & Jerry's, which of course makes the ice cream flavor Cherry Garcia. (Rovell)

And something that drew national attention during the 2010 World Series between the Giants and the Texas Rangers was the astonishment of Texas reporter Newy Scruggs at Giant fans in Candlestick Park who were openly smoking marijuana. The website for San Francisco radio station 99.7 (NOW!) headlines the piece, "Texas Thinks Giant Fans are a Bunch of Hippies."

Thus, not only does Hippie culture get some credit for a World Series championship team, but this Hippie-Giant connection should help us appreciate that event even more; after all, one of the owners of the defeated Texas Rangers was neocon former President George W. Bush, prominent in the Texas stands as his Rangers were crushed in five games. The "outlaw" Counterculture, then, outperformed the respectable Rangers (named, of course, after the Texas law officers), and Hippie-America beat Bush at his own game, trumping Hippie-hating neoconservatism in America's national pastime. Thus, the 2010 World Series transcended mere sports to become a chapter in a larger, richer national drama.

Of course, there are now many long-haired, Hippie-looking pro baseball players, suggesting a larger Hippie-American presence in the sport.

* * *

The NBA: Having already mentioned Bill and Luke Walton, here I'll discuss only two more people and move on.

Phil Jackson: Here's another legend in the world of basketball. For thirteen years, he was a star NBA player for, first, the New York Knicks and, then, the New Jersey Nets. His greatest fame and accomplishments, however, have come as the head coach of, first, the Chicago Bulls and, then, the Los Angeles Lakers—both of these teams won numerous NBA championships. I'll let *Wikipedia* tell it:

> He also won two championships as a player, and holds the NBA record for the most combined championships (13) as a player and a head coach. He also has the highest winning percentage of any NBA coach (.704). Jackson won championships as a player with the New York Knicks in 1970 and 1973 . . . .

In 2007 Jackson was inducted into the Basketball Hall of Fame.

> In 1996, as part of celebrations for the National Basketball Association's 50th anniversary, Jackson was named one of the 10 greatest coaches in league history.

Jackson's Countercultural identity is common knowledge; thus, journalist Daniel Burke in a 2008 profile for *The Washington Post* writes of Jackson's playing days with the New York Knicks, "[Jackson] became known as the hippie rebel who backed up teammate and future senator Bill Bradley." Burke adds of Jackson's spiritual journey: "That path took Jackson to the Lakota Sioux, who adopted the lanky Westerner and dubbed him 'Swift Eagle.' He also experimented with LSD and marijuana. Eventually, Jackson found his unique blend of myriad traditions; he now calls himself a 'Zen Christian.'"

Or one may find on-line an article by a Senior Lecturer in Sports Coaching at the University of Hertfordshire, David Turner, entitled, "Phil

Jackson: Zen and the Counterculture Coach." So, establishing Jackson's Hippie-American identity is a slam dunk. **HICR: 10**

Joakim Noah: Now, one of the biggest stars in the NBA, Joakim Noah came to national attention in the NCAA Final Four, leading his University of Florida Gators to national championships in 2006 (when he was picked NCAA Tournament Most Outstanding Player) and 2007. Since 2007, Joakim Noah has been the center of the Chicago Bulls, and in 2013, he was selected for the NBA All-Star Team.

Establishing Joakim Noah's Hippie identity is a snap. First, he has Hippie parents: his father is reggae singer and former tennis star Yannick Noah; the father has always had long hair, often a kind of dreadlocks. He married a former Miss Sweden, Cecilia Rodhe, who self-describes; thus, a profiler for the *Chicago Sun-Times* writes, "Ask about how she raised her children and she'll say, 'With hippie love'" (Konkol). And, of course, Joakim Noah looks Hippie with his very long hair, usually wrapped in a topknot, and facial hair. (Surprisingly, for an NBA star and a Hippie, he has no visible tattoos, far as I can tell.) And a 2008 web article is headlined, "Joakim Noah Confirms the Blindingly Obvious, Gets Busted For Weed" (Bodog-beat). Yes, his Hippie identity *is* pretty obvious, and Joakim Noah is, in fact, a self-identifier; thus, he tells an interviewer, "I'm just a chill kind of guy— a hippie that likes to go to the beach and go to concerts and do hippie things (Neumann). **HICR: 10**

As with pro baseball, one can now see many long-haired, bearded, Hippie-looking players, implying that there are numerous Hippie-Americans playing pro basketball.

* * *

> "At the University of South Carolina, Coach Paul Dietzel would not tolerate long hair on his football team. 'You cannot wear these girl haircuts,' he ordered, 'because I like to make sure we are coaching boys.'"
> —LeRoy Ashby

Let us now turn our attention to what we Americans call **football**, again both college and pro. While I acknowledge that long hair on males is not the sole or even foremost identifier of Hippie identity, when I watch football today, I see a note-worthy contingent of long hairs—you can see it sticking out of their helmets.

Again, years ago, coaches forbid long hair and often facial hair as well. LeRoy Ashby writes of 1969, "To the Notre Dame football coach, Ara Parseghian, hippies were simply 'scum.' At the University of South Carolina, Coach Paul Dietzel would not tolerate long hair on his football team. 'You cannot wear these girl haircuts,' he ordered, 'because I like to make sure we are coaching boys'" (370).

As part of a larger athlete-rights movement that started in the late Sixties, things have changed, and all these current long-haired football players suggest that the National Football League and the college leagues harbor a number of Hippie-Americans.

Let's begin here by mentioning some of the long-hairs in the NFL: among others, Mike McKenzie of the New Orleans Saints, Troy Polamalu of the Pittsburgh Steelers, Casey Matthews (brother of Clay Matthews) of the Philadelphia Eagles and the following, all employed by the Green Bay Packers: Clay Matthews, Al Harris, Brandon Chillar, Nick Barnett, Josh Sitton, AJ Hawk, Brett Swain, possibly quarterback Aaron Rodgers, who used to have long hair and facial hair (**see Photo #35**) and coach (former player) Kevin Greene.

The primary evidence I found of Hippie identity (aside from long hair on males) is that fans and sportswriters tend to see the long hair on male players as Hippie. Thus, a blogger says of Clay and Casey Matthews, "Where are all these Matthews hippie-freaks coming from?" (Wallace). Another says of Clay Matthews, "That no account, long hair, hippie type, no good sandal wearin' joker should be run outta' GB!!!!!!" (Vikingville). A Green Bay fan and blogger writes, "We sure have a lot of long haired hippies on our team!" (IluvGB). Many times, I found hostile comments directed towards long-haired players in the vein of, "Get a haircut, hippie!" I found a blog talking about "The First NFL Players who were Hippie" (Jorch). Also, a sportswriter says that a rule will be proposed requiring long-haired players to keep their hair inside their helmets; it's subheaded, "NFL Wants Damn Hippies Off Their Lawn" (Chand).

So, in the public mind, there seems to be the same conclusion I've drawn about many of these players with long hair and beards: they're Hippie. And this would hold true, no doubt, for college players as well.

Ricky Williams: Here's a player who's important not just because of his magnificent ball-carrying abilities, but because of what he represents—a Hippie who's been discriminated against. To summarize Williams' athletic achievements, in college, he won the Heisman Trophy.

Drafted by the New Orleans Saints in 1999, Williams' career soon skyrocketed. *Wikipedia*: "Williams was traded to the Miami Dolphins on March 8, 2002 for four draft picks, including two first-round picks. In 2002, his first season with the Dolphins, he was the NFL's leading rusher with 1,853 yards, a First-team All-Pro and a Pro Bowler [meaning he went to the Pro Bowl]." Williams was a sensation. Dolphin fans, in particular, couldn't get enough.

But in 2006, just before the public announcement of failing a drug test (he tested positive for marijuana), Williams left the Dolphins; he spent the 2006 season with a Canadian club, the Toronto Argonauts, whose former quarterback, the former NFL great Joe Theismann publicly castigated the Argonauts for taking Williams on: "Theismann claimed he was disgraced to be associated with a team that would knowingly sign 'an addict' such as Williams" (*Wikipedia*). The next season Williams returned to Miami, but apparently there were reports of additional failed drug tests. Somehow, Williams managed to keep playing, and he retired in 2011. My impression is that Williams was harassed and driven out of professional football prematurely due to his marijuana use.

Now, regarding Williams Hippie identity, yes, we've already discussed marijuana usage, but everything else points in that direction too: he has often worn long dreadlocks, he practices yoga, and he believes "Happiness comes from the inside, not from the outside." The best evidence here, however, is the *60 Minutes* profile of Williams by Mike Wallace in September 2005 ("Ricky Williams Opens Up"). Everything in the piece says Hippie. At one point, they even interview Williams, kicked out of the NFL, living on a beach in Australia—a Hippie beach in Australia. What I found marvelous about the interview is that when you see Williams on the field, he's scary looking. Heavily muscled, long dreadlocks, his head hidden in his helmet, he looks like some villainous creature from *Lord of the Rings*. Yet as the Wallace interview reveals, the real Williams is quite the opposite: soft spoken, intelligent, easy going—a gentleman in the truest sense of the word. It's so bizarre: think of all the professional sports players who've disgraced themselves by acts of violence against women or gun violence. And here's Ricky Williams, hounded out of the NFL, for being a marijuana user, for being Hippie.

*   *   *

> I remember watching a tennis championship on the television in the living room of a house I roomed in; as Bjorn Borg strode on-court and on-screen, I heard one of my bigoted housemates mutter in disgust, "Get the shotgun."

Professional Tennis: What's interesting about professional tennis is that, seemingly alone among sports, it's had apparently Hippie players for decades. Nowhere else were Countercultural athletes so prominent, so obvious. And that prominence has continued to this very day.

Well, as with football, our primary indicator of male Hippie identity here will be appearance. Rather than use HICR scores here, I'm simply going to caution the reader that in many of these instances, the scope of criteria I am using is limited. Also, I've edited this list, and there are many more not mentioned here.

Wikipedia: "[**Torben Ulrich**] was born on October 4, 1928. Ulrich played on the tennis tour from the late 1940s into the 1970s, and on the Tennis Grand Masters tour in the 1970s and 1980s. In 1976 he was the top-ranked senior player in the world. Ulrich played more than 100 Davis Cup matches for Denmark. In 1977, at a month shy of 49, he became the oldest Davis Cup player in history." Ulrich, incidentally, is the father of Metallica drummer Lars Ulrich, so he appears to have a Hippie son. see **Photo #36** of Torben Ulrich in his playing days. See father-son **Photo #37.**

Wikipedia: "[**Jim Courier**] is a former World No. 1 professional tennis player from the United States. During his career, he won four Grand Slam singles titles, two at the French Open and two at the Australian Open."

I'll tell an anecdote about Courier's probable Hippie identity: I was watching a tennis match on television; Brent Musburger of ABC was announcing when a voice over told us that Jim Courier, recently retired from pro tennis, was entering the ABC booth as a sort of guest commentator. I was surprised to see that Courier, not particularly long haired as a player, now had hair past his shoulders, parted in the middle. Musburger was apparently surprised as well, and rudely muttered to Courier, "So, what's with the hair, Jim?" to which Courier deftly responded, "Uh, can we talk about something else—like the match?" which he then did. I was unable to find a photo of Courier with that long hair.

I've mentioned Ulrich and Courier for interest; to save space, I've reduced the rest of this section to a list where I'll briefly mention anything besides appearance that might signal Hippie identity. The reader will find images of these players at HappilyHippie.net under "Book Images." As for the tennis accomplishments that have made these players famous, often legendary, I will refer the reader to *Wikipedia*; often, their achievements are so famous that in the tennis world, at least, they tend to be common knowledge.

John McEnroe of the USA; see **Photo #38**; here, the reader will see also what I mean by a headband being used as part of a larger Hippie look. In addition, he plays in a rock band. (In fairness, McEnroe doesn't appear Hippie today.)

Bjorn Borg of Sweden; see **Photo #39** of a very Hippie-looking Borg kissing the Wimbledon Cup.

Yannick Noah of France; see **Photo #40**; today he is known as, among other things, a professional musician and the father of NBA star Joakim Noah.

Andre Agassi of the USA; see **Photo #41**, and note earring and headscarf.

Pat Cash of Australia; see **Photo #42**; note, please, Cash's earring.

Roger Federer of Switzerland; incidentally, while Federer has been consistently long haired and Hippie looking most of his career (see **Photo #43**), recently (2017), he's adopted a shorter-hair look.[101]

Guillermo Vilas of Argentina; **Photo #45** shows an older Vilas (right) with current star Rafael Nadal.

Rafael Nadal of Spain; see **Photo #45**.

Patrick Rafter; see **Photo #46** of a very Hippie-looking Pat Rafter, off court.

Marcelo Rios of Chile; see **Photo #47**, and note that in addition to consistent long hair, usually in a ponytail, Rios has facial hair—he looks very Hippie.

Gustavo Kuerten of Brazil; see **Photo #48**, and notice how his headband makes him look even more Hippie.

---

[101]   Is it coincidence? Is it some kind of Countercultural networking? On August 20, 2006, David Foster Wallace had a piece published in the *New York Times* called "Roger Federer as a Religious Experience."

Any **women professional players** with Hippie identity? The problem here is that often, you can't just look at a female tennis player and see evidence of Hippie identity the way you often can with males. So far, at least, I can't find any; it's probable there are Countercultural women tennis players, but I'm, at this point, unable to document that.

Okay, let's wrap up pro tennis: First, yes, I am leaning heavily on appearance here; still, even I am shocked by how many Hippie-looking men there are in this sport, how often these players have been the sport's very best. Individually, their accomplishments are often legendary; in aggregate, we see a stupendous array of tennis ability and greatness

* * *

Hippie Olympians: As Hippie culture has evolved, its youth have cultivated particular sports, particularly boarding sports; surfing, skateboarding and snowboarding seem to have a Countercultural connection. Hippie surfers,

> **As Hippie culture has evolved, its youth have cultivated particular sports, particularly boarding sports; surfing, skateboarding and snow-boarding seem to have a Countercultural connection.**

of course, are neutral stereotypes. And there's another neutral stereotype, I think, of the adolescent Hippie skateboarder. As we'll see, Shaun White, for instance, got his start as a skate boarder—presumably the sport is more accessible than surfing or snowboarding. *Sports Illustrated* tells us, "Snow-boarding is a sport with a proud heritage of 'freethinking, creative people who often fall a bit outside the status quo,' says Mark Sullivan, publisher of *Snowboard* magazine" ("US"). These terms sound like euphemisms for *Hippies* to me. And the US Olympic Halfpipe coach Bud Keene is quoted as saying, "The stereotype for snowboarders is they come from a hippie upbringing and all that that entails" (Swift).

The biggest name in snowboarding is **Shaun White**, aka, The Flying Tomato, so known for his long mane of red locks (**see Photo #51**) and because he flies though the wintry air with the greatest of ease. He won Olympic Gold in the Half-pipe, and he did that two Winter Olympics in a row, Torino in 2006 and Vancouver in 2010. There is now an entire snow-boarding tour, full of medal-awarding events; White has won medals in all of them, apparently, and usually gold. Austin Murphy of *SI* calls him "the Michael Jordon of extreme sports." A *60 Minutes* interview with White at his personal training site somewhere deep in the Rockies revealed White also has a small financial empire that yields several million a year (CBS News). Let me finish by noting that one reason White is so dominant in his sport is because he keeps developing new "tricks," keeps pushing the envelope in a sport that's still growing (CBS News); so, in his sport, he's having an historical impact.

Proving White's Hippie identity is fairly easy. First of all, he's always looked very Hippie, on course and off. Also, White has been on the cover of the *Rolling Stone* twice. My research showed him apparently hanging out with Counterculturists, and I even found a fun photo of White with Richard Branson—so there does seem to be some Countercultural networking here. And a web search shows that people regularly recognize White as Hippie. **HICR: 9.75 to 10**

Next, consider another great American snowboarder, **Hannah Teter** of Vermont. In the Half-Pipe, Teter won Olympic Gold in Turin in 2006 and the Olympic Silver in Vancouver in 2010. She regularly wins medals on the pro snow-boarding circuit.

Her parents are Vermont Hippies; Teter describes her background: "A different kind of family, I guess. . . . I guess you call them hippies. They met at a music festival in Colorado. Dad was leaning against a tree, playing a flute, and Mom walked by and caught his eye." (Quotes Daddy). Also, she has a Ben & Jerry's Ice Cream flavor named after her: Maple Gold (her family runs a maple-syrup business that she remains involved in) (AP, "Ben"). *SI* had a photo of Teter with a psychedelic pattern on the bottom of her board, and she speaks in a sort of Hippie lingo, telling an interviewer, for instance, how she'd had a chance to "really chill out" and how something else "blew me away." People tend to see Teter as Hippie; thus, an interviewer writes, "That's typical Teter; she's a little rambling, a bit of a hippie, and quick to slip into stereotypical snowboard-speak. She drops more 'rads' than a surfer" (Gregory). Also, *Time* notes she now eats organic food ("it makes me feel purer and more powerful") (qtd. in "Shaun White"). And Teter is quite the accomplished humanitarian. Thus, she writes on her website, Hannah's Gold, "Currently, I am focusing on raising funds for a huge clean water project . . . and buying plots of land for homeless AIDS victims that we met in Kirindon, Kenya, the town we've been sponsoring for 3 years. Through donating all my contest winnings, through selling maple syrup and organic cotton/hemp sweatbands, I hope we can accomplish the goal of supporting my community with beautiful, clean water!" (Teter). Hannah Teter makes me proud to be Hippie-American! **HICR: 10**

Wikipedia: "**Apolo Anton Ohno** . . . is an American short track speed skating competitor and an eight-time medalist (two gold, two silver, four bronze) in the Winter Olympics. He is the most decorated American Winter Olympic athlete of all time." You may have seen Ohno on television's *Dancing with the Stars* where he is also a champion, winning the 2007 season with partner Julianne Hough. He's written *A Journey: The Autobiography of Apolo Anton Ohno* (2002); he's also a motivational speaker who's written *Zero Regrets: Be Greater Than Yesterday* (2010).

As for evidence of Hippie identity, I'll lean heavily on looks here. Ohno—with his consistently longish hair, goatee, and trademark bandanna headband when skating—has always looked Hippie (**see Photo #52**); if he's not Countercultural, how do we explain his appearance? He has, in addition, an interest in nutrition and healthy eating; in particular, *Wikipedia* tells us, he developed and sells a line of supplements, 8 Zone, and he's been working on a "healthy" cookbook with chefs in Seattle. Also, Ohno does community service; he seems very philanthropic (*Wikipedia*). Call the skating god Hippie-Japanese-American. **HICR: 9.25**

Wikipedia: "[**Ben Agosto**] is an American ice dancer. With partner Tanith Belbin, Agosto is the 2006 Olympic silver medalist, a four-time World medalist, the 2004–2006 Four Continents champion, and 2004–2008 U.S. champion."

As for Hippie identity, I'll again rely heavily on looks: as noted, a ponytail on a man (Agosto skates wearing one) is a strong indicator of Hippie ethnicity. **Photo #53** shows a an off-rink Agosto with long hair, a mustache and goatee, and he's carrying a guitar over his should, communicating Counterculturality. Plus, Agosto has a green reputation; thus, the website EarthDay.org says of Agosto in "Our Artists and Athletes," "Passionate supporter of all things green, Ben [Agosto] now supports Athletes for the Earth™" (Artists and Athletes for the Earth). Again, it would be nice to know more about Agosto; suffice it to, to say, we probably have enough here now to call him Hippie-Puerto-Rican-American, or something like that. **HICR: 9.25**

There are probably other Countercultural Olympians, but for now, we'll stop with these. A parting comment: bigots believe

Hippie-Americans are anti-American, that the Counterculture has let down, even betrayed, the USA. Let me point out that every one of the above-mentioned Hippie-American Olympians has done a sort of patriotic duty, has brought honor and glory to our nation.

* * *

Consider the English footballer (what the USA calls a *soccer player*) **David Beckham**. He's been runner up for best player in the world twice, and considering how many nations play football and how popular the sport is, that's something. He's probably the best known footballer in the world—lots of advertising deals, male-model looks, married to a former Spice Girl rock star. The couple is s sort of royalty, and *Wikipedia* puts their net worth at $125 million; both have high-profile lives. David Beckham, then, is a legend as in the film *Bend It Like Beckham* (2002).

Now, Hippie identity: I'll do this largely on looks. I found several photos of Beckham with long hair, sometimes a beard and lots of tattoos, looking very Hippie. In **Photo #54**, readers will find a particularly nice image of a Hippie-looking Beckham. **HICR: 9.0**

* * *

Race-car driver **Leilani Münter** is an American race car driver and environmental activist. She drives in the ARCA Racing Series, and previously drove in the Firestone Indy Lights, the development league of IndyCar. Prior to her debut in open-wheel racing, she was a stock car driver in the NASCAR Elite division." The website *Vegetarian Star* comments, "Race car driver Leilani Münter comes in as the #1 eco athlete on Planet Green's Planet 100. Leilani Münter is on a mission to ensure every race car uses clean, renewable biofuels and every race track has a recycling program." (*Wikipedia*).

> "Leilani Münter is on a mission to ensure every race car uses clean, renewable biofuels and every race track has a recycling program. "Her motto: "Never under-estimate a vegetarian hippie chick with a race car."

So, she's a woman making a difference. She self-identifies: her motto: "Never underestimate a vegetarian hippie chick with a race car" ("Race"). **(See Photo # 55.) HICR: 10**

* * *

There are sports that Hippiedom has pioneered and developed—brought to life, so to speak. Given that Hippies seem to have an affinity for mountains, it should come as no great surprise that such a sport is **Rock Climbing.**

The Counterculture didn't invent rock climbing (*Wikipedia* says it's existed since the mid 1800s), but it *has* re-invented it; Hippiedom has done with rock climbing as it did with yoga and meditation, turning something rare into something relatively common, especially if you consider the recent popularity of that outgrowth of rock-climbing, indoor climbing walls.

And, no, not every successful rock climber is Hippie. For example, I ran a search on the newest women's sensation in *free climbing* (without ropes, pitons, etc.), Sasha DiGuguilian; an interviewer reports that off the rocks, she has "a preference for pink and nail polish" (Spalding). I say . . . probably not Hippie.

Still, there are a lot of accomplished climbers—many, pioneers in the sport—who *are* Hippie. Also, the history of modern rock climbing seems so intertwined with the Counterculture that its newfound prominence can be considered a contribution of Hippiedom to the larger world.

One early group of Hippie rock climbers were known as the Stonemasters, and climber/writer John Long has written a book about them: *The Stonemasters: California Rock Climbers in the Seventies* (2009), and in **Photo #56,** see a fine image of these young men, taking a break on the rocks, all looking very Hippie. Reviewer Courtney Eldridge writes:

> [T]his long-haired band of bros from Southern California, who, armed with little more than frayed cut-offs, dark shades and folded bandanas, heralded the golden age of American rock climbing. They called themselves the Stonemasters—cheeky, but deserved—in their stripped-down, bare-bones approach to climbing, they devised revolutionary techniques, underscored by their renegade attitudes. Balancing intensity and exuberance,

the Stonemasters were a team of some of the most innovative daredevils the world has ever seen, and in the early 1970s, these laid-back originators of adventure sports were risking life and limb . . . .

Eldridge also calls them "hybrid pioneers bound by a communal spirit" and (I like this) "surfers of stone."

And what's been true for the US has apparently been true in other nations, particularly the UK. ClimbMagazine.com tells us, "Forty years ago, when Martin Crocker led his first routes on the compact grey limestone of the Avon Gorge, he had little idea that this . . . crag would kick-start his career as one of the leading pioneers in late twentieth century British rock climbing" (Crocker, editor).

Crocker himself writes:

It was a hippy idea, and it suited the times. The year was 1974 . . . to improve the odds I took to the belay a ghetto blaster with a strange brew of Hendrix, Al Green, Price Buster, and Pink Floyd. The strategy was to float weightlessly up on cosmic chords . . . .

Thus, we can date heavy Hippie involvement in and leadership of rock climbing from the late 1960s onward. Also, I was able to establish likely Hippie identity for a number of today's rock-climbing stars, male and female. Generally, the Counterculture has so influenced and dominated this modern sport that, some non-Hippie climbing stars aside, we might say we "own" it.

*   *   *

Mountain biking: Consider how many mountain-biking trails or multi-use trails that include mountain biking there now are, and this is true in parks and recreational areas across America and much of the world. And, of course, there's now an entire racing circuit of mountain-biking events. Mountain biking, then, is significant, something that's made its mark on American and international life.

So, where does mountain biking come from? Yes, Hippie culture. There is a documentary film about how Hippiedom developed the modern mountain bike and effectively created a new sport/recreation; directed by

Billy Savage, it's called *Klunkerz: A Film about Mountain Bikes (They Re-Invented the Wheel)*. In a piece entitled "Stoned Hippies, Crappy Bikes, and the History of Mountain Biking," reviewer Josh Cohen writes:

> Last night I watched *Klunkerz*, a 2007 documentary that traces the roots of mountain biking back to late-1960s Marin County, California. Mountain biking was spawned by a group of hippies and scofflaws[102] (including current industry big-wigs Joe Breeze and Gary Fisher) who enjoyed getting high and bombing through the woods around Mount Tamalpais.

I'll dispense with doing Hippie identifications on individual mountain bikers; for now, suffice it to say that this blessing to humanity has been brought to us courtesy of a bunch of Hippie scofflaws.

* * *

Our accomplishments in the world of sports are impressive. Not only do we have a plethora of likely Countercultural athletes who are very successful and prominent in their sports, sometimes legends, sometimes Olympic-medal winners, but we have Hippiedom inventing or at least re-inventing and developing some very popular contemporary sports: snowboarding, rock climbing and mountain biking. You can't help but be impressed, and, hey, I didn't even have to mention hacky-sacking.

* * *

Next, we're going to look at some **Hippie-created businesses and institutions[103];** we'll consider entire realms of the economy that the Counterculture has pioneered and developed as well as the striking careers and creations of some distinguished Counterculturists. Since we just ended a section on Hippie contributions to two outdoor sports, let's begin by looking at the modern outdoor-outfitting business, now referred to as the "adventure-gear" industry. We're going to look at several such

---

[102] This means "a contemptuous law violator"; I assume it's used here humorously.

[103] We could add here all the natural/organic grocers and related companies, but we've covered them.

companies, beginning with the national brands JanSport, The North Face, Patagonia, and REI.

Why **JanSport**? As *Wikipedia* tells us, "JanSport is the world's largest backpack maker, and together, JanSport and The North Face sell nearly half of all small backpacks sold in the United States. . . . JanSport innovated with a panel-loading daypack, unlike traditional top-loading packs. In 1975 it introduced the first convertible travel pack as well as its signature daypack."

> **Co-founder Skip Yowell credits JanSport's astounding success to the application of Hippie values: "nurturing others, speaking well of others, and assisting others."**

Now, think how common backpacks are today—every student has one, from pre-schoolers on up. We take them for granted and seldom ask, "Where did backpacks come from, anyway? Well, JanSport developed them—and made other very important innovations in this field. The modern camping tent with a dome design was a JanSport creation,[104] tested, like all JanSport products, in arduous conditions. And JanSport designed the first external-frame pack in the early 1970s—another innovative and revolutionary design of an ancient human tool. Think of it: the modern backpack, the dome tent and the external-frame pack. In their field, JanSport has been genius.

And it turns out, they've also pioneered a Hippie business model and shown how Countercultural values can lead to success in business. One of the founders of JanSport, Skip Yowell, has written a book called *The Hippie Guide to Climbing the Corporate Ladder & Other Mountains: How JanSport Makes It Happen* (Naked Ink, 2006).[105] As the title makes clear, JanSport was founded by Hippies: (Yowell, his cousin Murray Pletz, and Pletz' wife, Janice "Jan" Lewis, from whence derives the

---

[104] JanSport co-founder Skip Yowell writes: "Keep in mind that the concept of a dome was not new. In fact, we traced its origins back to pre-Ice Age man. But it was JanSport that introduced this tensioned dome structure to the backpacking community, and since its introduction into the market in 1972, our Dome (with external pole system) has in one form or other been adapted throughout the industry" (86).

[105] Incidentally, I recommend this book—an interesting, fun read that has lessons to teach, and not just about business, but about lives well lived.

company name). And what a great ride it's been. Yowell and company created tools for lives lived to the fullest—*carpe diem*, boys and girls! And by insisting that JanSport products be rigorously field tested, the Hippies at JanSport have had amazing experiences, from climbing the highest peaks to having an early prototype of a tent fail during a blizzard—a treasure trove of great stories and memories. And Yowell credits JanSport's astounding success to the application of Hippie values: "nurturing others, speaking well of others, and assisting others" (138). It should come as no great surprise, then, that JanSport has done great community-service work, too.

Well, JanSport is a tough act to follow, but let's next look at a now-famous company with a rock-climbing-derived name, **The North Face**. First, a quick description from *Wikipedia*:

> The North Face, Inc. is an American outdoor product company specializing in outerwear, fleece, coats, shirts, footwear, and equipment such as backpacks, tents, and sleeping bags. . . . In addition to selling through department stores and outdoor retailers, The North Face operates over 40 retail locations in the United States, 18 locations in the United Kingdom and many others worldwide.

The North Face is a widely recognized brand—so much so that they've endured numerous infringements of their name (*Wikipedia*).

Here's a story demonstrating The North Face's Hippie identity: it seems the two 2012 Republican presidential hopefuls, Mitt Romney and Veep nominee Paul Ryan, have a penchant for The North Face jackets—so much so this attracted media attention. I suppose they feel it makes them look heroic or something: Mitt Romney, the rugged billionaire, after a hearty breakfast, briefly exits the Mittmobile to scale a cliff with his bare hands. A portion of the piece:

> The pair [Romney and Ryan] even flashed matching North Face logos when they stood side by side Friday at a rally in Lancaster, Ohio. It's a choice that North Face founder Kenneth "Hap" Klopp finds "ironic." "We started in Berkeley in the late 60s . . . We were a hippie brand," said Klopp, who hasn't been in contact with the campaign. "When we started, the concept was an iconoclastic approach." (Fox)

If we needed further evidence that The North Face has Hippie roots, the company has a "mantra": "Never Stop Exploring" (*Wikipedia*).

Next, **Patagonia**. Like The North Face, here's a well-known brand with a reputation for producing quality outdoor wear and equipment. *Wikipedia*: "Patagonia, Inc. is a Ventura, California-based clothing company, focusing mainly on high-end outdoor clothing. . . . It was founded by Yvon Chouinard in 1972." And Patagonia is important also because it's environmentally active, doing its best to push the green envelope, to practice what it preaches.

Are they Hippie? Well, a look at their website (Patagonia.com) shows a scene littered with evidence of Hippie identity. They seem touchy about that website being quoted without permission, so I'll just say that on occasion a Patagonia employee, at work, might be barefoot. And we see the green emphasis noted above. Also, people—outsiders—tend to see Patagonia as Hippie and speak of it that way as if it were common knowledge. Thus, journalist/ pundit Anne Murphy responds to an *Inc. Magazine* cover article on "countercultural entrepreneurs":

> The four ["countercultural"] companies mentioned in the article were the $130 millions, publicly traded, Ben & Jerry's ice cream business, founded by hippies Ben Cohen and Jerry Greenfield; Anita and Gordon Roddick's the Body Shop business based in England; Patagonia, the high scale outdoors outfitter founded by Yvon Chouinard; Smith and Hawken founded by Paul Hawken.

"The Seven (Almost) Deadly Sins of High Minded Entrepreneurs" is the title of the *Inc. Magazine* July 1994 issue cover story. The subtitle: "A generation of countercultural entrepreneurs struck out to change the world in the 1980s by building socially responsible businesses and made getting filthy rich look like good clean fun. (Murphy)

Yes, call Patagonia (not to mention Body Shop, Smith & Hawken and, of course, Ben & Jerry's) Countercultural.

Let's next look at another renowned adventure-gear company: **REI.** I found lots of evidence tending to identify REI as Hippie, so much, in fact, that we might call its Countercultural character common knowledge. But in this quote from an article where the author calls REI "hippie," we find an interesting twist: "By now the news of Obama's nomination of Sally Jewell, the current President and CEO of every hippie's favorite outdoor gear store, REI, to head the Department of the Interior has reached those of us in the Tundra" (The Northern Right). Yes, the head of this Hippie company did become the 51st Secretary of the Interior.

Now, if you're wondering, where's Columbia,[106] the answer is that a bit of research regarding Hippie identity was unpromising: it's probably not a Hippie company.

Also, there are a lot of **smaller national companies,** which the reader may learn about by looking at an article by Anna Brones "Top 10 adventure gear companies you should know and why". These companies both produce quality gear and are environmentally active and green. They are Patagonia; "Canada's popular outdoor gear cooperative, Mountain Equipment Co-op"; international producer of "performance gear," Marmot; Canadian producer of "high end outdoor gear," Arc'teryx; shoe and boot maker, Timberland; Colorado-based backpack maker, Osprey; Big Agnes, which makes camping equipment, including tents and sleeping bags out of recycled plastic bottles; Mountain Hardware, maker of outdoor clothing; MountainSmith, which makes packs, partly from recycled plastic; and the Portland-based shoemaker Keen. Probably most of these companies are Countercultural; also, some such companies remain local.

Let's conclude this section by noting the profound impact Hippiedom has had on the adventure-gear/outdoor sporting industry. We invented large parts of it, and we revolutionized its tools and techniques. Also, this Hippie-dominated and developed industry is particularly green; often, it displays progressive business models, and it shows again how creative and practical Hippies are.

* * *

Let's look at another burgeoning area where Hippie-Americans are predominant: **microbreweries**. The tendency in the mainstream American beer market has been towards centralization, towards the big-fish companies and distributors eating the little-fish companies and distributors, towards national brands as opposed to local brands.

Accompanying this has been the kind of "white-bread effect" mainstream American culture has on things we eat and drink— employ a lowest-common denominator appeal, increase its shelf life

---

[106] The company, not the country.

with preservatives, ignore nutritional aspects, and narrow the whole experience to something very conformist, safe and predictable.

The American microbrewing industry appears almost the opposite. First, it tends to be very local—thus, the word "micro" in the title. These are small businesses not necessarily looking to conquer the beer-drinking world. Generally, these microbrews are more natural than their mainstream competitors, and lately, I'm occasionally seeing "organic beer" from micro-breweries. And of course, the microbreweries specialize in homemade variety; it's made right there on the premises, and there's often a changing variety of unique brews.

I also think that, being local, these microbreweries tend to be much more a part of their communities—to be more present, in a way—than the corporate behemoths of Big Beer.[107]

Hippie identity? From what I see around Boulder and environs, it's pretty obvious that modern American microbreweries are a Countercultural innovation. The Mountain Sun in Boulder, for instance, has now spawned another four stores, expanding into Denver and nearby Longmont. The Suns are more than microbreweries; they're restaurants too—brewpubs.

"These men and women, better known as "hop-heads" (an offhand reference to "Deadheads," the eponymous followers of the Grateful Dead), had extensive knowledge of the brewing process," says professor Neil Rieck, and they launched a Hippie-American microbrew industry.

They're overtly Hippie, and they've always been very successful and popular—in a large part, I think, due to their Hippie environment and atmosphere, including exemplary customer service.

When I did a web search using the term *microbreweries Hippie*, I got many hits, suggesting that Hippie brewpubs dot America and are

---

[107] *Wikipedia* ("Microbrewery") notes there are specific guidelines that keep a microbrewery (also called a "craft brewery") relatively small and local; it cannot, for instance, be more than 24% owned by another company that is not also a craft brewery. Note, however, that microbreweries often bottle and sell their products, usually locally.

prominent in heavily Hippie areas.[108] May I suggest that the curious reader do such a search. Some sound Countercultural in their self-description: "Rogue Meeting Halls are not cookie cutter corporate creations but like Americans come in all shapes and sizes . . ." (Rogue Ales). That's right: "meeting halls."

Finally, I found a semi-scholarly webpage: "More than Water, Hops, Barley, and Yeast: Authenticity and the Microbrew Revolution" by one Neil Rieck, apparently a professor of American Studies at the University of Virginia. He writes of the origins of America's modern microbrew industry:

> The people who were largely involved in the craft brew phenomenon, Baby Boomers who had grown up in the liberating 60's, had finally "found" them-selves in the 70's. . . . Emphasizing personal experience, self-discovery and a resistance to established institutions, the "seekers" of the Seventies looked inward for enlightenment as New Age religion and a "back to nature" aesthetic gained popularity. Communes sprang up in Northern California and Oregon as the 60's came to an end. The foothills of the Sierra Nevada and Cascade Mountains, as well as the valleys and beaches that spread out to the west welcomed many more nature-lovers and "hippies" who were searching for a genuine experience away from the "grim routine of the workaday world" (Schulman). The maverick spirit of the West, a strange yet potent bedfellow with the communal ideologies of the "hippie generation," drives the desires of the microbrewers to stay small and not become associated as a corporate conglomeration with the likes of the major breweries.
>
> These men and women, better known as "hop-heads" (an offhand reference to "Deadheads," the eponymous followers of the Grateful Dead), had extensive knowledge of the brewing process, the proper proportions of the ingredients in different beers, and could detail specific tastes in each beer.

---

[108] Since my research also showed an occasional brewpub owner who didn't look Hippie, I'm not claiming a Hippie monopoly in this field. I'm also not claiming that in other nations (the UK, for instance) the brewpub industry is as Hippie as here in the USA.

Thus, in the USA, at least, Hippiedom dominates this thriving field.

*   *   *

Mary-Kate and Ashley Olsen/Fashion: The Olsens were once those television twins who played one adorable child on *Full House*; soon, they were making wholesome Disney-like films that sold by gajillions, and eventually they became two of the wealthiest females in entertainment. Then, they grew up and became important fashion designers and trend setters. When I researched this in *Wikipedia*, I was impressed. Let me quote a bit (minus source citations):

> As the sisters have matured, they expressed greater interest in their fashion choices, with *The New York Time* declaring Mary-Kate a fashion icon for pioneering her signature (and now popular among celebrities and fans alike) "homeless" look. The style, sometimes referred to by fashion journalists as "ashcan" or "bohemian-bourgeois," is similar to the boho-chic style popularized in Britain by Kate Moss and Sienna Miller. The look consists of oversized sunglasses, boots, loose sweaters, and flowing skirts, with an aesthetic of mixing high-end and low-end pieces.

Add to this contracts with major merchandisers, their own fashion label ("The Row") and the 2008 publication of *Influence*, which *Wikipedia* describes as "a compilation of interviews with many of the most prominent people in the field of fashion," among other accomplishments.

If the Olsen twins are powers in the world of fashion, is fashion important? Well, "man does not live by bread alone," and if we need art, then fashion is one of the most accessible and immediate arts in that it's the art we wear and see every day. Yes, it is important for that and other reasons.

As for cultural identity, as you might have guessed from the above description of the Olsen fashion sense, they are Hippie-American. I consider their Hippie identity common knowledge; thus, an article on the website *Celebuzz!* is called "Fashion FTW: The Olsen Twins Are True Hippies . . . (Celebuzz!). There are numerous other pieces online substantiating and repeating that identification, and far as I can tell, everything about the Olsens says "modern Hippie." **HICR: 10**

Now, I've begun here with the Olsen twins because they give me a very specific example of Hippie culture applied to the world of fashion with great success. But the Olsens are the tip of a Countercultural iceberg here. What would we see if we considered the impact that Hippie culture has had on American and world fashion over the last fifty years? As mentioned, probably blue jeans (and jeans in general) have entered mainstream wear through the Counterculture. And again, we've had a positive effect on the way people dress in terms of lessening the formality of clothing and pushing towards more natural fabrics—that and probably in other ways that I'm not well-qualified to write about. For now, then, let's say Hippiedom's contributions here are noteworthy; this area would be a suitable subject for a book by an author interested in our impact on fashion.

*   *   *

Craigslist: Wow, how this seemingly simple, unpretentious website has changed our everyday lives! It creates a local cyber marketplace as well as providing other services (people meeting people, for instance), and it does it for free and without advertisements. That's right, what we used to have to pay for to advertise and sell in a local newspaper, we can now do for free and ever so easily. Craigslist is marvelous, and I laugh when I see occasional snotty comments about it from wannabe internet competitors.

How do I know Craigslist is Hippie? Well, under "Craigslist/About/Craig," I found a short biography and personal description of Craig Newmark: he's a "philanthropist, and a strong advocate of the use of technology for the public good." He's lived in San Francisco for twenty-plus years and is a bit of an activist, doing work for veterans' organizations, "open government, public diplomacy, back-to-basics journalism and fact-checking, consumer protection, and technology for the public good."

Craig Newmark, then, would seem to evidence several Hippie values, and in the webpage's accompanying photo, Newmark looks somewhat Hippie too. Well, not to sweat it here: in my computer's Favorites menu, I have "Craigslist," and in front of the name, apparently part of the logo, is a purple peace sign. So, that's the first thing Craigslist tells someone who uses it regularly, and it's essentially Hippie self-identification. **HICR: 10**

*   *   *

> *Wikipedia* **seems to live out much of those early ideals of community and public service that Hippie cyber pioneers laid out decades ago. A free service to users,** *Wikipedia* **seems like a scene from that cyber** *Brigadoon* **Stewart Brand spoke of.**

Wikipedia is wonderful. The claim that anyone can edit a *Wikipedia* entry as easily as snapping their fingers is inaccurate; while *Wikipedia* has had embarrassing error issues in the past, apparently that situation has been remedied, and a 2012 column in PCWorld.com reports, "[T]here are no recent relevant studies showing that *Britannica* is more accurate than *Wikipedia*" (Ionescu). As Clay Shirky notes in the UK *Guardian*:

> Many of *Wikipedia*'s critics have focused on the fact that the software lets anyone edit anything; what they miss is that the social constraints of the committed editors keep that capability in check. As easy as the software makes it to do damage, it makes it even easier to undo damage . . . Every single day for the last 10 years *Wikipedia* has gotten better because someone— several million someones in all—decided to make it better."

Let's think, then, of *Wikipedia*'s past problems as growing pains, and agree that, at the end of the day, *Wikipedia* is a boon to humanity.

Now, my hypothesis here was this: *Wikipedia* seems to live out much of those early ideals of community and public service that Hippie cyber pioneers laid out decades ago. A free service to users, *Wikipedia* seems like a scene from that cyber Brigadoon Stewart Brand spoke of. So, it's likely Hippie inspired; it's likely Hippie.

First, I found reporters and bloggers who find *Wikipedia* Hippie-ish; Giles Hattersley of the London *Sunday Times* speaks of founder Jimmy "Wales's hippie-tastic dream of access for every-one" (Hattersley). Wales himself writes, "This is a common pattern—to posit that yes, in the early days, *Wikipedia* was an anarchist dream, a hippie commune, a little bit of socialism or communism that actually worked— but over time, it had to grow up, to institute controls." Wales, then, seems to be recognizing some Hippie roots in *Wikipedia*.

On the other hand, that doesn't automatically make *Wikipedia* a Hippie institution today. First, Wales says, "I am not a hippie" though it seems clear from the context that he sees "hippie" as a left-leaning philosophy (Wales); Wales is apparently a rightist, an Ayn Rand disciple (Smart). Yet, as noted, there are conservative Hippies. And when I ran an image search on Wales, I found photos where he appears in Asian dress; in some, he's attired in that Hippie classic, the Nehru jacket, and suffice it to say, Wales doesn't appear racially Asian. Here, then, we have some limited evidence of potential Hippie identity.

I also found some evidence of *Wikipedia's* Hippie roots in the person of one Richard Stallman who resigned from MIT in 1984 to start something called the GNU project, a precursor of *Wikipedia*; a Google image search reveals numerous images of an obviously Countercultural Stallman. In *Jimmy Wales and Wikipedia*, Susan Meyer writes:

> The name "Nupedia" came from a combination of the word "encyclopedia" and something called the GNU public license. The GNU public license was an idea formed largely by a computer programmer named Richard Stallman. He shared many of Wales' ideas that information should be open to all people [37-38] . . . . He [Wales] would go on to use the idea of free information and open content sharing in Nupedia [which lasted until 2003] and ultimately, *Wikipedia*. (39)

Also, the personality that many people are now (2013) associating with *Wikipedia* is that of "*Wikipedia* programmer" Brandon Harris; that's because Harris has become the public face of *Wikipedia's* on-site fund-raising campaign.[109] Harris looks very Hippie with his long hair and facial hair; an image search showed several photos of Harris strumming a guitar—almost stereotypically Hippie. Okay, so let's call Harris Countercultural.

In *How a Bunch of Nobodies Created the World's Greatest Encyclopedia: The Wikipedia Revolution* (2009), Andrew Lih tells us that Ward Cunningham "was the creator of the wiki concept, the radical idea of allowing anyone to openly edit any page of a Web site" (2), laying the intellectual basis for *Wikipedia*. He describes Cunningham as "A tall and portly gentleman . . . with the trusty hacker look—gray beard, button-down shirt, round stomach, and tan Birkenstocks" (2).

---

[109] As of early 2016, this is no longer the case.

Well, sounds Hippie to me. Lih then mentions one of the "folks who built *Wikipedia* from nothing . . . Erik Moeller, a German user with the trademark ponytail of a computer hacker" (3). And Lih notes, "The computing culture at MIT and other top scientific schools [like where Richard Stallman came from] was one of sharing and openness. These institutions were full of people, after all, who were pursuing software programming not for dollar profits, but for the love of discovery and pioneering new solutions to problems" (24). Again, that sounds fairly Hippie to me.

If we looked in more depth at this amazing institution, I'm sure we'd find more Hippie influences and Hippie participation among the many who have created and care for *Wikipedia*. On the other hand, let's not assume everyone involved in this project is Hippie, either.[110] For now, let's say that *Wikipedia* is a child dreamt of by the Hippie parents of the PC, by the Countercultural pioneers of cyber culture. Hippiedom was certainly the cultural force behind and a major developer of *Wikipedia*, and that's something we should be immensely proud of. Well done, Counterculturists! **HICR: 9.0**

* * *

Steve Jobs: We earlier talked about how Steve Jobs, along with partner Steve Wozniak, created the first marketable personal computer. And Jobs' Hippie identity is common knowledge. Why discuss him again? Well, he's now left his body, and as the July 15, 2012 *60 Minutes* revealed, Jobs' co-creation of the Apple II "home computer" was only the first among many astounding achievements in what people increasingly regard as a great life. *60 Minutes* reporter Steve Kroft: "In his best-selling biography of Jobs, Walter Issacson writes that he revolutionized or re-imagined seven industries: personal computers, animated movies, music, telephones, tablet computing, digital publishing and retail stores" (CNET). That's a broad impact on society. Let's briefly look at some of these contributions, bearing in mind that our categories are going to get mixed, and that's because Jobs was a genre-bender:

---

[110] For example, a major player in *Wikipedia's* history is Larry Sanger, who doesn't appear, at least, Hippie.

First, as noted, Jobs was a personal-computer pioneer—as important as anyone in that process.

"Animated movies"—think Pixar, the small studio Jobs bought from *Star Wars* director George Lucas and turned into one of the most popular and successful entertainment businesses in the world. Pixar animations are astounding. The three dimensionality, the realism of motion, the life-likeness of the characters—previous

> **Because Steve Jobs had clear Countercultural identity, and because much of his success seems to have Hippie roots and reasons, we can credit Jobs' many contributions to the world not just to Steve Jobs the individual but to the ethnicity from which he hailed: Hippie-America.**

types of animation seem to pale in comparison. Next time you're being amazed by the sophistication of a Pixar-type animation, remember, it's brought to you by a Hippie-American.

Music—in "4 Ways Steve Jobs and Apple Changed the Music Industry," Max Blau lists four basic contributions: Musical Consumption Patterns, Accessibility of Recording and Production Tools, Online Retail and Distribution Models, and Live Electronic Performance Becomes Reliable.

Regarding telephones, Apple's iPhone, developed and introduced by Jobs in 2007, integrated phone functions into multi-function machine (*Wikipedia*, "iPhone"). That integration of different functions has also been a signature feature of other Jobs-pioneered Apple technologies.

"Tablet computing" is related to the next area, "digital publishing" because one major form of digital publishing is books and other materials geared for electronic reading tablets. A *60 Minutes* episode, "Apps for Autism," explores how a Jobs-created computing tablet has dramatically changed the world for "autistic people whose condition prevents them from speaking." *60 Minutes* correspondent Leslie Stahl reports, "When Steve Jobs unveiled the iPad, there's no way he could have predicted what it would mean to people with autism; it turns out it may be the perfect device to unlock the isolation many with autism feel by helping them communicate in ways they couldn't before."

The program then shows such a man in a restaurant; instead of struggling to speak his order, with a few simple touches, his Ipad, replete with speaker and computerized voice, can order those bacon and eggs with a side of hash browns for him—and thank the server afterwards. For vocally challenged autistics, this iPad app is a miracle.

These are some of the important contributions to modern society made by Steve Jobs. And because Jobs had clear Countercultural identity, and because much of his success seems to have Hippie roots and reasons, we can credit Jobs' many contributions to the world not just to Steve Jobs the individual but to the ethnicity from which he hailed: Hippie-America.

HICR: 10

Another possibly Hippie high-tech giant is **Google**, one of the largest, most successful cyber businesses on the planet. Presumably, we all know of Google, so let's talk Hippie identity. An article called "Rise of the Hippie-Crat" says, "Sergey Brin and Larry Page started Google with the tag line: 'Don't be evil.' Despite being two of the richest guys in the world they were regular attendees to the Burning Man festival, which really is a great big hippie-fest" (BradP). A BBC piece profiling Google's two founders speaks of their "hippie mantra" ("Don't be evil") (Smale). Also, a July 2013 piece in *Wired*, "Enlightenment Engineer: Meditation and mindfulness are the new rage in Silicon Valley. And it's not just about inner peace—it's about getting ahead," discusses how meditation and Mindfulness have become a major part of Google's corporate culture, and while mentioning that some in the company reject this "hippie bullshit" (Shactman), it is apparent that the company has a strong Countercultural influence; in addition to the meditation, *Wired* mentions the company's "free organic meals" for its employees (Shactman). The BBC notes that Google's head chef used to cook for the Grateful Dead (Smale).

So, without assuming that each and every Google employee is Countercultural, let's place Google in the general realm of Hippiedom. **HICR: 9.0**

Richard Branson: He's well-known to be Hippie-English; thus, *Travel Agent* magazine, for instance, refers to his airline, Virgin, as a "Counterculture Carrier" (Cardona). In 2007, *Time* rated this Englishman one of the 100 Most Influential People in the World (*Wikipedia*). A highly successful entrepreneur, his Virgin Group owns over 400 companies, including Virgin Airlines, Virgin Records, Virgin Trains, etc. *Wikipedia* says of him, "According to the Forbes 2012 list of billionaires, Branson is the 6th richest citizen of the United Kingdom, with an estimated net worth of US\$4.6 billion." Branson is also involved in space exploration (*Wikipedia*). He has pledged three billion dollars to fight global warming[111] and is involved in many humanitarian causes—a true citizen of the world. **HICR: 10**

Ben and Jerry's: Ben Cohen and Jerry Greenfield have created a huge ice-cream and frozen-yogurt chain with stores around the globe. Of course, their products are available in grocery stores as well. Yes, everyone's heard of, and eaten, Ben & Jerry's. The business has always been openly Hippie, socially active and politically progressive. **HICR: 10**

Rolling Stone: *Wikipedia*: "*Rolling Stone* [*RS*] magazine . . . was initially identified with and reported on the hippie counterculture of the era. . . . In the very first edition of the magazine, [founder Jan] Wenner wrote that *Rolling Stone* 'is not just about the music, but about the things and attitudes that music embraces'"—in short, the culture surrounding the music. The magazine remains Countercultural, and I think *RS*'s Hippie identity is common knowledge.

And just as Hippie culture never died, neither has *Rolling Stone*. Since its inception in 1967, it has become not only the most important and influential music-related magazine ever, it's become a major light in American journalism by doing serious investigative reporting, by holding the feet of "The Man" to the fire. Today, in an era characterized by a housebroken, compliant corporate media, *RS*, though a fairly large corporation itself, maintains an independent voice with journalistic integrity—they continue to report the tough anti-establishment stories that the likes of *60 Minutes* are increasingly reluctant to touch. As I recall, when President Obama ran for re-election in 2012 and wanted *RS*'s endorsement, he came to *their* offices. Yes, *Rolling Stone* is powerful and important. **HICR: 10**

"Alternative" newspapers: At one time they were known as "underground newspapers," and everyone knew they were Hippie—authentic, homegrown media. Today, there are hundreds of such local newspapers across the US and the world. Most have Hippie roots, and some remain Hippie, some not; some are in the closet. I will not attempt to inventory every "alternative newspaper" in America; suffice it to say that for the existence of these papers in general and the great good they do in providing a locally owned and often-independent media voice, we

---

[111]   Journalist Naomi Klein accuses Branson of not delivering on this promise (Goldenberg).

are largely endebted to the Counterculture. **HICR: 10 early on; today, it would depend on the individual newspaper.**

Julian Assange: Here, in my opinion, is one of the greatest world citizens of our time. He is the founder and main activist of *Wikileaks*, that website so hated by Washington, London and the Establishment throughout the world. His creation is a breakthrough in terms of democracy, transparency and in holding the powerful responsible. It does this by doing what a serious press should do:[112] publishing the secrets of powerful public and corporate parties with something to hide. Thus, *Wikileaks* has released thousands of files from government/ military/corporate whistleblowers, allowing the public to hear, in their own words, the powers that be discussing what and why they do what they do. The Establishment is enraged: they've been publicly embarassed and humiliated at being caught in so many lies, at having so much of their hypocrisy and illegality exposed.

Of course, many have claimed that *Wikileaks* has endangered US national security, and as of April 2017, the Trump Administration has filed public criminal charges against Assange on that basis, but they've failed to prove this, and when one of *Wikileaks'* main sources, Bradley/ Chelsea Manning, was tried, he/she was acquitted of the charge of "Aiding the Enemy" (DemocracyNow! "Bradley Manning"). *Wikileaks* vets the documents they publish, and there's no evidence that a single US soldier or civilian has ever been killed or wounded from a *Wikileaks* release—that's demagogic propaganda. Because people throughout the world can more easily discover the truth about the forces that shape their lives, their nations and the fate of this planet, the world is a far better place for Julian Assange.

Is Assange Countercultural? Writers David Leigh and Luke Harding say his mother is Countercultural and describe Assange in high school: "His exceptional intelligence and blond, shoulder-length hair marked him out."

Wikileaks is a cyber creation that embodies many of the ideals that those Countercultural founders of the personal computer held; in

---

[112] Actually, to their credit, many important and prestigious newspapers have collaborated with *Wikileaks* in releasing these once-private documents, but strangely the US government has only gone after *Wikileaks* and Julian Assange.

particular, empowering individuals in the face of an overweaning corporate power and pushing us in the direction of a more humane and just world. Thus, Leigh and Harding write, "A computer hacker . . . dreaming up a scheme for an idealistic information insurgency . . . Assange's early commitment to free information, and free software, would soon evolve into Wikileaks." Also, some journalists see Assange as Hippie; thus, Alex Moore speaks of "Julian Assange's countercultural mission."

The length of his hair varies, but in a 2015 interview with *Democracy Now!*, Assange has shoulder-length hair partially tied back—he looks very Hippie ("Britain Challenges"). **HICR: 9.5**

* * *

The range and depth of Countercultural contributions to society are impressive. In contrast to ugly stereotypes of Counterculturists wasting their

> **Hippiedom has been a cultural dynamo, a pantheon of success stories, and if we look at the world since the mid-1960s, we see that Hippiedom has in myriad ways made life genuinely better. If the Counterculture was an individual, we would say she or he was "the genius of the age."**

lives sitting stoned on the couch, we are astonishingly accomplished. Hippiedom has been a cultural dynamo, a pantheon of success stories; if we look at the world since the mid-1960s, we see that Hippiedom has in myriad ways made life genuinely better. If the Counterculture was an individual, we would say she or he was "the genius of the age."

Chapter Nine

"Now, Lay Back on the Couch, Please":
Healing Your Inner Hippie

"No one can make you feel inferior without your consent."
> —*Eleanor Roosevelt*

"This above all else: to thine own self be true."
> — *Shakespeare*

Continuing with our Hippiedom-as-an-individual analogy, yes, we might say she or he was the genius of the age, but we might also note some more troubling traits in our "genius": a lack of self-esteem, a tendency to be self-demeaning, a certain uncertainty about her or himself. No, we aren't asking this person to be cocky or condescending, to assume she or he is better than others. At the same time, people need to feel a sort of healthy pride—to have high self-esteem, to be able to respect themselves and thus to like and love themselves.

As I've shown, there's a tremendous amount of bigotry, stereotyping, condescension[113] and hatred directed at Hippiedom. Of course assuming that Hippies are "just a thing of the Sixties," that humiliating notion makes post-Sixties Hippies a lot of silly Rip Van Winkles, is *de rigueur*. And don't forget the widespread belief (prejudice, really) that adult Hippies are just "kids who never grew up." Then, of course, we're allegedly all a bunch of dirty, irresponsible, welfare-bum drug addicts who lost the War in Vietnam for America and then spit on our brave returning veterans, this, when weren't busy burning the flag or aborting babies. Generally, there's a lot of social shaming and abuse.

Thus, our self-esteem becomes related to how we feel about our ethnic identity and how society feels about it. Basically, if people are constantly stereotyping you, it's probably going to take its toll.

*   *   *

Here are six tales of, I think, Countercultural **low self-esteem and psychological, self-identification issues**:

---

[113]   Can you say "hippy dippy"?

First, a social example of probable low self-esteem by Hippie-Americans: Ever seen Tommy Chong on *That 70's Show* playing a stereotypical Hippie? We see a silly, inarticulate fool. Now, though I've never met him, I doubt Tommy Chong is actually like that in real life, so why does he behave this way on screen? And I don't think this is an isolated case. The stereotype of a Hippie/marijuana user screams silly, irresponsible and foolish.[114] But here's what's strange: many of these stereotypical images of Hippie-Americans are self-generated; that is, Hippie-Americans themselves are creating them. Why are we doing this? Why do so many Hippie-Americans seem uncomfortable with the idea of taking themselves seriously, as if their Hippie identity could never be anything more than a joke?

Second, the outdoor dinner table had been set, and the aromas of the almost-done food were alluring. A ready four of us had seated ourselves; I'd just been asked about my then-website, so I now proffered some business cards. To my right sat Emma. From the way she dressed, I assumed she was Hippie-American; in fact, later in the evening, she acknowledged that. But when she read the card—"www.HappilyHippie.com: Promoting Ethnic-Hippies Theory and Countercultural pride"—she was clearly uncomfortable, this masked by a hollow, shrieking laughter. She sort of flipped out; she seemed angry, disgusted. When I asked why she was "laughing," she snorted, "Well, it's a *joke*, isn't it? I mean, what else could it be *but* a joke?!" Okay, but if it's a joke and if she's Hippie, then that must mean she sees herself as a joke too, right? Her enraged, hateful response seemed both inappropriate and extreme—not to mention, rude. Later it hit me: the nasty voice I'd heard was probably her repeating all the nasty Hippie-demeaning things that had been said to her, those ugly voices she'd internalized and then repeated to herself. Reproachful, damaging and defeating—her tone was as hurtful as she was hurt.

Third, five of us were sitting in a rec-center sauna. Earlier, I had seen two of them outside—twentyish males, apparent Hippie types. One

---

[114]   *Boulder Weekly* columnist Leland Rucker:
There are plenty of people, myself included, who would like to see the image people have of marijuana users move beyond Cheech and Chong comedy sketches, stoner movies and dumbed-down TV characters. The National Cannabis Industry Association, which is lobbying Congress on medical marijuana and banking bills in committee, last month fired Tommy Chong as a celebrity activist for this very reason ("Cannabis Cup").

had shoulder-length hair parted in the middle and a goatee; the other had his brown hair pulled back in a ponytail, a mustache and a small earring in his left earlobe. They looked possibly transient. We had some idle conversation. Not wanting to bother anyone but at the same time in research mode, I wanted to ask the second, who sat beside me, a question: How did he feel about the word *Hippie*?; politely as possible, I asked. He said that he wasn't a Hippie. "Do you find the term offensive?" I asked. "I mean, if other people call you a *Hippie*, how do you feel about that?"

"Oh," he shrugged, "it doesn't bother me." I wondered if he was being honest.

"So, what do you call yourself?" I asked.

"A gypsy," he said in a seemingly practiced manner.

"A gypsy?" I repeated. "Do you have any gypsy blood in you?"

"No," he said somewhat defensively, "but when I was little my parents moved around a lot." This struck me as a *non sequitur*; after all, many people moved around a lot when they were kids—"army brats," for example. So why call himself a "gypsy"? He mentioned that he had some Puerto Rican ancestry, but I don't suppose calling himself Puerto Rican would've explained the ponytail and the earring, and somehow, he thought "gypsy" did.

"You know, I consider myself a Hippie," I offered, wanting to be sure he didn't perceive me as a threatening outsider or a bigot.

"Do you think I'm a Hippie?" he asked.

"Based on your long hair, facial hair and earring," I replied in my own practiced manner,[115] "yeah, I suppose I would. If we gave a photo of you to a cross section of 100 Americans and asked each to list five words describing you, I'd bet that for almost all, one of those five words would be *Hippie*."

Sounding ever more defensive—cornered, perhaps—he retorted a bit wildly, "Hey, having long hair and an earring doesn't make me a Hippie!"

In for a penny, in for a pound, I calmly responded, "If you were of some other distinctive ethnicity where males wore long hair—say Native American—that might make sense, but given that you're not, I think it's reasonable to see you as a Hippie type."

---

[115] Hey, book research takes moxie!

"Well," he said, "if those people saw me with my gold chains on [he raised his hands to indicate a small, not-particularly-gold necklace], they wouldn't say that." His response struck me as another *non-sequitur*, but I didn't press the point: I could see he was getting angry; the conversation soon ended.

So again: a serious fight-or-flight response to what should be non-threatening. Also, since gypsies are an ethnicity, what we have here is a sort of displaced ethnic identity—*Don't call me Hippie; call me gypsy, instead*—this, as if *gypsy* conferred more legitimacy or authenticity than *Hippie.*

Fourth, a few years back, in Boulder's Mountain Sun, an obviously Hippie-American brewpub, I met a man about 35 from Cleveland. He was wearing an Allman Brothers "Eat a Peach" baseball cap. He was excited about what he saw at The Sun; he seemed delighted with the Countercultural atmosphere in general; with the many microbrews, in particular. When I told him there was a sister brewpub, The Southern Sun, in southern Boulder, he was eager to go there and asked for detailed directions. He told me he was in Boulder for a week at a nutritional conference; among other things, he was vegan. Well, given these things and some comments he'd made, I concluded he was Countercultural. I then inquired about his town: "So, is there a Hippie community in Cleveland?" . . . Oops. . . . Apparently, I'd used the H-word, and this guy acted like I'd groped him or something. Immediately uncomfortable, he muttered, "Well, I don't think I'd hang around with *that* crowd!" and made a hasty exit.

Fifth, I contacted someone I knew many years ago. I saw her as Hippie then, and since that time, she'd married a man who was visibly Hippie, and she now has two grown children, both with what I'd call Hippie names. Yet, when I made a comment about what I had assumed was her Hippie identity, she was evasive, noting that while she had once worked in an organic bakery, making little money, she had then gone back to school and gotten a new career, and that she apparently didn't consider herself Hippie anymore because she was now "working within the system." This all struck me as strange. Okay, she went back to school and got a better job that isn't in a Hippie business, but how has *she* changed culturally? In fact, I'm told that she hasn't. What we see here, I think, is someone grasping at straws in a feeble attempt not to have that noose of a name thrown over her head.

Often, I think, Counterculturists have spent much of their lives living in fear, terrified that someone will "accuse" them of being Hippie and wondering how they'll respond or explain themselves. And because of that, they've often carefully cultivated a story—a dodge, really—that they'll use to rescue themselves in event of such an uncomfortable situation. It's sort of like they've practiced for a really difficult job-interview question they might be asked. Their response, then, often sounds painfully stiff, carefully rehearsed, usually irrational, and the point is always to avoid the H-word.

Lastly, I had, for example, a conversation with an individual who looked very Countercultural; we found ourselves discussing the definition of *Hippie*. "Hippies ended with the Sixties!" he scoffed, apparently angry. "There aren't any Hippies today." I nodded towards an overtly Counter-cultural couple standing twenty feet away:

"Okay, so if there are no Hippies today," I asked, "what do you call those people?"

"I don't know *what* you call them," he responded bitterly, "but you *can't* call them Hippies!"

> **For Hippie-Americans, assimilation seems, at least, a very viable option. I'm arguing it isn't, that while fleeing Hippie identity and the Counterculture might seem a natural, sensible response—a sort of survival instinct—it has, in fact, all sorts of hidden costs that outweigh its seeming benefits.**

If such people had mentioned some other term besides the H-word that they preferred, found less threatening, less demeaning, that might make some sense, but they didn't.

Also, if you have no word for people, no actual name, then they truly are invisible, and without even a word to use for themselves or their culture, they're socially hamstrung.

Now, let me say that I sometimes have such conversations with people who actually seem happy, sane and not put off by the subject, but the salient thread that runs through the above stories is the extreme and inappropriate emotionality involved, and those emotions are anger and fear—fight or flight. Being asked to admit to Hippie identity is like having the proverbial hot potato thrown into your lap; it's a question that must be answered *very* carefully as if one's self-esteem, reputation and safety depended on it.

Can you say *internalization of oppression*? I would argue that if you have the objective traits of a Hippie, and you wince at the word as applied to yourself, and yet you have to demonstrable alternative to that hated term, you, my friend, are in the closet. And of course, unlike people of color, those who are racially set apart, it's a whole lot easier for Hippie-Americans to assimilate—to "fit in."

For Hippie-Americans, assimilation *seems*, at least, a very viable option. I'm arguing it isn't, that while fleeing Hippie identity and the Counterculture might seem a natural, sensible response—a sort of survival instinct—it has, in fact, all sorts of hidden costs that outweigh its seeming benefits. It's bad for individual Hippies, bad for their Hippie kids, bad for the larger Countercultural community, bad for the nation and bad for the world.

Let's begin with **why the assimilationist/closet course is bad for the individual Hippie and how ethnic-Hippies theory and the Hippie-pride alternative work better.**

For starters, this flight from and denial of Hippie identity is largely unnecessary. Let me make a literary analogy. In Stephen Crane's realistic novel of the Civil War, *The Red Badge of Courage*, the young protagonist, Henry Fleming, belongs to the 304th New York Regiment of the Union Army. During a Confederate assault on his regiment's position, Henry, in the vernacular of the time, "skeedaddles." As he flees, he sees other Union soldiers holding their ground. In the bell jar of his hysteria, he thinks them absolutely crazy; he sees himself, by contrast, as absolutely sane—the simple, instinctual preservation of life and limb have dictated his course, and only a fool or a lunatic would behave otherwise.

What does it say about one-self, for example, to self-describe as an "ex-Hippie" as many Counterculturists now do? When you talk about yourself, you sound like a ghost; your life, a sort of funeral that never ended; you, a remnant, a leftover, a loser—an inferior.

Now, if someone, say, trying to write a book about Henry Fleming's regiment had at that moment approached Henry and in a perfectly neutral tone asked him, "Do you know anything about the 304th New York Regiment? Say, are you one of them?" Henry would have furiously denied it: "What? The 304th New York Regiment? Are you kidding me? Those losers? Oh, no! Why I'd be ashamed to be seen with them. This must be some sort of joke, right? Heh, heh. These clothes I'm wearing?. . .Why . . . I'm . . . I'm . . . a Cub Scout! Just because I'm wearing a Union uniform that says 304th New York Regiment on it doesn't mean I'm a member of the 304th New York Regiment! How presumptuous of you!" Of course, Fleming later discovers that his regiment has actually beaten back the enemy assault and remains intact.

So it is with Hippie culture: Yes, we have been under siege, we have been assaulted, but we've "held." In fact, as I lavishly illustrated in Chapter Eight, we've prospered; our successes are many and stunning. Saying "the Sixties are over with" over and over is Henry Fleming assuming his regiment has been routed. Stepping out of our analogy, in today's world, being Hippie, or having Hippie traits, is increasingly accepted—look at all those long-haired male athletes I mentioned. Likewise, Hippies have hidden in the closet because for so long having Hippie identity meant you were a drug-addicted criminal; yet, in today's America,[116] eight states have legalized marijuana, and many more are likely right behind. Increasingly, people realize that the late Steve Jobs was Hippie; yet, he's become an American hero. Yes, there's still scapegoating, discrimination, repression and hatred directed towards Hippie-Americans, but the notion that one simply can't be identified as Hippie and survive, well, that's Henry Fleming's panic. Please return to your regiment.[117]

Not only is this assimilationist course largely unnecessary, it has debilitating psychological effects for the individual. What does it say about oneself, for example, to self-describe as an "ex-Hippie" as many Counterculturists now do? When you talk about yourself, you sound like a ghost; your life, a sort of funeral that never ended; you, a remnant, a leftover, a loser—an inferior. Why should some be so doubtful or embarrassed about their cultural identity, so uncomfortable with the mere mention of it, so unable, fundamentally to even speak about it? It seems evidence of low self-esteem, and if you can't respect and love yourself, you won't be able to respect and love others. That's right: you'll have to throw away all your Beatle albums.

Here's the thing: when we feel that hurt at being labeled "hippie," when we accept that ugly stereotypical definition of the word, it's because

---

[116]   2017.

[117]   In this "army," we don't shoot "deserters": we welcome them home.

we've made a terrible choice. "No one," said Eleanor Roosevelt, "can make you feel inferior without your consent." She was right. When we squirm at the sound of *Hippie*, when we distance ourselves from Hippie identity, when we deny the Counterculture both within us and without us, we submit to the forces of forced assimilation; we *give* consent to feel inferior, embarrassed and ashamed. We have, in fact, internalized society's contempt for the Counterculture. Denial, shaming and invisibility directed at the Counterculture are often mirrored by denial, shame and "closet" attitudes within Counterculturalists.

And to be unsure or ambivalent about one's cultural identity is to be unsure of and ambivalent about oneself. When the simple question, "Who are you?" is posed, either externally or internally, the dissembling and euphemizing begins. Psychologically, it's not healthy; it's not clean.

Now, you may think you don't have issues in this area or that if you do, they must be minor. Well, you might be right; on the other hand, you might be in denial. You'll have to decide. But let me point out that the reason it seems so impossibly difficult to have simple, straight- forward discussions about Hippie identity, the reason that in the anecdotes above we saw such extreme and unwarranted emotional responses, usually fear and anger, is precisely because so many Hippies *do* have serious issues about their Hippie identity—open wounds that are hypersensitive to the touch.

> **Denial, shaming and invisibility directed at the Counterculture are often mirrored by denial, shame and "closet" attitudes within Counterculturalists.**

Part of the pain is probably the frustrating inability to even know how to talk about Hippie identity, or for that matter, to define *Hippie*—"What is a 'hippie,' anyway? How do I explain myself?" I believe many Counterculturists have a recurring bad dream, you know, like that one where you're sitting in class in your underwear—fearful, embarrassed, ashamed, about to be humiliated. Only in this dream, some bigot is harassing you, insisting that you explain your appearance, to justify yourself. And in what seems a nightmare, you can't. You don't know how to explain yourself—and it *is* humiliating.

Let me point out two things: first, no one has the right to insist you explain your appearance or yourself to them; second, with EHT, you do indeed have a reasonable explanation, suitable for others if needed but especially suited for yourself. Okay, wake up from that bad dream. If you've been embarrassed or humiliated that way in the past, it doesn't have to be that way in the future. Now you have a sensible answer, an understanding of your cultural identity.

Here's another common barrier to healing our inner Hippies: many Hippies with "straight" parents have had serious **issues with** their **families of origin** regarding their Hippie identity. I know I did. I was regularly told by my father that I was an embarrassing disgrace to him and our family. And I know dozens of Hippies carrying similar emotional baggage. It's a hard thing to forgo the love and respect of parents and siblings that we're born to need; yet, I'd bet there are literally millions of Counterculturists to whom this has happened.

I know a man who I consider borderline Hippie. He wears his hair in a small ponytail, and while that may not seem like a big deal to you or me, it's apparently a very big deal to his elderly father. Indeed, my ponytailed friend is constantly harassed by his father when he visits him, and he's even seriously concerned about being cut out of his father's will because of his longish hair.

Here's a particularly weird family story: In a classroom discussion, I'd mentioned that far as I knew, no one had ever died from marijuana. A young man angrily corrected me, telling me that his uncle had been killed by pot: It seems he had several uncles, one of whom was apparently a Hippie cannabis user. Well, the uncles had been passing around a loaded gun, and according to the lad, his stoner uncle dropped the weapon, it went off, and it killed another uncle. The assumption here, of course, is that people who smoke pot are prone to dropping things and that if the Hippie uncle hadn't been a pot smoker, the other uncle would be alive.

Notice that this argument begs the question by assuming that marijuana makes people clumsy; often, when something being passed is dropped, there are two parties involved, and it's not always clear who's to blame. Oh, by the way, have the uncles never taken any gun-safety training? Don't they know not to pass around a loaded gun? Have they never heard of putting on the safety? Oh, no! Blame it on the irresponsible, murderous marijuana user! Well, apparently, that's pretty much what the Countercultural uncle's family thinks of him—"He murdered his brother because he's a hippie pothead!"

Most Hippies have experienced harassment; it seems reasonable to assume they have issues about it. And what about Hippies who've been more than harassed, those who've been arrested, bullied, beaten, or raped due to their Hippie identity? How could those people not have serious issues?

There's sociological term: *stereotype threat*; it means to have less confidence based on stereotypes of one's own group (Rhys). And the resulting low self-esteem can have a devastating impact in many areas of one's life, ones not directly related to Hippie identity. Are you a Hippie with, say, a drinking problem? Perhaps that alcoholism has been an outgrowth of low self-esteem, and perhaps that low self-esteem is at least partly based on feelings of the guilt and shame produced by anti-Hippie bigotry.

I'm reminded of the late Robin Williams, who publically spoke about his alcoholism. One of Williams' signature jokes was, "If you can remember the Sixties, then you weren't there!" implying that the Sixties (and thus Hippie culture) were nothing more than an extended episode in drug abuse, a particularly long Lost Weekend where nothing of value was accomplished. Yes, I know: he was joking. He was a comedian. Still, it's a self-demeaning comment that isn't true of either Hippie culture or of Williams' own astonishingly successful career which began in the Sixties.

* * *

Let's now consider **a different course, one of ethnic pride, one of becoming happily Hippie.** You know, it's one thing to feel bad about something bad you've done; it's quite another to feel bad about something bad you haven't done. A hostile society has treated Hippie identity as if it were a crime; now, many Counterculturists seem to feel that they really have committed some kind of crime by being Hippie.

Let's give ourselves a break; let's stop feeling ashamed about that which isn't shameful. Let's start respecting ourselves and insisting others treat us respectfully. The way we heal our psychic wounds is by first of all being clear that being Hippie isn't a crime, it isn't a sign of mental illness, it isn't being irresponsible or refusing to grow up, and it isn't anything foolish or bad. Being Hippie is an ethnic choice which everyone has the right to make—a human right. And if you ask me, it was a smart choice. You didn't so much drop out as you dropped into something really wonderful, something that can heal both individuals and society, something that might just save this troubled world we're living in.

Negative assumptions regarding Hippie identity are nothing more than bigotry. If you've been treated badly in your family of origin because you're Hippie, the problem isn't you; it's that you have bigots in your family of origin. They're the ones with a problem, and they owe you an apology, not the other way around. Period. Understanding that may not make your disrespectful relatives enlightened, but it is the first step in your understanding what's been happening to you, taking control of that ugly experience psychologically and healing yourself.

Here are some advantages of an EHT approach: First, it allows us to get comfortable with our ethnic identity by explaining it. Everyone has one or more ethnic identities; one of yours happens to be Hippie. All that embarrassment and psychic discomfort you've been feeling, kiss it goodbye. You don't need to go through life feeling like a freak. We also become comfortable in our Hippie skins when we realize that Hippie culture is an ethnicity, not a religious order, and none of us need feel phony or inadequate because we're not Gandalfs. Hippies are human beings who belong to a particular ethnic group, not living gods.

> **Hippiedom was born in the Sixties, and when we look at the other social movements that flowered in that decade—black nationalism, feminism, gay rights, Chicano rights and others—we see that those sibling movements have all grasped and developed the notion of pride.**

Also, regarding Hippies Were Just a Thing of the Sixties, that ubiquitous notion that demeans and delegitimizes us, EHT allows us to quit assuming that Hippie identity can only exist in bygone days that we nostalgically pine for. For older and middle-aged Hippies, EHT allows them to stop assuming Hippie identity means trying to relive your past—time to come home to your Hippie self here in the present.

Further, if we understand our ethnic identity correctly, then we understand that while it may tell us a lot about ourselves and our place in the larger society, culture is not character, and your ethnic identity won't tell you, for instance, how spiritually developed you are; being Hippie doesn't make you evil, but it doesn't make you a saint either. What EHT can do is to clear our vision by distinguishing character issues from cultural-identity issues, and this can help us grow as people.

And EHT allows us to reclaim our individuality and thus our full humanity by moving beyond external stereotypes and by reminding us that ethnicities are composed of a broad variety of individuals not masses of clones.

Lastly here, Hippiedom was born in the Sixties, and when we look at the other social movements that flowered in that decade—black nationalism, feminism, gay rights, Chicano rights and others—we see that those sibling movements have all grasped and developed the notion of pride; instead of being embarrassed and ashamed of themselves, they've learned to be proud, to resist stereotyping and all the other machinations of a bigoted, belittling society. They've all transcended invisibility and the closet. Isn't it time we followed suit?

*   *   *

Okay, ready to talk about **self-esteem in Hippie children**? As mentioned, Hippie parents tend to have Hippie kids and grandkids—not always, but often. It's well known that white supremacism has damaged the self-esteem of African-American children: studies showing so were part of the landmark Brown vs. Board of Education lawsuit that desegregated US schools. It stands to reason, then, that the self-esteem of Hippie kids is also at risk. Kids in tie dyes or wearing hemp jewelry, boys with long hair, girls with pierced noses, youngsters who like to meditate and eat natural foods—they'll likely be identified as Hippie and possibly be subjected to stereotyping. Today's film directors, for example, sometimes still use a ponytail to indicate a villain in much the way that directors of Westerns used to put a black hat on "the bad guy." What does this do to the self-image of a long-haired Hippie boy?

Likewise, I'm sure there are a number of assistant principals, police officers, social workers, judges and others who see Hippie identity in a child as a sign that she or he comes from a "bad family," is a "teen in trouble," is addicted to drugs, is a discipline problem, etc. That's discriminatory profiling, that's stereotyping, that's bigotry. Also, I'm sure that if we combed through the nation's juvenile records, we'd find kids who'd been thrown into some sort of prison or totalitarian "tough-love" facility based solely on emerging Hippie identity.

So, it's not just our inner Hippies that may need healing; it may be our children's too, and there are Hippie kids out there, not necessarily our own, who need our help and cultural protection.

How to do these things? Within the family, teach your children well: explain to them what an ethnic group is and that Hippiedom is one, meaning that they have Hippie identity—they inherited it to some extent, and they'll also be making decisions about whether to keep it.

"Why is our family Hippie?"

"Because your parents (or grandparents) chose Hippie identity. It's a right people have."

This should lead into a discussion of the benefits and accomplishments of Hippie culture, a talk that should teach ethnic pride. At some point, you'll also want to point out that some people hate Hippies, and that we call those people *prejudiced*. If your son is a pre-pubescent long-haired male, you might want to talk with him about how to handle situations where people think he's a girl, and for many males, how to handle that question, "Hey, why's your hair so long?" should it arise. For all kids, how to handle the bullying question, "Hey, what are you? Some kind of hippie freak or something?"

> **Think of Hippiedom as some potentially species-saving social mutation, or think of its birth as something divine; in any case, think of it as something hopeful and wonderful, as something to be celebrated.**

Generally, we should instill a sense of pride in the Counterculture. Here's how I sometimes think about it: It's the mid-1960s, and humanity is at a historical crossroads—a time of acute crisis. In particular, it's becoming clear that people are in serious conflict with our natural environment; add to that the looming threat of nuclear Armageddon and continuing war-making and carnage. Sure, war and violence is as old as humanity, but the world is in a kind of trouble it's never quite seen before: if we continue screwing up, we might make this planet unlivable for our species. In the midst of this disturbing scenario, something surprising happens: Hippiedom is born. At first, no one quite knows what to make of it. Why it's a silly and scandalous social spectacle—"flower children"!

Yet this same new culture is green, and its core values are peace and love; as outlandish as Hippie culture might once have seemed, this new culture has actually been astonishingly successful, so much so that it may actually save the planet—or play a big part of that salvation. Unusual as the Counterculture and its birth might seem, it's the right culture in the right place at the right time. Think of Hippiedom as some potentially species-saving social mutation, or think of its birth as something divine; in any case, think of it as something hopeful and wonderful, as something to be celebrated.

* * *

It seems reasonable to assume that as the trend towards legalization grows, DARE (Drug Abuse Resistance Education) and similar War on Drugs mis-education will eventually collapse. It's going to be harder and harder to demonize pot with state after state, municipality after municipality legalizing it, harder and harder to keep repeating the same old tired lies and hysteria. It falls to Hippie-American parents to begin developing an intelligent alternative to Reefer Madness!

Parents, then, need to be aware of what kind of drug education is going on in local schools. The Just-Say-No/abstinence approach has failed utterly in the realm of sex education; there's no reason to think it will protect our kids from drug abuse.

But not only is DARE ineffective, I suspect it's actually counterproductive—a menace to youth. I was in high school when our administration decided to march us all down to the gym to watch a Sonny and Cher drug-war propaganda film. At one point, an actor is shown smoking marijuana and then hallucinating a purple gorilla; the wiseacre sitting behind me cracked, "Hey, how come I can never find pot like that?"—general hilarity. And today's young people watch "Reefer Madness" for laughs.

I believe that in the manner of The Boy Who Cried Wolf, kids who are introduced to various drugs, some of which might be very dangerous, through DARE miseducation become inured to arguments against their use. How many young people, who when first offered a crack pipe or a chance to try heroin, have responded, "Hey, wait a minute . . . Isn't this stuff dangerous; couldn't it hurt me?" only to hear a foolish, peer-pressure response: "Oh, don't be such a wimp; remember all those fool stories you heard about marijuana?" The result is what the Drug Warriors have always accused marijuana of being: a Gateway to more dangerous drugs.

Also, an enlightened school district will understand that among the many minority communities it serves, among the many culturally distinctive children it teaches, there are Hippie-Americans. Let's make sure our schools are treating Hippie kids with the respect and understanding they would give members of any racial or ethnic minority and not as criminals or trouble-makers or delinquents.

* * *

There are other reasons why an ethnic-pride approach is best:

First, there's the matter of **protecting and preserving Hippie culture as a whole.** Hippiedom has done a great deal of good in this world and will continue to do so. It needs to be defended, its right to exist acknowledged, its institutions strengthened, its future guaranteed. We can't do any of those things if we're ashamed or embarrassed to be Hippie; indeed, the first step towards effectively defending Hippie culture lies in *your* Hippie head: step out of the closet; stand up for yourself, stand up for Hippiedom and our ethnic rights.

And **the effect on the nation and world** of "closet" thinking? Well, as discussed and documented at length in Chapter Three, closet Counterculturists become enablers of fascism. What's ironic is that in distancing themselves from the word *Hippie* and Hippie culture in general, most think they're being "smart," engaging in self-preservation. The thing is, even if by avoiding Hippie identity you do "escape," where is it you escape to? The answer: a society that increasingly resembles Nazi Germany.

Abandoning the Counterculture and/or toadying before bigots encourages, emboldens and strengthens them. Bigotry is like a cancer in the body politic; if you don't arrest it, it will sicken and destroy an entire nation. And what's bad for America; it's bad for an American-dominated world.

* * *

In conclusion, the answer to all the problems discussed above—individual issues with Hippie identity, the effects of bigotry on Hippie kids, the need to protect Hippie culture and its institutions, and the need to save our nation and the world it dominates—is a Hippie-pride movement, one that begins here and now, one that begins with *you*. Be happily Hippie.

Chapter Ten

Drug Laws and Hippie-America—
We Are Not Criminals:
We're a People Criminalized

"Til the heat come round and busted me for smiling on a cloudy day"
—Grateful Dead, "The Other One"

This three-part chapter is about drug-related matters. In the first section, we're going to apply ethnic-Hippies theory (EHT), the notion that Hippie culture is a living ethnicity, to the history of American drug laws, including those now targeting the Counterculture, and demonstrate how only a minority-persecution paradigm can adequately explain that history, those laws and how they're applied. Then, I'll show how the counterargument that the War on Drugs protects the public health doesn't work, particularly how drug laws fail to reduce drug use or abuse and how instead of protecting America's youth, the War on Drugs is punishing them; lastly here, I'll demonstrate how the War on Drugs is a fascistic social movement.

Second, although health arguments are actually irrelevant to the legalization debate, they have some place in the larger discussion. So here I'll debunk Gateway, discuss some of the many problems with War on Drugs "science," discuss the health and behavioral effects of two drugs (tobacco and alcohol) that the ignorant tend to falsely equate with marijuana and then quickly look at some evidence suggesting cannabis can cure cancer.

> **The real purpose and practice of these historic drug laws has been to persecute racial and ethnic minorities. Then, since the mid-1960's, drug laws have been used to persecute that ethnic minority I call Hippie-America.**

Third, if the War on Drugs is a fascistic social movement, what's the proper response to it? I'm going to argue that Hippie-America is the wind under the wings of a Legalization Movement that's lighting the way to a better America.

* * *

The history of drug laws in America: These laws have their roots in the cesspool of racism and ethnic chauvinism; that is, the real purpose and practice of these laws has been to persecute racial and ethnic minorities. Then, since the mid-1960's, drug laws have been used to persecute that ethnic minority I call Hippie-America. Because I'm arguing that drug laws are *not* primarily misguided public-health measures, for most readers, this minority-persecution approach means paradigm shift.

In his *Drugs and Minority Oppression*, scholar John Helmer traces the history of what he terms "drug hysterias" in America. Thus, America's first anti-drug laws, starting around 1875, outlawed opium; these laws were used to persecute Chinese immigrants, many of whom had been recruited to build Western railroads. Chinese in America were the targets of widespread contempt and bigotry; many were lynched. In 1882 and 1892, respectively, Congress passed two Chinese Exclusion Acts—this, the social context under which opium prohibition was enacted. Helmer comments, "There was no claim, for example, that it [opium] was harmful directly. Its use indicated, rather, how different, foreign, and inassimilable the Chinese were as a group" (32). Helmer quotes a California Senate report of 1877: "The whites cannot stand their dirt and the fumes of opium, and are compelled to leave the vicinity" (32); Helmer concludes, "The ideological role of the anti-opium campaign was to get rid of the Chinese" (32).

> **That the real reason opium was prohibited had nothing to do with public health doesn't necessarily mean that opium isn't unhealthy. The same could be said of all the other drugs we're about to discuss.**

Then, there were cocaine laws; a public furor over cocaine in the early 20th Century, Helmer tells us, was fueled by a stereotype of black coke-heads assaulting white women. "[C]ocaine is often the direct incentive to the crime of rape [of white women] by the Negroes of the South and other sections of the country" (47), declared Hamilton Wright who, appointed United States Opium Commissioner in 1908, was America's first drug czar. Helmer explains that the hysteria over cocaine use was "designed to justify and legitimize the repression with which black claims for equality were met" (53).

Here's a way US drug laws were used to persecute African-Americans and frustrate their demands for social equality as reported in a *Democracy Now!* interview with British journalist Johann Hari who's researched and written *Chasing the Scream: The First and Last Days of the War of Drugs.* Long-time commissioner of the Federal Bureau of Narcotics Harry J. Anslinger[118] was a racist fanatic, considered extreme even at the time, Hari notes. The fabled black singer Billie Holiday was addicted to heroin. She was also a courageous fighter for black rights who continued to sing the taboo song "Strange Fruit" that protested the lynchings of African-Americans, then, fairly common. Anslinger particularly hated Holiday, partly because she was a heroin addict, partly because she was black, but especially because she was a black activist who insisted on singing "Strange Fruit." According to Hardy, Anslinger knew of Holiday's addiction and used it to destroy her career and eventually silence her—as in premature death or possibly murder. So, however dangerous heroin might be, here the laws against heroin weren't used to protect public health but to persecute a black civil-rights activist (*Democracy Now!* "The Hunting").

Early marijuana legislation particularly targeted Mexicans. In *The Emperor Wears No Clothes* (11th ed.), marijuana researcher and writer Jack Herer tells us, "[T]he first marijuana prohibition law in America—pertaining only to Mexicans—was passed in Brownsville" Texas in 1903 (87). Helmer adds, "Public concern about marijuana grew because Americans wanted to drive the Mexicans back over the border, for reasons which had nothing to do with the nature of the drug or its psychological effects" (56), and among other evidence, he quotes a Colorado newspaper editor's plea used as testimony for the Marihuana Tax Act of 1937: "I wish I could show you what a small marijuana cigarette can do to one of our degenerate Spanish-speaking residents" (55).

Helmer notes that the first recorded strike of Mexican migrant laborers in the Southwest was in 1928 and writes, "[T]he problem of Mexican labor and the unemployed surplus after 1928 [in urban areas] is the key factor in determining what became public [marijuana] policy . . ." (56).

According to Herer, much American fear and hatred of Mexicans and marijuana stems from the days of President Woodrow Wilson: between 1913 and 1917, the US had troops in Mexico to help suppress the

---

[118] Anslinger was in office from August 1930 through May 1962; in this era, he was a sort of second J. Edgar Hoover in American law enforcement.

revolution being led by Pancho Villa; news reports of the time, probably accurate, noted that many of Villa's men used marijuana. President Wilson and Establishment America feared the Mexican Revolution, and this marijuana use was used to demonize Villa's troops (90).

And, of course, there's the etymology of *marihuana/marijuana*. The correct term is *cannabis*; yet, it's the Spanish/Mexican slang term that dominates public discussion, and Herer says it was "pounded" into American English by reactionary newspaper mogul William Randoph Hearst in sensational cannabis stories encouraging anti-Mexican bigotry (31).

Also in California at this time, marijuana laws were used to persecute "Hindoos" (East Indian immigrants of Sikh religion and Punjabi origin) in California. California NORML researcher Dale H. Gieringer writes:

> The Hindoos were widely denounced for their outlandish customs, dirty clothes, strange food, suspect morals, and especially their propensity to work for low wages. Aside from [Hamilton J.] Finger [an associate of Hamilton Wright and a founder of drug laws in California], however, no one complained about their use of cannabis. To the contrary, their defenders portrayed them as hard-working and sober. "The taking of drugs as a habit scarcely exists among them," wrote one observer.

A political cartoon appeared in the *San Francisco Examiner* in August of 1910 (**see Photo #58**). It shows a "Hindu" head attached to a snake's body trailing all the way back to Asia—evidence of the kind of racist scare then being created in California.

Thus, a smear campaign against this group of Asian immigrants was combined with a hysteria about Pancho Villa's pot-smoking revolutionaries and Mexican immigrants (Gieringer), and in 1913, California became the first state to outlaw marijuana—its prohibition, a model for other states and the future federal Marihuana Tax Act of 1937.

Anslinger declared, "There are 100,000 total marijuana smokers in the US, and most are Negroes, Hispanics, Filipinos and entertainers. Their Satanic music, jazz and swing, result from marijuana usage. This marijuana causes white women to seek sexual relations with Negroes, entertainers and any others" (qtd. in Wing); also, "Reefer makes darkies think they're as good as white men" (qtd. in Wing). Anslinger's prejudices were so overt and extreme, one can only conclude that his zeal in persecuting marijuana and other drugs was merely an extension of his zeal in persecuting racial and ethnic minorities.

Anslinger may be long gone, but the underlying dynamic of marijuana laws being used to target racial and ethnic minorities remains. Between 2001 and 2010, reports Dylan Matthews of the *Washington Post*, arrest rates for African-Americans were:

> three-to-four times the rate as whites; yet, . . . blacks usually only smoke a bit more pot per capita than whites . . . In the state with the biggest [racial discrepancy], Iowa, blacks are 8.34 times more likely to be arrested. [Washington] D.C. has the second biggest; in the District, blacks are 8.05 times more likely to be arrested.

And today's stop-and-frisk policies target and incarcerate minorities at a disproportionate rate. Thus, in November 2014, *DemocracyNow!* reported that in New York City, "Eighty-six percent of those arrested for marijuana possession in the first eight months of this year were African-American or Latino" (*DemocracyNow!* "New York").

American drug hysterias, then, have not been misguided campaigns of public health: they've been campaigns of racial and ethnic persecution sometimes disguised as campaigns of public health, particularly of public moral health. Generally, if you want to persecute a racial or ethnic group, go after their drugs. American drug laws have been engines of racism and ethnocide; the persecution of racial and ethnic out groups, their *raison d'être*.

> **American drug hysterias have not been misguided campaigns of public health: they've been campaigns of racial and ethnic persecution sometimes disguised as campaigns of public health, particularly of public moral health. Generally, if you want to persecute a racial or ethnic group, go after their drugs.**

(If the persecution of minorities is the primary cause of our repressive drug laws, there are some lesser causes as well: First, Helmer says the early American Medical Association (AMA) felt threatened by the so-called "patent medicine" business and played a role in the

281

prohibition of these patent medicines and the drugs in them (36). Second, Herer cites evidence that today's Big Pharma "would lose hundreds of millions, to billions of dollars annually" (42) if cannabis was legalized. Third, DuPont Chemicals and other wealthy interests, including timber and paper industries, saw cannabis as an economic rival (Herer, 26-27). Fourth, in his many newspapers, the infamous "yellow journalist" William Randolph Hearst ran a Reefer Madness! campaign that fueled/exploited racial and ethnic fears (Herer, 29, 30).

* * *

Let's now fast-forward to the mid-1960's; **enter the Counterculture**. Yes, America had laws against marijuana before America had Hippies. President Nixon could have changed those laws; indeed, the 1972 commission he appointed to investigate US marijuana policy, the Shafer Commission, to everyone's surprise, recommended legalization (*Marihuana: A Signal*). Nixon dismissed their report without comment and actually called for harsher penalties, this part of the nation's first "War on Drugs" (Baum, *Smoke*, 143). And according to a report by Common Sense Drug Policy (CSDP), based on Nixon's Oval Office tapes, "the President believed many of the myths about marijuana and tied it very closely to . . . blacks, Jews[119] and the counterculture." So, Nixon went after marijuana because he was a bigot in general, partly because he hated Hippies, in particular.

Former *Wall St. Journal* reporter, drug-policy researcher and author Daniel Baum reports on a 1994 interview he had with President Nixon's former Domestic Policy Advisor John Ehrlichman:

> I started to ask Ehrlichman a series of earnest, wonky questions that he impatiently waved away. "You want to know what this [the War on Drugs] was really all about?" he asked with the bluntness of a man who, after public disgrace and a stretch in federal prison [for Watergate crimes], had little left to protect.

---

[119] Apparently, Nixon didn't so much see Jewish-Americans as pot smokers as he felt that Jewish-American judges were pro-legalization. Baum writes, "Haldeman [Nixon's Chief of Staff] also recorded in his diary that Nixon wanted to know 'why all the Jews seem to be the ones that are for liberalizing the regulations on marijuana'" (54).

"The Nixon campaign in 1968, and the Nixon White House after that, had two enemies: the antiwar left and black people.... We knew we couldn't make it illegal to be either against the war or black, but by getting the public to associate the hippies with marijuana and blacks with heroin, and then criminalizing both heavily, we could disrupt those communities. We could arrest their leaders, raid their homes, break up their meetings, and vilify them night after night on the evening news. Did we know we were lying about the drugs? Of course we did. ("How to")

Here, I believe, is the true face of modern anti-marijuana zealotry expressed with refreshing honesty in a letter to the conservative *National Review*, a 1972 piece entitled "Marijuana and the Counterculture":

The case "against" marijuana . . . seems to me to be cultural, or perhaps cultural-anthropological. . . . Marijuana is indeed an integral part of the counterculture of the 1960's. . . . The meaning of marijuana—and, as I say, I care not a fig for its physical effects—has to do with this cultural symbolism. And though the laws may indeed by excessively harsh . . . the *meaning* of those laws in the current historical circumstance is plain enough. They aim to lean on, to penalize the counterculture. They reflect the opinion, surely a majority one, that the counterculture, and its manners and morals, and all its works are *bad*. Now I don't care much for all that 'free society' rhetoric. No reference to marijuana occurs in the First Amendment. . . . marijuana became an issue during the 1960's with the rise of the counterculture. It will cease to be one about six months from now with the death of that counterculture. (Hart)

We can find similar sentiments voiced by neoconservative drug warrior William Bennett; indeed, in its zero-tolerance zealotry, all of neo-conservatism echoes this theme of using marijuana laws to reign in Hippie-America.[120] Modern American marijuana laws, then, are aimed heavily at Hippies; their intent and practice is to punish the

---

[120] Remember, as we saw in Chapter Three, hatred of the Counterculture is one of the two ideological pillars of neoconservatism.

Counterculture, and this conforms to and extrapolates the minority-persecution model of drug laws in pre-1960s American history.

*   *   *

There are two other drugs associated with Hippie-America that we need to discuss to show how they too confirm the ethnic-persecution model: LSD and MDMA ("Ecstasy").

Now, among the victims of the War on Drugs are those who call themselves **"LSD prisoners."** As you might imagine, they are largely Countercultural. Thing is, the public-health argument is pretty weak here (yes, we've all heard the pseudo-scientific scare stories about LSD leading to birth defects, but there's no evidence that's true; if it were, we'd have seen a wave of post-Sixties birth defects among the Hippie population in particular, and there's no evidence of such). And as the LSD prisoners themselves point out, they've harmed no one. One, Matt Cappelli, writes from prison: "Who Is My Victim? I have never imposed my will on others by intimidation, violence, theft, cheating, or any other unsavory methods. I have never victimized anyone to my knowledge. My definition of crime implies a victim was involved somehow. Yet I am now in prison as a convicted criminal!?! (qtd. in *Relix*, 11). Another, Robert Kitchin, adds, "Consenting adults should be able to do whatever they want to with their bodies. Destroying people's lives with prison because they happen to select LSD as their drug of their choice rather than cigarettes or alcohol is insane" (qtd. in *Relix*, 9).

That insanity is particularly apparent when you consider the severe sentences the War on Drugs has been exacting from convicted LSD users. *USA Today* (December 17, 1992) published a chart of comparitive sentences (minimum and maximum) for various federal crimes: "LSD Possession: 10.1 to 13.9 years; Attempted murder with harm: 6.5 to 8.1; Rape: 5.8 to 7.2; Armed robbery with a gun: 4.7 to 5.9; Kidnapping: 4.2 to 5.2 . . . (qtd. in *Relix*, 7).

Thus, these LSD prisoners are simply people who've made a choice about seeking a particular experience and who've harmed no one unless you swallow William Bennett's moral sophistry that such people are "contagious" and contaminate society (Baum, *Smoke*, 273). Incidentally, in his *Can't Find My Way Home: America in the Great Stoned Age, 1945-2000*, Martin Torgoff points out that in his case, as with tens of thousands of other "trippers"/"acid heads," they often sought religious/spiritual experiences. Here we have a perfect example of Hippies who aren't truly criminal; rather, through the use of LSD laws, they've been criminalized—viciously, cruelly, unjustly.

* * *

Discovered in 1985, **MDMA (Ecstasy)** at first had exclusively therapeutic uses. In his excellent *Smoke and Mirrors: The War on Drugs and The Politics of Failure*,[121] Baum writes, "[A] handful of psychiatrists from around the country reported phenomenal success with MDMA, a little white capsule that dramatically reduced inhibitions and made it possible for people to confront personal issues they previously could not. 'Like a year of therapy in two hours,' one patient said" (*Smoke*, 212). Apparently, *Newsweek* wrote a very positive piece about MDMA, noting that it "is not a hallucinogen, and it doesn't interfere with thinking . . ." (qtd. in Baum, *Smoke*, 212). The drug was soon saddled with the streetname Ecstasy. "It also," Baum adds, "wasn't the protected offspring of a publicly traded pharmeceuticals corporation but had been created by independent chemists" (*Smoke*, 213). Soon, a homemade Esctasy industry grew up, and the drug became the center of a type of party scene, "Raves"—generally Countercultural,[122] I think. Within weeks, the DEA banned Esctasy, saying it posed "a serious health threat" though Baum is quick to point out that DEA Chief Jack Lawn offered not a shred of evidence (*Smoke*, 213), and far as I can tell, there's no evidence of a single Ecstasy death up to this point.

Nowadays, we *do* have occasional "Ecstasy" deaths, including of teenagers. There seem to be two basic reasons: First, unregulated, street "Ecstasy" isn't always pure MDMA; for example, in cases of death caused by heart failure (hyponatremia), some "suspect that the

---

[121] Much as I respect Baum's book, the title represents a problem all too common in the legalization argument: that the War on Drugs has "failed" because it's failed to reduce the number of users. Well, if that were the true purpose of the War on Drugs, the "failure" accusation would be true, but since its true purpose is to persecute minorities, we can only say that the War on Drugs is an astounding success—it has, after all, filled our jails with a variety of minorities and given the US the highest incarceration rate in the world.

[122] Among other things, it seems the "ravers" are very much into love and a larger spiritual communion with other "ravers."

deaths might be largely due to impure Ecstasy cut with amphetamines," writes Benjamin Wallace-Wells (qtd. in Lane, 45); ampethamines, of course, make heartrate skyrocket. Second, some street "Ecstasy" either seems to trick users into thinking they're horrifically thirsty, or in other cases (usually involving a crowded dance floor), users are overheating (hyperthermia); on occasion, these people drink so much water that the brain swells greatly, and they die. The result has been "Ecstasy" "drowning" deaths; however, as clinical psychologist John A. Henry notes, these deaths are "due mainly to the circumstances in which it [the drug] has been abused" (qtd. in Lane, 46-7).

How dangerous is today's Ecstasy? I found a website called www. TheDEA.org—no, this clearly isn't a government DEA site though the source for its tables and statistics is listed as the US Substance Abuse and Mental Health Services Administration (SAMHSA). The author begins by noting that "One of the more exaggerated aspects of Ecstasy (MDMA) use is the perceived rate of death and injury. . . . Out of a total of 76 deaths involving MDMA reported in 2001 [for the US], only 9 involved only MDMA" (TheDEA.org), and presumably these would include preventable "drowning" deaths.

Incidentally, TheDEA.org adds regarding Ecstasy prohibition, "The government failed in both respects: They were unable to stop the growth of usage, and they refused to provide useful drug education to young people." Yes. So a few years back in Boulder, CO, a high-school girl "drowned" while using street Ecstasy. In such a situation, the drug warriors say, "See! This is *exactly* why we need to keep drugs illegal— they're killing our kids!" But those same laws didn't keep this child safe, and intelligent, honest drug education willing to go beyond "Just Say No" could've saved this girl's life. Thus, the protecting-the-public-health paradigm doesn't really explain MDMA laws; the persecution-of-a-minority paradigm does: Ecstasy laws unecessarily and deliberately put Counterculturists in jail.[123]

* * *

---

[123] In Holland, I'm told, there's an unofficial network where buyers of street Ecstasy can go online and get information about the "lot" of a particular drug beforehand. The book *Ecstasy* also shows an Ecstasy-testing booth set up at a rave (Lane). The point is, there are reasonable and effective ways of dealing with Ecstasy's potential health issues besides criminalization.

Add to the actual drug laws targeting the Counterculture a whole set of **bizarre related policies**—a convicted murderer might well get federal college aid, but a convicted marijuana user likely won't;[124] in September 20011, the ATF announced it wouldn't let medical marijuana users buy guns or ammunition (Volz); and so on—and we have a variety of laws designed to hurt, harass and discriminate against Hippie-Americans. So whatever high-minded rationales are raised for drug laws, in practice, they remain engines of racism and ethnocide. The birth of Hippiedom hasn't changed the nature of American drug laws; rather, the powers that be are the same old dog doing the same old trick only with a new toy.

* * *

Part of understanding the minority-persecution paradigm for American drug laws is seeing how historically the public-health issue has often been elided with **the moral-health issue**, which was integral to the overt racism and ethnic chauvinism of past drug hysterias; that is, the essential argument made to a largely white-supremacist American public was "Wanna keep white people healthy? Then, keep 'em moral. Keep 'em away from the coloreds. Don't let them be dragged down by Negroes and other inferiors."

Well, the same holds true today regarding the larger society and how it regards Hippie-America. Courtesy neoconservatism and bigotry in general, Americans have been taught to see the Counterculture as the essence of immorality and contagion, Sodom and Gomorrah staggering around with a bong in its hand—"Yeah, your kids will stop bathing, start smoking pot and become sleazy, America-hating, welfare-bum drug addicts with fleas in their dreadlocks!"

* * *

War on Drugs apologists assume that drug prohibition is curtailing drug use and abuse and thus protecting the public health, especially that of minors. It's crucial, then, to understand that **drug illegalization does not reduce drug use**. In a piece called "Do Drug Laws Affect Drug

---

[124]   In October 1998, President Clinton signed a bill denying "federal student loan assistance" to anyone ever convicted of a marijuana crime (NORML).

Use Rates? Evidently Not," David Borden, executive director of Stop the Drug War.org explains:

> Study after study has failed to find any increase in marijuana use following the passage of decriminalization laws in many US states . . . Add one more study to the pile—an important one ["Toward a Global View of Alcohol, Tobacco, Cannabis, and Cocaine Use: Findings from the WHO World Mental Health Surveys"—2008]. This study, carried out in conjunction with the most recent World Health Organization "Mental Health Surveys," boasts nineteen authors—yes, nineteen—from eighteen different countries on every continent. . . . This diverse, respectable group of academics from around the world determined that "[d]rug use does not appear to be related to drug policy, as countries with more stringent policies (e.g., the US) did not have lower levels of illegal drug use than countries with more liberal policies (e.g., The Netherlands)."

In short, the social scientists report there's no correlation between a drug's legal status and the extent to which people use it.

Likewise, the US War on Drugs has failed to reduce use or abuse of drugs. Thus, Mara Szalavitz writes for *Time*:

> Then [the early 1970s], the drug budget was in the tens or hundreds of millions per year. Now [2013], it's $20 billion annually. And the single largest category of arrests reported to the FBI today involve drug law violations—and of these, 82% are for simple possession. Half of those arrests are for marijuana use. The increase in spending and incarceration, however, has not been accompanied by a parallel drop in addiction or even drug use (including marijuana).

Also, the American Civil Liberties Union states, "Drug prohibition has . . . failed to curb or reduce the harmful effects of drug use . . ." (ACLU).

A webpage affiliated with Stanford University reports: "The United States has focused its efforts on the criminalization of drug use. The government has, to no avail, spent countless billions of dollars in efforts to eradicate the supply of drugs. Efforts of interdiction and law enforcement have *not* been met with decreases in the availability of drugs in America (emphasis added) ("America is at war").

Conversely, legalization doesn't necessarily increase use. Consider this regarding **the effects legalization has had on kids in Colorado**, mid-summer 2016, as reported by Sarah Haas of the *Boulder Weekly*:

> Last week's release of the long-awaited 2015 Healthy Kids Colorado Survey, issued jointly by the state departments of health, education and human services, surveyed about 17,000 students from state middle and high schools. *The data suggests that youth use and access [to marijuana] has remained steady since legalization* [in 2014] [emphasis added] . . . .
>
> Mason Tvert, the Denver-based director of communication for the Marijuana Policy Project, who co-directed the 2012 campaign to regulate marijuana like alcohol, [said] in a press release. "Colorado is proving that you do not need to arrest thousands of responsible adult marijuana consumers in order to prevent consumption by teens."

Far as I can tell, then, among scholars, journalists and the general public, it is common knowledge that our modern War on Drugs has failed to curtail use or abuse of drugs, and there's no reliable historical evidence, in general, showing that laws impact the extent to which society or individuals use/abuse a drug.

> **The public-health argument that's so long dominated the marijuana debate, absorbed so many federal dollars in pseudo-scientific attempts to show marijuana's unhealthy effects, is an argumentative red herring.**

All prohibitionist arguments rest on this argument: "Make it illegal so people will stop using it; then, we'll protect the public's health." But if there is no correlation between a drug's legal status and the extent of its usage, that argument collapses. Thus, the public-health argument that's so long dominated the marijuana debate, absorbed so many federal dollars in pseudo-scientific attempts to show marijuana's unhealthy effects, is an argumentative red-herring—a highly emotional issue that's largely irrelevant to the debate. Again, if drug laws curtailed use, the

protecting-the-public-health argument might be relevant. They don't;
it isn't.

*   *   *

Drug War apologists always say, "We're doing it for the kids," claiming
that the War on Drugs is necessary to save our nation's youth, our future,
but mostly, they've just been putting them in prison, **damaging the
futures of countless American kids**, sometimes killing them.

Democracy Now! broadcast a report about how the War on Drugs
actually works, this as part of a larger story on the documentary "Kids for
Cash" by Robert May that tells, "the shocking story of how thousands of
children in Pennsylvania were jailed by two corrupt judges who received
$2.6 million in kickbacks from the builders and owners of private prison
facilities" ("Kids for Cash"). The two judges, Mark Ciavarella and
Michael Conahan, both now in prison, were busted in a federal tax sting;
a primary way in which these predatory jurists ensnared their young
victims was drug laws, including, of course, marijuana laws. Among the
victimized was 17-year-old Ed Kenzakoski. A star wrestler at his high
school, Kenzakoski was respected; a college scholarship was expected.
His was a bright future—until his previously promising life ran headlong
into the War on Drugs.

Kenzakoski's mother, Sandy Fazo, explains, "You know, he had a
girlfriend at the time that was telling me stuff about him experimenting[125]
and, you know, just getting a little bit out of control." Fazo was alarmed
and spoke to Kenzakoski's father, who offered to help. Fazo continues:

> . . . he [the father] had friends that he graduated with that were
> cops, so he talked to them, and they were going to go in and put
> some, you know, paraphernalia on him just to get him caught,
> get him a slap on the wrist . . . .
> Amy Goodman: They planted drug paraphernalia?
> Sandy Fazo: Drug paraphernalia, marijuana pipe.
> Amy Goodman: In his truck?
> Sandy Fazo: Yes. . . .

---

[125]   I'm guessing this means he tried marijuana.

The legal system is set up, apparently, to discourage parents from getting a lawyer for their kids; in one case, a police officer told the family of an accused teenager that if they got an attorney, he would raise the charges to something seriously criminal. So, Kenzakoski's parents eschewed legal assistance, but instead of a promised "slap on the wrist," Judge Ciavarella gave Kenzakoski, according to his mother, "Three months. He went in there [jail] for three months. And then, from there, because Ciavarella said he had a drug problem, then he would have to go to Clearbrook, which was, you know, a rehabilitation for addictions . . . And we stood there, and in 30 seconds he was cuffed and shackled and taken away."

Nor was Ciavarella shy about his "no-nonsense, zero-tolerance" zealotry;[126] at one point, the film shows him lecturing an about-to-be-sentenced teen: "Whatever sins you have committed, you can't go back and undo it. You are going to experience prison. I'll be glad to put you there."[127]

"There," according to Fazo, turned out to be:

> Northwestern Boot Academy, an hour away from our house, total military. They couldn't speak. They couldn't do anything. They were dressed in military attire. He was with, you know, people from all over that committed actual—when he would tell me the crimes that were committed, this is whom my son was in with. They broke you down, I mean tore you apart, humiliated you. He wouldn't tell me what happened when he was in there.

On release, Kenzakoski, who had received "equivalent schooling" while incarcerated, wasn't allowed to return to his high-school or wrestling, and of course, his scholarship hopes vanished. He got a job and tried to get on with his life. Traumatized by his experience, probably angry and still in prison mode, Kenzakoski got into a fight with another

---

[126] This, from local television reporter Terrie Morgan-Besecker: "He [Ciavarella] always jailed kids."

[127] Filmmaker Robert May interviewed Ciavarella over a period of months; the interviews are astounding: Ciavarella claims to have been misrepresented and martyred. He seems utterly shameless. It's a stunning example of denial-and-projection thinking—evil is everywhere but inside of him.

teen—nothing particularly serious, apparently, but Judge Ciavarella sent him back to "camp." Kenzakoski, of course, lost his job, and he spent a total of five months in jail, the last two in a state prison.

Kenzakoski's mother adds:

> [H]e came out of there [jail] a changed person. Like I said, he was a 17-year-old, free-spirited boy, and he came out a hardened man that wouldn't even talk about what in—so, to this day, I don't know what happened to him in there, but he would never talk about it. But he was just a different person. You know, he—very bottled up, you know, wouldn't speak, and no respect for the justice system at all. He knew he was wronged. He knew what was taken away. He lost his little girlfriend while he was in there. She left him for somebody, you know. He just lost, in that age, at that impressionable age, way too much. He had way too much taken from him, everything his—everything he had, really.

Kenzakoski apparently decided to finish what the War on Drugs started; five months after getting back out of jail, he took his own life—shot himself in the heart.

Fazo concludes:

> And, I mean, I was—never in my wildest dreams would I think these people that are supposed to have—you know, they were the professionals. They have your child's interest at best—best at heart. And these are the people that you trust, and everything's going to be OK. You know, he's going to learn a little lesson, and everything will be fine. . . . He went there as a free-spirited kid. He came out a hardened man, I'd say.

*   *   *

In April 2017, *Democracy Now!* reported:

> "In what may be **the single largest dismissal of wrongful convictions in U.S. history**, Massachusetts prosecutors announced Tuesday they would throw out 21,587 criminal drug cases . . . all prosecuted based on evidence or testimony

supplied by a former state chemist who admitted to faking tests and identifying evidence as illegal narcotics without even testing it. The chemist, Annie Dookhan, pleaded guilty in 2013 to tampering with evidence during her nine years working at a state crime lab in Boston." ("Massachusetts")

Popular with prosecutors for her amazing turnaround time in consistently returning positive results, Dookhan told one, "I have the same attitude . . .get them [drug users] off the streets" ("Meet"). Many of the Dookhan defendants/ victims are minorities; particularly, it appears, African-Americans.

*   *   *

Let's now tally **the enormous damage that drug-war criminals have done to America.** First, the War on Drugs is but the modern chapter in what has always been a pretext for a vicious war on American minorities. Second, one of the most hurtful things you can do to a person is put him or her in jail, and courtesy of the War on Drugs, the USA has the highest incarceration rate in the developed world. Third is all the deadly violence associated with the illegality of drugs—just as it was with alcohol during American Prohibition. As many have correctly pointed out, the vast majority of the violence associated with drugs is a direct result of its illegality—drug gangs shooting it out in public (murdering innocent bystanders, as well), and in the case of some Latin American nations, terrorizing entire societies.

To these liabilities, let's add the terrible toll the War on Drugs has taken on our rights; thus, Baum writes, "conservative Justice John Paul Stevens lamented in writing that the Supreme Court had become little more than a 'loyal foot soldier in the War on Drugs'" (*Smoke*, 178), and "dissenting John Paul Stevens vented that the Court was converting 'the Bill of Rights into an unenforced honor code that the police may follow at their discretion.' [Justice] William Brennan went further. 'The Court's victory over the Fourth Amendment,' he wrote, 'is complete'" (*Smoke*, 203). Also, the financial cost has been staggering—literally hundreds of billions of dollars of public monies spent. Yes, that's a lot of very unhealthy history resulting from the War on Drugs.

The **drug warriors** pose as pillars of morality, but their **behavior is utterly shameless.** They say they're concerned with public health, but they destroy public health by incarcerating millions for victimless crimes. They say they're protecting our kids, but their idea of "tough love" is jail time, and it's the War on Drugs that's killing our kids, not marijuana. They boast they're going to demonstrate "personal responsibility" and be models of right living, yet, as with Judge Ciavarella, they seem unable to accept responsibility for their own actions, which are often corrupt. They claim to "Just Say No" to drugs, but in their private lives, they're often exposed as drug users and abusers. They claim to be defending minority communities from the scourge of drug abuse, yet their War on Drugs has devastated minority communities. They pose as defenders of law and order, yet their ethnocidal and racist practices are in conflict with international laws that protect minorities and human rights, and they seem to have no conception of justice and individual rights. They posture as pious students of William Bennett's *Book of Virtues*, but in practice, they're vicious and venal.

The modern War on Drugs is more than a well-intended mistake; it's a fascistic, predatory social movement. It and other drug scares in American history might be compared to a lynch mob or a witch hunt—a sort of psycho-political acting out that allows followers to feel holy by projecting evil onto others. By giving the little people a scapegoat to hate and

> **Atticus Finch, please come home! There's a large crowd gathering in front of the Elks Club on Main Street. They're chanting, "We're doing it for the kids! We're doing it for the kids!" and things look ugly. ("Say, I love your torch and pitchfork!"**
> **"Thanks! I got 'em at Jared!")**

vilify, the powers that be also politically distract and manipulate them and deflect the anger from below that social injustice creates. Consider the following comments made by the leadership of the War on Drugs; notice in particular how they aren't about protecting the public health.

Baum quotes John Walters, deputy drug czar from 1989 to 1993: "Between 1977 and 1992 a conservative cultural revolution occurred in America. It was called the drug war" (qtd. in Baum, *Smoke*, 104). Carlton Turner, President Reagan and President George H.W. Bush's drug czar, declared, "I was hired by the President of the United States to clean up America" (qtd. in Baum, *Smoke*, 137); he planned to do this by, in the words of a Turner supporter, "turning the nation away from the wretched

Drug Culture that is rotting it at the core" (qtd. in Baum, *Smoke*, 146). Turner adds, "We have to create a generation of drug-free Americans to purge society" (qtd. in Baum, *Smoke*, 152). Baum says of Ian Macdonald, a prohibitionist pamphleteer who in 1984 was appointed "manager of federal drug treatment and prevention":

> [He] further shared [Carlton] Turner's view that adolescent drug use was a cultural problem as much as a health problem. The Woodstock era had condoned a tendency in young people to reject authority, a malignant legacy that lingered fifteen years later. An entire generation of children seemed to believe that whatever their parents told them was wrong, that they could make up their own minds about what was safe and acceptable. (*Smoke*, 199)

Baum adds:

> In an article titled "White House Stop-Drug-Use Program—Why the Emphasis is on Marijuana," the magazine *Government Executive* profiled Turner, summarizing his views this way: "Marijuana, like hard-rock music, torn jeans and sexual promiscuity," was a pillar of "the counter culture" (*Smoke*, 154).

Turner himself adds that marijuana and drug use in general is more than a health issue:

> Drug use is also pattern that has sort of tagged along during the present young-adult generation's involvement in anti-military, anti-nuclear power, anti-big business, anti-authority demonstrations; of people from a myriad of different racial, religious or otherwise persuasions demanding "rights" or "entitlements" politically while refusing to accept corollary civic responsibility [this, I'm guessing, means drug use or protesting the War in Vietnam]. (qtd. in Baum, *Smoke*, 154)

Baum writes, "[William] Bennett freely admitted drug enforcement is but an instrument in a wider agenda, calling for 'the reconstitution of legal and social authority through the imposition of appropriate consequences for drug dealing and drug use,'" and Bennett said, "The drug crisis is a crisis of authority[128]. . ." (qtd. in Baum, *Smoke*, 266). In addition, Bennett believes, "[The drug problem] comes from this tradition of freedom and liberty, which gets distorted into license[129] and 'do your own thing' and the gospel of the sixties" (qtd. in Baum, *Smoke*, 291). Eventually, in 1989, Bennett told CNN interviewer Larry King, "I have no problem with beheading marijuana users only legal ones" (qtd. in Herer, 122). However carefully or philosophically you may parse your comments, when you start talking about beheading people, your moral train has gone off the tracks.

"Conservative counter revolution," "clean up America," "reconstitution of legal and social authority," "purge society," "beheading marijuana users"—these are euphemisms for fascism, the rhetoric of an institutionalized lynch mob attacking, primarily, Hippie-America.

Bigots, as sociologist Jack Levin told us in *The Functions of Prejudice*, seek a sort of intellectual security, a world without ambiguity; as such, they find this vapid self-righteousness appealing, even inspiring. They hear William Bennett blathering about "beheading marijuana users," and instead of being horrified, they're impressed—"Gosh, the courage! The moral greatness of the man!" Likewise, many Americans have come to believe that a person's use or non-use of marijuana is a simple way to judge his or her character: people who use marijuana are evil; those who don't are virtuous.

Bigots, Levin adds, also need to feel above others, and War on Drugs zealotry allows them to feel morally superior ("*We* are a higher form of life. We're the good guys; they're the bad guys"), and he notes, bigots also need a place to displace their anger, and hating all those "druggie dirtbags" works well for that.

Politics is to a large extent the act/art of mobilization: of getting people grouped, getting them emotionally and psychologically invested in an issue, and then moving them in a political direction with like-minded others. Through demagoguery, manipulation, Orwellian

---

[128] Can you say, "authoritarian personality"?

[129] For those unfamiliar with the traditional liberty vs. license distinction, generally *liberty* is seen as legitimate freedom that's socially responsible and doesn't impose on or violate the rights of others; *license* is seen as irresponsible freedom that does impose on or violate the rights of others. An example of *license* would be littering.

brainwashing and scads of money, the War on Drugs has been mobilizing America very successfully; unfortunately, the direction they've been moving us in is towards the far right—destination, fascism.

To participate in the War on Drugs is to participate in a national lynch mob. You may have been tricked into joining that lynch mob as a concerned parent worried about your child; nonetheless, it is a lynch mob; it has blood on its hands. Fascist

> **The War on Drugs is a modern American fascist movement. It is an ongoing crime against humanity.**

bullies seek minority victims, and racism, ethnic chauvinism and other forms of bigotry can lay the groundwork for genocide, the ultimate crime. God and history will remember as foolish, weak and wicked those who through the years were in that lynch mob, screaming (or nodding with approval as others screamed it), "Stretch the Chinaman's neck!" "Kill the Hindoo!" "String up the nigger!" "Teach that Mexicano. a lesson!" or post-Sixties, probably, "Give that hippie a haircut!"—only in this case, the "haircut" turned out to be a beating or a prison sentence for a victimless crime.[130]

*   *   *

Now, public-health arguments may be a red herring in the legalization debate, but with that important reservation in mind, there's a place here for discussing **some health-related marijuana and War on Drugs issues**.

The star of prohibition arguments and a staple of DARE has been **Gateway**, the notion that people start with a "softer" drug, like cannabis, grow bored with or inured to it, and soon "graduate" to harder drugs like heroin. Well, there are so many problems with Gateway that only in the Orwellian environment of the War on Drugs would this flimsy argument be taken seriously.

First, there *is* a Gateway effect from marijuana to harder drugs. According to Baum, the federal government has not produced any

---

[130] Incidentally, if you asked those historic lynch-mobbers why they were doing what they were doing, they would explain themselves much as the War on Drugs does: "We're doing this for the kids! We're doing this for the health and safety of our community! We're doing this for God and Country! We're doing this to save Western Civilization!"

scientific evidence for Gateway save one study conducted by an anti-pot researcher at the University of Kentucky. Here's the corker: yes, the study did demonstrate a limited Gateway effect, but it was the result of pot prohibition; that is, when marijuana users are forced into an underground criminal economy where pot and heroin might be sold alongside each other, that creates a limited Gateway effect.[131]

Logically, Gateway is an irrational mess, containing three clear causal fallacies. First, there's a *cause-effect* fallacy: the assumption that because A preceded B, A caused B—that because marijuana use may have preceded heroin use, the marijuana use caused the heroin use. No; that confuses chronology with causality. Second, there's *oversimplification*: the refusal to look at *all* the causes of an effect and to focus instead on just one. I mean, even if the cause-effect fallacy wasn't here, even if they'd proven that pot in some way leads to heroin, there might still be numerous other causes which are being ignored in place of a prejudicial emphasis on cannabis use. Finally, there's a *slippery slope*: the notion that A will lead to B which will lead to C—a downhill domino effect where the first step, innocent as it may seem, creates a *fait accompli*. It's a fallacy when there's no real evidence showing how each domino will inevitably fall into the next domino—when the domino effect is assumed. That's how Gateway is presented: all those intermediate steps between pot and heroin are glossed over, assumed. Gateway, then, is an intellectual embarrassment.

> **Gateway is illogical and ridiculous—an argumentative embarrassment pounded into the American brain by the War on Drugs.**

And when we examine the relation between cannabis usage and heroin usage, we see numerous problems; particularly, as Baum notes, even though marijuana use has increased since the 1960s, heroin-use rates haven't: "The number of Americans who have smoked

---

[131] Baum:
"Even the Kentucky researcher quoted in *Science News* conceded it is the act of criminalizing pot smokers, rather than the pharmacological properties of the drug itself, that is the real gateway to harder drugs. 'By throwing subjects into a subculture that elicits heroin use,' he said, 'even moderate marijuana use can weld the first link of a casual chain leading to heroin'" (*Smoke*, 153).

pot has skyrocketed in the past thirty years—to as many as 70 million—while the number of heroin addicts is about the same in the mid-1990s as it was in 1970: about half a million" (*Smoke*, 153).

If Gateway's promise of pot use leading to heroin addiction is true, then for the last several decades, we should've seen a national wave of heroin addiction and deaths as all those pot users "graduated." It didn't happen. However, *Time* reported in February 2014, "Heroin use has been rising since 2007, growing from 373,000 yearly users to 669,000 in 2012, according to the Substance Abuse and Mental Health Services Administration (SAMHSA)" (Gray, "Heroin Gains"). It sounds like the answer to a prohibitionist prayer, doesn't it? "Gateway finally kicked in!" Thing is, the article discusses the causes of this heroin-use spike—a purer, cheaper product that doesn't need to be injected, an emphasis on the heroin market by Mexican drug gangs, and a growing section of the public having prior experience with prescription pain killers, which is believed to predispose heroin use. *Nowhere is there any mention of marijuana.*

And the notion that pot smokers become bored with marijuana has problems. If that's true, then people would eventually quit cannabis, and marijuana-usage rates should be crashing. They aren't. Of course, the prohibitionists also argue that marijuana is psychologically addictive. Okay, explain to me how someone can be simultaneously bored with something and psychologically addicted to it. That would seem a contradiction.

In addition, Gateway assumes that marijuana, alleged intermediate drugs and heroin are on a simple continuum, that all have the same effects, the same "high" just in heavier ("harder") doses. Thus, when one gets bored with cannabis and quits using it, one will find what was lost in the next "harder" Gateway drug. Now, imagine we were hearing this argument about three popular *legal* drugs: caffeine, alcohol and nicotine. We'd be told that one of these drugs (say, caffeine) is the starter drug, the original Gateway; then, we'd be told, people grow bored with caffeine and seek something "harder," say alcohol, which people, in turn, become bored with and then graduate to nicotine which eventually kills them.

Most would respond, "That's the dumbest argument I ever heard; there are so many things wrong with it, I don't know where to start." Well, as badly as this Gateway argument would fare with legal drugs, so it fares with illegal drugs. The alleged Gateway drugs all have significantly different effects, different "highs," nor do users become bored with drugs.

And Gateway has been used in the most shameless ways; for instance, in recent years, drug warriors have been arguing that pot use can lead to tobacco addiction. Their evidence, apparently, is that they've found cases of pot use preceding tobacco use. Putting aside the obvious cause-effect fallacy here, historically, this is ridiculous. Look at America in the late 1950s, early 1960s: tobacco ads everywhere, smoking ubiquitous—a nation of tobacco addicts, many of whom would die from lung or throat cancer. Are we going to blame tobacco deaths on pot use when widespread tobacco use preceded widespread pot use by several decades? This contemptible claim is just more silly scapegoating of marijuana.

Also, **Gateway and War on Drugs propaganda don't understand addiction**. Dr. Carl Hart, a Columbia neuroscientist, is an African-American who started his career believing that drugs were devastating the kind of inner-city communities he hailed from. He changed his mind:

> I discovered that 80 to 90 percent of the people who actually use drugs like crack cocaine, heroin, methamphetamine, marijuana—80 to 90 percent of those people were not addicted. I thought, "Wait a second. I thought that once you use these drugs, everyone becomes addicted, and that's why we had these problems." . . . . Another thing that I found out is that if you provide alternatives to people—jobs, other sort of alternatives— they don't overindulge in drugs like this. I discovered this in the human laboratory as well as the animal laboratory. (Goodman, "Drugs Aren't")

Hart describes an experiment featured in *The New York Times*:

> I had read the literature, the animal literature, showing that when you allow an animal to self-administer, self—press a lever to receive intravenous injections of cocaine—they will do so until they die. But then, when I looked at the literature more carefully, if you provide that animal with a sexually receptive mate, with some sweet treats like sugar water or something of that nature, they wouldn't take the drug. (Goodman, "Drugs Aren't")

Thus, addiction is caused by a variety of factors and usually results from a lack of choices, of opportunity. Often, Hart says, "People get addicted because that's the best option available to them" (qtd. in Goodman, "Drugs Aren't"). This view directly contradicts simple-minded War on Drugs propaganda which asserts that the drug itself is almost entirely to blame, that if someone tries a drug even once, all his or her free will immediately evaporates and that person becomes a slave to that drug.

Basically, there are people who have so much pain, stress and anxiety in their lives that for them, addiction becomes a viable coping mechanism, a lesser evil. In those circumstances, some people are going to get addicted one way or another. If they start using heroin and become addicted to it, it's not the fault of marijuana. In fact, they probably sought out heroin precisely because of its notorious ability to narcoticize, to make one "feel no pain." Likewise, when stressed and depressed people with addictive personalities meet alcohol, you get an alcoholic; are we going to blame alcoholism on previous pot use? So Gateway and War on Drugs propaganda tend to scapegoat marijuana: no matter what the ugly result, somehow cannabis is always to blame.

* * *

Consider, please, **the bias in the pseudo-scientific studies allegedly showing the health hazards of marijuana**. That era which future historians will call The War on Drugs won't be seen as a bright spot for American science and medicine. Sadly, what we've seen is both professions doing their allegedly patriotic duty, much the way patriots are supposed to in any war; after all, they think, it's a crusade to save our youth from the horrors of drugs and the nation itself from moral rot. "How can *we* help?" American science and medicine have obligingly asked, to which neoconservatism and the government have replied, "By churning out a never-ending stream of research showing how unhealthy and dangerous marijuana is, by helping us portray pot as a menace of the first order."

To understand US marijuana-and-health research, we need to know some history. Harry Anslinger, the long-time head of the Bureau of Narcotics and racist nut job mentioned above, banned any government research on medical marijuana. Anslinger retired in 1962, and soon Herer writes, "Reports of positive effects and new therapeutic indications for cannabis were almost a weekly occurrence in medical journals and the national press. (41); thus, starting in 1966, there was what some call a "golden decade" of legitimate US research. Then, in 1974 at the Medical College of Virginia, journalist Raymond Cushing reports, researchers "who had been funded by the National Institute of Health to find evidence that marijuana damages the immune system, found instead that THC slowed the growth of three kinds of cancer in mice—lung and breast cancer, and a virus-induced leukemia."

Oops! Apparently, this publicized cancer-cure finding threw a scare into Big Pharma and the War on Drugs zealots, and Herer adds, "Following this remarkably positive discovery by the Medical College of Virginia, orders were immediately handed down by the DEA [Drug Enforcement Administration] and the National Institute of Health to defund all further cannabis/tumor research and reporting" (46).

Then, Herer writes:

[T]he research ban was accomplished when American pharmaceutical companies successfully petitioned the federal government to be allowed to finance and judge 100% of the research . . . the Ford Administration, NIDA [National Institute of Drug Abuse] and the DEA said, in effect, no American independent (read: university) research or federal health program would be allowed to again investigate natural cannabis derivatives for medicine. . . . [later] the Reagan/Bush/Clinton administrations absolutely refused to allow resumption of real (university) cannabis research. (41)

Apparently, this situation remains largely in place today although California, the Marijuana Policy Project reports, has been doing independent marijuana research since 2010 through its Center for Medicinal Cannabis Research (CMCR).

Generally, any potentially positive research about cannabis has been suppressed by both NIDA and the drug companies; as such, to find reliable scientific evidence regarding the effects of marijuana, we have to look to at US research from the decade of 1966-1975, at the few positive post-1975 US studies that can be considered admission-against-interest sources, [132] at CMCR research since 2010, or look to other nations. Most importantly, War on Drugs "science" regarding the evils of marijuana is biased science—not really science at all since its purpose is not a disinterested discovery of the truth but to act as an instrument of a reactionary political agenda. So, when reading or hearing newscasts about negative post-1975 US marijuana studies, the fair-minded and well-informed will understand that those studies usually can't be trusted—as evidence, they should be off the table.[133] And if for no other reason, we should know this because the results of such research are so often goofy, hysterical and suspicious.

Here's **an example of a War on Drugs-sponsored experiment** that seems valid—until we look closely at it and do a bit of critical thinking. A 2006 article on the website *New Scientist* called "Why teenagers should steer clear of cannabis," reports: "Adolescents' use of marijuana may increase the risk of heroin addiction later in life, a new study suggests. Researchers say the work adds to 'overwhelming' evidence that people under 21 should not use marijuana because of the risk of damaging the developing brain" (Vince). That's right: pot use leads to heroin, *and* it ruins kids' minds! The evidence is "overwhelming"!

Let me describe the experiment: there were two groups of "teenage" rats, six each, and one group was given doses of THC, the equivalent, reportedly, of smoking "one joint every three days." The other adolescent rats were a control group. Okay, so are we really going to say that rats and humans are so much alike that we can take a part of a rat's lifespan and say, "Hey, these days are its Wonder Years"? Logically, and I think scientifically, this is a stretch. Dr. Hart says of addiction experiments utilizing rats, "But when you start to talk about drug addiction and the complexities [of it], drug addiction is a human sort of ailment, not an ailment in rats. What you can do in rats is maybe model one component, maybe two components of drug addiction, but understand that that model might be quite limited" (Goodman, "Drugs Aren't").

---

[132] That is, these studies were originally funded to prove health hazards but they tended to prove the opposite.

[133] Herer notes (2007) another problem with War on Drugs "science": "Some 10,000 studies have been done on cannabis, 4,000 in the U.S., and only about a dozen have shown any negative results and *these have never been replicated*" (emphasis added) (43).

Okay, after 21 days (these are supposed to correspond to the human years between 12 and 18), the pot party was stopped, and those rats were rested for a week. Then "catheters were inserted in all 12 of the adult rats, and they were able to self-administer heroin by pushing a lever" (Vince). To read the news coverage of this experiment, you'd think it was supporting Gateway; in fact, the researchers forced the heroin onto the rats; the "teenage" rats didn't start using heroin because they were bored with pot, now did they? Instead of proving Gateway, the scientists simply assumed it. And then, the researchers monitored how much heroin the rats self-administered, and it turns out the six reefer rats were using higher doses; this, in turn, is cited as proof that their previous pot use had inured some of the pleasure centers in their brains, and this, in turn, is seen as proof that they were more prone to heroin addiction.

Notice that whatever the reported results, the experiment doesn't actually address the issue of why people, unlike rats, choose to use heroin, or in any way prove that previous marijuana use would make that choice more likely. The experiment *might* show that if you take an adult who smoked pot as a teen, take his or her pot away, force a catheter into the adult's arm and allow him or her to self-administer heroin, then adults who previously smoked pot *may* self-administer more heroin than adults who didn't smoke pot before, but even that is a best-case interpretation.

What we have here is a tortuous argument filled with logical leaps and silly assumptions. Yet, preposterous as this study seems, it was widely reported in the media—a leading story in the national news— as "overwhelming" proof that marijuana is a menace to children. Parents hear such "scientific" reports, and many, without a jot of critical thinking, apparently, jump onto a drug-hysteria bandwagon alleging that marijuana is killing their kids—"Gasp! And, oh, gasp again!!"

304

Another infamous example of War on Drugs pseudo-science is **studies claiming to show that marijuana makes adolescent boys grow breasts**. Although this disturbing accusation has been around for decades, as recently as 2013, a claim of such by Detroit plastic surgeon Andrew Youn was making headlines. The studies allegedly showing this apparently used mice, and Youn is merely reporting on these previous studies, repackaging them in an exclusive article for CNN: "Dr. Youn says that in animals, marijuana results in falling testosterone levels, shrinking testicles and abnormalities in sperm.

> **In their eagerness to serve the War on Drugs, the scientific and medical communities have frequently disgraced themselves, often acting with no more integrity than a bunch of Nazi quacks helping Hitler prove Jews were allegedly inferior.**

The effects of cannabis on testosterone in humans are not as clear, he says [emphasis added]," reports Emma Innes for the UK's DailMail.com. Apparently, there are a number of factors claimed to reduce testosterone levels in males, but since marijuana is said to be one, this pseudo-story becomes a sensational headline grabber even though, as Innes admits, "the association between marijuana and gynaecomastia [male breasts] hasn't been conclusively proven."

Okay, so look around you; where are all those busty boys? Shouldn't we be seeing young pot-smoking males who are, pardon me, stacked? It's a ridiculous assertion contradicted by everyday reality; I'd bet that if we measured the extent to which this phenomenon occurs in populations of marijuana users versus non-marijuana users, we'd find no measurable difference. Yet, this study (which just coincidentally echoes stereotypes about Hippie males being unmanly) is considered another weighty scientific indictment of the evils of marijuana; in fact, it's just another shameless, melodramatic attempt to portray children as marijuana victims.

As we can see, in their eagerness to serve the War on Drugs, the scientific and medical communities have frequently disgraced themselves, often acting with no more integrity than a bunch of Nazi quacks helping Hitler prove Jews were allegedly inferior. War on Drugs pseudo-science is unreliable, and apparently the American people are increasingly deducing this. Go figure: after decades of War on Drugs propaganda, after spending billions of our tax dollars urging the scientific and medical communities to spew out research demonizing marijuana, the drug warriors are losing and losing badly.

* * *

Many Americans are what we might call "marijuana virgins"; that is, they've never used marijuana, and they tend to be ignorant about it. They'll likely try, then, to understand cannabis by comparing it to drugs they are familiar with—**tobacco and alcohol**—and these faulty analogies also tend to permeate the national debate.

Now, it's true that in some ways **marijuana and tobacco** are similar: both are usually smoked; both make the user feel good by "relaxing" them.

But, that's where the similarities between tobacco and marijuana end. We've heard sensational claims that marijuana has "10 times the tar that tobacco does." Apparently, pot does have more tar than tobacco (though a web search shows it's more likely about four times as much); thing is, while tobacco tars cause cancer, apparently, marijuana tars don't.

As such, **there's no documented link between marijuana smoking and lung cancer or emphysema** (Herer, 110). As evidence, Jack Herer interviewed and cites the work of the eminent Dr. Donald Tashkin of UCLA: "[H]e [Tashkin] and other doctors had predicted 20 years ago, their certainty that hundreds of thousands of marijuana smokers would by now (1997) have developed lung cancer" (111).[134] Yet, when asked how many of Tashkin's "long-term, cannabis-only smokers" had developed lung cancer, Tashkin said, "That's the strange part. So far no one we've studied has gone on to get lung cancer" (qtd. in Herer, 111). According to Kathleen Miles of the *Huffington Post,* "Tashkin authored a . . . paper in 2006 that also found no link between marijuana use and risk of lung cancer," and in June of 2013, Tashkin again published a piece in *Annals of the American Thoracic Society* negating this link.

Lastly here, it's common knowledge that tobacco is a vasoconstrictor—it shrinks capillaries and thus tends to increase blood

---

[134] Notice how Dr. Tashkin's study began by expecting health hazards; this makes it "admission-against-interest."

pressure and stress.[135] But **marijuana is probably a vasodilator,** meaning it relaxes and expands capillaries. If that's true, then marijuana would likely lower blood pressure, and this vasodilation would be life giving: basically, everything in your body—from your brain to your sexual organs to an injury trying to heal— benefits from the abundant flow of healthy blood. Vasodilation could explain some of cannabis' reported health benefits and why people often claim marijuana increases their creativity. While I couldn't find conclusive evidence that marijuana vasodilates, many informed people believe it does; thus, Herer says, "While tobacco constricts arteries, cannabis dilates (opens) them" (49) though he cites no source. If this hypothesis is true, then marijuana likely has some very healthy effects.

* * *

One positive aspect of comparisons made between **marijuana and alcohol** is that the public seems to understand that not everyone who consumes alcohol is an alcoholic, that it's possible to "drink responsibly." When the public learns to think that way about marijuana, America will have come a long ways. At present, of course, DARE and other prohibitionist propaganda don't distinguish between use and abuse of marijuana; they consider all

With marijuana, intoxication doesn't necessarily equal impairment. In other words, getting high won't neces-sarily make you slur your speech, stagger around, get into car accident, or exhibit all the ugly symptoms of being "loaded."

---

[135] Incidentally, we might ask, if everyone agrees that nicotine is a vasoconstrictor, why does smoking "relax" tobacco users? The Australian website "Quit" explains:
Nicotine causes a spike in your heart rate and blood pressure making your heart work harder. The cigarette *appears* to relax you because the nicotine removes the uncomfortable withdrawal symptoms caused by smoking, and gives you a brief hit from the brain-reward chemical called dopamine. But because of this spike in heart rate and blood pressure it's difficult to achieve the level of relaxation and stress relief of a nonsmoker (emphasis in original). ("Stress and Smoking")

marijuana use "drug abuse" and stubbornly refuse to acknowledge that such a thing as responsible marijuana use exists.

On the other hand, there's **the naïve notion that a marijuana high must be like being drunk**. But with marijuana, intoxication doesn't necessarily equal impairment. In other words, getting high won't necessarily make you slur your speech, stagger around, get into car accident, or exhibit all the ugly symptoms of being "loaded." Let me support this with a quick overview of Dr. Andrew Weil's pioneering research at Harvard, a paper aptly entitled "What No One Wants to Know about Marijuana":

> There are three conditions under which marijuana can be shown to impair general psychological performance in laboratory subjects. They are:
>
> 1. by giving it to people who have never had it before;
>
> 2. by giving people very high doses that they are not used to (or giving it orally to people used to smoking it); and
>
> 3. by giving people very hard things to do, especially things that they have never had a chance to practice while under the influence of the drug.
>
> Under any of these three conditions, pharmacologists can demonstrate that marijuana impairs performance. (Weil)

Notice that in society as a whole, these three categories taken together would likely only comprise a very small percentage of "highs," of individual marijuana experiences. Weil continues:

> What pharmacologists cannot make sense of is that people who are high on marijuana cannot be shown, in objective terms, to be different from people who are not high. That is, if a marijuana user is allowed to smoke his usual doses and then to do things he has had a chance to practice while high, he does not appear to perform any differently from someone who is not high.

So, *being high on marijuana doesn't necessarily mean being impaired.*

It's interesting to apply these findings to things like people driving under the influence of marijuana; the law, of course, tends to treat these intoxicated pot-using drivers like drunk drivers. Here's Weil's take:

> [I]f I were given the choice of riding with one of the following four drivers:
>
> 1. a person who had never smoked marijuana before and just had [smoked marijuana];
>
> 2. a marijuana smoker who had never driven while high and was just about to;
>
> 3. a high marijuana smoker who had practiced driving while high; and
>
> 4. a person with any amount of alcohol in him.
>   I would unhesitatingly take driver number three as the best possible risk. . . .

Likewise, an argument the in-retreat drug warriors are using here in Colorado is to remind voters and legislators of a scientific correlation between marijuana and drunk-driving accidents for teens; the implication is that with legalization, we're going to see deadly teen-driving accidents spike. The thing is, correlation doesn't prove causation, and abusing alcohol is sufficient cause in and of itself for a driver to get into an accident. This argument, then, is another irrational scare tactic that scapegoats marijuana.

Let me finish this marijuana-and-health section by noting that there's **promising research that marijuana can cure certain types of cancer.** As we saw above, in 1974, researchers at the Medical College of Virginia (MCV) found that marijuana

Given that the health-care establishment and the federal government have spent billions on an elusive cure for cancer, that we've long had a possible cure for various cancers should be a shocker.

lessened cancerous tumors (Cushing). More recently, Robin Wilkey reports in the *Huffington Post*, "Last year [2012], a pair of scientists at California Pacific Medical Center in San Francisco found that a compound derived from marijuana could stop metastasis in many kinds of aggressive cancers, potentially altering the fatality of the disease forever." Columnist Leland Rucker mentions an August 2015 report from the National Cancer Institute which "admitted that cannabinoids can be used to inhibit cancer cells without harming healthy ones (a major side effect of chemotherapy and radiation)." He then quotes that report in part: "[C]annabinoids are useful in treating cancer and its side effects . . ." ("As it turns out").

Given that the health-care establishment and the federal government have spent billions on an elusive cure for cancer, that we've long had a possible cure for various cancers should be a shocker. The reason we've tended not to hear about marijuana's potential to cure cancer is that the War on Drugs has suppressed this research and its stunning findings; that's a terrible crime, possibly resulting in the unnecessary deaths of millions—the ultimate hypocrisy of a campaign pledged to promote public health.

*　　*　　*

If the War on Drugs is a modern fascist movement, how do we fight that fascism? The answer is in front of our faces: **the legalization movement, a political powerhouse on a roll**.

It's already made substantial US progress: Not only have 29 states legalized medical marijuana, as of May 2017, nine states have legalized all marijuana: Colorado, Washington, Alaska, Oregon, Nevada, Maine, Massachusetts, California and Vermont plus the District of Columbia and Guam.[136] Some major US cities have decriminalized cannabis, including Chicago (Nadelmann), Philadelphia (RT.com) and Brooklyn (Robbins). A late 2013 Gallup Poll shows 58% of Americans in favor of legalization (A. Swift); a Februrary 2017 Qunnipiac Poll shows that in response to the question, "Would you support or oppose the government enforcing federal laws against marijuana in states that have already legalized

---

[136] In 2014, Florida voters approved legalization by a 58% margin, but an undemocratic state law requires 60% for passage (CNN).

310

medical or recreational marijuana?" 71% are opposed." So, whatever the Trump Administration and Attorney General Sessions ultimately decide to do, the legalization movement is still dominating the political landscape; indeed, cannabis was legalized in Vermont in May 2017, several months into the Trump Administration.

*   *   *

What does EHT have to tell us about the legalization struggle? For starters, just as the modern War on Drugs is largely about persecuting Hippie-America, so the response to it, particularly marijuana legalization, is about the struggle of Hippie-America for an end to persecution and for social equality; thus, those leading and involved in the legalization struggle appear to be Hippie-Americans.

The lead organizer of the legalization campaign in Colorado, the spokesperson for a group known as SAFER (an acronym designed to echo the group's primary message that marijuana is a safer recreational drug than alcohol) is Mason Tvert. I once emailed Tvert, discussing some of the ideas in this book; in his response, he said that he used to have long hair and generally was Hippie looking (Tvert). Yet, to see Tvert on television or in the media, that probable Hippie identity is invisible—as Hippie-Americans are supposed to be. Like others in the legalization movement before, he likely believes that to be taken seriously in the public eye, he can't appear Hippie, that his likely cultural identity must be masked, that distancing oneself from Hippiedom is safest and most practical course. Nonetheless, that cultural identity is likely there; most of these legalizations activists are, in my opinion, Hippie-Americans fighting for something dear to their hearts, fighting for their people.[137]

In Washington state, one of the highest profile legalization activists/ activists is Rick Steves, a name known to most of us as the host/guide of PBS's long-running *Travels with Rick Steves*. Of course, you could watch dozens of Steves' overseas adventures and never guess he was Hippie. I did an image search on the web, searching *Rick Steves Hippie*, and quickly came across several photos that, based on appearance, strongly suggest Steves *is* Hippie-American.

---

[137]   Even if they wouldn't necessarily call them "Hippies."

311

See Photo #59 of a young Rick Steves on the road (and not only does he look Hippie, but I'm pretty sure the pose is Countercultural too—something from R. Crumb or a particular Countercultural album cover). I also found a more-recent photo of Steves addressing a Countercultural festival, Seattle Hempfest 2012 (Bienenstock). Considering that the photo is published as part of a May 2013 interview with *High Times* magazine, Steves' Hippie-American identity likely remains.

The same could also be said of much of the older leadership of the legalization movement, say, Keith Stroup of NORML, who with his longish hair, I've always thought looks a bit rock-star Countercultural. And a scan of the today's various cannabis-based magazines shows much the same: Hippie-Americans in leadership roles. The cover of *Dope Magazine*, for instance, carries a photo of a very Hippie-looking Steve DeAngelo. Thus, Rucker writes of, ". . . the counter culture from which NORML and the legalization movement came" ("Cannabis Cup").

So, even if the legalization-of-marijuana debate hasn't overtly been about social equality and respectability for Hippie-Americans, in an indirect way, it has been. Despite "Hippies Were Just a Thing of the Sixties," much of the public likely deduces that the legalization movement to a large extent represents Hippie-America. These legalization victories, then, are shaking things up, forcing all Americans to rethink things; in particular, they'll have to reconsider that social hierarchy that for five decades has put Hippie-Americans down near the bottom—people who, at best, don't really exist; who, at worst, are a bunch of criminals.

> Making marijuana legal makes Counterculturists legal and thus respectable; it turns "dirty hippies" into Hippie-Americans.

But legalization changes all of that; making marijuana legal makes Counterculturists legal and thus respectable; it turns "dirty hippies" into Hippie-Americans. For socially conservative bigots, of course, there's a terrible fear: the crutch of anti-Hippie prejudice they've been leaning on may get knocked away. Many Americans, on the other hand, are enjoying the fresh new political breeze. To some extent, they understand its social implications—social equality for minorities, particularly Hippie-Americans, and greater freedom for all—and they're stimulated by it. On a psycho-political level, that's what's happening in America today.

In short, underlying the legalization debate are social-justice and human-rights issues, and in fighting for those things, the legalization movement is fighting for a more American America, for the soul and body politic of this nation. That's what makes the legalization movement so important, such a potentially powerful change agent for a better America. Hey, this train is bound for glory, this train.

Chapter Eleven

Once Upon a Soapbox:
A Collection of EHT Essays

* * *

Weaknesses of the Counterculture:

Much criticism of the Counterculture is merely stereotyping and bigots projecting onto it all the things they fear and hate. On the other hand, Hippiedom isn't perfect, and I think there's a place for discussing some of the Counterculture's weaknesses—you can't fix problems until you first recognize them. Let's consider two: a sometime tendency of Hippie individuals to seek "*gurus*" and a sometime tendency towards mindless hedonism.

* * *

"Take Me to Your *Guru*"

"The function of leadership is to create more leaders, not more followers."
                                                                                            —Ralph Nader

At times Hippiedom or parts of it seem to have undemocratic tendencies; too often, individual Hippies have been on a search for "*gurus*," for know-it-alls they might uncritically follow. Now, as mentioned, a main Countercultural value is *question authority*, so, I'm not necessarily criticizing the entire Counterculture. Still, I think there's a problem here.

There have been rare times when I've felt ashamed of being Hippie-American; in particular, I am haunted by images of *guru*-smitten members of the infamous Manson family, jumping up and down and, like star-struck adolescent groupies, chanting over and over, "Charlie! Charlie! Charlie! . . ."—this as Manson, who'd carved an "X" into his forehead (which he later turned into a swastika), entered the courtroom. Soon, of course, three of Manson's female followers on trial with him "duplicated the mark" on their foreheads (*Wikipedia*, "Charles Manson")—"Hey, follow your *guru*." Then, in 1975, Manson

315

follower Lynette "Squeaky" Fromme threatened President Gerald Ford with a handgun. I know that I and the rest of Hippie-America are not responsible for the antics of these degraded cultists, of these violent looney-tuners, yet whenever they show up in the media and are identified as Hippies, I'm embarrassed.

Though I haven't thoroughly researched it, I'm pretty sure that many Counterculturists were with the Reverend Jim Jones (he'd moved his People's Temple to San Francisco in 1970) when his cult imploded in the infamous Guyana Tragedy of 1978 where over 900 people died in a mass cyanide-induced suicide—"Hey, follow the messiah!"

Once, I was looking at the bulletin board at a Boulder natural-foods market, and I saw a flyer with a photo of a handsome Hippie man. For no apparent reason, he saw himself as especially enlightened and was looking for an awed entourage. I've always wondered how well his ad worked—were there people foolish enough to hand their heads over to this pretentious narcissist, to this alleged holy man?

In my mind, as mentioned, there's a law of social life: treat others respectfully, insist others treat you respectfully, and you'll get along with people pretty well. Indeed, while I believe in the Hippie value of love, I find that without respect, "love" isn't worth much and that if we truly seek to love one another, we'll begin by respecting one another.

A *guru*-follower relationship—being "in awe" of someone or having someone be "in awe" of you—tends to be unequal and disrespectful.[138] It's not that we can never be a teacher to another or that we can never learn from another; it's that none of us is a higher form of life, none of us has all the answers—we learn from each other, and often, that's a two-way street. Also, we might think of spiritual development as learning to see our individual selves as part of a larger universal community—that you are me in another form, that I am you in another form. Increasingly, I see god as "Big Us," that larger thing we're all a part of on *equal* terms.

---

[138] Hippie culture has, of course, opened the Western door to the East; generally, that's been a very good thing. However, with the good things came, I suspect, this emphasis on *guru*-follower relationships, proving perhaps that just because something came from the East doesn't automatically make it enlightened and progressive.

Spiritual development, good mental health and healthy relationships, then, demand egalitarian values. When we assume another person is a higher form of life, we undermine Big Us, (psychologically, instead of building community, we're building hierarchy). We also debase ourselves, causing further problems. We find the answers to our personal issues— our "spiritual growth"—within ourselves; *guru* neediness, with its baggage of low self-esteem and codependency, doesn't help on that journey, nor does the misconception that someone else can sort it all out or do our spiritual/psychological work for us. We mustn't enmesh ourselves in disrespectful, unequal and unhealthy relationships, either as wannabe *guru* or as awe-struck admirer. In short, to "find" ourselves, we all may need some genuine help or teaching along the way, but generally, no one else can do it for us; no one else can realize the particular potentials that are each of our individual lives.

> **As a culture, we need to move away from "Take Me to your *Guru*" cults of personality and towards democratic and egalitarian relationships and organizations that build real human community, heal this world and genuinely contribute to Big Us.**

As a culture, we need to move away from "Take Me to your *Guru*" cults of personality and towards democratic and egalitarian relationships and organizations that build real human community, heal this world and genuinely contribute to Big Us.

* * *

"Sex, Drugs and Rock 'n' Roll!"

"We were right about a lot of things . . . , but we were wrong about the drugs."
—David Crosby

Another weakness in the Counterculture is embodied in the old Sixties slogan "Sex, Drugs and Rock 'n' Roll!" It is, essentially, the battle cry of unrestrained hedonism, and that would include unapologetic drug abuse.

Now, Hippie culture has emerged from and is to some extent a reaction to the Calvinism we find in mainstream culture, in Establishment morality. Flesh-hating is the logical conclusion of ideologies and values that see the body and the mind as opposed, which see God dwelling in the mind, the Devil embodied in the body. It's a crazed culture that often believes pleasure of any sort as wicked, and seeing pleasure as a good thing might actually be healthy. On the other hand, there's a point where pleasure seeking becomes destructive, and there's deadly drug abuse—in the case of the Counterculture, JimiJanisJim.

Of course, the slogan "Sex, Drugs and Rock 'n' Roll!" was not carefully crafted by some appointed Countercultural committee,[139] and let me note that if one examines the lyrics of many Countercultural songs, one will find a plethora of anti-drug abuse messages from Canned Heat's "Amphetamine Annie" (the chorus of which is "Speed kills!") to Neil Young's "The Needle and the Damage Done" ("Every junkie's like a setting sun") to Steppenwolf's "The Pusher" ("I said, 'God Damn! God Damn the pusher man!'") and many others. So, it's not like everyone in Hippiedom has always unreservedly argued for drug abuse; let's be fair here.

Still, I have met Hippies who seemed to believe that if you were unhappy or had a problem, well, you just hadn't found the right drug yet—or done enough of it. And of course, there's the recklessness with which some have experimented with drugs. A close friend of mine had a cousin he idolized; both were Hippie. When I met the cousin, I was impressed: Kevin had character, he was a gentleman, and he seemed together and fairly mature for his nineteen years. The friend, a huge Who fan, called him "Cousin Kevin," as in *Tommy*. Well, one day, freshman year in college, the awful news came: Kevin was dead. Seems he'd experimented with the wrong drug, heroin, and died of an overdose.

Although Hippiedom has no monopoly on drug abusers, sometimes people have seemed to use Hippie culture to rationalize their drug abuse—"Hey, it's what we do!"

Now, former cocaine abuser David Crosby says of Hippiedom, "We were wrong about the drugs." True and false. It's true that when Crosby

---

[139] "The chair will now entertain a motion to change the *or* in 'Sex, Drugs or Rock 'n' Roll!' to *and* . . . ."

ruined and almost lost his life to cocaine, yeah, "we" were wrong about the drugs. But it's also true that marijuana has turned out to be relatively healthy, its health risks, negligible. Likewise, many Counterculturists who've used LSD (such as the late Steve Jobs) don't look back on their drug experiences with regret.

In short, whether we say, "Sex, Drugs and Rock 'n' Roll!" or "We were wrong about the drugs," we're casting our net too broadly, not being specific enough. The issue is important because how we socialize people to use drugs can be a life-enhancing or life-ruining matter; it is particularly important regarding the reputation of Hippie culture and the extent to which we give bigots material to work with. As a culture, then, we need to start clearly distinguishing between drug use and drug abuse.

Easier said than done? No, I think that we need to begin with definitions of drug abuse such as suggested by Dr. Carl Hart, who I introduced in Chapter Ten: Drug Abuse is when usage of a drug impairs healthy, productive living. Let's also acknowledge that for some drugs, even one-time use may indeed be abuse.

Then, we need to distinguish between different drugs. One problem with War on Drugs propaganda and thus our public discussions about "drugs" is that we engage in the logical fallacy of *equivocation* where several different definitions of one term are juggled in the course of an argument: first, "drugs" means marijuana; then, it means heroin; then, it means opium; then, it means crystal meth—"Oh, what the heck, they're all *drugs* and they're all bad; it's just that simple!" On the other hand, common legal drugs—alcohol, nicotine and caffeine—often seem neglected in the rubric "drugs." For all these various substances, let's employ consistent criteria in our judgments—no more irrational double standards. Let's become the intelligent voice that, when confronted with yet another silly, equivocating conversation about "drugs," responds, "Okay, so what drug or drugs, exactly, are you talking about? And, oh, by the way, that steaming cup of coffee you're cradling—that's a 'drug' too."

As a conscious ethnicity, we need to take our weak spot (the public notion that Hippie-America promotes irresponsible drug abuse) and turn it into a strength by publically leading the way forward, by becoming the culture that gets it right about "the drugs."

* * *

Dumb Demagogues 'R' Us: The
Scariest Halloween Ever!

In 2014, Colorado and Washington became the first two states to legalize recreational cannabis. In the run up to the first post-legalization Halloween, the Denver Police Department and the anti-legalization group SmartColorado outdid themselves, running a state-wide campaign with billboards and Facebook pages showing two pieces of candy and dramatically asking, "Can you tell which candy is a marijuana edible?"

Actually, looking *would* tell us given that Colorado's marijuana edibles have always been carefully labeled.[140] No matter: the public was warned that post-legalization, young trick-or-treaters could be, would be, "poisoned" with marijuana—"Be afraid! Be very afraid!"

This scenario was, of course, preposterous: For starters, why at this time? If one was keen to do this, why wait until recreational-marijuana legalization? Coloradans had long been making marijuana edibles, particularly for the already-legal medicinal market.

Also, given that marijuana edibles are far more expensive than regular candy, who in his or her right mind is going to engage in such a prank?

The answer, of course, is depraved people who live to hurt your kids! They're just *bad*, that's all! Underlying all this nonsense, then, is the odious stereotype of marijuana users, of *hippies* with a small *h*, as fiends hell-bent on destroying our dear, innocent children.[141] Yet, as Denver's *Westword* reported, "[A]fter all that fear mongering (the story went national and international as well), there wasn't a single report of a kid being dosed with anything but sugar."

So, Colorado prohibitionists remain undaunted in their demonization of marijuana and in their demagogic claim that it's killing our kids. But legalization in Colorado is working: there's been no shocking upturn of people driving cars off bridges, of cannabis-crazed kids murdering Grandma and Grandpa for the sheer fun of it, of Western Civilization running lemming-like off a cliff. And buttressed by the first post-legalization surveys showing that cannabis use by Colorado kids hasn't increased (Haas), public support for legalization remains solid (Baca).

---

[140] And as a result of this scare campaign, they're now even more restrictively packaged.

[141] You know, like the witch in "Hansel and Gretel."

Politically, the Colorado prohibitionists have been undone. Like a fish that's jumped out of the water, they're flapping around mightily, desperately trying to survive, but increasingly, no one's paying much attention.

*   *   *

Fun Media Analysis with EHT:
Five Examples with Accompanying Ridicule

*   *   *

Media analysis: Take one![142]
Males with Long Hair, Bad Guys with Black Hats

The film *Pay it Forward*, directed by Mimi Leder, was released in 2000 to mixed reviews. It managed, however, to help start a sort of national movement of the same name. It's the story of a seventh-grade boy, Trevor McKinney (Haley Joel Osment) who has an alcoholic single mother (Helen Hunt). This school year, he also has an inspiring and altruistic social-studies teacher (Kevin Spacey) who's given his students a challenging assignment: figure out how to do something that will change the world for the better. And so Trevor does. He calls it "pay it forward," and it means that if someone does a great favor for you, instead of paying that person back, you do a great favor for three others, who, in turn, are supposed to do a great favor for three more others though I'm not entirely sure how it all works: if you talk someone out of committing suicide, as one character does, does that suicidal person have to agree in advance to greatly help three others before you'll talk that person out of committing suicide?

It all sounds very uplifting and progressive, right? Well, the film has a major problem: it appears to me that television and film directors often use long hair on a male, particularly a ponytail, to communicate evil, to say that the character is a villain in much the way that directors of Westerns have often identified the "bad guy" with a black hat—a

---

[142] (Klack!)

simple way of tipping off the audience that they shouldn't like or trust this person, that he's a villain.[143]

There is a villain in *Pay it Forward*: the leader of a group *Wikipedia* describes as "gangster-like children." Late in the film, this gang is again tormenting their victim of choice: a smaller boy disabled by asthma. Trevor had earlier witnessed this aggression but backed off from fighting the three bigger kids. Seeing it happen again, young Mr. Decent runs off to battle the bullies; their leader then "inadvertently" (*Wikipedia*) stabs Trevor with a switchblade he carries, and thus, in a completely unnecessary plot twist not in the least foreshadowed by Leder, Trevor dies. It's heartrending, but, hey, these things happen.

Well, what a coincidence—the killer kid is a boy with a very prominent samurai ponytail, and he's also the only male in the film with a ponytail. Then again, Trevor's alcoholic father, played by rocker Jon Bon Jovi, briefly returns home, and he has longish hair; of course, he's also an abusive sleaze.

Get it? Long hair on a male means a bad guy; a ponytail on a male means a particularly bad guy. Memorize that. It's a kind of Hollywood formula, and it will help you understand movies.

> **Long hair on a male means a bad guy; a ponytail on a male means a particularly bad guy. Memorize that. It's a kind of Hollywood formula, and it will help you understand movies.**

* * *

Media analysis: Take two!
Good Will Hunting Fights the Abominable Hippie!

The script for the 1997 film *Good Will Hunting*, written by then-unknowns Ben Affleck and Matt Damon, won an Academy Award. Alongside Affleck and Damon, Robin Williams stars in a particularly appealing role for which he won the Oscar for Best Supporting Actor.

---

[143] We already discussed this some in Chapter Seven when I mentioned the Hippie-as-villain sterotype and cited *Baywatch* as an example.

All the acting is excellent; the story is a relatively deep and interesting exploration of trauma and personal healing.

I have issues, however, with Damon's character, the brilliant Will Hunting: he's a rough-and-tumble Boston Southie, who hangs with the same. Yet, since Hunting is deeply versed in a variety of subjects, he has to be an avid reader. True, his math genius might be explained in part by natural talent, but it would take hours of scholarly research to be conversant in, for instance, Colonial American economics. Certainly, he must have spent the majority of his short, impoverished life sitting in a university library, not hanging out on mean streets. I don't see it; I don't see his peers accepting it.

More worrisome is the film's use of the above-mentioned stereotype equating Hippie appearance with evil or at least obnoxiousness. So, our working-class twenty-somethings have gone to a Harvard bar to meet women, drink and play darts. Handsome ladies man Chuckie (Ben Affleck) spies some "babes" and makes his move. Approaching Skylar (British pre-med Minne Driver) and a female companion, he pawns himself off as an Ivy Leaguer. It's harmless, and we admire Chuckie's gumption and fast-on-his-feet improvisation as he fields a friendly Skylar's getting-to-know-you, college-life questions.

It's a warm, fun scene until a handsome man, his long blond hair tied loosely back in a ponytail, intrudes. He verbally jumps Chuckie, asking which history class he was allegedly in, bullying Chuckie with his greater learning, and the guy just won't quit. He's a serious prick.

Then . . . Is it a bird? Is it a plane? No, it's SuperMind! in the person of Good Will Hunting who leaps in front of Academic Bully Boy, quickly wrestling his brain to the ground with a dazzling display of in-depth knowledge of Colonial American economics, employing "modalities" and other pedantic terms sure to impress the easily impressed. Wow, Will is devastating! Hunting follows up by publicly lecturing and humiliating the long hair about his boorish behavior towards Chuckie. Ouch!

Thoroughly routed, our antagonist now begs off with a sort of stereotypically Hippieish, "Hey, it's cool" to which Chuckie and Hunting both sarcastically respond, "Y-yeah, it's cool" only what they really mean is "Fuck you, asshole." Well, as least Good Will Hunting doesn't haul off and smash the longhair in the face 27 times like the guy we saw him viciously jump in a street fight (though if this character were consistently written, he would've).

A bystander then makes a smirking comment that the now-retreating snob has some kind of Michael Bolton complex, this a slighting reference to his long blond hair. Others nearby snigger appropriately.

Later, as the Southies head home, Hunting spots his nemesis in a bar, taps on the window to get his attention and then taunts him with the fact that *he* got Skylar's phone number, not evil Hippie boy. The scene seems superfluous, but Goldilocks is so distasteful, his comeuppance so satisfying, that director Gus Van Sant has apparently decided on a reprise. Hey, it's cool . . . yeah, modalities.

Yes, there are occasional glimpses of Hippie-looking males in classroom scenes in *Good Will Hunting*, but these actors are extras and have no lines. There's nothing here, then, to balance this very negative character, and once again, Hollywood sends the same insidious message: if a male has long hair or Hippie appearance, he lacks character, he's a bad guy, you should hate him.

* * *

Media analysis: Take three!
Farscape: How Bigotry is Born

One Saturday in 2006, I discovered Nine Network's bush-league attempt to combine *Star Trek* and *Star Wars: Farscape*. This episode, "Scratch n' Sniff,"[144] had space travelers landing on a supposedly Hippie planet, resulting in a showcase of stereotypes and anti-Hippie prejudice.

For starters, our voyagers (the clean-cut good guys) enter an apparently Countercultural scene—a *groovy* nightclub! Yeah, it's swinging party scene, man, with lots of deafening music and male extras wearing headbands. Their drinking and carousing attest to their hedonism.

And when their leader—a repulsive woman with a snow-white face filled with varicose veins and surrounded by anemic-looking dreadlocks—greets them, her inebriation is obvious: long pauses between each elongated syllable as if she were *r-e-e-e-al-ly* high. "The

---

[144] Why this title? I'm guessing it has something to do with Hippie-types allegedly being dirty, and therefore they scratch themselves and smell. At least, I'm at a loss as to what else it could mean.

Princess," as she's called, gives orders and is what passes for leadership here—obviously, Hippie types aren't very good at organizing anything, and funny, even though the atmosphere is allegedly anarchistic, it has a dictator, doesn't it? The message seems, not only is the Counterculture hypocritical, but it's not part of a "free" society either.

In case the slow-witted viewer has yet to make the Countercultural connection, after the voyagers leave the club, one mutters a derisive comment about "that Woodstock back there."

It gets better: it seems the Hippie residents are being forced to grow a plant for a dominating alien power, the Peacekeepers (the bad guys). The entire Hippie economy is based on it, and they labor in the fields, wearing straw "coolie" hats as they work. It's all very primitive and Third World (a suffering-peasant-in-Red China stereotype) and parallels the fears of bigots who believe this is what the USA would look like if the Counterculture had its way.

The plant is a drug to which the whole planet is addicted (read "marijuana"), and as it turns out, the plant produces a byproduct that the bad guys are secretly using for fuel (you mean, sort of the way that the marijuana trade allegedly fuels international terrorism?). But the Hippie types are too naive, trusting, and stupid to understand this, and the truth has to be forced upon them. Hey, they're not in touch with reality.

And, of course, since "hippies" are all mindless, submissive sheep, one of our clean-cut heroes now angrily lectures them about "blindly following" evil others. And when the truth about The Peacekeepers is finally made clear, the gullible Hippies can only bleat, "But we can't defend ourselves against them; we have no weapons . . . ." Yes, these space Hippies are weak, pitiful pacifists, and (oh, did you notice?), the men are all unmanly.

Similarly, all Hippies are helpless children, hapless victims, and like the denizens of this world, they need strong outsiders to fight for them. Billy Jack, where are you?!

One of the voyagers is briefly happy there, but his compatriots explain that he's just under the influence of the drug. Yeah, he's not in his right mind—"This is your brain on drugs." Later, the once-content creature ruefully admits his happiness "wasn't real." Yes, like Hippies and the entire Counterculture, his experience wasn't a part of the "real world"; it isn't legitimate.

Yes, *Farscape* is deep. I'm thinking of special ordering the *Cliff Notes* for the entire series.

Seriously, this *Farscape* episode shows us how anti-Hippie bigotry is created and fomented by mainstream media. Obviously, this show is fairly adolescent, and no doubt, that's what a good portion of its audience is: adolescents. They're young people learning how to think about the world—who to respect, who to admire, who to despise, who to feel superior to. *Farscape* teaches them to *dis*respect Hippie-Americans, and that would include many of their fellow adolescents, young Hippie-Americans.

The show's stereotyping, its negativity, its accusations, its condescension and contempt—these are the ugly stuff of prejudice and ethnic chauvinism, of stupid, self-serving bigotry.

* * *

Media analysis: Take four!

Fox's *24*: "Oh, the treasonous Counterculture!"

As we might expect, Fox's notoriously far-right television series, *24*, spews hatred of Hippies. First, as is fairly common in mainstream American entertainment media, the machine-gun toting thugs of the terrorists/drug dealers are often white males with ponytails; they look like muscular Hippie surfers from California.

More to the point, however, would be one episode (Season Four, 4am-5am) where the son of Secretary of Defense James Heller (William Devane) has a son who—with his denim jacket, shoulder-length hair, bangs hanging in his eyes, unshaven face and, when he enters, an amulet—looks like a twenty-something Hippie. Turns out, Richard Heller (Logan Marshall-Green) has let himself be picked up in a bar by a calculating terrorist couple. Well, it seems they all went back to his apartment to "get high," and young Richard—who pleads and cries

> **Of course, this bad seed represents the entire Counterculture: in addition to being "in bed" with terrorists, he's irresponsible, weak, whiney, cowardly, selfish, promiscuous, childlike, bitter, filled with self-pity, not a "real man," not a speck of dignity to him. And he's betrayed not just his own father and sister but his own country!**

piteously throughout—confesses in front of his father that he had sex with the terrorist *man*. Boy, does Dad look disappointed. This has all led to his godlike father and his good-and-decent sister being kidnapped by terrorists; they, in turn, had to be rescued by *24's* super-cool action hero, Counter-Terrorism Unit special agent Jack Bauer![145]

Oh, by the way, Richard Heller's not coming clean about his dirty little drugs-and-gay-sex tryst sooner has already led to terrorist attacks that have killed innocent Americans—"Hey, it's like *not cool* to expect Baby Richie to behave responsibly!" Of course, this bad seed represents the entire Counterculture: in addition to being "in bed" with terrorists, he's irresponsible, weak, whiney, cowardly, selfish, promiscuous, childlike, bitter, filled with self-pity, not a "real man," not a speck of dignity to him. And he's betrayed not just his own father and sister but his own country! Oh, how could manly and patriotic James Heller have spawned such a depraved and ungrateful son, a "hippie fag"?[146] Apparently, it's no less a mystery to neoconservatives than how so great and good a nation as the United States of America could spawn something as vile, disturbing and treacherous as Hippie culture. Well, what are you going to do? Agent Jack Bauer knows: he plans to torture the blubbering traitor—this, no doubt, to the delight of fans.

Gosh, *24* is great! Who would've thought nascent fascism could be so much fun?! The far-right's favorite action show, then, effectively communicates all the vicious stereotypes and virulent hatred they feel for Hippie-America—and they do it using a possibly Hippie-American star! How cool is that!

* * *

---

[145] Ironically, Keifer Sutherland, who plays Bauer, probably does fit an ethnic definition of *Hippie*—or at least, used to (see Chapter Eight and book website).

[146] The phrase is from popular discourse, not the episode of *24*.

Media analysis: Take five!

Happily Hippie's Hall of Shame Award: "And, the loser is . . ."

"Oh, the shark, babe, has such teeth, dear, and it shows them pearly white."
— *"Mack the Knife"*

"So, what've you guys got for me? Let's hear your pitch for this new show, and it better be good!" JB thundered from behind his massive mahogany desk.

"Well," said an anxious BJ, "it's going to star James Woods as Sebastian Stark, a single parent who used to be an unscrupulous high-end defense lawyer who successfully defended a rich guy on spouse-abuse charges, but then three days later, he killed his wife."

"Stark?"

"No, the rich guy. . . . Okay, so now Stark's decided to change sides and become a prosecutor in the LA District Attorney's Office."

"I see . . . a bad boy trying to go good. . . . I like it: it's deep, complex. Okay, so tell me: this James Woods, is he photogenic? Can he carry this show?"

"Is he photogenic?! Can he carry this show?! JB, the camera loves him! He has boyish good looks, and the man has *cha-ris-ma*! We feel he's perfect to play a character who's vain, immature, arrogant, and often foolish, but who in the end, always gets the bad guy."

"Well, I'm looking at your promo photos, and I must say, the man looks great in a suit—is that an Armani?"

"Yes, sir. And look at that shot of him in those shades."

"Yeah . . . very cool . . . . Okay, so what else have you got? We'll need more than Mr. Charismatic Bad Boy Gone Good to hold our rating share."

"Jeri Ryan, sir. You remember . . . *Star Trek's* Seven of Nine—you know . . . in that tight outfit."

"Yes, heh, heh, . . . I *do* remember that," JB leered, a faraway look in his eyes.

"Well, she plays Stark's boss, Jessica Devlin, who because of her deep desire to do right and get the bad guys left a six-figure job in the private sector to work as the District Attorney of Los Angeles, where she's been for 14 years. Of course, she still makes six figures."

"Of course . . . . Can Ryan play this part?"

"Can she?! Remember *Boston Public* where she was a school teacher who wore tight white sweaters over cross-your-heart bras, and you could see her nipples?! And she has this impossibly cool, ultimate-in-crowd air about her. She's like a Fox newscaster only sexier!"

"Yes," interjected CD, "and we're sure there'll be real chemistry between Ryan and Woods—frisson, JB, frisson!"

"Okay," mused JB, "it sounds like a law-and-order show for middle-aged Republicans who want to feel self-righteous *and* sexy. It *could* work. . . . What do you plan to call this thing?"

"Oh, that's the best part, sir," BJ said as he and CD eyed each other with smug satisfaction. "Shark! It's aggressive and deadly and sleek and sexy, *and* . . . it rhymes with his last name, Stark!"

"Willikers!" gasped JB in astonishment. "Shark! . . . Th-that's *genius*! Okay, boys, let's roll with it! We'll find a director and begin production ASAP!"

* * *

On January 18th of 2007, CBS's *Shark* ran an episode called "Wayne's World"[147]—yes, as in the *SNL* skit and the subsequent films starring Wayne (Mike Myers) and Garth (Dana Carvey). Only this wasn't comedy; it was high legal drama.

Sebastian Stark, "Shark," is prosecuting a serial killer accused of murdering five women; the suspect would've murdered a sixth, but she ran from his house; now, she's afraid to testify against him because the creep is acting as his own attorney and planning to cross examine her. Can you imagine this poor traumatized woman having to be questioned—to be "re-victimized"—by this monster!

The improbable story unfolds: The defendant is handsome, soft spoken and educated; we're tempted to believe that such a seemingly decent fellow couldn't do such a thing—except for one telltale clue: he has his long hair tied back in a ponytail, and he has a neatly trimmed beard. That's right! Neat or not, he's one of those Hippies! Now, as I understand it, before he murders his exclusively female victims, he reads

---

[147] My comments here are based on my remembrance of the show combined with information from *Wikipedia*.

them the details of their own, earlier molestations from their psychiatric diaries[148] as a way of torturing them—sort of like he now wants to do to the victim/witness in court. The fiend!

Since the accused is a college English professor and not a psychiatrist or a social worker, it's not quite clear how he got a hold of these diaries to begin with. Are they assignments for his English classes? ("Okay class, the third installment of your My Sexual Abuse Diary is due next Tuesday—five-hundred words, double spaced, no excuses.")[149] Not to mention that if you were a misogynist serial killer, this would sort of narrow your field of victims, wouldn't it? ("Sorry, I may be a dastardly sex criminal, but I do have my standards: I never murder a woman who doesn't first let me read her sexual-abuse diary.")

Never mind. Don't ask any hard questions. In the world of Wayne, anything is possible! The absurdly far-fetched plot is clearly intended to create a super-evil character: a "normal" serial killer would appear almost healthy by comparison.

And watching, I'm wondering, Who are these victims, anyway? These silly, flat-character females so lacking in a basic sense of self-preservation that they would go to this guy's house on a date? ("Yes, it's true: women in the neighborhood have been disappearing. . . . but, I wonder. . . should I bring wine?")

And in case we hadn't noticed the professor's long hair, it's also a prominent, identifying detail in the testimony of a prosecution witness. It isn't, then, just that the director has cast an actor with long hair to play the serial killer, it's that his long-hair is written right into the script. Wayne is, incidentally, the only male in the entire show with long hair; possibly, the only one with a beard.

Well, this Hippie sicko is so devious, clever and convincing that he almost gets away with it, especially when incorrigible bad boy Shark, who cut some legal corners and got caught, has to step back and let his boss, Jessica Devlin (Jeri Ryan), take over. Attired in a chic power

---

[148]   Do sexual-abuse therapists actually encourage such "diaries"? I doubt it, and wouldn't doing so make the therapists as hurtful and abusive as "Wayne"?

[149]   I'm not making fun of sexual abuse; I'm making fun of this preposterous television program.

suit, Devlin looks about 35, and she's been the LA District Attorney for 14 years (having, apparently, been elected at about 21).[150] Tough, contemptuous, cutting—Devlin bores in on the villain, until finally, unable to bear her verbal lashings another moment, he . . . *bre-e-a-aks* (!) and—in a violent outburst of misogyny—confesses to the crimes. Gosh, it was *so* dramatic! Television at its hard-hitting best!

Here, then, we have a heavy-handed attempt to equate long hair and a beard on a man, Hippie appearance, with the most unspeakable depravity. Well, speaking of depravity, let's recognize malicious stereotyping and bigotry when we see it.

Thus, our Happily Hippie Hall of Shame Award goes to . . . (long pause as envelope is opened) . . . (microphone sounds) . . . (more microphone sounds) . . . the creators of this execrable episode of *Shark*, "Wayne's World"! Congratulations! For now and evermore, may you and your vile ilk live in ignominious disgrace.[151]

*   *   *

Hippie-America and Vietnam: If Anything, Heroism and Social Responsibility

"It was the age of selfishness; it was the age of self-indulgence; it was the age of anti-authority; it was an age in which people did all kinds of wrong things; that was the start, really, of the drug problem in the United States."
—President Reagan's attorney general
Ed Meese on the 1960s

For Ed Meese and other neocons, one of those "wrong things" that happened in the 1960s was the mass movement against the War in Vietnam. And for many conservative Americans, the "irresponsibility" of the peace movement was the "irresponsibility" of the Counterculture: they see that anti-war movement and Hippiedom as one and the same.

---

[150] This, of course, after her six-figure-salary career in the private sector.
[151] A smattering of polite but restrained applause.

I've pointed out how that equation is false—there was overlap between the two, but they were separate entities.[152]

What I'll argue here, however, is that to the extent that Hippie-America *was* involved in the anti-war movement, that involvement is entirely to its credit, that actual history shows those who helped stop the War in Vietnam were highly responsible, that those in our government waging that war were probably the most irresponsible and dangerous people the world has ever known.

Let's step back to the early 1950's: Vietnam remained a French colony, but there was political and military resistance to this by the Vietnamese people led by Ho Chi Minh; its political character was a mix of nationalism and socialism. As that military resistance grew and challenged French colonial power, the United States began to support the French and by 1953 was paying for 80 percent of the French war (Gunnick). And when, in the spring of 1953, the Vietnamese forces finally surrounded the French army at Dien Bien Phu, the US offered the French nuclear weapons, which they encouraged them to use; Paris ultimately rejected Washington's offer (Morgan, "Nuclear Crisis #5"). Of course, the French lost at Dien Bien Phu, and Vietnam began suffering what Western policy makers call a "power vacuum," meaning that for a moment in history, no great world power was controlling Vietnam and using it like a colony. The 1954 Geneva Accords temporarily divided Vietnam and scheduled a unifying election for Vietnam in July of 1956.

However, the Eisenhower Administration canceled that election; President Eisenhower explained, saying, "A possible 80 per cent of the population would have voted for the communist Ho Chi Minh as their leader" (HistoryCommons). Washington then established, essentially, a puppet state in the south, and historian Howard Zinn tells us that the leaders of the new South Vietnam were mostly generals who'd the collaborated with French colonialism.

Historians seem to agree that the French presence in Vietnam was colonial, that the US was supporting French colonialism, especially late in the game, and that for all practical purposes, the US eventually took

---

[152]   I believe one reason we so often equate Hippiedom and the anti-war movement is that the latter was Hippie-baited by social conservatives and the mainstream media: if you wished to discredit that peace movement, it was easier if the nation saw it as "just a bunch of hippies."

over for France in Vietnam much the way that one corporation might take over the assets of another's as that chain goes out of business. Generally, the transition from French colonial occupation to US military intervention and occupation was seamless.

Yet, the notion that the US presence in Vietnam was in any way, shape or form colonial is taboo in America: "Who? Us? Colonial? Why, we went into Vietnam with only the most noble intentions—to lift those people up, to teach them democracy and promote human rights, to help protect the Vietnamese from Communist/terrorist bullies who were running amok in Vietnam, to save America and the world from Soviet/ Chinese expansionism, to, to . . . keep the world free!" Yes, anything and everything but admitting our War in Vietnam was part of expanding a *de facto* US empire.

It's common for hawks to compare Vietnam to WW II, but that's a faulty analogy: In WW II, we "picked on someone our own size," the formidable military forces of three industrialized nations gone fascist. Likewise, given the desire of Hitler to dominate the world and the Japanese attack on Pearl Harbor, there was a legitimate national-defense argument. And while there were certainly some imperial interests in Washington's WW II behavior, generally, we seemed to be on the side of democracy and human rights.

In Vietnam, on the other hand, we were in a war with the people of a Third World nation, a largely agricultural society—and no amount of "Communist aggression" rhetoric will change that. In Vietnam, we had no real national-defense case aside from the inaccurate charge that the Vietnamese revolution was merely a pawn of Moscow or Peking, that and a silly Domino Theory that said if Vietnam went Red, California was next. And arguing that our invasion and occupation of Vietnam was in defense of democracy and human rights—that's a hard row to hoe; after all, the US did cancel those 1956 elections. Also, it's historically clear that those South Vietnamese governments we created and supported were brutal abusers of human rights, that South Vietnamese "democracy" was a farce.

To show how faulty is the Vietnam-WW II analogy is, let's contrast the behavior of US troops in Vietnam and in WW II:

Far as we know, the behavior of US troops in WW II was exemplary—we're pretty sure there were no massacres of civilians, no systemic mistreatment or execution of prisoners. For decades now, the fine behavior of those troops has rightly been a source of great national pride.

Then there's Vietnam; in particular, there was the 1968 My Lai massacre. Some have tried to explain this difference by arguing or implying that the Vietnam generation of American troops just wasn't up to snuff. Nonsense. Vietnam was a fundamentally different type of war, one where, inevitably, the Vietnamese people (the great majority of whom didn't want the Americans occupying and running their country any more than they did the French) became the enemy.

Imagine: you and your unit are out hiking through rice paddies looking for Viet Cong, and "Charlie" does exactly what colonized and militarily overmatched people always do: set booby traps. With shocking suddenness, you watch parts of a buddy fly into the air. You're angry, terrified, and in your fear and frustration, you want to hit back somehow. You know full well that, to use the Maoist analogy, the guerrillas/fish swim in the pond of the people, and you see the local Vietnamese villagers as responsible. Add a large dose of racism, particularly among white "straight" soldiers; then, a few minutes later, your patrol wanders into a neighboring village . . . . That's how My Lai's happen.

America never won "the hearts and minds" of most Vietnamese. The very people we said we were there to "save" were actually the enemy. We claimed we were going to protect the Vietnamese from "Communist terrorism"; in fact the great majority of Vietnamese either supported or were those "Communist terrorists."

Now in WW II, we saw scenes of crying French, for instance, kissing and hugging American soldiers who (with Free French help) had just liberated Paris. In WW II, then, US troops usually had a healthy relationship with the civilians of the countries they occupied; thus, no WW II My Lai's.

So in Vietnam, we weren't re-fighting WW II; the US lost in Vietnam because it was fighting a neo-colonial war in a post-colonial era of history. Let's be honest about that and quit blaming the antiwar movement or the Counterculture.

Lastly—*and here's what is routinely ignored in the accusation that the anti-war movement lost the war for America and betrayed the nation*—we should consider what exactly was the conservative policy for winning the War in Vietnam, what Nixon called "peace with honor."

What follows is from the 2005 PBS documentary "The Sixties—The Years that Shaped a Generation":[153]

> A nationwide moratorium on October 15th, 1969, called for immediate withdrawal from Vietnam. With protests in every city across the country, it became the largest one-day demonstration, ever, in a Western democracy. Unknown to its participants, the moratorium would significantly alter Nixon's war plans. [Voice of the leaker of the Pentagon Papers, Daniel Ellsberg:] "He [Nixon] was making secret threats of escalation to North Vietnam, secretly from the American public, but not at all secret, of course, from the target of these threats; in short, he made those threats explicitly to the Soviets, for the Vietnamese, and directly to the Vietnamese, that he was prepared to use nuclear weapons. The march of the moratorium in cities across the country on October 15th, just before[154] his 'secret ultimatum' was too large, two million people on one day across the country convinced him, reasonably, that this was not the time to escalate the war, and in particular, not the time to use nuclear weapons for the first time since Hiroshima."

In short, Nixon's "secret plan" to end the war was in fact a plan to use nuclear weapons on North Vietnam, and as part of that strategy, Nixon did something terrifyingly reckless and provocative: attempting to intimidate the Soviets into pressuring the North Vietnamese to surrender, on October 1st, he placed our nuclear forces on the highest level of alert, DEFCON 1, "maximum force readiness," meaning, he had "Nuclear-armed B-52 bombers circle [the Soviet Union], Minuteman missiles prepared in the highest state of readiness and threat since [the Cuban Missile] Crisis," according

Neither the anti-war movement nor Hippie-America betrayed the nation during the War in Vietnam; rather, in one of the most dangerous moments of human history, we helped tip the balance, we helped save life on this Earth.

---

[153]   I found a number of sources corroborating this account.

[154]   Actually, as we'll see, it was *during* the "secret ultimatum."

to an article authored by David R. Morgan, National President of the Canadian group Veterans Against Nuclear Arms. He adds that Nixon kept the aggressive and provocative DEFCON 1 status active for 29 full days (Nuclear Crisis #12).

When hawks, then, argue that the anti-war movement kept the US from winning in Vietnam, what they really mean is that the anti-war movement kept the US from launching a nuclear attack that would've bombed North Vietnam "back to the Stone Age" and possibly led to a full-scale nuclear war with the Soviets. On an environmental level, it would've been horrific; of course, it could have led to nuclear Armageddon and the likely extinction of humanity.

This thwarted US policy would've been an unspeakable crime, the most extreme violation of human rights imaginable, and for it, in what may have been left of the world, the United States of America would have lived in infamy and eternal disgrace. Apparently, American conservatives believe that demonstrating against the Vietnam War or being Hippie-American were "wrong things" whereas maniacally flirting with the end of the world as we know it while trying to win an unwinnable neo-colonial war, was the right thing. What a *twisted* notion of morality and responsibility.

Thus, neither the anti-war movement nor Hippie-America betrayed the nation during the War in Vietnam. The truth is the opposite: any involvement Hippie-America had with the anti-Vietnam movement is solely to our credit; in one of the most dangerous moments of human history, we helped tip the balance, we helped preserve life on this Earth.

*   *   *

"Dirty Hippie Protestors" Spittin' on "Our Brave Boys"!

"I came back to the world and I see all those maggots at the airport! Protesting me! Spitting! Calling me baby killer!"
            —Rambo raging, near tears

Here in Colorado, there's a rock band called Chris Daniels and the Kings. A few of the members have long hair; generally, they look contemporary Hippie-American. Their taste in tunes would also seem to support that—a kind of bluesy electric folk-rock that I imagine most people would describe as "kind of Sixties"; so I suspect their audiences see Hippie-Americans onstage, however they might phrase that cultural identification. Chris Daniels and the Kings are fine musicians, they play well together, and I mostly enjoy their performances.

There is, however, a particular song they do, an original; it's melodramatically entitled "An American Tragedy," this a reference to "the peace-and-love generation" (read, Hippiedom) allegedly spitting on returning Vietnam veterans. A line that echoes throughout the song is ". . . and the spittin'!'"—this, said/sung in head-hanging shame.

But it's a myth, a popular falsehood, that Countercultural anti-war protestors routinely greeted our home-coming heroes with salvos of saliva.

First, imagine you were an anti-war protestor and you decided to spit on a real-life John Rambo. I mean, here's this guy boiling with rage, trained to kill with his bare hands, possibly unhinged by war violence he's experienced—and you're going to spit on him? No, only a self-destructive fool would do that.

So, just on the level of common sense, these spitting stories should be suspect. Among other things, they assume a level of submission and passivity among returning troops that defies reality. As for fictional Rambo, are we really to believe this volcano of violence just stood there, let himself get goobered, put his head down and shuffled away? Also, do you think protestors could just march into an airport reception area, begin harassing and abusing returning soldiers, and no one, no police or security, would stop them? That's ridiculous.

Then, there's the historical evidence: Sociologist and Vietnam veteran Jerry Lembcke researched and wrote *The Spitting Image: Myth, Memory, and the Legacy of Vietnam (1998).* "His research examined newspapers from New York and San Francisco, as well as police reports detailing the interaction between protesters and veterans. No spitting incidents were reported," says *The Veteran,* journal of Vietnam Veterans Against the War (Zutz).

Underlying the whole protestors-spitting-on-vets myth, of course, is the larger myth that our returning troops and the anti-war movement were mutually exclusive and that all of those returning vets were fiercely, "patriotically," pro-war. Yet, a Harris Poll of that time "reported that over 75% of returning vets were opposed to the war" (Zutz). *The Veteran* explains, "There is no place in the American memory for the factually accurate image of vets throwing their medals back at Congress. This image had to be changed if the United States ever wanted to go to war again" (Zutz). As a nation, apparently, we have a need to see martyred Rambos—righteous gung-ho killers *betrayed* by the anti-war weaklings! Now, there are Vietnam veterans who earnestly maintain they were indeed spit upon and otherwise abused by "peaceniks." The problem is, their stories don't check out; as such, both Lembcke and columnist Bob Greene in his 1989 book, *Homecoming* note unreliable, exaggerated or false accounts by veterans of being spit on (*Wikipedia*, "The Spitting Image").

Some examples: Well, it turns out that despite attempts by Lembcke to show reporters and editors at the *New York Times* that "the spittin'" is a myth, America's "newspaper of record" continues to propagate that myth. Thus, Lembcke reports on some *NY Times* coverage:

> The *New York Times* business section of November 2, 1998, carried the story, "A Bicycle Path From Wall Street to Vietnam," written by Laura A. Holson. The story was about Peter D. Kiernan, III, who organized a bicycle tour of Vietnam. Kiernan is a banker at Goldman, Sachs & Company. In her report, Holson wrote that Kiernan had been moved to organize the trip when he heard a Vietnam veteran talk about his coming-home experience. The veteran, identified in Holson's story as "a top executive," reportedly told Kiernan that he had returned from Vietnam on a stretcher with a bullet in his leg. He said, "college kids rushed up and poured rotten vegetables on him. They spat on him. He was so ashamed." (Lembcke, "Media Myth")

Lembcke responds: "It would have been impossible for protesters with rotten vegetables to get close to a wounded soldier returning from Vietnam" ("Media Myth"). Yes, I think so.[155]
Lembcke tells of another alleged account:

> In a November 11, 1998, Veterans Day story, [in the Worcester, Massachusetts *Telegram and Gazette*], James Collins claimed his plane from Vietnam was met at Clark Air Force Base north

---

[155]   Also, instead of feeling "ashamed," shouldn't this veteran feel enraged?

338

of San Francisco by "thousands of protesters throwing Molotov cocktails." Like many of the stories, Collins's had details that were factually wrong (e.g. there is no Clark Air Force Base in the Bay Area) or too implausible to be believed. ("Media Myth")

> **Here is my favorite doubtful account: "One veteran claimed a 'hippy chick' spat dog semen on him after giving her puppy a blow job."**

Here, from Lembcke ("Media Myth"), is my favorite doubtful account: "One veteran claimed a 'hippy chick' spat dog semen on him after giving her puppy a blow job."

I wrote a letter[156] to the Boulder *Daily Camera* about "An American Tragedy" and its lack of basis in fact; a Vietnam-era sailor responded[157] that "the spittin'" was indeed commonplace. He cited the example of US Admiral Elmo Zumwalt ordering his Navy people not to wear their uniforms off base as a precaution against such animosity—the writer claimed to know all about it, and his expertise seemed convincing.

Well, I checked out his account: first, it's reasonable to assume that if Admiral Zumwalt had issued such an order—the implications would be politically shocking, probably headline making—there must surely be a record of it. Yet, I was unable to find any such evidence. What I *did* find was that in the early 1970s, Admiral Zumwalt had issued an order allowing on-base Naval personnel to wear civilian clothes when off duty (Mishalov). In short, this righteous, detailed, first-hand account of protestor abuse turned out to be a figment of the writer's imagination. And so it goes.

According to what appears to be a very good *Wikipedia* article on this controversy ("The Spitting Image"), Greene believes some spitting-on-returning-vets incidents probably occurred; Lembcke does not. *Both, however, agree there are no verifiable reports of any such events.* What's happened here is that American reactionaries have created a market for I'm-a-veteran-who-was-abused-by-protestors stories, and we now have veterans who've "recovered" politically expedient memories of things that never happened.

---

[156]   Aug. 6, 2011.
[157]   Aug. 14, 2011.

Essentially, there is no solid evidence—and if it happened, there should be solid evidence—to substantiate the charge that our troops were welcomed home with salivary abuse.[158] Why, then, do the American people assume there was a broad trend of protestors spitting on returning Vietnam veterans, perceive a "historical truth" with no basis in fact?

Perhaps it began with the 1982 film "First Blood," the first of the Rambo series, which appeared shortly after the triumph of the "Reagan Revolution." In that movie, by the way, the bad guys aren't so much those "maggot" protestors as the local sheriff and his deputies; nonetheless, the film helped cement "the spittin'" myth; for the nation, protestor-abused Rambo became the War in Vietnam's Everysoldier, and America then guilt-tripped—"Oh, how could we have treated our brave boys so badly?!" and they blamed the anti-war movement, the "dirty hippie protestors."

And, of course, underlying all this myth-making are the political needs of social conservatives, who continue to repeat "the spittin'" claim long after the myth has been debunked. In particular, they seek to cure the nation of what they call the "Vietnam Syndrome"—essentially, the post-Vietnam reluctance of the American people to sacrifice their blood and treasure for yet another thinly disguised neo-colonial war. In this vein, they've been promoting what in Germany is called *Dolchstosslegende* (stab-in-the-back legend); that is, just as Hitler and his Nazis tried to blame Germany's loss in WW I on a Trojan Horse inside Germany (Jews, Socialists and Communists), American conservatives have been trying to blame America's loss in Vietnam on a Trojan Horse inside America (the anti-war movement, liberals and the Counterculture).

It's all that, and of course, it's also the usual rightist appeals to hierarchy and bigotry—"Dirty Jews/dirty hippies—let's place them beneath us." Finally, in terms of the far-right's need to get the "little people" pissed off at a scapegoat group, "the spittin'" works wonderfully; it sows the seeds of intense resentment, of ready-to-hurt-someone rage. In short, the far right has written another moving chapter in the silly pulp-fiction melodrama in which they, and now much of America, resides.

---

[158] Actually, there *are* police and media reports from the Vietnam years of spitting incidents; they don't involve vets and relate almost entirely to anti-war protestors being spit on by pro-war counter-protestors, "hawks" (*Wikipedia*, "The Spitting Image").

The insistence of the nation in propagating "the spittin'" myth, then, is like a child adamant about hearing a particular bedtime story:

"Please" pleads the child, "read *Rambo Returns* to me!"

"But, we've read *Rambo Returns*138 times; in fact, we read it just last night. By now, you must know every sentence in that story by heart, I'd think."

"I know, but I want to hear it *again* . . .," the child insists, savoring the sense of security the story gives. Even if it's not true, the child longs to hear it since it lends a sense of security and moral place by creating a simplistic world of strong, brave, virtuous heroes and weak, sniveling, cowardly villains.

"Please, please . . . read *Rambo Returns* again!" the child pouts.

"Okay . . .," the nagged parent relents, "*Rambo Returns* it is . . .":

> It was a dark and stormy night at the Mudville airport. America's brave heroes, clean-cut, dressed in crisp military uniforms with brightly polished shoes, were just returning from their noble quest to save the little brown people of Vietnam from terrorist bullies who had infested their nation. They were also keeping America free! Suddenly, dirty drooling hippies, surrounded by buzzing flies, shouting profanities and waving misspelled protest signs, stormed into the airport reception area. In their filthy, mucus-encrusted hands, the slovenly, smelly miscreants carried rotten vegetables, dead cats and tumescent puppies . . . .

"Say, . . . (quietly) are you asleep yet? . . . I see you sucking your thumb."

* * *

Slouching Towards the Third Reich

So far, our ethnic parallels have been limited largely to America, but ethnic persecution happens elsewhere also; certainly one of the most egregious non-American examples would be the persecution in Hitler's Germany of ethnic and racial others, particularly Jews. Although Hippie-Americans are not being systematically slaughtered, the manner in which

American bigots think about Hippies is disturbingly similar to the way German anti-Semites of the Nazi era viewed Jews: the bane of the nation.

A former Nazi prison guard explained that Germans were "taught to hate" the Jews and that he saw them ". . . as criminals, as subhumans and as the cause of our nation's decline" (Rees); I earlier documented the Hippie-as-subhuman stereotype and the notion that the Counterculture is responsible for America's alleged decline.

The phrase "dirty Jew" came as naturally to many Germans as the phrase "dirty hippie" comes to many Americans today.

And just as Jews were blamed by German anti-Semites for Germany's loss in WW I, "hippie protestors" are popularly blamed for America's loss in Vietnam.

"Patriotic" Germans of the era saw Jews as traitors, as the enemy within, as part of a larger "international Jewish conspiracy" attacking their homeland. "Patriotic" Americans, prodded by government propaganda linking "drug" use with terror, see Hippies as aligned with an international terrorism attacking our homeland, as a Trojan Horse.

And the Nazis used anti-Semitism to bring out the bully in society. Jews were seen as meek (Baron 133), as easy victims whose perceived pacifism only proved their weakness and inferiority—the exact attitude many Americans have towards Hippies.

Likewise, the Nazis didn't see Jews as real Germans. Though Hitler's Jewish victims had often been German for generations, the Third Reich saw only aliens; just so, many Americans don't see Hippies as real Americans.

Just as the Nazi state formulated laws to identify and repress Jews, to criminalize that people, so America's drug-testing policies seem designed to identify and repress Hippie-Americans, and for decades, governmental policies have criminalized the Counterculture.

And just as German science was whored by the Nazis, much American science has been bent to the will of the War on Drugs: the Nazis measured Jewish skulls to prove Jewish inferiority; America's drug researchers tell us marijuana makes adolescent males grow breasts. Both groups of scientists have acted as part of a crusade for moral and physical health, for national strength and purity.

If you asked "patriotic" Germans of the period about morality, they would likely have framed their answers in terms of evil being represented by Jews and goodness being represented by "Aryans," the "master race," themselves; the War on Drugs has created that kind of simplistic good guys/bad guys dualism in America.

Those Germans would likely have added that those actively persecuting Jews were the most moral of all since they were on a crusade against evil; just so, William Bennett is seen as a moralist, a great expert on the nature of "virtue." And just as those "moral" Germans thought their nation could only be lifted up when the Jews had been eliminated, so many of today's most "moral" Americans believe Hippies are evil, that the very survival of the nation depends on the "cancer" of the Counterculture being excised—"America has problems because America has Hippies."

Generally, the way that many non-Hippie Americans, particularly those on the right, have come to view the Counterculture much resembles the way "loyal" Germans came to view Jews.

Here's part of a column by Paul Jackson (associate editor of the Canadian *Calgary Sun*) that appeared in December 2004; it's called "Blame Hippies: Sixties counterculture eroded moral foundations of society." In it, Jackson is echoing and paraphrasing the ideas (and emotions) in a film called *The Siege of Western Civilization*, produced and marketed by one Herb Meyer, a former high-ranking CIA official in the Reagan Administration:

> Meyer . . . notes western civilization is under attack both from outside and within our borders. . . .
>
> Today, he sees the internal threat to our moral foundations stemming from the "hippie" counterculture of the 1960's.[159] The hippie movement spurned all that centuries of western civilization had spent building and safeguarding. Hippies rejected material success, and military strength. They loathed the consumer society,[160] and the moral values of the day. It really was sex, drugs and rock 'n' roll with no thought to the consequences of where their actions would take them. The

---

[159] You'll notice here the confused, contradictory way people talk about Hippiedom: It exists today, yet it was Just a thing of the Sixties, and they speak about it in past tense.

[160] Sorry, but I just have to ask: Is the "consumer society" really what "centuries of western civilization . . . spent building and safeguarding"?

historic Fourth of July holiday was abandoned in place of "Earth Day" or some other such nonsense. There was no God. . . .

What they do, says Meyer, is subvert the foundations of our free society.

We are now in the second American civil war, against those who want to put the American Revolution in reverse. . . . Meyer believes time is quickly running out for us unless we quickly tackle both the enemy outside our borders [Muslim 'extremists'] and the enemy within [Hippie culture]. . . . wake up now to the relentless undermining of our way of life.

Meyer himself adds, "We need to understand these threats, now, so we can set in place the right policies to lift this siege we are under—to save our country and by doing so to rescue Western Civilization itself."

True, Meyer calls for no extermination of Hippies, yet in their characterizations of the Counterculture, he and Jackson sound like Nazi ideologues discussing Jews sometime in the early-1930's when the Holocaust hadn't yet been planned.

To them, the Counterculture is the antithesis of virtue, the enemy within who they are pitted against in a life-or-death struggle—they're defending themselves and all that's good against annihilation.

> **The most reactionary elements in America today are fueling and feeding off of anti-Hippie prejudice, hating Hippies, much the way the Nazis of the 1930's fueled and fed off of anti-Semitism, hated Jews.**

Their us-or-them logic leads inexorably to this ferocious, nightmarish conclusion: "If the choices are you destroy us, or we destroy you, we're going to destroy you." That's how Jews, Gypsies and other "undesirables" ended up in Nazi gas chambers. And like the fascists of the Third Reich, these bigots see themselves as the saviors of their nation, the defenders of Western Civilization.

Of course, if you asked German Nazis, "Why are you attacking Jews?" they would have sputtered in astonishment, "We attack them?! Are you insane? They've attacked us! The Jews have betrayed our nation, stabbed us in the back! The Jews mean to destroy us!" And you would look at that person and think, "My God, you've turned reality on its head."

That same confusion of aggression with self-defense seems to run through the heads of Hippie-hating Americans. You can see it in Al Capp's widely read *L'il Abner* cartoons of the late 1960s and early 1970s: "Ignoble Savages" first shows Hippie protestors (and again, all of Capp's protestors are portrayed as Hippie) brutally assaulting campus officials— breaking protest signs over officials' heads, beating them with baseball bats, choking them, setting fires. An ineffectual police officer looks on then walks away as a protestor exults, "He won't dare lay a finger on us!!" (167). Later, after gangster thugs have taken over Harvard, they don brass knuckles to brutalize the demonstrators; one fleeing Hippie whines, "The new administration's playing dirty!! They're—sob!—treating us like we treated them!!" (169).

To live in Capp's world, you would think that at Kent State, Hippie protestors had shot four National Guardsmen dead and gone unpunished, that at the 1968 Democratic Convention in Chicago, exclusively Hippie demonstrators had manhandled police, that Hippies were—with impunity—bullying and beating on America.

Like the Nazi notion of "Jewish aggression" against Germany, here we have a denial-and-projection fantasy world, and in the minds of many, a "wicked counterculture" has viciously assaulted innocent America; thus, violence against Hippies is the righteous violence of self-defense.

No, as mentioned, America hasn't begun practicing mass murder on Hippies—and hopefully never will—but it is deeply involved in a concerted program of state-sponsored ethnocide, and the most reactionary elements in America today are fueling and feeding off of anti-Hippie prejudice, hating Hippies, much the way the Nazis of the 1930's fueled and fed off of anti-Semitism, hated Jews. Sadly, whenever such a dynamic is in place, it has the potential to spin truly out of control, pulling us all into the abyss.

*   *   *

The Infamous Case of Dr. Jeffrey MacDonald: "Helter Skelter" Meets "The Ballad of the Green Berets"

"Acid is groovy, kill the pigs!"—so the former Green Beret doctor Jeffrey MacDonald claims drug-crazed Hippies chanted as they assaulted him and murdered his wife and two daughters. The killings occurred in 1970, but given a new parole hearing for a convicted MacDonald,[161] the story is being revisited. For many, the case has become an emblem of culture wars: wicked Hippies attacking decent, patriotic Americans. But not only does MacDonald almost certainly belong in jail, the implication of an America under siege by a violent Counterculture is ugly propaganda.

CBS's *48 Hours Mystery* tells us, "[T]he MacDonalds were well on their way to a seemingly perfect life. But in 1970, life in America was far from perfect. 'This was an era of shock and counterculture rage in America' . . .," explains MacDonald's former attorney—this juxtaposed with an image of a Hippie protestor throwing a tear-gas canister at police[162] ("Jeffrey MacDonald"). No, it wasn't the War in Vietnam, race riots or the nuclear Sword of Damocles hanging over our heads that was keeping the nation "far from perfect"; it was those crazy, violent hippies!—"Oh! Why won't they just leave decent, God-fearing Americans alone?!"

> **MacDonald is almost certainly a liar. A major problem in his story is the LSD/"acid" claim.**

The storyline is straight out of Al Capp's hateful comic strip *L'il* Abner where Hippie protestors brutalize campus administrators (166-69), right out of *Forrest Gump* where at one point a female Hippie protestor, truncheon in hand, menaces a fleeing policeman. It's the world of the rightist *Washington Times* where Jimi Hendrix's rendition of "The Star Spangled Banner" is called an "assault on the national anthem" (Gaffney). It's a world steeped in the myth of Hippie protestors spitting on returning Vietnam veterans. It's the silly, self-serving fantasy world of anti-Hippie bigotry.

And MacDonald is almost certainly a liar. A major problem in his story is the LSD/"acid" claim. "Trippers" seek a psychedelic experience. That might mean everything from attempting to "see God" to watching

---

161 The *CBS* story I'm about to mention ("Jeffrey MacDonald: Time For Truth—Convicted Murderer Says New Evidence Will Exonerate Him") aired November 6th, 2006; at that time, MacDonald had a parole hearing coming up; indeed, the news story might be thought of as an attempt to influence the parole board.

162 What's strange here, of course, is that the "hippie protestor" is throwing the tear-gas canister *back* at the police, but no one would think of describing that time as one of "police rage" or "conservative rage."

pink mushrooms grow out of the carpet, but it usually means a peaceful setting.

Now, hand-to-hand combat is probably the most arduous thing a human being can do—adrenaline pumping, people fighting for their lives. LSD is not known as a performance enhancer; tripping is usually incompatible with ice-pick-wielding murder.[163]

As a nation, we tend to be ignorant and misinformed about LSD, and we've been trained by the War on Drugs and the mainstream media to stereotype LSD users[164]; this stereotype, in turn, has become part of a larger stereotype of Hippies as a whole. As such, some Americans have gone from seeing the Counterculture as a peace-and-love community to seeing it as a maniacal cult of psychopathic killers; some, apparently, fear Hippies on LSD coming to butcher them and their families.

Okay, what about the Manson-family murders? They were Hippies high on acid, right? Well . . . actually not. Countercultural author Ed Sanders researched and wrote *The Family: The Story of Charles Manson's Dune Buggy Attack Battalion*. As Martin Torgoff writes, "Sanders discovered that speed—the cold, hard drug of the Nazi *blitzkrieg*— and not LSD had been the killers' drug of choice on the night of the murders . . ." (241).

Speed—now that makes sense. Developed by Nazi scientists to supercharge Hitler's *wehrmacht* as it surged across Europe, amphetamines *are* the killer's drug of choice.

But if an LSD high isn't conducive to a coordinated attack involving hand-to-hand combat and if LSD wasn't involved in the Manson murders, why would those Hippies said to have slaughtered MacDonald's family have been chanting "Acid is groovy"? If MacDonald had claimed they were chanting, "Speed is groovy!" his story *might* be plausible.[165]

---

[163]　In an exception to this rule, there was an incident in Boulder in July 2015 where a man on LSD flipped out, grabbed a hammer and became violent, but the details of this incident would seem to undercut the MacDonald story: the guy was stark naked and out of his head—hardly in a position to coordinate any kind of sustained and murderous attack, particularly with others in a similar state (Stanley).

[164]　One way to combat this stereotype is to remind people that the great Steve Jobs used LSD.

[165]　To my knowledge, this is a new argument regarding a significant problem in MacDonald's defense.

Most likely, in a shameless appeal to hysteria about Hippies, a panicked, post-bloodbath MacDonald made his Manson-copycats story up on the fly. It wouldn't be the first or last time a desperate murderer tried to blame an outgroup. And those erroneous details about the Manson murderers being on LSD were in a story in a blood-smudged copy of *Esquire* found at the MacDonald crime scene (*Wikipedia*, "Jeffrey R. MacDonald").

Thankfully, MacDonald's parole has been repeatedly denied. What's odd is that—given the obvious and serious problems in MacDonald's story, given that the courts have consistently upheld MacDonald's conviction—the myth of MacDonald's innocence and martyrdom persists. Many, I suspect, are determined to see him as a hero because it validates their warped perception of the world: Jeffrey MacDonald as a virtual Christ figure who's been cruelly victimized by a "permissive" society that let the Hippie killers get away while irrationally persecuting a noble Green Beret: "Mom, the military, apple pie—all that's good and decent in America crucified on the broken, upside-down cross of the Counterculture!"

But the evidence shows that Jeffrey MacDonald, his wife and two daughters were no more attacked by marauding Hippies than America itself has been victimized by a violent Counterculture. We are *not* the enemy.

*   *   *

A Love-Haight Letter to the Left:
The Devil Reads Pravda;[166] The Democrats
Usually Disappoint; The Center-Left Shines

If the reactionary right has shamelessly scapegoated and vilified Hippie culture,[167] often, the Old Left and mainstream liberals haven't done much better.

To begin with, what unifies Hippiedom is culture and values; politically, there are a wide variety of perspectives within the Counterculture. Reactionaries have both Red-baited Hippie culture and Hippie-baited the Reds; but the notion that the two are the same is silly. Despite the ravings of some of the far-right, Hippiedom isn't Bolshevism.

Regarding the attitudes of the far left towards Hippiedom, there are reports of persecution of our Countercultural cousins, Rastafarians, in contemporary Cuba where marijuana use remains illegal. And, as we discussed, the old Stalinist regimes of Eastern Europe severely repressed Hippiedom.

Also, in Salvador Allende's socialist Chile,[168] Hippies were frowned upon; as Chilean-born history professor Patrick Barr-Melej notes:

> . . . Hippies weren't popular with the left-leaning Allende . . . sexual liberation, smoking marijuana or listening to beat music was not the kind of "revolution" Salvador Allende wanted in Chile. He wanted youths to be clean-cut and marching in the ranks of Marxist parties, and he deplored any form of revolution outside of the one he was building. . . . Hippies were actually repressed during this time period and . . . Allende's government

---

[166] *Pravda* was/is the official newspaper of the Communist Party of the Soviet Union/Russia.

[167] While I address this piece to the left, of which I feel a part, in fairness, let me note that the libertarians have been wonderful in their consistent and principled opposition to the War on Drugs and support for legalization of marijuana.

[168] These criticisms of Salvador Allende's Chile should in no way be seen as an endorsement of or excuse for the Nixon Administration's criminal overthrow of that democratically elected government in 1973.

and the Pinochet regime shared much of the same cultural conservatism that, in many ways, permeates Chilean society today.

Likewise, when the Old Left talk about "drugs," we often hear the same shallow rhetoric we would expect from a neoconservative: little distinction is made between different drugs, no distinction is made between use and abuse, the insight that American drug laws are not about protecting public health but are about ethnic/racial persecution is usually missed, Gateway is assumed, and underlying the whole mess are the same Calvinist assumptions about the "degenerate" or "counter-revolutionary" nature of pleasure.

> When the Old Left talk about "drugs," we often hear the same shallow rhetoric we would expect from a neoconservative.

Generally, because the Counterculture hasn't turned out to be the "revolutionary combat party" of Marxist-Leninist wet dreams, the far left has condemned the Counterculture or, worse still, engaged in its persecution.

Jumping to the right, we find mainstream liberals. In the past, at least, they've tended to trivialize legalization-of-marijuana issues—failing to see their civil-rights nature; politically, of course, the Democrats have been a willing partner of the Republicans in the War on Drugs, better known as the War on American Minorities. And when you explain to mainstream liberals that Hippies are being persecuted in a national campaign of ethnic cleansing, they splutter, "Well, I've checked here in my *Handbook of Political Correctness*, and I just don't see any listing for *Hippies*; it just says they ended with the 1960s; therefore, this can't be a legitimate issue I should take seriously."

Sometimes, they're smug and bigoted: I knew a liberal white attorney, for instance, who thought an African-American targeted by racist drug laws is a scandalous violation of human rights, but a Hippie-American persecuted by bigoted neoconservative drug laws is a "distraction from real people with real problems." Often, they have a sectarian outlook in which newly recognized members of the oppressed are unwelcome, even threatening; often, they lack a politically outgoing, "internationalist" perspective that realizes an injury to one is an injury to all, that new potential allies make them stronger, not weaker.

Now, in 2014 (the reason for the "usually" in the title of this piece), President Obama and his Attorney General Eric Holder did well in crafting an intelligent response to state marijuana legalization; indeed, their enlightened approach of letting the states decide largely for themselves whether or not to legalize represents a giant step forward for the national Democratic Party. Increasingly, some important Democrats correctly see marijuana legalization as a civil-rights issue.

On the other hand, *Rolling Stone* reports that Hillary Clinton believes in Gateway (Dickinson), and here in Colorado, narrowly re-elected Democratic Governor John Hickenlooper has been widely quoted as calling our marijuana legalization "reckless" and vowing to "regulate marijuana to death." Yes, there has been some significant progress by the Obama Administration, and many progressive Democrats have been supportive of legalizing marijuana; still, as a whole, the party's been bigoted towards Hippiedom and deeply complicit in the War on Drugs.

Fortunately, here in the US, tucked between the far left and the mainstream liberals, are the center-left; these groups are already more enlightened, more ready to grow in their thinking about Hippie-America. Internationally, I notice that Uruguay, now led by a liberation-theology-inspired former priest, was the first nation in the world to legalize marijuana. Here at home, I am pleased with the way the center-left website/news show *Democracy Now!* takes legalization issues seriously and devotes excellent coverage to them, with their awareness that the War on Drugs is a war on American minorities, and with their apparent respect for Hippie-America—interviews with Willie Nelson, Neil Young, Patti Smith and such. Also, Senator and presidential candidate Bernie Sanders has been very progressive regarding legalization of cannabis; he introduced a Senate bill called "Ending Federal Marijuana Prohibition Act of 2015" (Graham).

Here's what *all* progressives need to learn: Hippie-Americans are an ethnicity; ethnicities have inherent rights, and undefended ethnic minorities are prey for fascism. Anti-Hippie bigotry feeds fascism; if you want to beat the far right, take away their food.

* * *

Seeing "Redneck":
Country-Western Culture as an American Ethnicity

"Proud to be redneck."

—bumper sticker

Created in 1569, the Mercator map gave us a false view of the world, one where land masses furthest north and south of the equator, particularly European colonial nations, appeared disproportionately large. In our view of society, Americans' cultural map is skewed; our inability to see our society as it is, to have an accurate map of American racial/ethnic minorities, impairs our understanding of our nation.

I've argued that Hippie-America is a sizable chunk of US demography that's been socially invisible—"Just a thing of the Sixties"—and is in fact a living ethnicity. But I believe there are other distinct cultural populations that we should consider as ethnic minorities, and that in so doing, we see our world more clearly; in particular, we should see those I'll call "Country Western,"[169] in homage to the musical genre/style, as a major, modern ethnic group here in the good old US of A.

Let's first quickly apply the extended definition of ethnic group I created in Chapter Two based on the *Harvard Encyclopedia of American Ethnic Groups* 17-point definition. How well does Country-Western culture fit that definition? Admittedly, I'm not Country-Western, but I'll give it a shot:

Common geographic origin: Yes, they do hail from a relatively common geographical area: the rural (country) and Western parts of the USA.

Language or dialect: Probably: CW culture may not have a full-fledged dialect as linguists define it, but they have something that seems equivalent, and you can hear it right there in the twang in the singers' voices.

Ties that transcend kinship, neighborhood, and community boundaries: Yes, CW culture is broader than any of these three things.

---

[169] I will take the liberty of using the acronym *CW*, and I understand that many simply use the term *Country*, but for my purposes here, I prefer *Country-Western* and hope I offend none by its use.

Shared traditions, values, and symbols: I'm too ignorant to document this first item, but I think it's safe to guess there are several. CW culture is widely seen as culturally conservative, as having conservative values, though I imagine closer inspection would also show many others. As for symbols, you know, I don't think I've ever seen a photo of CW star Tim McGraw without a cowboy hat. That headgear is symbolic of CW identity.

Literature, folklore, and music: Is there contemporary CW literature? In the past, perhaps, Louis L'amore and other writers of Westerns. Regarding, folklore, I'm guessing CW culture has something similar; if nothing else, tales of the roots of, say, Loretta Lynn or Dolly Parton would probably do; of course, the music category is easy.

Food preferences: I see barbeque, for example, as a part of or strongly associated with CW culture. My guess is, you could also find CW-type cookbooks. When I Googled "Country-Western food," I came up with several examples.

Settlement and employment patterns: For settlement, we could again refer to mostly rural and western areas; as for employment, I suppose a disproportionate percentage of CW people are involved in farm, ranch or other rural work.

Institutions that specifically serve and maintain the group: Sure, the Grand Ole Opry, the Country Music Hall of Fame and possibly others.

An internal sense of distinctiveness: A good example of this is comedian Jeff Foxworthy's "You Might be a Redneck If . . ." routine. It's clear Foxworthy is talking about and sees himself as part of CW culture; it's clear that "redneck" is a sort of epithet that's been directed at CW people and that Foxworthy is now using that term much the way a Hippie-American comedian might speak of "freaks" or an African-American comedian might speak of "niggers."

An external perception of distinctiveness: Definitely, and part of this is stereotyping and bigotry directed at CW people, everything from things like bigoted New Yorkers screaming "dumb cowboy" at Jon Voight's character in *Midnight Cowboy* to bumper stickers reading "Stop Inbreeding: Ban Country Music."

Ethnic costume: Absolutely: cowboy hats and boots. A local hardware store, Jax, has an entire clothing section that's CW, and I've seen other CW clothing stores.

Cultural artifacts: Okay, I'm stumped here, but I'd be shocked if there weren't; perhaps, we could use CW clothing here.

Distinctive drugs or recreational substances: CW culture hardly has a monopoly on whiskey, for instance; still, whiskey, particularly brands like Jack Daniels, have been associated with CW culture, whether it was Hank Williams' alcoholism or song lyrics like "She's actin' single; I'm drinkin' double."

Generational transfer: You bet: CW people have CW kids; it's about that simple. I know a CW woman, and I've seen photos of her family— her husband and son are wearing black cowboy hats and boots; the two girls are wearing pink cowboy hats and boots. They're a beautiful family.

Then, let me point out a few other things about CW culture: in NASCAR racing, it seems to have largely its own sport. The fans, the drivers—they seem disproportionately CW. There are certain types of vehicles associated with CW culture, particularly, four-wheel drive trucks of the kind used in farm or ranch work.

As mentioned, CW people are subject to bigotry and stereotypying. My father grew up on a farm and for much of his career with John Deere, he worked with farmers; nonetheless, I remember hearing disrespectful remarks about rural people from my parents— "coots" and "hicks," for example. And Elvis Presley was dismissed out of hand as "dumb." In response, perhaps, I think we're seeing a quiet CW pride movement; I suspect many CW people now see their culture as a source of authenticity, as a source of strength and identity.

So, seeing Country Western culture as ethnic or as a "minority" may seem novel, but it's not unreasonable. That, however, begs some questions: Why do it? What's the point? Hopefully, it gives us new ways to understand and heal contemporary America.

Think of ethnicities as individual children in a larger society. The "parent" or rulers of that society will often set ethnic or racial groups against each other for their own selfish divide-and-conquer purposes, creating a sort of sibling rivalry between minorities. So, these same manipulative and selfish social forces, the true elite of society, have helped pit CW culture and Hippie-America against each other. Hippie-Americans have been taught to see CW people as a bunch of "dumb rednecks," who are extremely bigoted towards them[170]; CW people have

---

[170] The Hippie song lyric, "Up against the wall, redneck mother" comes to mind.

been taught to resent and hate Hippies, [171] to see us as the antithesis of everything they hold dear, as people who are disrespecting them, and in their disgust and resentment, they've been encouraged to be violent towards us.

That's a rift that needs healing; a good example of how that can happen would be the evolution of CW singer Merle Haggard who's gone from singing "Okie from Muskogee," with its Hippie- hating lyrics, to being an activist in the legalization movement. Hey, I will *gladly* fix your flat tire anytime, Merle! It is in the interests of both Hippie-America and Country-Western-America that we end this rivalry. The basis for doing that is pretty simple: mutual respect.

One way of fostering that mutual respect should be the avoidance of *redneck* within Hippie culture to describe a violent, Hippie-hating bigot. Yes, in this book, I've struggled (unsuccessfully so far) to find a simple word to use for anti-Hippie prejudice and someone who practices it. Well, *redneck* isn't the answer. In practice, it will be seen as an epithet for and stereotype of CWers and will unnecessarily taint our relations with CW-America. Let's jettison that language.

Lastly, Hippie-Americans sometimes object to Country-Western-Americans because they seem so conservative, so often bigoted. I mean, here's a culture that greeted its own, The Dixie Chicks, with ostracism and death threats for publically snubbing George W. Bush and his War on Iraq.

Here's the thing: many non-conservative Hippie-Americans may be at odds with the rightist politics of many CW people; we have that right. We do not have the right, however, to be dismissive, condescending or disrespectful of their culture. When we indulge in bigotry against CWers on that "progressive" pretext, we only make things worse.

First, in our bigotry, we lose any moral high ground we may have had. Secondly, yes, I agree that *generally* being prejudiced corresponds with being socially conservative. Conservatives today are usually uncomfortable admitting it, but the right has always been aligned with racism, ethnic chauvinism and other movements seeking to preserve social inequality. Yet, as sociologist Jack Levin confirmed, bigotry is often a function of insecurity; generally, the more insecure people are,

---

[171]   Think of CWers at the Grand Ole Opry in 1968 infamously booing the Countercultural band The Byrds.

the more vulnerable they are to leaning on the crutch of bigotry. Being dismissive towards CW people, then, will only exacerbate that insecurity, fueling further bigotry directed at, among others, Hippie-America.

Want to disagree with the social conservatism often seen in CW culture? Feel free; just separate their often conservative politics[172] from their culture, and if we tend to disagree with the former, let's be careful not to disrespect the latter.

* * *

Paul's Addiction

It was sometime in the 1980s. I was irked with myself: I need to be productive, and I wanted to get more done. But it was a hot, wearing summer, and I had a tendency to be a sleepy-head. I wanted some kind of help, a mild stimulant, perhaps. Then, one day as I pushed a grocery cart past the coffees and teas, I spied it: a large glass jar with a bright-yellow, generic label: Instant Tea. "Hmm," I thought, "what could be easier? You toss a teaspoonful into some water, stir, add ice, and away you go. It's inexpensive, and millions of people use it. I'm going to buy a jar and try some."

Well, I was happy with my new drug. I mean, I would wake up early, make a glass, and within minutes, I felt wide awake, ready to take on the world. And I was getting things done. "Great stuff," I thought; soon, instant tea became a part of my life. This continued for some months when I started to notice some side effects: while that first glass in the morning seemed righteous, after an hour, I needed a second glass. And while the second glass was good, it wasn't quite as good as the first. And come to think of it, the third glass wasn't quite as good as the second . . . . Years later, when a recovering friend explained to me the psychological aspects of his cocaine addiction, I related to his description

---

[172] Of course, there are CWers who aren't rightist; besides the aforementioned Dixie Chicks, an example would be liberal pundit Jim Hightower who hails from Texas and sports a cowboy hat. Also, remember that prejudice and stereotyping are usually unable to recognize individuality and that CW culture, like any ethnicity, has a great deal of individual diversity within it; common culture doesn't mean strict ideological uniformity.

of a coming-down-the-stairs effect— each new dose doesn't get you quite as high as the last; by the end of the night, you're burned out and can't "get off" anymore.

Also, iced tea gave me an edge—but not necessarily a good one. I was pushy and irritable. Clerks would take one look at me, sense my annoyance and impatience, and tense up. I scared people. I recall with embarrassment how rude I sometimes appeared—even when I was trying very hard not to be.

The thing is, I was in pain. I mean actual physical pain: all that caffeine was giving me headaches.

And it got worse: When the headaches became serious, I would try headache medicines, but I found that the

> I looked around and saw the peculiar clutter with which I now lived: there on the kitchen table, there on the desk, there on the radiator shelf—a partly drunk glass of tea, the dark dregs thickening at the bottom. Like little toxic-waste dumps, like a junkie's used syringes, they littered my apartment.

only products that helped contained caffeine. Yes, the only way I could escape my caffeine-induced headaches was to take more caffeine; I was like the alcoholic who drinks to relieve a hangover.

And after a while, it seemed like I'd had a headache for weeks; I had to *do* something. I realized I was acting like a drug addict: I either had too much caffeine in my system or not enough, and it was like I was trying to do "maintenance doses"—and not succeeding. *I never felt good anymore.* I looked around and saw the peculiar clutter with which I now lived: there on the kitchen table, there on the desk, there on the radiator shelf—a partly drunk glass of tea, the dark dregs thickening at the bottom. Like little toxic-waste dumps, like a junkie's used syringes, they littered my apartment. "Okay," I concluded decisively and with a great deal of relief, "Let's get this stuff out of my life."

For the next three days, I went through withdrawal. Oh, it wasn't gut-wrenching like the withdrawal from heroin or something, but it was physical withdrawal—a sort of extended low-level hangover. Then, I began to get my old life and self back, and I haven't touched instant tea since.

Yes, I was an abuser/addict, and in addition to all the matters mentioned above, I know I was an abuser because even today, my body remembers: if I open a jar of instant tea and sniff, at the very top of my head, I feel a sharp pain—a tiny, intense headache like someone had pricked my brain with a pin. It's the only time I feel pain there, and it only happens when I smell instant tea.

Would I ever go back to my drug habit? Not on your life. Now, I rarely have headaches; in addition, I've learned ways to energize myself that aren't drug induced. Clerks no longer fear me, and I find it far easier to behave the way I'd like. Goodbye and good riddance.

So, drug abuse isn't necessarily the province of Countercultural drugs or illegal drugs; as likely as not, it's the province of legal and socially sanctioned substances. As a nation, our double standards on drugs don't just unfairly target certain substances, they also help blind us to the potentially harmful ones in front of our faces.

* * *

Mr. Paulie's Psychedelic Experience: Toto, We're not in Kansas Anymore!

"Have you ever been experienced? Not necessarily stoned, but, uh, . . . beautiful."
—*Jimi Hendrix*

Many Hippies have had intense and formative psychedelic experiences, mostly with LSD. I did acid a few times and never really liked it. It made me physically uncomfortable, the hangover was like the aftermath of a tropical storm, and the deep thoughts and insights I was supposed to have while tripping? Not happening. No, I had my life-altering experience with another hallucinogen: MDA,[173] a cousin, apparently, of Ecstasy (MDMA).

I was 21, living in a dorm of a Midwestern university. Hillcrest was heavily Hippie; when you walked its hallways, you smelled marijuana. Most halls had one or two marijuana dealers. Mine was an affable, academically capable computer-science major, Dave. I tell people that one of the first "drug dealers" I ever knew was an Eagle Scout, and he was. He sold pot only and was liked and trusted by his neighbors/customers.

---

[173] I'm not advocating experimentation with MDA here. Remember, what is sold as "MDA" might be something else. Rather, this is an honest attempt to reconstruct a personal experience and draw some lessons from it.

At the Hillcrest's other end lived several other Hippies I knew. Frank was a friend from high school, now a driven pre-med student; he hung around with Matt—dark, haunted, angry and mercurial. His very long hair parted in the middle, a mustache and wire-rimmed glasses, Frank's roommate, Mike, was another computer-science whiz and a dealer. He was experienced with drugs of various sorts and well respected. A bit older than the three of us; he seemed an elder.

Mike sold more than pot. I didn't know him well, but I found myself alone with him in his room one day, and he showed me a "hit" of MDA wrapped in aluminum foil. "Look, you're really going to like this," he said, "I did it myself, and it's great. Hey, I have one hit left, and I want you to try it." He was firm with me. Leery of what I called "chemicals," I was hesitant, but he reassured me it was safe, and he wanted me to do this drug as if he had decided to do me a favor. Opening the foil, he displayed the fine brownish powder. "It's cut with Nestle Quik," he explained. I paid him two dollars and planned to do it that night, Friday.

We had no grand plans—I would meet Frank and Matt in Frank/ Mike's room. Mike was out. We three would hang: chess and perhaps pizza. They had no MDA, I would be flying solo though in the company of friends. A bit anxious at first, when I put the powder in my mouth, its sweet and chocolaty taste reassured me. Frank and Matt huddled over the chess-board; I watched, detached.

A half hour later, my MDA experience was defining itself. Frank asked how I was doing, and I told them fine—I was feeling comfortable with the emerging high.

Physically, I felt fine— no weird LSD queasiness, no annoying amphetamine buzz. More noteworthy were the

> **Imagine a place beyond fear, insecurity, neediness and anger. A place where you feel content, happy to be alive, quietly aglow with warmth, joy and kindness.**

psychological effects. Imagine a place beyond fear, insecurity, neediness and anger. A place where you feel content, happy to be alive, quietly aglow with warmth, joy and kindness. In later years, I would hear a New Age minister speak of "masters," those capable of being happy "completely independent of external circumstances." That night, I remember thinking, "You could shut me in a dark closet, and it wouldn't even faze me." It was a bit like coming home—a place where you feel comfortable, natural and good. You don't say, "Oh my God, this is amazing!" you say, "Oh, of course; hey, I knew this."

If I "saw God," God wasn't what we expect: a bolt of lightning from some supernatural patriarch, an aching insight into a deep universal mystery—or at least a really good hallucination. No, more like a current of life or light flowing through me. It wasn't sensational; it didn't have to be. Apparently, real happiness doesn't require stage gimmicks. My "wild" drug experience was anything but.

Now, if that's what my experience looked like inside, what was happening outside? Surely, I must have been about to leap off a ledge, crying, "I can fly!" right? Well, I was lucid and calm, completely in my senses; indeed, our threesome wasn't always so harmonious, yet that night I was putting out such a good vibe, seemed so clearly together, I appeared to be playing a leadership role, modeling how to be. It was like I was suddenly more secure and mature, and it showed.

The "trip" lasted about six hours—as I'd been told it would. Around two, I walked back to my room; I remember that corners of the hallway seemed slightly distorted, but that was all. I went right to bed. I wasn't exhausted; it was just time to retire. I slept well. The next morning, I awoke early, refreshed. As I inhaled the fresh spring air wafting through the raised windows, as I admired the impressive oak trees now in bloom and the shadows they cast over the sunny grass, a robin chirped. "God," I thought, "I'm so happy to be alive."

You know, one way to gauge the health effects of any drug is to see how you feel after you use it: if you're hung over in some way, that might tell you something. The way I felt that morning told me that whatever I'd done was apparently kind to my body. I felt wonderful.

Over the next several months, I tried to have a similar experience, and did "MDA" twice more. But unregulated street drugs are unreliable; the last "MDA" I bought was a fraudulent mix of amphetamines and baby powder. *C'est la vie.*

Do I regret my drug experience? Obviously not. It was a gift, possibly the

> **Theologians seem to think God is an intellectual construct, a really complex equation, and if you square both sides and multiply by the Holy Ghost and add a catechism, you may get it right. But what if God isn't a dogma? What if God is a feeling?**

nicest gift anyone ever gave me. Mike the drug dealer turned out trustworthy. In some spiritual communities, they speak of a "tuning-fork memory"—a recollection of a time when one felt at peace and in harmony with life. This has been a tuning-fork memory for me: it has stabilized me, given me buoyancy, and like a kind hand on the shoulder, it helped me grow up.

Theologians seem to think God is an intellectual construct, a really complex equation, and if you square both sides and multiply by the Holy Ghost and add a catechism, you may get it right. But what if God isn't a dogma? What if God is a feeling?

As for "drugs," yes, there are dangerous drugs, and we should beware of them and of drug abuse. There are also positive drug experiences, things so valuable that a nation that outlaws them is foolish and repressive.

* * *

My Hippie Dream: A Life Where Soul Meets Body

"I want to live where soul meets body."
—Death Cab for Cutie

"I had a dream last night; what an amazing dream it was.
I dreamed we all were alright, happy in a land of Oz."
—John Sebastian at Woodstock

Since the early Greeks, there's been a divide in human thought: philosophical idealists, like Plato, believed that the material world was but the shadow of an idea, that mind precedes matter; philosophical materialists, like Socrates, believed that ideas arise out of the material world, that matter precedes the mind. In more modern days, of course, the disagreement has played out along God vs. Science lines. Underlying and accompanying this debate are disagreements about the relative importance of environment and free will in human conduct, and beyond that is often a liberal-vs.-conservative divide, with liberals stressing the need to change ugly environmental influences and conservatives stressing the role of free will and personal responsibility—"The problem isn't a bad environment: it's bad people."

That same divide has run through Hippiedom. On the materialist side have been the politicos and activists; on the idealist side have been the metaphysicists, the spiritually inclined, those known as New Agers.

Now, the Hippie politicos and activists, and I would include myself among them, have always been a prominent part of the Counterculture; this would mean not just those participating in legendary anti-Vietnam War protests but in many other types of activism also—from protecting the environment to women's rights to homeschooling to perhaps building a Hippie ethnic organization. For many, political activism is a part of their Hippie identity. "We can change the world . . ." rings the chorus of a Graham Nash song, and for many of us, that confidence that we *can* change the world for the better is what's kept us alive and growing—still hopeful after all these years. To me, in that material-world activism and hope for positive social change, there's something divine.

The argument for political activism and a materialist approach is basically this: Don't beat the dog. So, you can take an abused dog. You can send that dog to some kind of church. That dog can learn spiritual lessons and with great effort and much meditation, perhaps someday that beaten dog will "come to Jesus" and find inner peace; indeed Fido might eventually become some kind of swami or holy dog. Unfortunately, such creatures take a tremendous amount of work, and even if that work is successful, they will always constitute only a tiny minority of abused dogs.

Or you could change the dog's environment to begin with: be proactive and give that dog a loving, nurturing and respectful home. That will produce a "divine" dog virtually every time, and it's so much easier than trying to reform a traumatized and degraded Fido. In short, don't assume that environmental factors are just excuses for bad behavior, that trying to change the world is a quixotic waste of time. Stop beating the dog.

Of course, there's the other half of the argument: activism rings hollow if you never deal with your personal issues, never experience true maturity or spiritual growth, if, say, you go through your entire life angry, never able to love others or to love yourself—"Let there be peace on earth, and let it begin with me." I knew someone who was very insecure and angry and who bullied those around her with her temper; yet, just as some people "wrap themselves in the flag" or become Bible beaters who claim every evil thing they do is for God, her progressive politics became the rationalization for her ugly personal behaviors. In fact, I've met that person several times.

In what I call the "sectarian left," instead of "Holier than thou," it's often "More politically correct than thou"—essentially an exercise in insecurity and one-upmanship that has nothing to do with improving this world. And if you never deal with your issues, chances are that no matter how you vote or what kind of progressive activism you engage in, on a personal level, at least, you'll probably make the world a worse place, not better.

On the other hand, to march further along on the philosophically idealist path, into the realm of what I'll call "metaphysical extremism" seems silly. Generally, the extreme metaphysicists seem to believe that there is no such thing as objective reality; it's sort of like saying that because some people are colorblind, there's no such thing as blue— "Absolutely everything is subjective."

An anecdote about a metaphysical extremist: One day, during normal chit-chat, I made some comments to a friend about the thunderstorms we'd recently had. She said the harsh weather had probably been the result of the subjective state of mind of particular individuals (possibly me, possibly herself, possibly the vast majority of people living in this area—she didn't specify) who, apparently, are upset and putting out bad vibes. When I pointed out the many and obvious problems with her meteorology, she was unfazed and adamant—as certain that human emotions and moods cause weather as most of us are that dropping an egg will cause it to break.

I once got into an editorial fisticuffs with a metaphysical-extremist writing for a local New Age magazine. Among other things, she claimed that there is no injustice in the world; that's right: everything that happens is divine; the universe is a perfect and just place where people only get exactly what they deserve. Thus, the secret to prosperity is to put out good vibrations, to always be overflowing with gratitude, to be vehemently positive on all occasions.

There's a book/film called *The Secret* (2006) that promotes this message.

While a grateful attitude can help you prosper in and enjoy life, and while we can to some extent make choices, to engage in healthy

Mindfulness,[174] the obvious flaw with this argument regards the bad things that happen to people: remember, if good things are a response to positive energy, bad things must then be a response to negative energy. In short, regarding every horrific thing that's ever happened to any individual or group since the dawn of time, those people must have been emitting and attracting negative energy; their misfortune and suffering has only been the meta-physical chickens coming home to roost.

One of Hippiedom's foremost values is kindness. One problem with extreme metaphysics is that, if actually followed, it leads to unkindness. Thus, if we see injustice or unnecessary suffering in this world, instead of being our brother's/sister's keeper, we are apparently to say, "Clearly, that person's pain is only the Universe's response to the negative energy he or she is radiating; I can do *nothing* to help him or her except to act as an example of someone who emits positive energy, nor should I try."

Generally, I think we need to live in both realms, the spiritual and the practical, and if we seek spiritual peace and enlightenment, to be "above" this world, it should be partly so that we can bring that divine state back to this world and heal it—"On Earth as it is in Heaven." If these differences between philosophical idealism and materialism at first seem a troubling contradiction within Hippie culture, in the end, the desire and ability of most Counterculturists to fuse, understand and practice both the spiritual and the practical/ political is one of our greatest strengths.

> **Here's my "Hippie dream," and I suspect it's the dream of most Counterculturists: I want to be personally happy and spiritually developed; I want to make this world a better place. I want to live where soul meets body.**

On the cover of his recent book,[175] Neil Young has a small sign in his headband reading "Hippie Dream." Well, here's my "Hippie dream," and I suspect it's the dream of most Counterculturists: I want to be personally happy and spiritually developed; I want to make this world a better place. I want to live where soul meets body.

---

[174]   As Lincoln said, "I reckon people are about as happy as they choose to be."
[175]   *Waging Heavy Peace: A Hippie Dream* (2012)

Chapter Twelve

A Problem's Solution:
Building a Hippie-American Ethnic Organization

"It's not so much the quality of the leader that counts:
it's the quality of the leader's vision."

—*Anonymous*

"If you build it, they will come."

—*"Field of Dreams"*

This book is not just an argument proving that Hippie culture is a living ethnicity. The book's intent is to make this world a better place, to, in singer/songwriter Jackson Browne's words, "hotwire reality." Theory should lead to practice. Ethnic-Hippies theory, the theory that Hippie-Americans are a living ethnicity, leads to the case for creating some kind of ethnic organization, [176] a sort of NAACP or NOW, if you will, for Hippie-Americans. In this chapter, I'll be sketching out what such an organization might look like, what functions it might serve, and how it might be formed.

Why do we need such an organization? Let me make a military analogy: In most battles, there are battle lines, and the general wisdom is, if the opposition punches a hole in your line, they win. Now, nascent American fascism is searching for scapegoats/victims; it feeds off them. There are, of course, numerous possibilities: African-Americans, Mexican-Americans, Jewish-Americans, Muslim-Americans, gays and lesbians, feminists, "liberals," and others, including Hippie-Americans. Those potential target groups form the battle line for Progressive America, but for the last several decades, reactionaries have been pouring through a hole in that line, which represents Hippie-America. Vilified though we are, we're not organized and are thus unable to effectively fight back. An injury to one is an injury to all, and because Hippie-America is unorganized and vulnerable, all those other target groups, the American majority, too often lose. We need to plug that hole in the line.

---

[176] Another way to conceptualize this would be a *democratic-rights* or *civil-rights* or *social-equality* organization.

So, **what is an "ethnic organization," anyway?** It's not a political party since the basis of a political party is an ideology, but remember, there is no "Hippie philosophy," just Hippie values that might manifest as a broad range of ideas. Although ethnic organizations might be involved in politics, might lobby, they don't usually run candidates for office, and inside the organization, there's the understanding that there are ideological and political disagreements. The glue that holds the organization together is cultural.

The primary goal of such a civil-rights organization is generally to promote the interests of the group (in particular, to create social equality and respectability for group members), and this might be done in many ways. When discussing the nature of an ethnic organization, we wander into the traditional left-right debate on the size of government; only in this case, it's the size of the organization, its scope. At the very "big" end of the spectrum, you'd have an organization that might, for example, provide insurance, retirement homes and a virtual social-security net for its members; at the "small" end, just an organization that fights stereotyping and scapegoating of the group, possibly lobbies and not much more.

In this chapter, I'll be brainstorming, thinking aloud about what a Hippie-American Ethnic Organization, an HAEO, might look like. Any discussion of potential organizational functions assumes that an HAEO would likely start out smaller, not bigger, and a potential organizational function that might seem impractical at first might make more sense later on. And underlying that potential is, of course, how much money the organization either has or can raise—big things require more money.

* * *

Let's begin, however, by making the case for an **HAEO—what good would it or could it do?** Why is it necessary?

In Chapter Three, we discussed how by Hippie-baiting, how by using stereotypes of Hippies as a foil, reactionary politicians have shoved America to the far right. Generally speaking, in election after election since the mid-1960s, Republicans have demagogically exploited anti-Hippie prejudice, wooing voters through a campaign of Hippie-hating or by essentially saying that "The Democrats are just a bunch of hippies!"—Hippie-baiting.

Remember also that the obituary for the "Godfather of Neoconservatism," Irving Kristol, showed that one of the two main pillars of neoconservatism was contempt for the Counterculture (Associated Press). Anti-Hippie bigotry, then, has been the food that neoconservatism feeds on, the source or much of its power and seeming political magic.

And the successful results of this Hippie-hating demagoguery have been as devastating as the rightist policies it's empowered from an aggressive foreign policy, such as the War in Iraq, to the further thinning of the American middle class at the behest of the super-wealthy, to a disdain for the environment, to a repressive War on Drugs.

There are other reasons for an HAEO which we'll discuss below, but that's the most important: the widespread existence of anti-Hippie bigotry has a direct, powerful and ugly impact on American politics; so, an HAEO isn't just about saving the Counterculture from those who would destroy it: it's about saving the United States of America from those who would destroy *it*—make the Founding Fathers roll over in their graves. Want to be true patriot? Build an HAEO; help roll back the trend towards American fascism.

> Civil-rights, social-equality movements often change the nation more dramatically, in deeper ways, than a presidential election, for instance. A particular election seems more on the surface and shorter term whereas successful struggles for social equality seem to move society's tectonic plates, to have a more lasting and fundamental impact.

Also, civil-rights, social-equality movements often change the nation more dramatically, in deeper ways, than a presidential election, for instance. A particular election seems more on the surface and shorter term whereas successful struggles for social equality seem to move society's tectonic plates, to have a more lasting and fundamental impact.

* * *

Possible functions of a.n HAEO

First and foremost, a Hippie-American ethnic organization should **attack the stereotyping and scapegoating of Hippie-Americans.** Think of it as an education effort. Specifically, where demagogic bigots are Hippie-hating and Hippie-baiting, an HAEO should be calling those people "bigots" and pointing out that they're making divisive appeals to prejudice. Happily, Americans increasingly see appeals to prejudice as evil. We need to open the eyes of American voters so that when they see the usual attempts at Hippie-hating and Hippie-baiting, they understand that also is evil.

That "education" will mean everything from showing that stereotypes of Hippie-Americans are indeed stereotypes to debunking myths like "Hippies didn't fight in Vietnam" or "Hippie protestors spit on returning Vietnam veterans" or "Marijuana users are evil people who menace America's children." It might also mean complaining to television networks and such when they run programs that seem to stereotype or scapegoat Hippie-Americans. It might mean discussing with school boards and educational publishers how textbooks and such portray Hippie-Americans and our history. I've imagined television spots where a prominent and respected Hippie-American might say something like, "I'm _____, and I'm proud to be Hippie-American." Let's change the ways people think about us.

In particular, we should attack Just-a-Thing-of-the-Sixties notions that make us socially invisible and dead. We need to point out that when the 1960s ended, a majority of today's Counterculturalists hadn't yet been born. We need to change the way the media habitually speaks about us, with the constant implication and assumption that contemporary Hippie-Americans are "throwbacks," the leftovers of the 1960s too spaced out to know the party ended long ago. It's the language of disrespect, the language of contemptuous trivialization, the language of social invisibility, the language of ethnocide.

And we need to make America understand that there are Hippie-American families, that Hippie identity is often trans-generational. As things stand, rightist demagogues preaching "family values" have made Hippie-America[177] out to be the enemy of the American family; we need to make it clear that is not so.

Generally, we need to change the way Americans think about Hippie-Americans—to move beyond the stupid stereotypes and start seeing us as an accomplished cultural group that deserves respect and social equality. We need to re-educate them and shift their paradigms.

---

[177] Along with gays and lesbians.

Next up on our functions list would be **political lobbying.** That might mean endorsing particular candidates or parties or ballot initiatives. Many Hippie-Americans belong to third parties, say, the Libertarians or the Greens. Okay, so perhaps the power of an HAEO could be directed towards making American democracy more democratic and not just a monopoly of two parties, neither of which, voters increasingly feel, represents them. Or, of course, such an organization might also decide to endorse a Democrat or even (given their ugly Hippie-baiting history, it pains me to say this) a Republican.

Naturally, an HAEO would want to involve itself in **the legalization movement**—to legalize marijuana is to legalize Hippie-America, to bring us within the law and make us respectable. And we need an amnesty for those incarcerated for marijuana and other drug crimes.[178] Also, an HAEO could lobby on particular issues.

I think there could be legislation (either at the local, state or national level) **prohibiting discrimination against Hippie-Americans.** At present, many anti-discrimination laws apply only to things like race, religion and gender. We need to get those laws broadened to include "ethnicity," with the understanding that that category includes Hippie-Americans.

Current hiring law usually involves the criterion of "mutability"; in other words, if the prospective employee has it in his or her power to mute or change that which is objectionable to the prospective employer, then the prospective employee can't claim discrimination.

This notion involves what I call "Archie Bunker thinking." Archie Bunker was, of course, the nationally televised bigot of that famous 1970s sitcom *All in the Family.* There's an episode where Bunker says, as I recall, "Hey, I ain't got nothin' against the blacks. After all, they can't help it." The joke, of course, is that Blacks have nothing to help. Thus, these "mutability" laws are a sort of extrapolation of that bigoted attitude in that they say to job-hunting Hippie-Americans, in effect, "Hey, you *can* 'help it.' You *can* change to meet our bigoted and discriminatory hiring standards; therefore, you must." As a nation, we should be steering towards an egalitarian, non-discriminatory society, a place where there are no second-class citizens, not finding legal excuses for the prejudicial policies of the past.

---

[178] I am happy to report that California's 2016 law legalizing marijuana has such a provision.

Other things an HAEO can accomplish: Well, the NAACP has an annual **Image Awards Dinner.** Activities that recognize important achievements within our community should be promoted; we could have awards such as Hippie-American of the Year. Who might win that? Mia Farrow, Willie Nelson, Bruce Springsteen, Hannah Teeter, Bill Walton, Alicia Silverstone, Drew Barrymore, some non-celebrity Hippie-American who's done something special—you tell me.

A **newspaper:** An organization needs an "organ," some kind of magazine, newspaper or website to give the group a voice that's heard by members on a regular basis, something that by discussing relevant controversies, reporting on relevant issues and profiling people in the organization or in the larger culture builds community and coherence.

In this neighborhood, I have another idea though it's towards the "big" end of the spectrum: start our own **television station.** It could create new programming, including things like variety shows—a new *Smothers Brothers Comedy Hour*, perhaps—but also programs not derivative of the 1960s, dramas that include contemporary Hippie-Americans, for instance. A place on the airwaves, a television channel of our own would give us real power, presence and visibility—exactly the opposite of the social invisibility that those intent on destroying Hippie culture have forced onto American society.

Things that **maintain group history:** An HAEO would be interested, probably, in founding museums and other venues for preserving Hippie history and presenting that history to the public in a respectful, honest and intelligent manner. That might even mean looking after certain Hippie figures who we

> An HAEO gives Hippie-America an official voice. And part of that official voice will be the messages we send to our fellow Americans, how we portray ourselves and how we orient towards other groups, particularly other American racial and ethnic minorities.

might consider "institutions." Hey, if Grace Slick or Wavy Gravy fall on hard times, I think we should take care of them. Let's start treating each other like members of a healthy family.

Things that **build cultural community:** An HAEO could also be a place for networking, seminars, and so forth. I documented the great many Hippie-American athletes; yet, you may have noticed that despite their many accomplishments, apparently, they aren't always treated respectfully.[179] And of course, there's the whole issue of drugs in sports: steroids might be tolerated, but an athlete who uses marijuana off the field—scandalous! We need some kind of forum or association where Countercultural athletes can meet, discuss their issues and perhaps organize in some way.

An HAEO gives Hippie-America **an official voice.** And part of that official voice will be the messages we send to our fellow Americans, how we portray ourselves and how we orient towards other groups, particularly other American racial and ethnic minorities. How, for example, should Hippie-America relate to African-America, or Mexican-America, Country-Western America, Jewish-America, Native-America or various Asian-American communities? How should Hippie-America relate to various other movements for social equality such as gay-rights groups or the women's movement?

I believe our approach to all should be basically the same: create the same types of relationships that create healthy relationships between individuals—relationships based on mutual respect, relationships that build trust, relationships that stress common interests. And offer them all the same basic deal: we'll do everything in our power to discourage prejudice, scapegoating and other disrespectful attitudes and behaviors directed towards your group members within our group and in society as a whole; in return, your group will do everything in its power to discourage prejudice, scapegoating and other disrespectful attitudes and behaviors directed towards Hippie-Americans within your group and in society as a whole. In short, we start/continue the writing of a new social contract, and by enacting that new social contract, we create a healthier, more fair and egalitarian America; we grow Big Us.

Also, if Hippie ethnic organization form elsewhere, we would **maintain symbiotic relationships with those civil-rights organizations.**

Let's consider a few other things that a larger HAEO might do. There's a novel about a **retirement home** for aging Hippies.[180] I find the idea perfectly reasonable; after all, other ethnic groups have done this; there are, for example, Jewish-American retirement homes. A Hippie-

---

[179]   Gustafson gives an example of Luke Walton being hassled in the locker room for his Hippie identity

[180]   The 2007 novel by Tim Sandlin is called *Jimi Hendrix Turns Eighty.*

American retirement home would place older Hippies in an environment where they felt comfortable and hopefully happy. I imagine they could use marijuana, eat organic/natural foods, be environmentally friendly, live in a sort of communal manner, have tie dyes hanging in the dining room, emphasize natural healing, and when people die, cremate them or bury them in a simple, environmentally friendly manner.[181]

And here's an idea for possibly the "biggest" organization of them all: We need to dramatically reduce the emission of greenhouse gasses; in particular, we need to create a **functioning biodiesel industry** here in the United States of America, the nation with the largest environmental footprint on the planet. Yes, an HAEO could lobby for this, but here I'm discussing the possibility of using a "big" HAEO to actually create or help create such an industry. Part of that would likely be legalizing marijuana and developing a reborn US hemp economy to produce biofuel, but it's other things too, like ensuring that a majority of Americans can buy a diesel car or have their current vehicle somehow refitted. Government help for the latter would be crucial: give Americans a tax break or a stipend to go diesel. Fact is, the creation of a web of biodiesel filling stations accessible to average Americans would likely involve billions of dollars.

Again, what happens when our current government, run by two political parties beholden to Big Oil, just doesn't seem up to the task? And the private sector, controlled by Big Oil and its partners, has a different plan— something about continuing to suck every last drop of fossil-fuel out of the earth and burn it until they've rung every cent of profit out of it? What do we do then?

Well, it's a situation where a large enough, wealthy enough, and determined enough HAEO could begin this important work, show leadership where other American institutions have failed.

I am not advocating a sprawling and expensive bureaucracy, but at the bigger end of the spectrum, to some extent an ethnic organization can create paying **jobs for group members**. Hippie-Americans have long suffered job discrimination in the larger society. It is so unreasonable to, then, use the HAEO to give a few Hippie-Americans a bit of shelter from the economic storm, particularly if they're working hard and well and doing valuable work that needs being done?

---

[181] Green funeral businesses are now being created—a "natural" burial that doesn't require a "magnificent" coffin and that costs a fortune (Miller).

Other big-organization ideas/possibilities: We could have our own **fashion house/clothing industry.** We could make and market hemp or other natural/organic fiber clothing. Personally, I'd like to see an HAEO or someone create a sort of "professional Hippie" look, clothing that's Countercultural yet appropriate for the workplace. Let's create business attire that goes beyond the tired male suit-and-tie; let's create a new look that's appropriate for work yet sensibly casual. Let's free society from the necktie and uncomfortable "plastic" clothing.

It's also possible that when marijuana becomes fully legalized, a "big" HAEO could decide to **invest in industrial-hemp or marijuana production.**

Generally, for an organizationally related business idea to be taken seriously, it should meet three criteria: one, fill some kind of need or niche in a market in a way that makes America and the world a better place; two, create quality jobs for Hippie-Americans or others; three, be mostly financially self-sustaining and have the potential to one day turn a profit which could then be used to fill organizational coffers. And an organization that has solid funding and a treasury is an organization that's powerful, an organization that gets taken seriously, an organization that can undertake challenging tasks.

* * *

Let me now open a discussion about **the form of an HAEO.** Lots of issues here: democracy vs. cult of personality; volunteer vs. paid work and staff; elections vs. appointment/hiring of staff; cyber vs. real-life contact; who to allow into the organization and who should it represent; and no doubt others.

Let's start with the democracy vs. cult-of-personality dichotomy. Well, I suppose there are other ways that an organization can be less than democratic besides being a cult of personality. In most organizations with at least some paid staff, for example, there's the tendency towards bureaucracy and in-crowdism. In any case, we should take **the democratic route;** the more democratic the organization is, the more invested in and satisfied with the organization members will be; conversely, an organization that degenerates into a cult of personality or celebrities or a bureaucratized in-crowd alienates a majority of its members, and an organization is greatly weakened when it becomes about a tiny minority instead of a manifestation of Big Us. For starters, it loses its moral authority.

As you read this book, you may assume that I would be the president of this potential organization. Not necessarily; in fact, it's possible the group wouldn't have a president (though I think it probably should); instead, it could have some kind of group leadership, a board of directors, or—my preference—it could have both: a president or such who reports to a board of directors. In any case, those leadership positions could be elected and rotating.

Generally, we want to strive for **an organization that would be as diverse as is Hippiedom;** thus, even if Hippie-America is largely white, there are Hippie-Americans of various races, and the organization should reflect that. We discussed the political and ideological differences within the Counterculture, and an HAEO should have liberals as well as libertarians—or whomever. Remember, we need to agree on the matters relevant to an HAEO and on achieving social equality and respectability for Hippie-Americans, but that doesn't mean we have to agree on everything.[182]

In particular, an HAEO must never become a boys club; if the organization is to succeed and prosper, it needs to be an organization that **involves Hippie-American women** and that includes them in leadership positions. If Hippie-American women don't feel welcome or equal in an HAEO, the organization will fail.

> **An HAEO must never become a boys club; if the organization is to succeed and prosper, it needs to be an organization that involves Hippie-American women and that includes them in leadership positions.**

This discussion of diversity raises the issue of **quotas;** that is, do we want to fill elected or appointed positions according to strict percentages? I would say, no. If members understand the importance of diversity—racial, gender, gender-preference, political, etc.—to the organization's image and effectiveness, I think we'll achieve our diversity goals well enough. On the other hand, I like the idea of having a governing board that's half female.

---

[182] And the truth is that, despite differing political approaches to things, the center-left and the Libertarian right agree on a surprising number of things.

Paid staff vs. volunteer labor: the strength of volunteer labor is, of course, it requires no funding; personally, I think an all-volunteer organization isn't really feasible—it would need more structure than, "Hey, whoever's here on Tuesday will do it—I'll leave a note . . ." It's probably obvious that a nationally functioning organization would need both volunteer workers and paid staff.

Which leads us to the matter of **how people might volunteer or participate in the organization;** one way could be through the internet. We could be a heavily cyber organization. One way of paying your member "dues," for instance, might be to volunteer to spend two hours a month working on a particular committee. Let's say the organization decides it needs a logo, and you have experience with graphic design and—brilliant and creative you!—you have logo ideas. You join that committee and then working online, your committee creates two-or-three logos. Later, perhaps, the larger group could by vote choose one of those logos or approve the committee's choice.

Which leads us to another matter: it's entirely possible to conduct **democratic elections** using a simple cyber system: have members log in and then vote once on a particular issue.

In education nowadays, there are what they call FLEX courses, meaning that sometimes the class meets in person; other times, the class is conducted online. I'm thinking an HAEO could function similarly; that is, at times we would perhaps have **live meetings** in a particular area with group members; other times, we'd **conduct business online.**

Of course, there could also be a **convention** to found the organization. We could consider having a political/organizational Woodstock of sorts.

Another issue is how we decide **who can be a member.** I think this is easier than we might suppose: anyone can join who wants to. Given the stigma placed on Hippie identity, I really doubt that anyone who doesn't feel they are indeed Hippie-American will join. Yes, there may be some pranksters and saboteurs, but you have to be a pretty dedicated prankster to participate on any extended basis. Of course, at the live meetings, you'll have to put on a real act. I mean, I doubt this is going to be a problem.

Then, there's the matter of **how members should relate to the larger group,** how working in an HAEO should make them feel— empowered, involved and respected. The personal relationships built there should be valuable; the organization should nurture and create community; it should build Big Us at a local level.

Part of this is **filling jobs** with people who are particularly qualified for them—let their work in the organization help them fulfill themselves, develop their particular talents, bring out the best in themselves, hopefully. And if you can consistently create situations like that, you'll never have any trouble getting people to stay involved at some level. They're going to be saying, "I don't just work in this organization because it makes the world a better place, though it clearly does; I work in this organization because I enjoy it: it allows me to be creative; it allows me to grow; it allows me to work with amazing people who I respect and enjoy, it allows me to be part of our growing sense of cultural community." Generally, the organization should be professional and take itself seriously, yet it should also reflect and embody Countercultural values, including fun, informality and creativity.

Well, I used to think I wanted as many people in an HAEO as possible—if there are thirty-some million Hippie-Americans, I thought, let's get thirty-some million Hippie-Americans involved. Of course, that's unrealistic and increasingly, I think, undesirable. Yes, the bigger and more inclusive the organization, the better, but then again, people are people; thus, on occasion, I've had discussions about Hippie-identity issues with people who seemed Countercultural, and I've found myself thinking, *This person is so difficult to even talk with that I don't think they'd be an asset to any organization*, and I've concluded, "So, step around such people. There will be others who will agree that Hippie-America needs an ethnic organization, who will rise to the call and be the kind of people that will make a great organization—mature, responsible, thoughtful people, team players with energy and ideas. Build the organization around them, and don't worry so much about others who for now will probably only hold us back. Further down the road, especially as they see a functioning organization emerge, they may join us and be of value."

There's an old baseball story: a catcher who's mentoring a pitcher tells him, "Don't just throw at the strike zone: throw at a particular spot in the strike zone." In other words, we shouldn't strive just to have an ethnic organization; we should **strive to have an excellent ethnic organization**—innovative, effective, world class.[183]

---

[183] One thing that might give Hippie-America an edge here is that, although I admit I have no hard evidence to prove this, I suspect we are a well-educated population.

How excellent an organization is, of course, is related to its funding. Question: **how to raise funds?** Well, there could be membership dues. There could also be a fundraising wing of the organization. You know, there are several very wealthy Hippie-Americans, including a few billionaires; these would include rock stars and others. The extent to which wealthy Counterculturists are willing to donate to and support an HAEO will make a vast difference. Also, imagine major Hippie rock bands or musical acts, for instance, willing to do national fundraising/ organizational tours.

If wealthy Counterculturists do contribute, that can also create a problem: the organization must remain democratic and not simply controlled by wealthy donors; otherwise, the non-wealthy will come to feel alienated, similar to the way in which many non-rich Americans feel alienated from our bought national "democracy."

At some point this prospective **organization will need a name;** my idea is to use the title of this book: Happily Hippie. It's positive, non-threatening and embodies Hippie values. Of course, the organization's name is not my decision to make, necessarily; ideally, it would be democratically decided upon.

*　　*　　*

Lastly here, let's deal with a crucial problem that has long bedeviled me: **how to actually start an HAEO.** Well, setting aside for the moment the whole question of reader paradigm shift and convincing Hippie-Americans to build an organization, how would we actually get started?

There are many possibilities, but here's my idea: **We'll begin with a website: HappilyHippie.net** for the present, at least.

We'd begin by **getting endorsers.** Get a list of Hippie-Americans who are out of the closet, who agree that we need an ethnic organization and who are willing to publicly say so. It's like signing the Declaration of Independence—"We pledge our lives, our fortunes and our sacred honor"; only, we're not asking that much from you: we're just asking you to acknowledge your Hippie identity and to stand up for the Counterculture—an act of courage admittedly, but one most Hippie-Americans should be able to handle.

Now, **who would we want as endorsers?** Any Hippie-American would be welcome. Still, since celebrity and name recognition in this culture carry a certain amount of power, prestige and respect, those who are better known would be particularly helpful. Though they haven't been democratically elected, there are those who because of their fame already play a leadership role in Hippie culture. Imagine thirty-or-fewer famous and thus influential and powerful Hippie-Americans openly claiming Hippie identity and endorsing the idea of an HAEO. That, I believe, would be a solid basis for building a serious organization.

How to become an endorser? We'd begin with HappilyHippie.net. Here's my idea: write a short essay telling us three things: First, you've agreed to publicly claim Hippie identity and to stand for a Hippie ethnic organization. Second, explain why you support the creation of a Hippie ethnic organization. Three, you might want to list or explain any particular talents or skills, if any, you might be interested in contributing. *One of the first things I'd like to do is create a small committee of people who want to read and filter those endorser applications.*

> I can't build an organization by myself. I need people who will say, "I agree with your idea; we do need such an organization, and I'm interested in helping. Let's do this."

Generally, **I could use some help;** I can't build an organization by myself. I need people who will say, "I agree with your idea; we do need such an organization, and I'm interested in helping. Let's do this." Eventually, a committee of endorsers would agree to lay the basis for an organization.

That's as far as I've thought these matters through; may my ideas here give readers—hopefully the future members of an HAEO—food for thought, ideas on how to begin, how to make the vision a reality.

Chapter Thirteen

The End of a Book, The Start of an Organization

"Let's get together before we get much older."
—Pete Townshend

"You don't have to see the whole staircase, just take the first step."
—Martin Luther King, Jr.

I began this book by promising paradigm shift, that I was going to give readers a pair of see-the-world glasses with a better prescription. Let's now retrace our footsteps by discussing paradigms hopefully shifted and common ideas rethought.

I began by changing the very language of the topic, introducing *Hippie-America/Hippie-American, Hippie,* moving us from a meaning of insulting stereotypes to that of being a member of an ethnic group with all the rights that entails—a respectful definition. For many, I think, the idea of taking Hippies seriously requires a paradigm shift as we been trained to disrespect and trivialize.

A primary paradigm shift in this book is understanding that Hippies Were Just a Thing of the Sixties is, in fact, a socio-political construct which has made a post-Sixties Counterculture socially invisible and shoved many Hippie-Americans into the closet. I pointed out how it's exceptional to argue that Hippiedom never even though Hippie-America lives, even thrives. That's important because it moves our discussion of Hippiedom into the present and makes it more clearly relevant.

Part of understanding that Hippie culture transcends the 1960s is the realization that Hippie culture is often transmitting generationally, that Hippie parents frequently have Hippie kids and eventually, perhaps, Hippie grandchildren.

Hippie culture, then, is comprised of several generations and people of all ages. When the 1960s ended, a majority of today's Counterculturists had yet to be born.

I made estimates of the number of Hippie-Americans (over ten percent of the population) and of the international Counterculture: roughly 100 million people.

Of course, the central thesis of this book is that Hippie culture is a modern American ethnicity. Ethnicity involves volition; ethnicities are dynamic. Hippiedom is an ethnicity created through non-traditional, technological means, particularly mass media; it is the outgrowth of a choice to join what sociologists call a *revitalization movement.* Hippiedom is a synthetic ethnic minority both in how it was formed in its eclectic content.

The subject of Hippies and their social status is not trivial but of the utmost importance since it has a direct affect on US society and politics. Generally, Republicans have claimed that Democrats were just a bunch of hippies and in so doing have pushed the nation towards fascism. As is most bigotry, Hippie hating is about rightist political opportunism; we can't really understand modern American history without Ethnic-Hippies Theory.

Hippie culture is not an ideological movement; there is no Hippie philosophy. Rather, there are common underlying values, and these lead to a variety of viewpoints. Particularly, it's a political stereotype to assume all Hippie-Americans are liberals with liberal opinions on all subjects.

Other common paradigms/definitions of Hippie culture such as "The Sixties Generation," Just a Phase of Life, or what I called the Mythic Definition (to be a true Hippie, you must be a Gandalf) don't work and should be abandoned.

Society has treated Hippiedom much the way it has treated traditionally recognized racial and ethnic minorities; generally, regarding the Counterculture, American bigots are the same old dog doing the same old trick only with a new toy. In particular, stereotypes of Hippies echo those of traditionally recognized minorities.

While neoconservatives and other bigots routinely portray an innocent America violently attacked by marauding Hippies, in fact, it's American society has been violent and aggressive towards the Counter-culture, and their distorted fantasy world here is denial and projection.

According to sociologist Jack Levin's *The Functions of Prejudice,* there are three causes of prejudice in individuals: one, the desire to feel superior to another; two, the inability to deal with ambiguity and the need to view people in simplistic good-or-bad terms which can be easily defined by race, culture or nationality; three, the need for a safe place to displace one's anger—if the powers that be (or mom and dad) have treated you badly, don't rebel against them; find a scapegoat, someone to see as below you on the social hierarchy, and hate them. These three qualities often signal something called the *authoritarian personality.*

These elements, all present in traditional forms of bigotry, seem present in Hippie-haters.

Hippie/Counterculture can be clearly defined and such individuals and institutions, identified.

Hippiedom has been phenomenally successful, including inventing the PC and making major contributions to the internet, building a booming natural/organic foods industry, creating Integrative

> **"Respectable" America has worked relentlessly to make contemporary Hippie-America invisible: constantly telling us either Hippie culture ended with the 1960s or questioning whether it ever existed to begin with. But that's not reality; that's a politically motivated social construct—a canard.**

Medicine, and beginning the greening of America. We have also made numerous contributions to arts, industry and the larger society, including healthy, progressive values. Far from being parasites, Hippies have been leaders in philanthropy. It's a slander that we are the essence of irresponsibility; generally, Hippie culture has been a boon to society.

Fat doesn't make you fat, and the Hippie diet has made America hands-down healthier.

Many "ex-hippies," etc. are in fact just middle aged Hippies who don't know how else to speak about their identity. Many such people are effectively "in the closet."

Many Hippies have self-esteem issues related to Hippie identity and would feel better with an attitude of Hippie pride and self-respect. Hippie-Americans shouldn't internalize oppression, then, but develop a pride movement. If Hippie culture hasn't been perfect, no culture has, and we have nothing, really, to apologize for.

One aspect of ethnicity is distinctive recreational substances/drugs. All cultures use drugs and always have. The real question, then, isn't so much whether a person or culture uses drugs: it's whether they are using them responsibly or abusing them. One reason we often can't see this is because of the pejorative manner in which the term "drugs" is used, too often excluding legal drugs such as caffeine, alcohol and nicotine. Also, American society, courtesy the War on Drugs, falsely assumes all marijuana use is abuse.

The legal status of a drug has no effect on the extent to which that drug is used or abused in society.

Ethnic-Hippies Theory gives us a consistent, necessary understanding of the modern War on Drugs.

Gateway—the notion that people will be seduced by even casual marijuana use, "graduate" to heroin addiction and likely then die—is the dumbest argument that ever fell off the turnip truck.

American drug-prohibition laws are not about protecting the public health but about persecuting minorities.

Unlike alcohol, marijuana intoxication doesn't necessarily mean impairment.

Playing their "patriotic" parts in the War on Drugs, American science and American medicine have often disgraced themselves. War on Drugs studies are biased, unreliable pseudo-science, the bought-and-sold propaganda of the "conservative cultural revolution."

> The War on Drugs is an American fascist movement; far from being a failure, it's been highly successful as its true purposes are to persecute minorities and drive the nation to the right.

Instead of saving America and Western Civilization, the War on Drugs has done it tremendous harm. The War on Drugs doesn't protect American children: it hurts them, particularly, minority children. The War on Drugs is an American fascist movement; far from being a failure, it's been highly successful as its true purposes are to persecute minorities and drive the nation to the right.

The War on Drugs is responsible for the vast majority of drug-related violence in the US and in much of the Third World, like Mexico.

The legalization movement is essentially an expression of Hippie nationalism and one more reason why we need EHT to understand modern American history.

American Country-Western culture is also an unrecognized ethnicity.

LSD seldom makes people violent, and since the Manson killers were actually on speed, not LSD, the Jeffrey MacDonald defense story is, once again, unbelievable.

The anti-War in Vietnam movement and Hippiedom were not one in the same. Where the two did overlap, this is to the Counterculture's credit since that anti-war movement was essentially right and helped save humanity from nuclear war.

"Hippie protestors" did not spit on returning Vietnam veterans. Hippie culture has two poles, the spiritual and the activist.

We need a Hippie American Ethnic Organization (HAEO); forming one is a necessary thing that can make America and the world better.

That building such an organization starts within the reader's head with paradigm shift and EHT—here and now. In the words of Bob Marley, "Emancipate yourself. None but ourselves can free our minds."

* * *

Let's now discuss the advantages of EHT for the individual and of an HAEO for the nation. My goal in writing this book has been to change the world. Let's begin with you, the reader.

First, whether you're Hippie or non-Hippie, wouldn't it be nice to live in a world that makes sense, a place where we don't have to constantly employ euphemisms and the strange duplicity of "Hippies don't exist"/"Hippies do exist"? Dispensing with pretense and moving beyond enforced dishonesty is liberating. For me, it's like some clutter in my mind has been organized and made sense of, and I feel better for it. So, let's first use EHT to free our minds.

In our bigoted society, Hippie identity brings with it heavy baggage: shaming, stereotyping, scapegoating, intimidation, violence, hatred, and legal persecution—the behaviors and policies of attempted ethnocide. America, misled and bullied by neoconservatism, has vilified us. But remember the words of Eleanor Roosevelt: "No one can make you feel inferior without your permission." Let's not give that permission. Why should we let small-minded, angry and insecure people decide our course in life? Thus, we can defer to the bullies, to the bigots, to American fascism, or we can set a saner course.

In the world of the oppressed, that saner course is known as a "pride movement." We didn't lose the War in Vietnam for America or spit on returning Vietnam veterans. We didn't get the neighbor kid hooked on heroin. We didn't burn the flag. We didn't destroy America's moral fiber. Let's stop acting like we're guilty of crimes we didn't commit, stop apologizing for things we never did.

Then, there's the other side of the coin: the amazing contributions of the Counterculture to the nation and the world. Our successes are stunning. Instead of being ambivalent about Hippie identity or relegating it to some questionable part of our younger lives, we should be celebrating it. As it turns out, we made a great cultural choice, one that may save ourselves and this planet; now, let's stop second-guessing ourselves. We need to be comfortable with our Hippie identity; we need to develop confidence in and an appreciation for it.

> **We didn't lose the War in Vietnam for America or spit on returning Vietnam veterans. We didn't get the neighbor kid hooked on heroin. We didn't burn the flag. We didn't destroy America's moral fiber. Let's stop acting like we're guilty of crimes we didn't commit, stop apologizing for things we never did.**

One way the reader can start this psychological transformation is in her or his use of language. Become comfortable with terms like *Hippie-American*. Also, are you one who says, "I'm just an old hippie" even though you're not really old? Let's stop using language that assumes Hippies Were Just a Thing of the Sixties and all its demeaning, disrespectful corollaries.

Think of Hippie identity as something that you have now and will have in the future, and if you have children, there's a good chance they'll have Hippie identity too. This healing, then, isn't just for you, it's for them, and someday, maybe, for future Hippie generations. Let's stop accepting the ethnocidal assumption that Hippie culture either has died or soon will die. We have a bright future, a crucial role to play in human evolution.

Counterculturists so often support other oppressed outgroups and fight prejudice in general; when do we start supporting and standing up for ourselves? Let's stop being ashamed or embarrassed; let's start being proud, self-accepting and not afraid to take ourselves seriously.

Next, consider what the formation of a Hippie-American Ethnic Organization, could do for the larger society and this nation. Well, America has become almost a parody of what it's supposed to be. The American Dream no longer has much to do with building community or an egalitarian, democratic society or some shining spiritual city upon a hill; it now means simply the crass accumulation of great wealth by a fortunate few. Modern America is about transferring wealth upwards—making the filthy rich filthy richer at the expense of the great majority of society. To enable their shameless greed, the far right has had to demagogue it up at election time, and a large portion of what constitutes respectable, politically viable demagoguery in modern America is Hippie-hating and Hippie-baiting. We must change that.

And beyond elections, criminalizing over ten percent of the population has been instrumental in making America fascistic— a repressive place where hatred, cynicism and prejudice have grown. Ethnocide directed at the Counterculture has created a safe house for those launching attacks on the rights and civil liberties of all Americans.

Let's stand up for Hippie culture and its right to exist. Let's fight stereotyping and scapegoating. Let's connect with gay America; let's connect with Lesbian America. Let's cultivate Country-Western America. Let's stand by African-America and encourage African-America to stand by us. Let's ally with NOW and modern American feminism. Let's build a positive relationship with Hispanics, Mexican-Americans, in particular. Let's broker relationships with both Jewish-Americans and Arab/Muslim Americans. Let's connect with Counterculturists around the world.

We've been born into an age where humanity faces challenges unprecedented in world history—in particular, to save our traditional environment from sudden and traumatic climate change, to save this planet. We know how important a player the Counterculture has been in that struggle already, and that's another reason why Hippie culture needs to be organized—to be free and to flourish.

If Hippiedom began as a revitalization movement that evolved into an ethnicity, let's follow through and do as we first intended: let's continue revitalizing and transforming America, from the food it eats to the values it holds to how it treats Mother Earth. Let us find that path where soul meets body and then make that path our cultural destiny.

By creating an HAEO, we grow up, we come of age, we claim our rightful place in the multicultural tapestry that is modern America. And if in 1980, it was a scary time to be Hippie-American, it's not so scary today. Generally, we're living in a more sophisticated and tolerant society, and Hippie-America is far stronger, more stable and probably larger. If you decide to stand—and especially if we stand together—we won't be crushed. Rather, we will rise. Let us be happily Hippie.

Works Cited

Chapter One Works Cited
None

Chapter Two Works Cited
Ashby, LeRoy. *With Amusement for All: A History of American Popular Culture since 1830.* University Press of Kentucky, Lexington. 2006
Allstays.com. "Natural Food Store Locations." 1999-2013. www.Allstays.com. 1 May 2016 <http://www.allstays.com/c/health-food-store-locations.htm>.
Associated Press. "Bin Laden son aims to be 'ambassador of peace': Offspring of al-Qaida leader seeks understanding between Muslims, West." 21 Jan. 2008. MSNBC. 15 Jan. 2010 <http://www.msnbc.msn.com/id/22711392/ ns/world_news-terrorism//>.
Barker, Chris. "10 Rock Concerts which Resulted in Bloodshed." 19 Oct. 2012. Social Science Careers. 19 Jan. 2016 <http://www.socialsciencecareers.org/ 10-rock-concerts-which-resulted-in-bloodshed/>.
CDC. "Black or African American Populations." 31 July 2015. Center for Disease Control and Prevention. 15 Jan. 2016 <http://www.cdc.gov/minorityhealth/populations/ REMP/black.html>.
Country Boys. Dir. David Sutherland. PBS Frontline. WGBH, 2006.
Daniels, Stephen. "US organic food market to grow 14% from 2013-18." 3 Jan.2014. *FoodNavigator-USA.com.* 28 Oct. 2015. <http://www.foodnavigator-usa.com/ Markets/US-organic-food-market-to-grow-14-from-2013-18>.
Frick, David. "Phish Reunite Hippie Nation." Rolling Stone 2 April 2009.
Gitlin, Todd *The Sixties: Years of Hope, Days of Rage.* Bantam Books 1987
Haight-Ashbury Free Clinics. "Health Care is a Right—Not a Privilege." 2008. www. hafci.org. 15 Feb. 2010 <http://www.hafci.org/CD_Info.html>.
Hippies. Perf. Peter (narrator) Coyote. The History Channel. 2007.
"Hippy Havens." 10 Feb. 2010. Hippyland. Ed. Skip (webmaster) Stone. 16 Jan. 2016 <http://www.hippy.com/havens.htm>.
Huffington Post. "Best Colleges For Hippies In 2013-14 Ranked By Princeton Review." 12 Aug. 2013. www.huffingtonpost.com. 15 Jan. 2016 <http://www.huffingtonpost. com/2013/08/12/best-colleges-hippies-princeton-review_n_3741519.html>.
Madigan, Tim. "Vermont, the anti-Texas: It's grabbing headlines, but this little state of Zen and modern-day hippies wants no part of the rest of us." Fort Worth Star-Telegram (TX) 27 Nov. 2000: 1.
Markoff, John. What the Dormouse Said: How the 60s Counterculture Shaped the Personal Computer Industry. New York: Viking Penguin, 2005.
McManis, Sam. "Mighty 'dyno' mite." Boulder Weekly 18 June 2009: 33-34.
Nickum, Ryan. "17 Best U.S. Cities for Hippies." 7 July 2013. blog.estately.com 12 Jan. 2016 <http://blog.estately.com/2013/07/17-best-u-s-cities-for-hippies/>.
Nieves, Evelyn. "Attacks on a Gay Teen-Ager Prompt Outrage and Soul-Searching." New York Times 19 Feb. 1999: A12
Powell's Books. "Wild Child: Girlhoods in the Counterculture by Chelsea Cain." Powell's Books.com. 15 Jan. 2010 <http://www.powells.com/biblio/9781580050319>.
Powers, Ann. "A New Variety of Flower Child In Full Bloom: Music and the Internet Nourish a Counterculture." New York Times 19 Feb. 1999: E1.

Ryan, Christopher. "Fascinating Figures: Andrew Weil." 16 Oct. 2009. www.psychologytoday.com. 5 Feb. 2015 <https://www.psychology today.com/blog/sex-dawn/200910/fascinating-figures-andrew-weil>.

"San Marcos Journal; A Move for Marijuana Where the 60's Survive."10 April 1991. New York Times. 3 Dec. 2015. http://www.nytimes.com/1991/ 04/10/us/ san-marcos-journal-a-move-for-marijuana-where-the-60-s-survive.html

Stone, Skip. "Hippies from A to Z: The Young Hippies." 2015. *Hippyland* http://www.hipplanet.com/books/atoz/young.htm. 3 Dec. 2015.

Smith, Gene. "Hippies Praised for Plant Work." New York Times 22 Dec. 1969: 54.

Swanson, Ana. "Justice Scalia suggests asking a hippie about gay marriage. Here's how to find one near you." 26 June 2015. www.washingtonpost.com. 11 Jan. 2016 <https://www.washingtonpost.com/ news/wonk/wp/2015/06/26/justice- scalia-suggests-asking-a-hippie-about-gay-marriage-heres-how-to-find-one-near-you/>.

"The Counterculture." *World Book*, 2009.

The Doors. Dir. Oliver Stone. Perf. Meg Ryan Val Kilmer. 1991.

The Roots of Rock n' Roll. Dir. Arthur Forrest. 1981.

www.boston.com. "Hippie by Barry Miles." 2004. www.boston.com. 20 Dec. 2009 <(http://www. boston.com/ae/books/articles/ 2004/12/05/ from_jackie_o_to_hippies _a_bumper_crop_of_gift_books/)>.

Chapter Three Works Cited

Associated Press. Irving Kristol, 'Godfather' of Neo-Conservatism, Dies at 89. 18 September 2009. 24 March 2010 <http://www.foxnews.com/us/2009/09/18/ irving-kristol-godfather-neo-conservatism-dies/>.

Balko, Radley. "Drug War Terrorsim." 26 Sept. 2002. FoxNews.com. 7 Feb. 2005.

Baseball, Vol. 6. By Ken Burns and Geoffrey C. Ward. Dir. Ken Burns. Prods.Ken Burns and Lynn Novick. 1994.

Baum, Daniel. The War on Drugs and the Politics of Failure. Boston: Little Brown and Company, 1996.

Broder, David. "Swift Boats and Old Wounds." Washington Post 24 Aug. 2004: A17.

Brokaw, Tom. "Interview, Jimmy Carter." Rolling Stone 3-17 May 2007: 55-58.

Bump, Philip. "Defying Reagan, Obama Returns Solar Panels to the White House." 13 August 2013. www.thewire.com. 11 Jan. 2016 <http://www. thewire.com/ politics/2013/08/defying-reagan-obama-returns-solar-panels-white-house/68381/>.

Byrne, Carol. "Another fiery populist from earlier political era: Echoes of Wallace emerge in Buchanan." Star Tribune (Minneapolis, MN) 5 March 1996: Metro edition, 1A.

Caban, Ana. "Feeling right at home outside the mainstream." Milwaukee Journal Sentinel (WI) 3 March 2002: 2A.

Campbell, Duncan. "Bush tars drug takers with aiding terrorists: Mandatory jail makes a drugs Gulag." 8 Aug. 2002. www.guardian.co.uk. 15 Jan. 2005.

Cannon, Bob. "Banned on the Fourth of July (the Beach Boys)." Entertainment Weekly 9 April 1993: 64.

CNN. "Nancy Reagan: First Lady, First Friend." CNN.com. 6 Dec. 2009 <http:// www.cnn.com/SPECIALS/2004/reagan/stories/first.lady/index.html>.

Common Sense for Drug Policy. "Marijuana." DrugWarFacts.org. 6 Dec. 2009 <http:// www.drugwarfacts.org/cms/node/53>.

Common Sense for Drug Policy. "Nixon Tapes Show Roots of Marijuana Prohibition: Misinformation, Culture Wars and Prejudice." 2002. www.csdp.org. 24 March 2002 <www.csdp.org - www.drugwarfacts.org>.

Curt. "Fred Thompson – Kill The Terrorists & Punch The Hippies!" 18 Dec. 2007. www.floppingraces.net. 2010 17 June <http://www.floppingaces.net/2007/ 12/18/ fred-thompson-kill-the-terrori/>.

DeFrank, Thomas. "McCain bashes Schumer, Hil for Woodstock memorial." 22 Oct. 2007. New York Daily News on-line. 30 Oct. 2007 <http://www. nydailynews.com/news/wn_report/2007/ 10/22/2007- 10-22_mccain_bashes_ schumer_hil_for_woodstock_-2.html >.

Dowd, Maureen. "Cultural Drifter." 3 Oct. 1999. New York Times. 4 Dec. 2015 <http:// www.nytimes.com/1999/10/03/opinion/liberties-culturaldrifter.html>.

___. "President Frat Boy?" New York Times 7 April 1999: A21.

___. "G.O.P.'s Rising Star Pledges to Right Wrongs of the Left." New York Times 10 Nov. 1994: A1.

___. "Ozone Man Sequel." 28 Feb. 2007. NYTimes.com. 25 Oct. 2015. <http://www. nytimes.com/2007/02/28/opinion/28dowd.html?_r=0>.

Eakman, Beverly. "The Smell of Battle." 31 Oct. 2004. www.newswithviews. com. 21 March 2005 <http://www.newswithviews.com/Eakman/beverly18.htm>.

Eskenazi, Joe. "Democratic Candidate Portrays San Francisco as Haven of Dirty Hippies." 13 Oct. 2010 www.sfweekly.com. 1 Jan. 2016 <http://www.sfweekly. com/thesnitch/2010/10/13/democratic-candidate-portrays-san-francisco-as-haven-of-dirty-hippies>.

George Wallace: Settin' the Woods on Fire. By Steve Fayer, Daniel McCabe and Paul Stekler. Dirs Daniel McCabe and Paul Stekler. Perf. David (host) McCullough. PBS: The AmericanExperience. WGBH Boston, 2000.

Geraghty, Jim. "He Should Have Punched More Hippies." 22 Jan. 2008. National Review Online. 16 June 2010 <http://www.nationalreview.com/ campaign-spot/ 10621/ he-should-have-punched-more-hippies>.

Goodman, Linda. "More proof of Kerry's treason." 17 Oct. 2004. Linda-Goodman.com. 4 Dec. 2015 <http://www.linda-goodman.com/ubb/Forum16/HTML/000711.html>.

Gordinier, Jeff. "Mr. Gump Goes to Washington: The connection between Forrest Gump and Newt Gingrich." 10 Feb. 1995. Entertainment Weekly. 31 Aug. 2009 <http:// www.ew.com/ew/article/0,296004,00.html>.

Graham, Michael. "John Kerry: Not So Swift." 25 Aug. 2004. www.Pittsburg.com. 3 Sept. 2004 <http://www.freetimes.com/Usual_Suspects/suspects.html>.

Grant, Peter. "Texaco Hits 4 in Race Scandal." 7 Nov. 1996. NY Daily News.com 18 Feb. 2010 <http://www.nydailynews.com/ archives/ news/1996/11/07/1996-11-07_texaco_hits_4_in_race_scandal.html>.

Jacobs, Ron. "Long Live People's Park!: Showdown in the Counterculture Corral." 23 March 2003. Counterpunch.org. 18 Feb. 2010 <http://www.counterpunch.org/ jacobs05232003.html>.

Kennedy, Robert. "Was the 2004 Election Stolen?" 1 June 2006. Originally published in Rolling Stone.18 Nov. 2009 <http://www.truthout.org/article/robert-f->.

Klein, Edward. The Truth About Hillary: What She Knew, When She Knew It, and How Far She'll Go to Become President. New York: Sentinel (Penguin), 2005.

Krugman, Paul. The Conscience of a Liberal. New York: Norton, 2007.

Levin, Jack. The Functions of Prejudice. New York: Harper and Row, 1975.

388

Mojoey. "Are we all terrorists?" 14 July 2007. Blog: Deep Thoughts: Sometimes I Just Have to Speak My Mind. 18 Mov. 2009 <mojoey.blogspot.com/2007_07_01_archive. html>.

Montopoli, Brian. "New McCain Ad: "Love"." 8 July 2008. CBS News. 12 Feb. 2010 <http://www.cbsnews.com/blogs/2008/07/08/ politics/horserace/entry4240647. shtml>.

Murray, Shailagh. "Clinton Dealt a Bummer on Woodstock Museum." 18 Oct. 2007. Washington Post on-line. 6 Dec. 2009 <http://voices. washingtonpost. com/44/2007/10/18/clinton_dealt_a_bummer_on_wood.html>.

Osborn, Scott. "WIKILEAKS: Hippie Hillary Clinton's Gas Guzzling Hippie Van Has a Bed; Mood Lighting!." 19 Oct. 2016. JoeForAmerica.com. 9 April 2017 <http://joeforamerica.com/2016/10/wikileaks-hippie-hillary-clintons-gas-guzzling-hippie-van-bed-mood-lighting/>.

Plumer, Bradford. "The Divided States of America." www.inthesetimes.com. 13 June 2008 <http://www.inthesetimes.com/article/ 3743/the_divided_states_of_america>.

Reagan Quotes. 11 Feb. 2010. 11 Feb. 2010 <http://www.geocities.com/>.

Reel Bad Arabs: How Hollywood Vilifies a People. By Jack Shaheen and Jeremy Earp. Dirs. Jeremy Earp and Sut Jhally. IMBDbPro, 2006.

Roberts, Steven V. "The War Between Reagan and Berkeley." New York Times 25 May 1967: E13.

Rich, Frank. "Blowing In the Wind." New York Times 20 Nov. 1994: E15.

Rosin, Hanna. "Among the Hillary Haters." March 2015. TheAtlantic.com. 9 April 2017 <https:// www.theatlantic.com/magazine/archive/2015/03/among-the-hillary-haters/ 384976/>.

Rowland, Darrel. "Buchanan Assures Ohio Rally He's Not Giving Up." Columbus Dispatch (OH) 14 March 1996: 3A

Ryan, Joseph J. "Career flip-flopper Kerry's voting record places him on far left of the Democratic Party." Bucks County Courier Times (Levittown, PA) 17 March 2004: 14A.

SFist. "Bill O'Reilly Spreads the Love." 18 Oct. 2006. www.sfist.com. 21 Oct. 2006 <www.sfist.com/archives/>.

Taibbi, Matt. "Mad Dog Palin." Rolling Stone 5 April 2010.

Torgoff, Martin. Can't Find My Way Home: America in the Great Stoned Age, 1945-2000. New York:Simon & Shuster, 2004.

UPI. "Watt says rock won't roll at July 4 bash." Daily Iowan (Iowa City) April 1983: 1+.

Waldman, Paul. "Hillary Clinton, Bill Clinton, and the Long But Fading Shadow of the 1960s." 18 Feb. 2015. TheAmericanProspect. 9 April 2017 <http://prospect.org/ waldman/ hillary-clinton-bill-clinton-and-long-fading-shadow-1960s>.

Will, George F. "About That 'Sixties Idealism': Meet Wolfgang and Lisa Von Nester who 'did their own thing'." Newsweek 21 Aug. 1995: 72.

Chapter Four Works Cited

"Concepts of Ethnicity." Harvard Encyclopedia of American Ethnic Groups. Cambridge: Belnap/Harvard, 1980. 240-42.

Hawkes, Rebecca. "'Lovely California girl': Beach Boys pay tribute to Nancy Reagan at concert in Texas." 8 March 2016. www.telegraph.co.uk. 9 April 2017 <http:// www.telegraph.co.uk/music/news/lovely-california-girl-beach-boys-pay-tribute-to-nancy-reagan-at/>.

Helmer, John. Drugs and Minority Oppression. New York: The Seabury Press, 1975.

Roszak, Theodore. The Making of a Counter Culture, Reflections on the Technocratic Society and its Youthful Opposition. Garden City (NJ): Anchor Books, 1969.

Chapter Five Works Cited

Abrahams, Roger D. "Folklore." The Harvard Encyclopedia of American Ethnic Groups. Ed.Thermstrom et al. Belnap Press/Harvard University Press,1980. 370-71.

Adler, Jerry and Shawn Doherty. "The Graying of Aquarius: Some people cling to the values of the '60s—and they're still called hippies." Newsweek 30 March 1987: 56-58.

Baum, Daniel. The War on Drugs and the Politics of Failure. Boston: Little Brown and Company, 1996.

Belasco, Warren J. Appetite for Change: How the Counterculture Took On The Food Industry 1968-1988. Ithaca: Cornell University Press, 1993, Updated ed.

Boyle, T. Coraghessan. Drop City. New York: Viking, 2003.

Brown, Patricia Leigh. "Museum Gives Hippie Stuff The Acid Test." New York Times 16 Dec.1999.

Brumberg, Joan. "Review of Appetite for Change: How the Counterculture Took on the Food Industry, 1966-1988 by Warren J. Belasco." The Nation 9 April 1990: 494.

Burns, John F. "Off Canada, The Hippies Are Evolving." New York Times 19 Aug. 1987: 3.

Daniels, Charlie (and band). "The Ballad of Uneasy Rider." Essential Super Hits By Charlie Daniels. 2004.

Dreman, Craig. "Hippie ethnobotany." Whole Earth Review Fall 1989.: 25.

Guthrie, Arlo. "Alice' Restaurant." Alice's Restaurant. Reprise, 1967.

Hager, Stephen. "History of the Cannabis Cup: Steven Hager tells the tale of the world's foremost marijuana competition." 17 June 2002. High Times. 16 June 2005 <http://www.cannabiscup.com/ht/cancup/content.php?bid=9&aid=9>>.

Hagle, Louiser and Dorothy R. Bates, eds. The New Farm vegetarian cookbook. Summertown: Book Pub., 1989.

Haight-Ashbury Free Clinics. "Health Care is a Right—Not a Privilege." 2008.www.hafci. org. 15 Feb. 2010 <http://www.hafci.org/CD_Info.html>.

Hedgepeth, William and Dennis Stock (photographer). The Alternative. Collier Books, 1970 (1st ed.).

Helms, Chet. "About this event . . ." 3 April 2010. www.summeroflove.org. 3 April 2010 <http://www.summeroflove.org/event.html>.

Herer, Jack. The Emperor Wears No Clothes: Cannabis and the Conspiracy Against Marijuana 11th ed. Phoenix: Paper Master, 1998.

"Introduction." The Harvard Encyclopedia of American Ethnic Groups. Ed. Stephan et al. Thermstrom. Cambridge: Belnap Press/Harvard, 1980. i-ix.

Katzen, Mollie. The Moosewood Cookbook: Recipes from Moosewood Restaurant, Ithaca, New York. Berkeley: Ten Speed Press, 1977.

Kennett, Francis with Caroline MacDonald-Haig. Ethnic Dress: A Comprehensive Guide to the Folk Costume of the World. New York: Facts on File, 1995.

Kesey, Ken. One flew over the cuckoo's nest. New York, N.Y.: New American Library, 1989, c1962.

Kruh, Nancy. "'90s Kids Follow the Lead of '60s Parents: 30 Years Later, Counterculture Ideals Hold Appeal." The Seattle Times 9 Sept. 1997: L5 (Scene).

Madigan, Tim. "Vermont, the anti-Texas: It's grabbing headlines, but this little state of Zen and modern-day hippies wants no part of the rest of us." Fort Worth Star-Telegram (TX) 27Nov. 2000: 1.

Miller, Joel. "Subtracting the 4th Amendment." 11 Sept. 2000. World Net Daily. 16 Jan. 2005 <http://www.worldnetdaily.com>.

Petersen, William. "Prejudice." The Harvard Encyclopedia of American Ethnic Groups. Ed. Stephan Thermstrom et al. Cambridge: Harvard University Press, 1980. 234-42.

Powers, Ann. "A New Variety of Flower Child In Full Bloom: Music and theInternet Nourish a Counterculture." New York Times 19 Feb. 1999: E1.

Reich, Charles. The Greening of America: How the youth revolution is trying to make America livable. New York: Random House, 1970.

Sanders, Ed. "The Illiad." Sanders Truckstop. Collector's Choice Music, 2008.

Schaefer, Richard T. Racial and Ethnic Groups, 6th ed. New York: HarperCollins College Publishers, 1996.

Sobran, Joseph. "Woodstock Reality: Mass-Marketed Loners." 20 Aug. 1989. www.VictoriaAdvocate.com. 8 April 2010 <http://news.google.com/newspapers?nid=861&dat= 19890820&id=AGQdAAAAIBAJ&sjid=R1kEAAAA IBAJ&pg=3016,4039156>.

Taylor, Mike. "The natural wonder of Boulder: "We're going to revolutionize the way people eat."." www.cobizmag.com (Colorado Business Magazine). 22 March 2005 <http://www.cobizmag.com/articles.cfm?article_id=284>.>.

Tie Died: Rock 'n Roll's Most Dedicated Fans. Dir. Andrew Behar. Cathay Sterling, Inc. & Padded Cell & Arrowhead Productions. 1995.

Time, Inc. (correspondents of). The Hippies. Ed. J.D. Brown. New York, 1967.

"Tradition." American Heritage College Dictionary, 3rd ed. 1993.

Vecoli, Rudolph J. "Introduction." Gale Encyclopedia of Multicultural America. 1995.

Waters, Mary C. Ethnic Options: Choosing Identities in America. Berkeley:University of California Press, 1990.

Weiner, Rex and Deanne Stillman. Woodstock Census. New York: Viking, 1979.

Will, George F. "About That 'Sixties Idealism': Meet Wolfgang and Lisa Von Nester who 'did their own thing'." Newsweek 21 Aug. 1995: 72.

Wilson, Wes, Bonnie MacLean, Victor Moscosco et al. The Psychedelic Experience: Rock Posters from the San Francisco Bay Area, 1965-71. Denver Art Museum, Denver, CO.

Wolfe, Tom. The electric kool-aid acid test. New York: Bantam, 1968.

Zinsser, William. On Writing Well: An Informal Guide to Writing Nonfiction, 2nd ed. New York: Harper & Row, 1980.

Chapter Six Works Cited

Adamy, Janet. "Behind a food giant's success: An unlikely soy-milk alliance." 2 Feb. 2005. The Wall St. Journal.com. 10 June 2010 <http://www.marconews.com/news/2005 / feb/02/ndn_behind_a_food_giant_s_success__an_unlikely_soy/>.

Adler, Jerry and Shawn Doherty. "The Graying of Aquarius: Some people cling to the values of the '60s—and they're still called hippies." Newsweek 30 March 1987: 56-58.

Anderson, Christopher. "Former Nederland cop charged in '71 'hippy' slaying." Boulder Daily Camera 13 Sept. 1997: 1A.

Anti-Hippie Action League. Suppressing Hippie-Dom World Wide. 21 Jan. 2008. 21 Jan. 2008 <http://www.devo.com/tft/hippie/index.html>.

Baron, Reuben M. "An Ecological View of Accuracy." Stereotype Accuracy: Toward Appreciating Group Differences. Ed. Yuah-Ting et al Lee. Washington, DC: American PsychologicalAssociation, 1995.

Baum, Daniel. The War on Drugs and the Politics of Failure. Boston: Little Brown and Company, 1996.

Baywatch, "River of No Return". Perf. David and Pamela Anderson Hasselhoff. Prod. David et al Hasselhoff. NBC, All-American Entertainment, 1989-2001.

Belasco, Warren J. Appetite for Change: How the Counterculture Took On The Food Industry, 1968-1988. Ithaca: Cornell University Press, 1993, Updated ed.

«Bernie Hayzy.» <www.ukcia.org/culture/users.php>.

Big Hawaii. Dir. Lawrence Doheny et al. Perf. John Dehner and Cliff Potts. NBC. 1977-1978.

Brainyquote. "John Wayne quotes." 2016. www.brainyquote.com. 16 April 2016 <http://www.brainyquote.com/quotes/quotes/j/johnwayne383173.html>.

Brislin, Tom. "Exotics, Erotics, and Coco-Nuts: Stereotypes of Pacific Islanders." Images that Injure: Pictorial Stereotypes in the Media. Ed. Paul Martin Lester. Westport: Praeger, 1996 35-40.

Brown, Michael E. "The Condemnation and Persecution of Hippies." The Anti-American Generation. Ed.Edgar Z. Friedenberg. Chicago: Aldine Pub. Co., 1971.

Brown, Toni A. "Editorial." Relix: Music for the Mind Feb. 1994: 5.

Callum-Penso, Lillia. "A Hippie Wedding?" 2 Aug. 2004. Greenville online.com. 14 Jan. 2005 <http://www.upstatelink.com/people/weddings/8-3.htm >.

Capp, Al. The Best of L'il Abner. New York: Holt, Reinhart and Winston, 1978.

"Concepts of Ethnicity." Harvard Encyclopedia of American Ethnic Groups. Cambridge: Belnap/Harvard,1980. 240-42.

Conrad, Chris, Mikki Norris and Virginia Resner. Human Rights and the US Drug War: A treatise based on the UN Universal Declaration of Human Rights and the US Bill of Rights. El Cerrito (CA): Creative Xpressions, 2001.

Davis, Jimm. "Letter to the editor." 27 March 2002. www.csindy.com (The Independent— Colorado Springs). 22 May 2005 <http://www.csindy.com/csindy/2002-04-04/ letters.html>.

Dodd, David. "The Annotated "Ripple"." 1 September 2006. artsites.ucsc.edu. 2 June 2010 <http://artsites.ucsc.edu/gdead/agdl/ripple.html>.

Easy Rider. By Dennis Hopper, Peter Fonda and Terry Southern. Dir. Dennis Hopper. Perf. DennisHopper, Peter Fonda and Jack Nicholson. Columbia, 1969.

"Eating Up: As Shoppers Grow Finicky, Big Food Has Big Problems." Wall St. Journal 21 May 2004: A1.

Gaffney, Frank J., Jr. "Counterculture assault on the military." Washington Times 30 June 1998: 15.

Ganje, Lucy A. "Native American Stereotypes." Lester, Paul Martin (editor). Images that Injure: Pictorial Stereotypes in the Media. Westport, CN: Praeger, 2003. 41-46.

Griffith, Winthrop. "People's Park—240' x 430' of Confrontation." New York Times 29 June 1969, National ed.: SM5.

Guinness, Os. Dust of Death: The Sixties Counterculture and How It Changed America Forever.Wheaton, IL: Crossway Books, 1994.

Healy, Jim. Des Moines Register 28 June 1983.

Herer, Jack. The Emperor Wears No Clothes: Cannabis and the Conspiracy Against Marijuana. 11ᵗʰ ed. Phoenix: Paper Master, 1998.

Krassner, Paul. "The Communal Truth." 8-14 Nov. 2006. New York Press. 24 June 2008 <http://www.nypress.com/18/32/books/paulkrassner.cfm>.

Krassner, Paul. "Why Was Peter McWilliams Murdered?" 2000. www. jeffpolachek. com. 25 Nov.2014<http://www.jeffpolachek.com/ petermcwilliams.info/articles/ WhyWasPeterMurdered.html>.

Kurlansky, Mark. 1968: The Year That Rocked the World. New York: Random House, 2004.

Levin, Jack. The Functions of Prejudice. New York: Harper and Row, 1975.

Levinson, David H. "Introduction." Ethnic Groups Worldwide: A Ready Reference Handbook. Phoenix: Oryx Press, 1998. vii-xxvii.

Lind, Angus. "Cool, man! It's a hippie dictionary." 10 June 2004. San Diego Union-Tribune online. 28June 2010 <http://www.signonsandiego.com/ uniontrib/20040610/ news_1c10hippy.html>.

Lopresti, Mike. "Red Sox proving to be a fine hair band." 25 Oct. 2004. USA Today. http:// usatoday30.usatoday.com/sports/columnist/lopresti/2004-10-25-lopresti-series_x. htm. 5 Dec. 2015.

Martindale, Carolyn. "Newspaper Stereotypes of African Americans." Images that Injure: Pictorial Stereotypes in the Media. Ed. Paul Martin Lester.Westport: Praeger, 1996. 21-25.

Miller, Joel. "Subtracting the 4ᵗʰ Amendment." 11 Sept. 2000. World Net Daily. 16 Jan. 2005 <http://www.worldnetdaily.com>.

Moyers, Bill. "America on the Road." 13 June 1984. BillMoyers.com. 5 Dec. 2015 <http:// billmoyers.com/content/america-road/>.

My Big Fat Greek Wedding. By Nia Vardalois. Dir. Joel Zwick. Playtone, HBO, 2002.

NORML. "Report: One In Eight Federal Drug Prisoners Serving Time For Marijuana Offenses." 12 Nov. 2015. NORML.org. 16 April 2017 <http://norml.org/ news/2015/11/12/report-one-in-eight-federal-drug-prisoners-serving-time-for-marijuana-offenses>.

National Youth Anti-drug Media Campaign (Office of National Drug Control Policy). "Pool." 16 March 2005. www.freevibe.com. 21 March 2005. <http://mediacampaign. org/mg/television/html>.

National Youth Anti-drug Media Campaign (Office of National Drug Control Policy). "Wallet." 16 March 2005. www.freevibe.com. 21 March 2005. <http:// mediacampaign.org/mg/television/html>.

Nelson, Cletus. "Looking for a few good Dudes: Potheads take up arms in the war on Drugs." Boulder Weekly 15 Oct. 1998: 12-13.

Oakdancer. "Some kinda heathen wedding . . ." 27 March 1999. 14 Jan. 2005 <http:// oakdancer.com/hfast/HeathenWedding.htm>.

Omang, Joanne. "A Mother Searches for Answers; Son's Death in El Salvador Starts Personal Crusade." Washington Post 8 Feb. 1983: A12.

Out of Ireland. By Paul and Kerby Miller Wagner. Dir. Paul Wagner. Shanachie. PBS, 1997.

Pettigrew, Thomas V. "Prejudice." The Harvard Encyclopedia of American Ethnic Groups. Ed. Stephan Thermstrom et al. Cambridge: Harvard University Press, 1980. 820-829.

Posner, Richard A. "The Moral Minority (review of One Nation, Two Cultures by GertrudeHimmelfarb)." New York Times 19 Dec. 1999.

Republican Rebel, The. Hippies: A Moral and Spritual Crisis. Ed. Johnny Lee Clary. 2008. 02 June 2010 <www.republicanrebel.com/hippies.htm>.

Ross, Susan Dente. "Images of Irish Americans: Invisible, Inebriated, or Irascable." Images that Injure:Pictorial Stereotypes in the Media. Ed. Paul Martin and Susan Dente Ross Lester. Westport: Praeger, 2003. 131-138.

Saparito, Bill. "Holy Sox!: How a lovable bunch of 'idiots' overcame their demons to win the title Boston has coveted for generations." Time 08 November 2004: 42.

Savage, Michael. The Savage Nation: Saving America from the Liberal Assault on Our Borders, Language, and Culture. Nashville: WND Books, 2002.

Schaefer, Richard T. Racial and Ethnic Groups, 6th ed. New York: HarperCollins College Publishers,1996.

Shenton, James P. "Introduction." The Great Contemporary Issues: Ethnic Groups in American Life. Ed. Gene Brown. New York: Arno Press, 1978. vii.

Sloan, Gary. "The 'good old days' weren't." San Francisco Examiner 18 October 2000.

Swanson, Ana. "Justice Scalia suggests asking a hippie about gay marriage. Here's how to find one near you." 26 June 2015. www.washingtonpost.com. 11 Jan. 2016 <https:// www. washingtonpost.com/news/wonk/wp/ 2015/06/26/justice-scalia-suggests-asking-a-hippie-about-gay-marriage-heres-how-to-find-one-near-you/>.

Talbott, Cliff. "An Offensive Defense." Colorado Daily 24-26 Oct. 1997: 10-11.

Taylor, Mike. "The natural wonder of Boulder: "We're going to revolutionize the way people eat." www.cobizmag.com (Colorado Business Magazine). 22 March 2005 <http://www.cobizmag.com/articles.cfm?article_id=284>.>.

The Godfather. Dir. Francis Ford Coppolla. Perf. Marlon Brando, Al Pacino andJames Caan. ParamountPictures, 1972.

Time. The Hippies. Ed. J.D. Brown. New York: Time, Inc., 1967.

Torgoff, Martin. Can't Find My Way Home: America in the Great Stoned Age, 1945-2000. New York: Simon & Shuster, 2004.

Vecoli, Rudolph J. "Introduction." Gale Encyclopedia of Multicultural America. 1995.

Washington, Roxanne. "A green wedding: From cakes to clothes, couples opt to go organic." 26 March 2003. Cleveland (Plain Dealer) Online. 14 Jan. 2005 <www. cleveland.com/weddings/pdmore/green.html>.

Waters, Mary C. Ethnic Options: Choosing Identities in America. Berkeley: University of California Press, 1990.

Weiner, Rex and Deanne Stillman. Woodstock Census. New York: Viking, 1979.

West, Diana. "Counterculture president: Why upstate New York sniffs at Bill Clinton." Washington Times 24 September 1999: 19.

Whole Foods Market. "Our History: Celebrating 25 Years, 1980-2005 Whole Foods Market." 26 June2005. WholeFoods.com. 15 July 2005 <http://www. wholefoodsmarket.com/company/history.html>.

Will, George F. "About That 'Sixties Idealism': Meet Wolfgang and Lisa Von Nester who 'did their own thing'." Newsweek 21 Aug. 1995: 72.

Woodbury, Marsha. "Jewish Images that Injure." Images that Injure: Pictorial Stereotypes in the Media. Ed. Paul Martin Lester. Westport: Praeger, 1996. 48-53.

Woolfolk, John. "Drifting Grateful Dead followers bite the handouts that feed them." San Jose Mercury News 8 August 1996

Chapter Seven Works Cited

Ashby, Leroy. With Amusement for All: A History of American Popular Culture Since 1830. Lexington:University of Kentucky Press, 2006.

"Concepts of Ethnicity." Harvard Encyclopedia of American Ethnic Groups. Cambridge: Belnap/Harvard,1980. 240-42.

Diamond, Jared. Guns, Germs and Steel: The Fate of Human Socieites. New York: Norton, 1999.

Hager, Steven. "An ad for "Freedom Fighters." High Times 17 June 2002.

Krassner, Paul. "The Communal Truth." 8-14 Nov. 2006. New York Press. 24 June 2008 <http://www.nypress.com/18/32/books/paulkrassner.cfm>.

Kurlansky, Mark. 1968: The Year That Rocked the World. New York: Random House, 2004.

Moyers, Bill. "America on the Road." 13 June 1984. BillMoyers.com. 5 Dec. 2015 <http://billmoyers.com/content/america-road/>.

Partridge, William. The Hippie Ghetto: The Natural History of a Subculture. New York: Holt, Reinhart and Winston, 1973.

Weiner, Rex and Deanne Stillman. Woodstock Census. New York: Viking, 1979.

Westhues, Kenneth. Society's Shadow: Studies in the Sociology of Countercultures. Toronto; New York: McGraw-Hill Ryerson, 1972.

Chapter Eight Works Cited

420 Magazine. "Celebrity Toker: Steve Martin." 420 Magazine. 15 July 2011 <http://www.420magazine.com/forums/celebrity-tokers/80737-steve-martin.html>.

____. "Quentin Tarantino Smokes Weed With Brad Pitt In France." 13 Sept. 2009. 420 Magazine. 29 Dec. 2010 <http://www.420magazine.com/forums/ celebrity-tokers/101215-quentin-tarantino-smokes-weed-brad-pitt-france.html>.

5min.com. "Julia Louis Dreyfus Interview." 2011. 5min.com. 26 Feb. 2012 <http://www.5min.com/Video/Julia-Louis-Dreyfus-Interview-287670568>.

7th Annual Utah Bioneers: Revolution from the Heart of Nature. "Bioneers History." 14 Nov. 2010. Utah Bioneers. 14 Nov. 2010 <http://conference.usu.edu/bioneers/2010/History.cfm>.

929 Radio (Perth). "Celeb Yummy Mummies?" www.929.com.au. 14 Dec. 2015 <http://www.929.com.au/entertainment/celebrity/galleries/celeb-yummy-mummies?selectedImage=6>.

99.7 (NOW!). "Texas Thinks Giant Fans are a Bunch of Hippies." 10 Oct. 2010. 99.7 (NOW!). 20 Jan. 2013 <http://997now.cbslocal.com/2010/ 10/29/giants-fan-are-a-bunch-of-happy-hippies/>.

Adler, Jerry and Shawn Doherty. "The Graying of Aquarius: Some people cling to the values of the '60s—and they're still called hippies." Newsweek 30 March 1987: 56-58.

AFP. "Oprah tells India love of books central to her life." 22 Jan. 2013. tribune.com.pk. 27 March 2016 <http://tribune.com.pk/story/ 325459/oprah-tells-india-love-of-books-central-to-her-life/>.

Aldrich, Amy. "The Muppets Take Disney World." March 1990. University of Maryland. 28 Nov. 2010 <http://www.newsdesk.umd.edu/ images/Henson/Articles/InquiryArticle.html>.

All Day Energy Greens. "Excess Acid Stored inside your Fat Cells . . ." All Day Energy Greens Newsletter Special Edition 2014: 9, 10.

395

Amazon.com. "DVD Today: Live 8." 27 Nov. 2010. Amazon.com. 27 Nov. 2010 <http://www.dvd-today.com/top/music/dvd.html>.

———. "Review of LA Leche League: At the Crossroads of Medicine, Feminism, and Religion by JuleDeJager Ward." 6 Nov. 2010. Amazon.com. 2010 6 Nov. <http://www.amazon.com/Leche-League-Crossroads-Medicine-Feminism/dp/0807847917#_>.

American Beauty. Dir. Sam Mendes. Perf. Annette Benning Kevin Spacey. 1999.

AMG All Movie Guide. "Steve Martin." 2012. Answers.com. 25 March 2012 <http://www.answers.com/topic/steve-martin#ixzz1nduMnHoh>.

ANI. "Michael Douglas calls for marijuana legalization." 2 May 2009. www.FreeLibrary.com. 14 Dec. 2015 <http://www.thefreelibrary.com/Michael+Douglas+calls+for+marijuana+legalization.-a0199351367>.

———. "Russell Brand to play 'sexy hippie' in President comedy." 14 Nov. 2011. Yahoo!Lifestyle. 15 Dec. 2015 <https://in.lifestyle.yahoo.com/ russell-brand-play-sexy-hippie-president-comedy-130941494.html>.

Answers.com. "Does jeff bridges smoke pot?" 20 Feb. 2011. Answers.com. 20 Feb. 2011 <http://wiki.answers.com/Q/Does_jeff_bridges_smoke_pot>.

———. "Did al pacino take drugs?" Answers.com. 17 April 2011 <http://wiki.answers.com/Q/Did_al_pacino_take_drugs>.

AP. "Ben & Jerry's names new flavor after Hannah Teter." 21 Nov. 2009. KIMATV.com. 16 March 2013 <http://www.kimatv.com/news/business/70701537.html>.

———. "New memoir recounts early days of 'SNL'." 7 April 2009. MSNBC.com. 1 March 2011 <http://today.msnbc.msn.com/id/30087072/ns/today-books/>.

Appleyard, Brian. "Interview: Nunn the wiser." 4 April 2004. TheSundayTimes.co.uk. 28 Dec. 2014 <http://www.thesundaytimes.co.uk/sto/culture/article36843.ece>.

———. "Trevor Nunn and Tom Stoppard." 12 June 2011. BryanAppleyard.com. 28 Dec. 2014 <http://bryanappleyard.com/trevor-nunn-and-tom-stoppard/>.

Artis, Julie E. "Breastfeed at Your Own Risk." Fall 2009. ASA (American Sociological Association). 14 Nov. 2010 <http://contexts.org/ articles/fall-2009/breastfeed-at-your-own-risk/>.

Artists and Athletes for the Earth. "Our Artists and Athletes." EarthDay.org. 17 March 2013 <http://www.earthday.org/athletes-and-arts-for-the-earth>.

Ashby, Leroy. With Amusement for All: A History of American Popular Culture Since 1830. Lexington: University of Kentucky Press, 2006.

Atomica.com. "Celebrities you didn't know are hippies." Atomica.com. 14 Dec. 2014 <http://www.atomica.com/article/1241627/ celebrities-you-didnt-know-are-hippies>.

Avatar. Dir. James Cameron. Perf. Sam Worthington Zoc Saldana. 2009.

Ayoub, Chuck. "Kiefer Sutherland Biography." 2004-06. www.The-Planets.com. 7 Jan. 2001 <http://www.the-planets.com/star-biography/Kiefer_Sutherland_Biography.htm>.

Azula, Roberto. "Inglorious Basterds: Review." 29 Aug. 2009. LowDownCinema.com. 29 Dec. 2010 <http://www.lowdowncinema.com/tag/inglorious-bastards/>.

Barley, Lisa. "Stacking up white vs. wheat bread." March 2005. Vegetarian Times. 17 Oct. 2010 <http://findarticles.com/p/articles/mi_m0820/is_329/ai_n12938278/>.

Beatles, The. The Beatles: Love. Prod. George Martin and Giles Martin. Apple, Capitol, EMI, 2006.

Begley, Sharon. "What the Beatles Gave Science: Their visit popularized the notion that the spiritual East has something to teach the rational West."10 Nov. 2007. Newsweek.com. 3 Nov. 2010 <http://www. newsweek.com/2007/11/10/what-the-beatles-gave-science.html>.

Behr, Jim. "Bill Murray's Greatest Role: Marijuana Drug Trafficker." 9 Sept. 2010. 4 20 Magazine. 25 May 2011 <http://www.420magazine.com forums/celebrity-tokers/128680-bill-murrays-greatest-role-marijuana-drug-trafficker.html>.

Belasco, Warren J. Appetite for Change: How the Counterculture Took On The Food Industry, 1968-1988. Ithaca: Cornell University Press, 1993, Updated ed.

Bend It Like Beckham. Dir. Gurinder Chaha. Perf. Parminder Nagra. 2002.

Bertodano, Helena de. "I'm still a Hippie Chick": Susan Sarandon Interview." 4 Oct. 2010. The Telegraph. 30 Jan. 2011 <http://www.telegraph.co.uk/culture/ 8023313/ Im-Still-a-Hippie-Chick-Susan-Sarandon-interview.html>.

Bioneers. "The Organic Revolution: From Hippie to Hip to Scale." 2015. Bioneers.org. 19 Jan. 2016 <http://www.bioneers.org/the-organic-revolution/>.

Biskind, Peter. Down and Dirty Pictures: Miramax, Sundance, and the Rise of Independent Film. New York: Simon & Shuster Paperbacks, 2004.

Biskind, Peter. Easy Riders, Raging Bulls: Easy riders, raging bulls: How the sex-drugs-and-rock'n'roll generation saved Hollywood. New York:Simon & Schuster, 1998.

Blau, Max. "4 Ways Steve Jobs and Apple Changed the Music Industry." 11 Oct.2011. mashable. com. 17 Dec. 2015 <http://mashable.com/2011/10/11/apple-changed-music/#hBX_ DbJq95qw>.

Blum, Linda M. At the Breast: Ideologies of Breastfeeding and Motherhood in the Contemporary United States. Boston: Beacon Press, 1999.

Bodog-beat. "Joakim Noah Confirms the Blindingly Obvious, Gets Busted For Weed." 26 May 2008. GamblingBeat.com. 23 Feb. 2013 <http://www.gamblingbeat.com/ sports/joakim-noah-confirms-the-blindingly-obvious-gets-busted-for-wee-62994. html>.

Bodroghkozy, Anita. "The Smothers Brothers Comedy Hour." 2012. The Museum of Broadcast Communications. 20 May 2012 <http://www.museum.tv/eotvsection. php? entrycode=smothersbrot>.

Bosworth, Patricia. Marlon Brando: A Penguin Life. New York: Viking/Penguin, 2001.

Boyle, T. Coraghessan. Drop City. New York: Viking, 2003.

BradP. "Rise of the Hippie-crats." 26 March 2013. Shape of Things to Come. 16 Jan 2014 <http://sottc.net/2013/03/>.

Brand, Russell. Revolution. New York: Ballantine Books, 2014.

Brand, Stewart. "We Owe It All to the Hippies: Forget antiwar protests, Woodstock, even long hair. The real legacy of the sixties generation is the computer revolution." Time Spring (Special Ed.) 1995: History.

Brando, Marlon (with Robert Lindsey). Brando: Songs My Mother Taught Me. New York: Random House, 1994.

Brigette. "The Samurai look conquered Hollywood." www.brigitte.de. 23 Dec. 2015 <http://www.brigitte.de/kultur/lifestyle/maenner-dutt-1209626/>.

Brones, Anna. "Top 10 Adventure Gear Companies You Should Know and Why." 22 Sept. 2008.matadornetwork.com. 16 Dec. 2015 <http://matadornetwork.com/goods/ top-10-adventure-gear-companies-you-should-know-and-why/>.

Brown, Mick. "BB King: last of the great bluesmen." 15 May 2015. www.
telegraph.co.uk. 14 Dec. 2015 <http://www.telegraph.co.uk/ culture/music/
rockandpopfeatures/5343853/BB-King-last-of-the-great-bluesmen.html>.

Brumberg, Joan Jacobs. "Rev. of Appetite for Change: How the Counterculture Took on
the Food Industry, 1966-1988, by Warren J. Belasco." The Nation 9 April 1990: 494.

Bryan, Steve. "Hollywood Celebrities who Embody the Hippie Lifestyle." 19 April
2001. OMG from Yahoo! 19 Feb. 2012 <http://omg.yahoo.com/news /hollywood-
celebrities-embody-hippie-lifestyle-204500529.html>.

Burke, Daniel. "Spiritual Journey Leads Lakers Coach to Serenity, NBA Finals." 14 June
2008.Washington Post. 06 Feb. 2013 <http://www.washingtonpost. /wp-dyn/content/
article/2008/06/13/AR2008061303290.html>.

Burnett, Bob. "Rock 'n' Roll: Art or Politics?" 9 Sept. 2006. The Huffington Post.
28 Nov. 2010 <http://www.huffingtonpost.com/bob-burnett/rock-n-roll-art-or-
politi_b_30262.html>.

Cahill, Tim. "The Rolling Stone Interview—Jack Nicholson (April 16, 1981)." 12 Jan.
2011. www.JackNicholson.org. 12 Jan. 2011 <http://www.jacknicholson.org/
1981RollingStoneInterview.html>.

Californality.com. "www.californaity.com." 6 Dec. 2009. Famous San Francisco
Quotations. 28 Dec.2010 <http://www.californiality.com/ 2009/12/famous-san-
francisco-quotations.html>.

Cardona, Mercedes M. "Counterculture carrier: Virgin is celebrating new U.S. gateways,
access to Heathrow and healthy profits. ." Travel Agent 8 April 1991: 24(2).

Carlson, Raymond. "For Trudeau, road to comic fame began on York Street." 11 April 2008.
YaleDailyNews.com. 14 Dec. 2015 <http://yaledailynews.com/ blog/2008/04/11/
for-trudeau-road-to-comic-fame-began-on-york-street/>.

Caton, Hope. "Canada's salt of the earth." 21 Aug. 2008. Guardian.co.uk. 30 July 2011
<http://www.guardian.co.uk/travel/2008/aug/21/canada.green>.

CBS. "Madonna Interview David Letterman 2009 Part 1." 2 Oct. 2009. YouTube.com. 29
Jan. 2011 <http://www.youtube.com/watch? v=1QysEBANCa0&feature=related>.

CBS News. "Bush's Final Approval Rating: 22 Percent." 16 Jan. 2009. CBSNews. 9 April
2017 <http://www.cbsnews.com/news/bushs-final-approval-rating-22-percent/>.

CBS News. "Shaun White's Olympic Secret." 19 Feb. 2010. CBSNews.com (60 Minutes).
16 March 2013 <http://www.cbsnews.com/8301-18560_162-6219801.html>.

CBS, 60 Minutes. "Steve Jobs, Apps for Autism." 23 Oct. 2011. Tv.com. 17 Dec. 2015
<http://www.tv.com/shows/60-minutes/october-23-2011-steve-jobs-apps-for-
autism-642014/>.

CEIBA (China Europe Internatonal Business School). ""High-Wire Balancing Act":
Cirque Du SoleilExec Shares Secrets to Success with CEIBS." 27 Aug. 2007.
CEIBA.com. 6 Dec. 2010 <http://www.ceibs.edu/media/archive/21391.shtml>.

Celebslam.com. "What a Wierdo: Alicia Silverstone." 2010. Celebslam.com. 30 March
2011 <http://celebslam.celebuzz.com/2009/08/alicia-silverstone-hippy-1.php>.

CelebStoner.com. "Acid Queen: Helen Mirren's LSD trip." 27 Sept. 2006. CelebStoner.
com. 27 Feb. 2011 <http://www.celebstoner.com/20070926362/news/celebstoner-
news/acid-queen-helen-mirrens-lsd-trip.html>.

____. "Bill Murray." May 20 2009. CelebStoner.com. 25 May 2011 <http://www.celebstoner.
com/ 200905202274/celebstoners/top-celebstoners/bill-murray.html>.—

___ "Jack Nicholson: Pot's a "Curative"." 1 Feb. 2001. CelebStoner.com. 3 Feb. 2011 <http:// www.celebstoner.com/201102015711/news/celebstoner-news/jack-nicholson-on-pot.html>.

Celebuzz! "Fashion FTW: The Olsen Twins Are True Hippies (PHOTOS)." 27 May 2010. Celebuzz.com.24 March 2015 <http://www.celebuzz.com/ 2010-05-27/ fashion-ftw-the-olsen-twins-are-true-hippies-photos/>.

Chand, Rick. "NFL Wants Damn Hippies Off Their Lawn." 27 March 2008. Deadspin. com. Feb. 28 2013 <http://deadspin.com/nfl-wants-damn-hippies-off-their-lawn/>.

Chicago Blues Guide. "Eric Clapton's Crossroads Guitar Festival 2010." July 2010. ChicagoBluesGuide.com. 25 May 2011<http://www.chicagobluesguide. com/ reviews/live-reviews/crossroads-2010/crossroads-2010-page.html>.

ChronicCandy.com. "Alicia Silverstone Getting Gorgeous with Hemp." 11 Jan.2011. ChronicCandy.com. 30 March 2011<http://www.chroniccandy.com/2011/01/ aliia-silverstone-getting-gorgeous-with-hemp/>

.___. "Chronic Candy's 10 Sexiest Celebrity Stoners." 31 Dec. 2010. ChronicCandy.com. 16 April 2011 <http://www.chroniccandy.com/ 2010/12/ chronic-candys-10-sexiest-celebrity-stoners/>.

Clayton, Dave. "Lord of the Rings: The Fellowship of the Ring." 28 Dec. 2010.

CNET News Staff. "Jobs biographer sits down with '60 Minutes'." 23 Oct. 2011. www.cnet.com. 17 Dec.2015 <http://www.cnet.com/ news/ jobs-biographer-sits-down-with-60-minutes/#!>.

Cohen, Josh. "Stoned Hippies, Crappy Bikes, and the History of Mountain Biking." 5 April 2010. www.seattlemet.com. 25 March 2013 <http://www. seattlemet.com/news-and-profiles/ publicola/articles/stoned-hippies-crappy-bikes-and-the-history-of-mountain-biking>.

ContactMusic.com. "Jim Carrey - Carrey Quits Marijuana." 18 Feb, 2004. ContactMusic.com. 19 Feb. 2012 <http://www.contactmusic.com/news-article/ carrey-quits-marijuana>.

Cooper, Charles. "Perspective: Do We Owe It All to the Hippies?" 13 March 2005. CNET News. 9 Oct. 2010 <http://news.cnet.com/Do-we-owe-it-all-to-the-hippies/2010-1071_3-5705499.html>.

Corliss, Richard. "The Power of Yoga." 15 April 2001. www.Time.com. 3 Nov. 2010 <http://www.time.com/time/health/article/0,8599,106356,00.html>.

Crocker, Martin. "Bristol Style." December 2011. ClimbMagazine.com. 23 March 2013 <http://www.climbmagazine.com/issues/82/articles/bristol-fashion>.

Crumb. Dir. Terry Zwigoff. Perf. Robert Crumb. 1995.

Crumb, Robert. The R. Crumb Coffee Table Art Book: Crumb's Whole Career, from Shack to Chateau! Ed. Peter Poplaski. Boston: Little, Brown, 1997.

Daily Mail Showbiz Reporter. "An offer he couldn't refuse: Al Pacino reveals Marlon Brando kept him in The Godfather when Francis Ford Coppola wanted to sack him." 12 Dec. 2010. DailyMail.co.uk.16 April 2011 <http://www.dailymail. co.uk/tvshowbiz/article-1336468/ Al-Pacino-reveals-Marlon-Brando-kept-The-Godfather–Francis-Ford-Coppola-wanted-sack-him.html>.

Darcangelo, Vince. "Denver Art Museum spotlights psychedelic rock posters in new exhibit." 19 March 2009. BoulderWeekly.com. 2009 June 2010 <http://www.dailycamera. com/news/2009/mar/19/Denver-Art-Museum-psychedelic-rock-posters-exhibit/>.

Daurer, Gregory. "The Green Man: Tom Robbins." 12 June 2002. HighTimes.com. 10 Dec. 2010 <http://hightimes.com/entertainment/ht_admin/152>.

399

Davis, Tom. 39 Years of Short-Term Memory Loss: The Early Days of SNL from Someone Who Was There. Grove/Atlantic, Inc., 2010.

DemocracyNow! "Bradley Manning Sentenced to 35 Years In Prison." 31 August 2013. DemocracyNow!23 Dec. 2015 <http://www.democracynow.org/2013/8/21/bradley_manning_sentenced_to_35_years>.

____. "Britain Challenges Julian Assange's Asylum in Ecuadorean Embassy as Sweden Vows to Continue Inquiry." 14 Aug. 2015. DemocracyNow! 17 Dec. 2015 <http://www.democracynow.org/2015/8/14 /britain_challenges_julian_assange_s_asylum>.

DeMontigny, Nate. "Sarah Jessica Parker: Hollywood's Newest Jew-Bu?" 22 Aug. 2008.

Precious Metal: The Road to Nirvana is Paved with Samsara. 8 May 2011

Deutschman, Alan. "The Gonzo Way of Branding." Fast Company Oct. 2004: 90-96.

Drunk, Stoned, Brilliant, Dead: The Story of the National Lampoon. Dir. Douglas Tirola. 2015.

Dubner, Stephen J. "Steven Spielberg, in Black and White (from NYT Magazine)." 14 Feb. 1999. Selected journalism by Stephen J. Dubner. 28 Dec. 2010 <http://stephenjdubner.com/journalism/021499.html>.

DuDell, Michael Parrish. "Madonna Insists Children Eat Macrobiotic, Vegetarian, Organic Diet." 12 Nov. 2008. Ecorazzi: The Latest in Green Gossip. 29 Jan. 2011 <http://www.ecorazzi. com/2008/ 11/12/madonna-insists-children-eat-macrobiotic-vegetarian-organic-diet/>.

Duffy, Paula. "Drunk, Stoned, Brilliant, Dead preview: National Lampoon's History and Legacy (Video)." 16 Jan. 2016. TVruckus.com. 24 April 2016 <http://tvruckus.com/2016/01/22/ drunk-stoned-brilliant-dead-preview-national-lampoons-history-and-legacy-video/>.

DVD Review. "HD-DVD Reviews: Animal House (1978)." 5 Aug. 2006. www.dvdreview.com. 2 Jan. 2011 <http://www.dvdreview.com/reviews/pages/2399.shtml>.

DVD Talk. "YourOlympicHero." DVD Talk. 20 Feb. 2012 <http://forum.dvdtalk.com/archive/t395566.html>.

Easy Rider. By Dennis Hopper, Peter Fonda and Terry Southern. Dir. Dennis Hopper. Perf. Dennis, Hopper, Peter Fonda and Jack Nicholson. Columbia Pictures, 1969.

Eells, Josh. "Seth Rogen at the Crossroads." Rolling Stone Dec. 18th through Jan. 1 2014, 2015: 53-57,86.

Ekarius, Carol. "Farm Aid History and Reflection Featuring Interview with John." 17 Aug. 2008. mellencamp.com. 27 Nov. 2010 <http://www.mellencamp.com/index. php?page=news&n_id=218>.

Eldridge, Courtney. "Master Class: The Epic California Rock Climbers of the Seventies. 29 July 2011. TheSelvegeYard.wordpress.com. 23 March 2913 <http://theselvedgeyard.wordpress.com/2011/07/29/ master-class-the-epic-california-rock-climbers-of-the-seventies/>.

Enzinna, Peter. "David Foster Wallace and Antonin Scalia's unlikely common ground." 12 July 2012. NYDailyNews.com. 8 April 2017 <http://www.nydailynews.com/blogs/pageviews/ david-foster-wallace-antonin-scalia-common-ground-blog-entry-1.1638812>.

Eventful.com. "Michael Douglas: Does anyone look as good in the moonlight?" 13 Jan. 2011. Eventful.com. 13 Jan. 2011 <http://eventful. com/performers/michael-douglas-/P0-001-000166886-4>.

Everett-Haynes, La Monica. "A Different Type of Hippie Hype." 19 March 2008. UA News (University of Arizona). 13 Nov. 2010 <http://uanews.org/node/18838>.

Fahey, Todd Brendan. "Twentieth Century Neuronaut: Timothy Leary: The Far Gone Interview." 28 Sept. 1992. wwwl.fargonebooks.com. 9 Oct. 2010

Francis Coppola Winery. "Rustic: Francis' Favorites." 8 Feb. 2011. www. franciscoppolawinery.com. 8 Feb. 2011

Fears, Darryl. "Alarming 'dead zone' grows in the Chesapeake." 24 July 2011. www. washingtonpost.com. 9 Jan. 2016 <https://www. washingtonpost.com/national/ health-science/alarming-dead-zone-grows-in-the-chesapeake/2011/07/20/ gIQABRmKXI_story.html>.

Feaster, Felicia. "Peter Jackson keeps the cloying tone of The Lovely Bones intact: Trippy Adaption." 13 Jan. 2010. Charleston City Paper. 28 Dec. 2010.

Female First: Celebrity Gossip & Lifestyle Magazine. "Lisa Kudrow Based Phoebe on Aniston." 1 Aug. 2009. Female First: Celebrity Gossip & Lifestyle Magazine. 27 March 2011 <http://www.femalefirst.co.uk/movies/movie-news/ Jennifer+Aniston-69924.html>.

Fox, Emily Jane. "Romney, Ryan love North Face. Founder finds it 'ironic'." 16 Oct. 2012. money.cnn.com. 27 March 2013 http://money.cnn.com/2012/ 10/16/news/economy/ romney-north-face/index.html>.

FrankDiscussion.net. "Celebrity Cannabis Consumers." Frank Discussion: Cannabis Activism, Info & Resources. 3 April 2011 <http://frankdiscussion.netfirms.com/ who_celebtokers.html>.

Franken, Al. "Small, Beginning and Organic Farmers." Al Franken: U.S. Senator for Minnesota. 9 May 2011 <http://franken.senate.gov/?p=issue&id=59>.

FreakingNews.com. "Whoopi Goldberg Pictures Gallery." 18 Feb. 2012. www.Freaking News.com. 20 Feb. 2012 <http://www. freakingnews.com/Whoopi-Goldberg-Pictures—-3116.asp>.

Friends of Cannabis. "Madonna's Marijuana Confession." 1 March 2008. FriendsOfCannabis.com. 29 Jan. 2011 <http://www.friendsofcannabis. com/ directory/index.php?option=com_alphacontent&section=23&cat=368&task=view &id=395&Itemid=58>.

Gadsby, Ephriam. "Monty Python's Flying Circus: Live at Aspen: Love Them Pythons." 15 June 2006. IMDb. 28 Nov. 2010 <http://www.imdb.com/title/tt0287570/ usercomments>.

Gilchrist, Todd. "Alice in Wonderland—Film Review." 5 March 2010. HMonthly.com. 31 Dec. 2010 <http://www.hmonthly.com/ 2010/03/05/alice-wonderland-film-review/>.

Goodreads. "Michael Pollan quotes." 17 Oct. 2010. www.Goodreads.com. 17 Oct. 2010 <http://www.goodreads.com/author/quotes/2121.Michael_Pollan>.

Gosselin, Laura. "Francis Ford Coppola and His Eco Friendly Resorts." 9 Dec. 2009. The Sustainability Ninja. 23 March 2011 http://www. sustainabilityninja.com/sustainable-alternative-materials/francis-ford-coppola-and-his-eco-friendly-resorts-19820/>.

Goldenberg, Suzanne. "Richard Branson failed to deliver on $3bn climate change pledge." 13 Sept. 2014. TheGuardian.com. 22 Oct. 2015.

Granju, Katie Allison. "The midwife of modern midwifery: From her Tennessee commune, Ina May Gaskin almost single-handedly inspired the rebirth of midwifery in the United States." 1 June1999. Salon.com. 6 Nov. 2010 <http://www.salon.com/ people/bc/1999/06/01/gaskin>.

Gravett, Paul. "Creator Profile: Art Spiegelman." PaulGravett.com. 14 Dec. 2015 <http:// www.paulgravett.com/profiles/creator/art_spiegelman>.

401

Gregory, Sean. "Winter Olympians: Hannah Teter." 4 Feb. 2010. Time.com. 16 Dec. 2015
<http://content.time.com/time/specials/ packages/article/0,28804,1958645_1958459
_1958773,00.html
Go n Try. "Jim Carrey." 2009. Go n Try. 19 Feb. 2012 <http://www.gontry. com/Celebrity/
CelebrityDiet/CAT3/CEL46/Jim-Carrey.aspx>.
Grierson, Tim. "Best Rock Band Cameos on 'The Simpsons'." 23 Dec. 2010. About.com.
23 Dec. 2010 <http://rock.about.com/od/top10lists/tp/simpsonsrock.htm>.
Gross, Michael. "Madonna: Catholic Girl, Material Girl, Post-Liberation Woman."1985.
Vanity Fair interview. 29 Jan. 2011 <http://www.mgross.com/MoreThgsChng/
interviews/madonna1.html>.
Gurvis, Sandra. Where Have All the Flower Children Gone? Jackson: University Press
of Mississippi,2006.
Harris, Richard. Photo. 23 Dec. 2015 <http://harrypotter.wikia.com/wiki/Richard_Harris>
Harris, Scott. "George Clooney Is the Other Smothers Brother." 11 Dec.
2011. NextMovie.com. 20 May2012 <http://www.nextmovie.com/ blog/
george-clooney-smothers-brothers/>.
Hattersley, Giles. "The Wiki Snobs are Taking Over." 9 Feb. 2009. The Sunday Times. 14
April 2013 <http://www.anglonautes.com/voc_ it_main/voc_it_www_wikipedia_1/
voc_it_www_wikipedia_1.htm>.
Hepp, Kyle. "Hippie dressing Madonna uses maiden name to buy a house." 27
April 2008. StyleList. 29Jan. 2011 <http://www.stylelist.com/ 2008/04/27/
hippie-dressing-madonna-uses-maiden-name-to-buy-a-house/>.
Hershberg, James G. "Just Who Did Smash Communism?" 27 June 2004.
WashingtonPost.com. 24 Nov. 2010 <http://www.washingtonpost.com/ ac2/wp-dyn/
A7328-2004Jun26?language=printer>.
____. "Outlook: The Reagan Effect." 28 June 2004. WashingtonPost.com. 24 Nov. 2010
<http://www.washingtonpost.com/wp-dyn/articles/A5739-2004Jun25.html>.
High Times. "Brad Pitt Gets Quentin Tarantino Stoned in France." 23 Jan.
2014. High.Times.com. 14Dec. 2015 <http://www.hightimes.com/ read/
brad-pitt-gets-quentin-tarantino-stoned-france>.
____. "High Times Interview: David Carradine." 5 June 2009. HighTimes.com. 14 Dec.
2015 <http://hightimes.com/read/high-times-interview-david-carradine>.
Hill, Doug and Jeff Weingrad. Saturday Night: A Backstage History of Saturday Night
Live. New York:Beach Tree Books, 1986.
Hippies. By Dennis Kleinman. Dir. Scott Reda. The History Channel. Lou Reda
Productions. 2008.
Holden, Stephen. "Star Trek: Insurrection (1998)—Movie Review." 11 Dec. 1998.
TheNewYorkTimes.com. 13 May 2012 <http://movies.nytimes.com/movie/review?
res=9505E2DB103AF932A25751C1A96E958260>.
Hogg, Trevor. "The Man and His Dream: A Francis Ford Coppola Profile (Part 2)." 10
Nov. 2010. FlickeringMyth.com. 23 March 2011 <http://flickeringmyth. blogspot.
com/2010/11/man-and-his-dream-francis-ford-coppola_10.html>.
Horn, Barbara Lee. The Age of Hair: Evolution and impact of Broadway's first rock
musical. New York: Greenwood Press, 1991.
Hot Momma. "Hot Momma Gossip." 6 June 2006. HotMommaGossip. 20 Feb. 2011
<http://www.hotmommagossip.com/2006/06/05/woody-harrelson-is-a-hippie/>.

Icons: A Portrait of England. "Icons: Portraits of England: Monty Python." 28 Nov. 2010. icons.org.uk. 28 Nov. 2010 <http://www.icons.org.uk/theicons/ collection/ monty-python/biography/the-basics-finished>.

IluvGB. "One for the Girls." 19 Dec. 2010. PackerForum.com. 16 Dec. 2015 <https://www. packerforum.com/threads/one-for-the-girls.24061/>

Ionescu, Daniel. "Has Wikipedia Beaten Britannica in the Encyclopedia Battle?" 14 March 2012. PCWorld.com. 15 April 2013 <http://www.pcworld.com/article/ 251796/has_wikipedia_beat_britannica_in_the_encyclopedia_battle_.html>.

Jewster, Punky (citing High Times). "Quentin Tarantino and Sofia Coppola— Pot-Smoking Love Monkeys." 23 April 2005. www.shoomery.org. 29 Dec. 2010 <http:// www.shroomery.org/forums/showflat.php/Number/4087865>.

Johnson, Ken. "Mr. Natural Goes to the Museum." 9 Sept. 2008. NewYorkTimes.com. 20 Dec. 2010 <http://www.nytimes.com/2008/09/05/arts/design/05crum.html>.

Johnson, Neala. "Annie Leibovitz goes on the other side of the camera." 8 Nov. 2007. HeraldSun.com.au. 26 Dec. 2010 <http://www.heraldsun.com.au/ entertainment/ movies/fame-by-frame-for-leibovitz/story-e6frf9h6-1111114823189>.

Jones, Alison. "Robin Williams, the happy hippie." 6 Dec 2006. Birmingham Post. net (UK). 30 July 2011 <http://www.birminghampost.net/life leisure-birmingham-guide/birmingham-culture/tm_ headline=robin-williams—the-happy-hippy&met hod=full&objectid=18219318& siteid=50002-name_page.html>.

Jorch, Noraree. "The First NFL Players Who Were Hippies." 20 Sept. 2012. CoastGab.com—For Art Bell Fans. 28 Feb. 2013 <http://coastgab.com/index. php?topic=3447.0>.

Keilberger, Craig and Marc. "Mia Farrow stars in role as activist." 25 Feb. 2008. The Toronto Star. 27 Nov. 2010 <http://www.thestar.com/comment/columnists/ article/306547>.

Kelly, Katherine E., ed. The Cambridge Companion to Tom Stoppard (Cambridge Companions to Literature). Cambridge: Cambridge University Press, 2001.

Kelly, Kevin. "One-Eyed Aliens! Suicide Booths! Mom's Old-Fashioned Robot Oil!: Kevin Kelly tours the theme park inside Matt Groening's brain." 2 July 2004. Wired. com. 23 Dec. 2010 <http://www.wired.com/wired/archive/7.02/futurama_pr.html>.

Kirk, Andrew G. Counterculture Green: The Whole Earth Catalog and American Environmentalism. Lawrence, Kan: University Press of Kansas, 2007.

Kirk, Jane and Michael. "Access to Tools." 9 Dec. 2007. The New York Times, Sunday Book Review. 14 Nov. 2010 <http://ebookpedia.net/Counterculture-Green—-Andrew-G—Kirk—-Books—-Review—-New-York——.html>.

Kitchen, Denis. "BIO - R. CRUMB." 2016. www.deniskitchen.com. 1 Feb. 2016 <http:// www.deniskitchen.com/mm5/merchant.mvc?Store_Code=SK&Screen=CTGY Category_Code=C.BIO.RC>.

Klein, Matthew. "Classic Ten - Iconic Hollywood Hippies." 26 Aug. 2009. AMC. filmcritic.com. 7 Jan. 2011 <http://www.filmcritic.com/ features/2009/08/ top-ten-movie-hippies/>.

Klunkerz: A Film about Mountain Bikes (They Re-Invented the Wheel). Dir. William Savage. 2007.

Konkol, Mark. "Joakim Noah's mom hopes son 'enjoys the journey'." 7 May 2011. posttrib.suntimes.com. 23 Feb. 2013<http://posttrib.suntimes.com/news/5241659-418/joakim-noahs-mom-hopes-son-enjoys-the-journey.html>.

Krantz, Michael. "The Way They Were." 6 June 1999. Time.com. 14 Dec. 2015 <http://content.time.com/time/magazine/article/0,9171,26471,00.html>.

Kristopher. "Meet Art Spiegelman." 1 Dec. 2008. GraphicMaelstrom.blogspot.com. 15 Dec. 2015 <http://graphicmaelstrom.blogspot.com/2008/12/meet-art-spiegelman. html>.

Kurlansky, Mark. 1968: The Year That Rocked the World. New York: Random House, 2004.

Landry, Aaron. "Al Franken on the Environment." 27 April 2008. Aaron Landry. 8 May 2011 <http://s4xton.com/1729/al-franken-on-the-environment/>.

Larsen, Brooke Thorsteinson and Dana. "Ocean's 420." 1 Jan. 2005. www.cannabisculture. com. 3 Jan.2016 <http://www.cannabisculture.com/content/2005/1/4/4030>.

Larsen, Dana. "Celebrity Stoners." 8 July 2002. www.CannabisCulture.com. 17 Jan. 2011<http://www.cannabisculture.com/articles/2404.html>.

Learyfan. "Today in Counterculture History." Jan. 2008. Mushroomery: Magic Mushrooms Demystified. 30 July 2011 <http://www.shroomery.org/forums/ showflat.php/Number/13750963>.

Lengel, Allan and Martin Weil. "Hunter S. Thompson Dies at 67." 21 Feb. 2005. WashingtonPost.com.11 Dec. 2010 http://www.washingtonpost.com/wp-dyn/ articles/A40737-2005Feb20.html>.

Leigh, David and Luke Harding. Wikileads: Inside Julian Assange's War on Secrecy. London: Guardian Books, 2013.

Levine, David. "The Fuelish Things: Jerry Robock's long, strange trip has taken him from the '60s counterculture to the forefront of the biofuel revolution." 17 July 2008. 14 Nov. 2010 <http://www.hvmag.com/Hudson-Valley-Magazine/August-2008/Going-Green/David Levine>.

Liebing, Ben. "The Top Five: David Foster Wallace." 21 Feb. 2014. ThePubScout. 16 Dec. 2014 <http://thepubscout.com/the-top-5-david-foster-wallaces/>.

Lih, Andrew. The Wikipedia revolution: how a bunch of nobodies created the world's greatest encyclopedia. Pymble, NSW, 2009.

Lipworth, Elaine. "Michael Douglas: 'I am consumed with being a father'." 2 Oct. 2010. www.Guardian.co.uk. 13 Jan. 2011 <http://www.guardian.co.uk/ lifeandstyle/ 2010/ oct/02/michael-douglas-cancer-catherine-zeta-jones>.

Liquori, Irene J. Summer 1999. BuffaloSpree.com. 3 Jan. 2007<http://www.buffalospree. com/archives/1999_summer/summ99toles.html>.

LiveNewsIndia.com. 27 Feb. 2012 <http://www.livenewsindia.com/regional-news/ rajasthan-news/does-exotic-rajasthan-equal-short-term-shaadi/>.

MacLeod, Terri. "Chace Crawford's Good Jeans, Gwyneth Paltrow's Yoga Practice, and Julia Louis Dreyfus' Green Diet." 28 Feb. 2009.TreeHugger.com. 26 Feb. 2012 <http://www.treehugger.com/culture/chace-crawfords-good-jeans-gwyneth-paltrows-yoga-practice-and-julia-louis-dreyfus-green-diet.html>.

Markoff, John. What the Dormouse Said: How the 60s Counterculture Shaped the Personal Computer Industry. New York: Viking Penguin, 2005.

Martin, Steve. "When you believe in God, but not church." 3 Feb. 2007. www.Helium.com. 15 July 2011 <http://www.helium.com/ items/147825-when-you-believe-in-god-but-not-church>.

Mercola, Dr. "The Very Real Risks of Consuming Too Much Protein." 12 Sept. 2014. articles.mercola.com. 9 Jan. 2016 <http://articles.mercola.com/ sites/articles/ archive/ 2014/09/03/too-much-protein.aspx>.

404

Meyer, Susan. Jimmy Wales and Wikipedia. New York: Rosen Publishing, 2013.
Mitchell, Joni. "Big Yellow Taxi." Ladies of the Canyon. By Joni Mitchell. 1968.
Monty Python's The Meaning of Life. Dir. Terry Jones. Perf. John Cleese, et al. 1983.
Moore, Alex. "Julian Assange: Life is Hard in a World Without Hippies." 23 Oct. 2010.
    www.deathandtaxesmag.com. 25 May 2017 <http://www.deathandtaxesmag.
    com/33545/ julian-assange-life-is-hard-in-a-world-without-hippies/>.
Moore, Victoria. "Queen of the Hippies." 2 March 2007. The Mail Online. 27 Feb. 2011
    <http://www.dailymail.co.uk/femail/article-439739/Queen-Hippies.html>.
Morgan, David. Monty Python Speaks: A Complete Oral History of Monty Python. New
    York: Harper-Collins, 1999.
MovieStarBody.com. "Jennifer Aniston's Diet." 6 Nov. 2010. MovieStarBody.com. 19 Jan.
    2011 <http://moviestarbody.com/jennifer-aniston%E2%80%99s-diet/>.
Muñoz, Lorenza. "'Simpsons' Show Global Appeal." July 2007. BanderasNews.com. 23
    Dec. 2010 <http://www.banderasnews.com/0707/ent-simpsons.htm>.
Murphy, Anne. "The Rise and Fall of Politically Correct Businesses." No date. www.ewtn.
    com. 27 March 2013 http://www.ewtn.com/library/business/risefall.htm>.
Murphy, Austin. Sports Illustrated 20 Feb. 2006. NBDA. "Industry Overview 2014." 2015.
    NBDA.com. 16 Dec. 2015 <http://nbda.com/articles/industry-overview-2014-pg34.
    htm>.
Neumann, Thomas. "Playbook runs the break with Joakim Noah." 1 Nov. 2012. ESPN.
    go.com. 6 Feb. 2013 <http:// espn.go.com/blog/playbook/ fandom/post/_/id/10867/
    playbook-crashes-the-boards-with-joakim-noah>.
Nesteroff, Kliph. "The Comedy Writer That Helped Elect Richard M. Nixon." 19
    Sept. 2010. WFMU's Beware of the Blog. 20 May 2012 <http://blog.wfmu.org/
    freeform/2010/09/richard-nixons-laugh-in.html>.
Newsweek. "Stop-Rocks." 24 July 2006. Newsweek.com. 24 Nov. 2010 <http://www.
    newsweek.com/2006/07/24/stop-rocks.html>.
Nieves, Evelyn. "Attacks on a Gay Teen-Ager Prompt Outrage and Soul-Searching." New
    York Times 19 Feb. 1999: A12.
Nonprophet81. "Xanga weblog." 26 Oct. 2004. One last entry for the night. 20 Feb. 2012
    <http://nonprophet81.xanga.com/149189512/item/>.
NotStarring.com. "Roles turned down by Johnny Depp:." 23 March 2011. www.
    NotStarring.com. 23March 2011 <http://www.notstarring.com/actors/depp-johnny>.
NPR. "Intersections: T.C. Boyle's Rock 'n' Roll Muse." 8 March 2004. NPR
    (National Public Radio). 11Dec. 2010 <http://www.npr.org/templates/story/story.
    php?storyId=1741159>.
NYMag.com. "Vulture Giveaway: Watch Francis Ford Coppola Talking Pot Cookies,
    Win the Three-Disc Apocalypse Now Blu-ray." 10 Oct. 2010. NyMag.com. 8 Feb.
    2011 <http://nymag.com/daily/entertainment/2010/ 10/vulture_giveaway_watch
    _a_clip.html>.
Ohno, Apolo Anton with Nancy Ann Richardson. A Journey: The Autobiography of
    Apolo Anton Ohno. New York: Simon & Schuster Books for Young Readers, 2002.
Ohno, Apolo Anton. Zero Regrets: Be Greater Than Yesterday. New York: Astria Books,
    2010.
Organic Lifestyle Magazine. "Healthy Sugar Alternatives: Understanding both
    Healthy & Unhealthy Sugars with their Glycemic Index." 16 Oct. 2010. www.
    organiclifestylemagazine.com. 16 Oct.2010 <http://www. organiclifestylemagazine.
    com/blog/healthy-sugar-alternatives.php>.

O'Rourke, Jill. "Our 12 Favorite Celebrity Hippies, In Honor Of Earth Day." 22 April 2014. www.crushable.com. 14 Dec. 2014 <http://www.crushable. com/2014/04/22/ entertainment/celebrity-hippies-alternative-lifestyle/>.

Pacino, Al. "Al Pacino's inspriational speech." PersonalGrowth4U.net. 17 April 2011 <http://www.personalgrowth4u.net/view-video-8.html>.

Padgett, John B. "The Mississippi Writers Page: Jim Henson." 17 Feb. 1999. University of Mississippi 28 Nov. 2010 <http://www.olemiss.edu/mwp/dir/henson_jim/index. html>.

Papenfuss, Mary. "Right-wingers Go Ballistic Over Avatar: Anti-military Sci-Fi "Hippies" Giving Conservatives Fits." 5 Jan. 2010. Newser.com. 2 Jan.2011 <http:// www.newser.com/story/77475/ right-wingers-go-ballistic-over-avatar.html>.

People Magazine. "Helen Mirren 'Utterly Disgusted' by Her Drunken Tattoo." 22 Jan. 2010. People.com.27 Feb. 2011 <http://www.people.com/people/article/0,,20338830,00. html>.

Perone, David E. American History through Music: Music of the Countercultural Era. Westport, CN: Greenwood, CN, 2004.

Platoon. Dir. Oliver Stone. Perf. Willem DaFoe, Tom Berenger Charlie Sheen. Hemdale Film Corp.,1986.

Polilla. "Julia Roberts is a Dirty Hippie." 5 Dec. 2008. liesandfairytales.blogspot.com. 3 Jan. 2016 <http://liesandfairytales. blogspot.com/2008/12/julia-roberts-is-stinky-hippie.html>.

Pollan, Michael. In Defense of Food: An Eater's Manifesto. New York: Penguin, 2008.

____. The Botany of Desire: A Plant's-Eye View of the World. New York: Random House, 2001.

Pop Blend. "Jim Carrey's Healthy Diet Keeps Him Young." 3 March 2008. CinemaBlend. com. 19 Feb 2012 <http://www.cinemablend.com/ pop/Jim-Carrey-s-Healthy-Diet-Keeps-Him-Young-9673.html>.

PopDirt.com. "Hilary Duff Fuming Over Alicia Silverstone's Pot Smoking." 11 April 2004. PopDirt.com.30 March 2011 <http://popdirt.com/ hilary-duff-fuming-over-alicia-silverstones-pot-smoking/27906/>.

Prague-Life.com. "The Plastic People of Prague: Rock'n'Roll Revolution." 2008. Prague-Life.com. 26 Nov. 2010 <http://www.prague-life.com/prague/plastic-people>.

Press Trust of India. "Keanu Reeves tries the hippie look." 12 Aug. 2009. NDTV Movies. 3 April 2011 <http://movies.ndtv.com/movie Story.aspx?id=ENTEN20090104875& keyword=&subcatg=>.

Quotes Daddy. "Hannah Teter." 2013. QuotesDaddy.com. 16 March 2013 <http://www. quotesdaddy.com/author/Hannah+Teter>.

Rader, Dodson. "Leonardo DiCaprio, Hollywood outsider." 11 Jan. 2009. The Sunday Times (London). 16 Feb. 2011 <http://entertainment. timesonline.co. uk/tol/ arts_and_entertainment/film/article5467287.ece>.

Reed. "Treknobabble #70: Across the Star Trek Universe." 8 July 2009. Film Junk. 13 May 2012 <http://www.filmjunk.com/2009/07/08/ treknobabble-70-across-the-star-trek-universe/>.

Reocities.com. "Dana Carvey on The Late Show." 1993. 15 July 2011 <http://reocities. com/Wellesley/3657/dc_dl.html>.

Reynolds, Grace. "Helen Mirren: Hippie Chic." 3 Jan. 2011. Style Goes Strong. 27 Feb. 2011 <http://style.lifegoesstrong.com/helen-mirren-hippie-chic>.

406

Rieck, Neil. "More than Water, Hops, Barley and Yeast: Authenticity and the Microbrew Revolution." Xroads.Virginia.edu. 8 April 2013<http://xroads.virginia.edu/~ma03/holmgren/microbrew/index.html#top>

Roberts, Soraya. "The new hippie Hollywood: From Gwyneth Paltrow to Shailene Woodley." 5 June 2013. Yahoo!CanadaCelebrity. 16 Dec. 2014 <https://ca.celebrity.yahoo.com/blogs/ celebrity-news/hippie-hollywood-gwyneth-paltrow-shailene-woodley-152653047.html>.

Rogue Ales. «Rogue Locations.» 2012. Rogue.com. 8 April 2013 <http://rogue.com/locations/locations.php>.

Rolling Stone. "Leonardo DiCaprio's Crusade: Inside the New Issue." 12 Jan. 2016. www.rollingstone.com. 13 Jan. 2016 <http://www.rollingstone. com/movies/news/leonardo-dicaprios-crusade-inside-the-new-issue-20160112>.

___. "Six Things You Didn't Know About David Foster Wallace." 27 Aug. 2012. RollingStone.com. 9 Jan. 2016 <http://www.rollingstone.com/ culture/news/six-things-you-didnt-know-about-david-foster-wallace-20120827>.

Rovell, Darren. "Jerry Garcia Night Already A Big Success." 10 Aug. 2010. CNBC. 20 Jan. 2013 <http://www.cnbc.com/id/38577418/Jerry_Garcia_Night_Already_A_Big_Success>.

Schulman, Bruce J. The Seventies: The Great Shift in American Culture, Society, and Politics. Cambridge, MA: Da Cappo Press, 2002.

Seal, Mark. "The New Adventures of Julia." 1 Feb. 2008. American Way (American Airlines). 20 Feb. 2012 <http://www.americanwaymag.com / julia-louis-dreyfus-seinfeld-brad-hall-bay>.

Sellers, Robert. The Life and Inebriated Times of Richard Burton, Richard Harris, Peter O'Toole and Oliver Reed. New York: St. Martin's Press, 2009.

Senda, Akihiko. Shakespeare and the Japanese Stage. Cambridge, New York: Cambridge University Press, 1998.

Seva Foundation. "Seva Foundation: Joining Together in the Spirit of Service." 27 Nov. 2010. Seva Foundation: Compassion in Action. 27 Nov. 2010 <http://www.seva.org/site/PageServer?pagename=about_seva>.

Shactman, Noah. "Enlightment Engineers." 18 June 2013. Wired.com. 16 Jan. 2014 <http://www.wired.com/business/2013/ 06/meditation-mindfulness-silicon-valley/>.

Shea, N. Beth. "Workouts of the Stars: Celebrity Moms Love Yoga & Pilates." 3 May 2010. CelebrityBabyScoop.com. 26 Feb. 2012 <http://celebritybabyscoop. com/2010/04/27/workouts-of-the-stars-celebrity-moms-love-yoga-pilates>.

Shirky, Clay. "Wikipedia - An Unplanned Miracle." 14 January 2011. guardian.co.uk. 14 April 2013 <http://www.anglonautes.com/voc_it_ main/voc_it_www_wikipedia_1/voc_it_www_wikipedia_1.htm>.

Silverstone, Alicia. "Alicia Silverstone's 3 Best Ways to Get Fit Inside & Out." 2010. Gaiam Life. 30 March 2011 <http://life.gaiam.com/article/alicia-silverstones-3-best-ways-get-fit-inside-out>.

Silverstone, Alicia. The kind diet: a simple guide to feeling great, losing weight, and saving the planet. New York: Macmillan, 2009.

Silverstone, Alicia. The Kind Mama. New York: Rodale, 2014.

Smale, Will. "Profile: The Google founders." 30 April 2004. BBC. 16 Jan. 2014 <http://news.bbc.co.uk/2/hi/business/3666241.stm>.

407

Smart, Maxwell. "Ayn Rand enthusiast Jimmy Wales wants your charity." 18 Nov. 2012. www.inthe00s.com. 14 April 2013 <http://www.inthe00s. com/archive/inthe00spolitics/smf/1290116248.shtml>.

Smith, Jada F. "Remembering Black Soldiers in Films." 24 May 2010. TheRoot.com. 14 Dec. 2015 <http://www.theroot.com/photos/ 2010/05/black_soldiers_in_films. html>.

Snelgar, Rhonda. "Gonzo Journalism." 10 Aug. 2010. Passion and Distraction:.11 Dec. 2010 <http://www.passionanddistraction.com/2010/08/gonzo-journalism.html>.

Snelson, John. Andrew Lloyd Weber. New Haven: Yale University Press, 2004.

Sommer, Elyse. "An Overview of Tom Stoppard's Career." 2008. CurtainUp.com. 28 Nov. 2010 <http://www.curtainup.com/stoppard.html>.

Sports Illustrated. "US Snowboarding Medalists." Sports Illustrated 27 Feb. 2006.

Stants, Carolyn. "Tribal Fusion." 4 Dec. 2010. Tribalternative: The ongoing evolution of dance, music, fashion, art, and life. 4 Dec. 2010 <http://www.tribalternative.com/ tribalfusion.html>.

Stape, Will. "Star Trek's Gene Roddenberry was a Big Hippie." May 14 2007. Yahoo!Voices. 13 May2012 <http://voices.yahoo.com/ star-treks-gene-roddenberry-was-big-hippie-339524.html?cat=38>

Stein, Joel. "The Science of Meditation." Time 4 Aug. 2003.

Strasser, Susan. Waste and Want: The History of Trash. New York: Henry Holt and Company, 1999.

Sullivan, Jeff. "A Few Thoughts On Those Sign-Bearing Phillies Fans." 17 Oct. 2010. LookoutLanding.com. 20 Jan. 2013 <http://www.lookoutlanding.com/2010/10/ 17/1758492/a-few-thoughts-on-those-sign-bearing-phillies-fans>.

Swift, E.M. "Eyes on the Prize." 16 Jan. 2006. SportsIllustrated.com. 16 March 2013 <http://sportsillustrated.cnn.com/vault/ article/magazine/MAG1108494/index. htm>.

Talbot, Margaret. "The New Counterculture: The rapid growth of the home-schooling movement owes much to the energy and organizational skills of its Christian advocates." Nov. 2001. The Atlantic Monthly. 6 Nov. 2010 <http://www.theatlantic. com/past/docs/issues/2001/11/talbot.htm>.

Taubes, Gary. Good Calories, Bad Calories: Fats, Carbs, and the Controversial Science of Diet and Health. New York: Anchor Books, 2007.

Teter, Hannah. "What Does Snowboarding Have to Do with Africa?" HannahsGold.com. 16 March 2013 <http://www.hannahsgold.com/>.

The Dictionary of Literary Biography. "Biography of T(homas) Coraghessan Boyle." 11 Dec. 2010. BookRags.com. 11 Dec. 2010 <http://www. bookrags.com/biography/ thomas-coraghessan-boyle-dlb2/>.

The Graduate. By Buck Henry and Calder Willingham. Dir. Mike Nichols. Perf. Dustin Hoffman, Katherine Ross and Anne Bancroft. United Artists, 1967.

The Northern Right. "Alaska Not Impressed with REI's Sally Jewell for Interior."6 Feb. 2013. The Northern Right. 27 March 2013 <http://northernright.com/ articles/front-page/2013/2/6/alaska-not-impressed-with-reis-sally-jewell-for-interior>.

The News Hour with Jim McNeil. "Biofuels as Oil Alternative." 2006 16 April. PBS. 14 Nov. 2010 <http://www.pbs.org/newshour/bb/economy/jan-june06/biofuels_4-13. html>.

The New York Times. "In Praise of the Counterculture." The New York Times 11 Dec. 1994: E1.

408

The Onion. "Area Woman Emotionally Invested In Jennifer Aniston's Well-Being." 10 Oct. 2006. TheOnion. 19 Jan. 2011 <http://www.theonion. com/articles/ area-woman-emotionally-invested-in-jennifer-anisto,2066/>.

ThinkExist.com. "Leonardo DiCaprio Quotes." 2009-10. ThinkExist.com. 16 Feb. 2011 <http://thinkexist.com/quotation/we-re_not_the_hippie_family_who_only_ eats_organic/154345.html>.

Thompson, Gary. "Director Oliver Stone Brings Iconic "Wall Street" Character Back." 15 Sept. 2010.Philly.com. 29 Dec. 2010 <http://www.philly.com/philly/entertainment /20100915_Director_Oliver_Stone_brings_iconic__Wall_Street__character_back. html>.

Tierra, Michael. "Review of Free Land: Free Love: Tales of a Wilderness Commune." 6 Nov. 2010. East West School of Planetary Herbology. 6 Nov. 2010 <http://www. planetherbs. com/other-items-of-interest/free-land-free-love-tales-of-a-wilderness-commune.html>.

Time. "Shaun White." 23 Jan. 2006. Time.com. 23 Dec. 2015 <http://topics.time.com/ shaun-white/articles/2/>.

Time. "The Way They Were: It's sex, war and microchips in a nifty movie." Time 14 June 1999: 222.

Tucker, Ken. "'Saturday Night Live' recap: Robert De Niro, better in drag these days." 5 Dec. 2010.Entertainment Weekly. 15 Dec. 2015 <http://www.ew.com/ article/2010/12/05/saturday-night-live-de-niro-diddy-deniro>.

Tumlin, Annie. "White vs. Whole Wheat Flour: White vs Wheat, Bleached vs Unbleached Differences." 19 Feb. 2010. Suite101.com. 17 Oct. 2010 <http://www.suite101.com/ content/white-flour-vs-whole-wheat-flour-a203963>.

Turner, David. "Phil Jackson: Zen and the Counterculture Coach." 2004. uhra.herts. ac.uk. 15 Dec. 2015 <https://uhra.herts.ac.uk/ bitstream/handle/2299/1346/900740. pdf?sequence=1>.

UBR, Inc. "Hunter S Thompson Quotes." 11 Dec. 2010. UBR, Inc. 11 Dec. 2010 <http:// www.people.ubr.com/authors/by-first-name/h/hunter-s-thompson/hunter-s-thompson-quotes/i-have-always-loved.aspx>.

US Department of State. "The Counter-Culture and Environmentalism." US Department of State (Country Studies). 14 Nov. 2010 <http://countrystudies.us/united-states/ history-134.htm>.

US Magazine. "Jennifer Aniston, Gwyneth Paltrow Spend Thanksgiving in Morocco." 27 Nov. 2009. www.USMagazine.com. 19 Jan. 2011 <http://www.usmagazine. com/celebritynews/ news/jennifer- aniston-gwyneth-paltrow-spend-thanksgiving-in-morocco-20092711>.

Vaugn, Adam. "Paul McCartney backs 'Meat Free Monday' to cut carbon emissions." 15 June 2009. guardian.co.uk. 2010 17 Oct. <http://www.guardian.co.uk/ environment/2009/jun/15/paul-mccartney-meat-free-monday>.

Vegetarian Star. "Celebrity Vegetarian Gossip And News." 10 June 2010. VegetarianStar. com. 17 March 2013 <http://vegetarianstar.com/tag/hannah-Teter/>.

Vegetarian Star "Race Car Driver Leilani Münter: One Of 10 Reasons To Love USA." 29 June 2009. Vegetarian Star. 16 Dec. 2015 <http://vegetarianstar.com/ 2009/06/29/ race-car-driver-leilani-munter-one-of-10-reasons-to-love-usa/>.

Vikingville, Trapped In. "Packer Forum." 31 Aug. 2012. PackerForum.com. 16 Dec. 2015 <https://www.packerforum.com/threads/clay-matthews-jokester.38646/>.

Voller, Debbi. Madonna: The Style Book. New York: Omnibus Press, 1999.

Wales, Jimmy. "What Was My Goal When I Came Up with the Idea of Starting a Free Encyclopedia for Everyone?" 22 July 2009. www.bbc.co.uk/blogs.14 April 2013 <http://www.bbc.co.uk/blogs/digitalrevolution/2009/07/what-was-my-goal-when-i-came-u.shtml>.

Walker, Jesse. "The Hippie and the Redneck Can Be Friends." April 2005. Reason.com. 8 Feb. 2011 <http://en.wikipedia.org/wiki/Francis_Ford_Coppola>.

Wallace, David Foster. "Roger Federer as Religious Experience." 20 Aug. 2006. www. NYTimes.com. 22 April 2014 <http://www.nytimes.com/2006/08/20/sports/playmagazine/20federer.html>.

Wallace, William. "Uncensored Play-By-Play Recap Of The BCS Championship Game." 11 Jan. 2011.www.saturdaydownsouth.com. 16 Dec. 2015 <http://www.saturdaydownsouth. com/2011/uncensored-play-by-play-recap-of-the-bcs-championship-game/>.

Walsh, Michael. "The Curiosity of Cats." Oct. 2007. Smithsonian.com. 28 Nov. 2010 <http://www.smithsonianmag.com/arts-culture/cats.html>.

Wenn.com. "Morissette reveals cannabis use." 31 Jan. 2010. CannabisFacts.ca. 30 March 2011 <http://frankdiscussion.netfirms. com/who_celebtokers.html>.

Whitmer, Peter O. and Bruce VanWyngarden. Return to Aquarius: Seven Who Created the Sixties Counterculture that Changed America. New York: Citadel Press, 1987.

Williams, Ricky. Ricky Williams Opens Up, 60 Minutes, Mike Wallace. September 2010.

Wiltwinny. "10 Food Rules to Live by." 10 Oct. 2010. 17 Oct. 2010 <http://healthmad.com/nutrition/10-food-rules-to-live-by/#ixzz12eil3ue7>.

WorkOutInfoGuru.com. "Julia Roberts Workout Routine & Diet Plan." 2015. workoutinfoguru.com. 3Jan. 2016 <http://workoutinfoguru.com/julia-roberts-workout/>.

WordIQ.com. "Barbara Hershey—Definition." 5 Jan. 2011. WordIQ.com. 5 Jan. 2011 <http://www.wordiq.com/definition/Barbara_Hershey>.

X17 Online. "Al Pacino Photos & Pics—Another Day Another Leather Blazer." 2008. X17online.com. 16 April 2011 <http://x17online.com/celebrities/ al_pacino/another_day_another_leather blazer-12312008 php>.

YouTube. "Smoking Weed." 18 March 2008. YouTube.com. 26 Feb. 2012 <http://www.youtube.com/watch?v=hMhAvLxRXmw>.

Yowell, Skip. The Hippie Guide to Climbing the Corporate Ladder & Other Mountains: How JansportMakes it Happen. Nashville, TN: Naked Ink, 2006.

Chapter Nine Works Cited

Crane, Stephen. The Red Badge of Courage. New York: Baronet Books, 2009.

Rhys, R. "Stereotype Threat: An Overview." unknown. diversity.arizona.edu. 7 April 2017<http://diversity.arizona.edu/sites/diversity/files/stereotype_ threat_overview.pdf>.

Rucker, Leland. "Cannabis Cup encapsulates the marijuana culture clash." Boulder Weekly 23 April2015: 59.

Chapter Ten Works Cited

ACLU. "Against Drug Prohibition." 2015. www.ACLU.org. 30 August 2015 <https://www.aclu. org/against-drug-prohibition>. "America is at war." web.stanford.edu. 30 August 2015 <https://web.stanford.edu/class/ e297c/poverty _prejudice/paradox/htele.html>.

Allahpundit. "Quinnipiac poll: 71% oppose enforcing federal marijuana laws in states where the drug is legal." 2 Feb. 2017. HotAir.com. 1 April 2017 <http://hotair.com/ archives/2017/02/25/quinnipiac-poll-71-oppose-enforcing-federal-marijuana-laws-in-states-where-the-drug-is-legal/>.

Baum, Daniel. "How to Win the War on Drugs: Legalize It All." April 2016. harpers.org. 17 April 2016 <https://harpers.org/archive/ 2016/04/legalize-it-all/>.

____. The War on Drugs and the Politics of Failure. Boston: Little Brown and Company, 1996.

Becker, Sam. "10 Countries Leading the Push for International Marijuana Legalization." 22 May 2015. CheatSheet.com. 22 Dec. 2015 <http://www.cheatsheet.com/politics/10-countries-that-have-or-will-see-marijuana-legalization.html/?a=viewall>.

Bienenstock, David. "The HIGH TIMES Interview: Rick Steves." 13 May 2013. HighTimes. com. 22 Dec 2015 <http://www.hightimes. com/read/ high-times-interview-rick-steves>.

Borden, David. "Editorial: Do Drug Laws Affect Drug Use Rates? Evidently Not." 11 July 2008. StopTheDrugWar.org. 6 April 2013 <http://stopthedrugwar.org/ chronicle/2008/jul/11/editorial_do_drug_laws_affect_dr>.

Brown, Toni A. "Editorial." Relix: Music for the Mind Feb. 1994: 5.

California NORML. 24 April 2014 <http://www.canorml.org/background/ca1913.html>.

CNN. "Ballot Measure: Florida (Florida Amendment 2)." 6 Nov. 2014. CNN. 15 April 2017 <http://www.cnn.com/election/2014/results/state/FL/ballot/01/>.

Common Sense for Drug Policy. "Nixon Tapes Show Roots of Marijuana Prohibition: Misinformation Culture Wars and Prejudice." 2002. www.csdp.org. 24 March 2002 <www.csdp.org-www.drugwarfacts.org>.

Cushing, Raymond. "Pot Shrinks Tumors; Government Knew in '74." 30 May 2000. AlterNet. 12 April2014 <http://www.alternet.org/story/ 9257/ pot_shrinks_tumors%3B_government_knew_in_'74>.

Democracy Now! "Massachusetts to Throw Out 21,000 Drug Convictions After State Chemist Tampers with Evidence." 19 April 2017. www. DemocracyNow.org. 7 May 2017 <https://www.democracynow.org/2017/4/19/ massachusetts_to_throw_out_21_000>.

____. "Meet Timothy Taylor, Convicted on Drug Evidence Handled by a State Chemist Who Falsified Tests." 19 April 2017. www.DemocracyNow.org. 7 May 2017 <https:// www.democracynow.org/2017/4/19/meet_timothy_taylor_convicted_on_drug>.

____."The Hunting of Billie Holiday & the Roots of the U.S. War on Drugs." 7 April 2015. Democracy Now! 26 April 2015 <http://www.democracynow.org/blog/2015/4/7/ johann_harri_the_hunting_of_billie>.

____. "New York City to Ease Response to Marijuana Possession After Arrests Rise Under de Blasio." 11 Nov. 2014. .org. 2015 6 Jan. <http://www.democracynow. org/2014/ 11/11 /headlines/nyc_to_loosen_ penalties_for_marijuana_possession_ after_arrests_rise_under_de_blasio>.

Goodman, Amy. "Drugs Aren't the Problem": Neuroscientist Carl Hart on Brain Science & Myths About Addiction." 6 Jan. 2014. DemocracyNow! 5 June 2014 <http://www. democracynow.org/ 2014/1/6/drugs_arent_the_problem_neuroscientist_carl>.

____. "Kids For Cash: Inside One of the Nation's Most Shocking Juvenile Justice Scandals." 14 Feb. 2014.DemocracyNow! 8 March 2014 <http://www. democracynow. org/2014/2/4/ kids_for_cash_inside_one_of>.

Gray, Eliza. "Heroin Gains Popularity as Cheap Doses Flood the U.S."4 Feb. 2014. Time.com. 18 March 2014 <http://time.com/4505/heroin-gains-popularity-as-cheap-doses-flood-the-u-s/>

Haas, Sarah. "Rate of use for youth stays steady, but arrest rates increase." 29 2016. BoulderWeekly.com. 15 July 2016 <http://www.boulderweekly.com/ features/ rate-of-use-for-youth-stays-steady-but-arrest-rates-increase/>.

Hari, Johann. Chasing the Scream: The First and Last Days of the War on Drugs. Bloomsbury, UK:Bloomsbury, 2015.

Hart, Jeffrey. "Marijuana and the Counterculture." National Review 1972, 24 ed.:1348.

Helmer, John. Drugs and Minority Oppression. New York: The Seabury Press, 1975.

Herer, Jack. The Emperor Wears No Clothes: Cannabis and the Conspiracy Against Marijuana. 11th ed. Phoenix: Paper Master, 1998.

Innes, Emma. "Does smoking marijuana give you MAN BOOBS? Plastic surgeon's claim." 5 Dec. 2013. DailyMail.com (UK). 10 May 2015 <http://www.dailymail. co.uk/health/article-2518807/Men-smoke-marijuana-likely-MAN-BOOBS-plastic-surgeon-claims.html#ixzz3Zn1vX1C3 >.

Kids for Cash. Dir. Robert May. 2013.

Lane, Stephanie. Ecstasy. Detroit: Lucent Books, 2006.

Levin, Jack. The Functions of Prejudice. New York: Harper and Row, 1975.

Marijuana Policy Project. "Federal Obstruction of Medical Marijuana Research." 2010 www.mpp.org. 26 May 2015 <http://www.mpp.org/ assets/pdfs/library/Federal-Obstruction-of-MMJ-Research-1.pdf>.

Matthews, Dylan. "The black/white marijuana arrest gap, in nine charts." 4 June 2013. WashingtonPost.com. 5 June 2014 <http://www.washingtonpost.com/blogs/ wonkblog/wp/2013/06/04/the-blackwhite-marijuana-arrest-gap-in-nine-charts/>.

Miles, Kathleen. "Marijuana Not Linked To Lung Cancer When Use Is Light Or Moderate, Unknown With Heavy Use." 20 June 2013. HuffingtonPost. 16 April 2014 <http:// www.huffingtonpost.com/ 2013/06/20/marijuana-lung-cancer_n_3474960.html>.

Nadelmann, Ethan. "Chicago to Decriminalize Marijuana." 27 June 2012. HuffingtonPost. com. 22 Dec. 2015 <http://www.huffingtonpost.com/ethan-nadelmann/chicago-to-decriminalize-marijuana_b_1632417.html>.

National Commission on Marihuana and Drug Abuse. Marihuana: A Signal of Misunderstanding. Washington, D.C.: U.S. Government Printing Office, 1972.

NORML. "Clinton Signs Law Denying Student Aid To Marijuana Smokers." 8 Oct. 1998. NORML.org. 6 April 2014 <http://norml.org/news/1998/ 10/08/ clinton-signs-law-denying-student-aid-to-marijuana-smokers>.

Quit Victoria. "Stress and Smoking." 2014. Quit.org.au. 1 March 2014 <http://www.quit. org. au/preparing-to-quit/understanding-your-smoking/stress-and-smoking>.

Relix "Tales from Behind Bars." Relix: Music for the Mind Feb. 1994: 8-13.

Robbins, Christopher. "Brooklyn DA Decriminalizes Marijuana Possession. For Some." 9 July 2014.gothamist.com. 22 Dec. 2015 < http://gothamist.com/2014/07/09/ brooklyn_ pot_decriminalize.php>.

RT.com. "Philadelphia becomes largest US city to decriminalize marijuana." 4 Oct. 2014. RT.com/usa. 22 Dec. 2015 <https://www.rt.com/ usa/192684-philadelphia-marijuana-decriminalize-pot/>.

Rucker, Leland. "As it turns out, marijuana doesn't like cancer." Boulder Weekly 27 Aug. 2015: 65.

____. "Cannabis Cup encapsulates the marijuana culture clash." Boulder Weekly 23 April 2015: 59.

Swift, Art. "For First Time, Americans Favor Legalizing Marijuana." 22 Oct. 2013. Gallup Politics. 1 March 2014 <http://www.gallup.com/poll/ 165539/first-time-americans-favor-legalizing-marijuana.aspx>.

Szalavitz, Maia. "Viewpoint: How Marijuana Decision Could Signal TurningPoint in the U.S. War onDrugs." 29 Aug. 2013. Time.com. 24 April 2014 <http://healthland.time. com/2013/08/29/ viewpoint-how-marijuana-decision-could-signal-turning-point-in-the-u-s-war-on-drugs/>.

TheDEA.org. "Ecstasy Statistics." TheDEA.org. 18 March 2014 <http://thedea.org/ statistics.html>.

Torgoff, Martin. Can't Find My Way Home: America in the Great Stoned Age, 1945-2000. New York:Simon & Shuster, 2004.

Tvert, Mason. Personal email. Denver, 17 Jan. 2006.

Vince, Gaia. "Why teenagers should steer clear of cannabis." 5 July 2006. New Scientist. 2014 Feb. 13 <http://www.newscientist.com/ article/dn9488-why-teenagers-should-steer-clear-of-cannabis.html#.Uv0ir8RDuSo>.

Volz, Matt. "Do medical marijuana users have right to bear arms? No, says ATF." 29 September 2011. NBCNews.com. 6 April 2014 <http://www.nbcnews.com/ id/44712648/ns/us_news-crime_and_courts/t/do-medical-marijuana-users-have-right-bear-arms-no-says-atf/#.U0Gzs8RDuSo>.

Weil, Andrew. "What No One Wants to Know about Marijuana." 1986. The Vaults of Erowid. 2 March 2014 <http://www.erowid.org/plants/cannabis/cannabis_writings6. shtml>.

Wing, Nick. "Marijuana Prohibition Was Racist From The Start. Not Much Has Changed." 25 Jan. 2014.Huffington Post. 18 Jan. 2016 <http://www. huffingtonpost.com/ 2014/01/14/marijuana-prohibition-racist_n_4590190.html>.

Wilkey, Robin. "Marijuana And Cancer: Scientists Find Cannabis Compound Stops Metastasis In Aggressive Cancers." 19 Sept. 2012. www.huffingtonpost.com. 20 Dec. 2015 <http://www.huffingtonpost.com/2012/09/19/marijuana-and-cancer_n_1898208.html>.

Chapter Eleven Works Cited

Auschwitz: Inside the Third Reich. Dir. Laurence Rees. PBS. KCET, Hollywood and the BBC, 2005.

Baca, Richard. "Poll shows little regret in Colorado over legalizing marijuana." 20 Sept. 2016. www.DenverPost.com. 1 May 2017 <http://www.denverpost.com/2016/09/20/ legalize-marijuana-poll/>.

Barr-Melej, Patrick. "Research briefs: Drugs, sex and rock 'n roll." 21 Sept. 2004. Iowa State University.22 July 2014 <http://archive.inside.iastate.edu/2004/0924/briefs. shtml>.

Capp, Al. The Best of L'il Abner. New York: Holt, Reinhart and Winston, 1978.

CBS: 48 Hours Mystery. "Jeffrey MacDonald: Time For Truth—Convicted Murderer Says New Evidence Will Exonerate Him." 6 Nov. 2006. CBSnews.com. 16 July 2014 <http://www.cbsnews.com/news/jeffrey-macdonald-time-for-truth/>.

Dickinson, Tim. "The War on Drugs is Burning Out." Rolling Stone 15 Jan. 2015: 33-37.

Gaffney, Frank J., Jr. "Counterculture assault on the military." Washington Times 30 June 1998: 15.

Graham, Luke. "Bernie Sanders files bill to legalize marijuana." 5 Nov. 2015. CNBC. com. 22 Feb. 2016<http://www.cnbc.com/2015/ 11/05/bernie-sanders-files-bill-to-legalize-marijuana.html>.

Gunnick, Ben. "Tim O'Brien." StFrancis.edu. 21 June 2014 <https://www.stfrancis.edu/ content/en/student/O'Brien/vietnam.htm>.

Haas, Sarah. "Rate of use for youth stays steady, but arrest rates increase." 29 2016. BoulderWeekly.com. 15 July 2016 <http://www.boulderweekly.com/features/ rate-of-use-for-youth-stays-steady-but-arrest-rates-increase/>.

HistoryCommons. "Context of 'July 1956: South Vietnamese President Blocks Unifying Elections'." HistoryCommons.org. 21 June 2014 <http://www.historycommons.org/ context.jsp?item=vietnam_637>.

Jackson, Paul. "Blame hippies: Sixties counterculture eroded moral foundations of society." 24 Dec. 2004. Calgary Sun. <http://www.canoe.ca/ NewsStand/ Columnists/ Calgary/Paul_Jackson/home.html>.

Lembcke, Jerry. "Debunking a spitting image." 30 April 2005. www.boston.com. 7 Feb. 2015 <http://www.boston.com/news/globe/editorial_opinion/oped/articles/2005/ 04/30/debunking_a_spitting_image/>.

Lembcke, Jerry. "Media Myth: Vietnam Vets and Spit." 7 Sept. 2000. TomPaine.com. 26 June 2014 <http://archive.today/ffOt2#selection-463.45-463.185>.

Lembcke, Jerry. The Spitting Image: Myth, Memory and the Legacy of Vietnam. New York: NYU Press, 1998.

Meyer, Herb. "The Siege of Western Civilization." 2003. Storm King Press. 21 March 2005 <www.stormkingpress.com>.

Mishalov, Neil. "Elmo R. Zumwalt Jr., Admiral Who Modernized the Navy, Is Dead at 79." 2000.www.mishalov.com. 27 Dec. 2015 <http://www.mishalov.com/Zumwalt. html>.

Morgan, David R. "Nuclear Crisis #5 in Year: 1954." 14 Oct. 2011. Victoria Peace Coalition. 21 June 2014 <http://www.colorado.edu/AmStudies/lewis/1025/16nuclear.pdf>.

____. "Nuclear Crisis 12 in Year: 1969." 14 Oct. 2011. Victoria Peace Coalition.22 June 2014 <http://www.colorado.edu/AmStudies/lewis/1025/16nuclear.pdf>.

Pay It Forward. Dir. Mimi Leder. Warner Brothers, 2000.

Rambo: First Blood, Part I. Dir. Ted Kotcheff. Perf. Sylvester Stallone. 1982.

Sanders, Ed. The Family: The Story of Charles Manson's Dune Buggy Attack Battalion. New York: E.P. Dutton, 1971.

Stanley, Deb. "Naked CU student killed by Boulder police was not properly hit with taser before shooting." 30 July 2015. www.thedenverchannel.com. 16 Jan. 2016 <http:// www.thedenverchannel.com/news/ front-range/boulder/naked-cu-student-killed-by-boulder-police-was-not-properly-hit-with-police-taser-before-shooting>.

The Secret. Dir. Drew Heriot et al. 2006.

The Sixties - The Years That Shaped a Generation (TV). Dir. Stephen Talbot. PBS. 2005.

Torgoff, Martin. Can't Find My Way Home: America in the Great Stoned Age, 1945-2000. New York: Simon & Shuster, 2004.

Young, Neil. Waging Heavy Peace: A Hippie Dream. New York: Blue Rider Press, 2012.

Zinn, Howard. A Young People's History of the United States. Seven Stories Press, 2009.

Zutz, John. "Debunking a Myth." VietnamVeteransAgainstthe War. 26 June 2014 <http:// www.vvaw.org/veteran/article/?id=215&print=yes>.

Chapter Twelve Works Cited

Associated Press. Irving Kristol, 'Godfather' of Neo-Conservatism, Dies at 89. 18 September 2009. 24 March 2010 <http://www.foxnews.com/us/ 2009/09/18/ irving-kristol-godfather-neo-conservatism-dies/>.

Gustafson, John. "Son King." 12 Nov. 2002. ESPN.go.com. 06 Feb. 2013 <http://espn. go.com/magazine/vol5no24walton.html>.

Miller, Elizabeth. "Dust to Dust." 29 April 2010. BoulderWeekly.com. 9 April 2017 <http://www.boulderweekly.com/news/dust-to-dust/>.

Chapter Thirteen Works Cited
None.

Index

419

423

Paul Dougan is a Hippie-American living in Boulder, Colorado. He is looking for those willing to rethink the concept of Hippies (especially the notion that Hippies Were Just a Thing of the 1960s) and to become endorsers for a Hippie-American ethnic organization, a civil-rights organization for Counterculturists.

To become an endorser of such an organization, to blurb this book, or to follow up on what you have read in *Happily Hippie: Meet a Modern Ethnicity,* visit HappilyHippie. net where you'll find activities (I am, for instance, trying to create of photo collection of Hippie-American families), a Wordpress column/ blog, book photos, book excerpts and supplementary book materials. See you there, Hippie-Americans!

Printed in the United States
By Bookmasters